# KNOW YOUR OWN MIND

A brave attempt to demystify and explain the contemporary jargon of psychology and psychiatry . . .as welcome as it is ambitious.
— Professor Anthony Clare

Jane Knowles' new book, *Know Your Own Mind*, is a treasure. For many, many years I have wished I had something to give to clients that described emotional distress in straightforward language yet addressed the client as an intelligent human being. This is exactly the book I have been waiting for. Dr Knowles begins with an encyclopedia of various psychological experiences, from absentmindedness and accident neurosis through womb envy and working through pain. She presents fascinating case examples for each condition, adding elements of humanity, richness, and depth. In later sections, she discusses etiology, diagnosis, and treatment.

This is a reassuring, compassionate, and above all, extremely informative book. Its tone is at once sensible and lively. Dr Knowles does not present a particular point of view, but rather a variety of points of view, leaving readers to reach their own conclusions about the true cause of a particular condition or the most appropriate treatment method. Unlike many psychiatrists, she does not push psychotropic medication, or psychoanalysis, or any other particular treatment. To her credit, she includes self-help groups as a viable treatment option.

I think this book will and ought to be widely read by family members, by mental health professionals no matter how experienced, and by students of psychology and psychiatry. Dr Knowles does indeed reach her stated goal of holding out her hand and being a true friend.
— Ellen Cole, Ph.D., Psychologist
Co-editor of *Women & Therapy*

Jane Knowles, MBBS MRCPsych., is a psychiatrist and psychotherapist in the National Health Service. She trained at St Bartholomew's before taking up positions in Southampton and Nottingham; she is currently Consultant Psychotherapist to Berkshire, where she specialises in the psychology of women. Jane Knowles is also the author of *Motherhood: What it Does to Your Mind* (Pandora), written under her previous name, Jane Price.

# KNOW YOUR OWN MIND

## The Complete Reference to Your Psychological Well-being

### Jane Knowles

Pandora
*An Imprint of HarperCollinsPublishers*

Pandora
An Imprint of HarperCollins*Publishers*
77 – 85 Fulham Palace Road,
Hammersmith, London W6 8JB

Published by Pandora 1991
1  3  5  7  9  10  8  6  4  2

A catalogue record for this book
is available from the British Library

ISBN 0 04440 646 0

Typeset by Harper Phototypesetters Limited,
Northampton, England
Printed in Great Britain by
Mackays of Chatham, Kent

# CONTENTS

## Appendices

# ACKNOWLEDGEMENTS

So many people have helped me over the years in acquiring the knowledge and experience reflected in this book that it is hard to pick out the few for special mention. However I would like to thank Dr John Grimshaw, who first initiated me into the mysteries and wonders of psychiatry, Dr Pamela Ashurst, whom I have considered my 'psychotherapeutic' mother (despite her assertions that she is not old enough!), Dr Mark Aveline for his tolerant tuition as I struggled to become a psychotherapist, Bernard Ratigan, who tackled the unenviable job of analysing me with such charm and (I hope) success, Dr Heinz Wolfe, whose courteous understanding of people was a shining example, and Mrs Meg Sharpe and 'the group', who furthered my analysis with so much love.

Colleagues past and present have supported my adventures in writing this book and have put up good-humouredly with my endless enquiries and requests that they read parts of the manuscript. In particular I would like to thank Dr Ellen Cole in the USA, Professor Anthony Clare in Ireland and Ms Carol Town in the UK. Carol deserves a medal for agreeing to read the entire manuscript while confined to hospital for four months. The section on drug treatment was greatly helped by friend and clinical pharmacist Ms Wendy Davies. Overall I could not have started, continued or finished this mammoth enterprise without the support and encouragement of my editors, Candida Lacey and Ginny Iliff.

Anyone reading this book will understand the great debt I owe to my patients, who have shared their experiences with courage, and without whom any knowledge would seem dry and uninteresting. They have made my decision to become a psychiatrist/psychotherapist the most sensible one of my life.

Finally yet again I find myself thanking my family for their tolerance towards my preoccupation with this project. I am so lucky to have their support and love, without which I could never have imagined myself capable of this undertaking.

Jane Knowles
April 1991

# How to Use this Book

The contents of this book have been divided into four sections, and hopefully this will help you find the parts which are most relevant for yourself more easily.

Part One (*What Does It Feel Like?*) makes up the central core of the book. It is an A to Z of thoughts and feelings, psychological experiences, symptoms, complexes and illnesses. Although not exhaustive, I hope that it covers the majority of those experiences which have worried or distressed you, as well as providing interesting reading about the normal psychological sensations and developmental stages through which we have all passed. You may want to look up a specific experience, in which case the alphabetical arrangement should make it easy for you to find what you need. Alternatively you may want to browse through many entries. I trust that the examples given will add enjoyment to your reading.

Part Two (*Why Does It Happen?*) deals with the origins of our emotional lives and experiences and the many theories we have to explain them. These explanations form the basis of our ability to diagnose such experiences on many parameters and I hope that Part Three (*What Is It Called?*), which covers the subject of diagnosis, will allow you a choice of ways in which to understand yourself and your own experiences. Finally, Part Four (*What Can Be Done?*), on treatment, explores the range of available options. I hope that each of these sections of the book conveys the fundamental fact that each of us needs to have a sense of choice about the way in which we (and others) perceive our experiences and their origins, and the help we may (or may not) want and need.

Throughout this book I have used examples drawn from clinical practice in order to illustrate various points in a way which, I hope, will allow others to identify the problems, experiences and situations discussed. Because I would wish to maintain the confidentiality of all my patients these examples were produced from a mixture of material, so that although they represent real people accurately, each example is an amalgam with details from several, even many, individual cases. If you think that you recognise someone, perhaps even yourself, it is because so many of our feelings are universal, so many of our experiences simply human, so many of our problems shared ones.

Writing this book has been a great pleasure, a true labour of love. Mental illness has been buried under an avalanche of fear and ignorance for far too long, and whilst we have become health-conscious about our bodies in recent years, our understanding of and kindness to our emotions lags way behind. In reading this book I would hope that much of the ignorance can be dispelled, reducing fear and opening up areas, which are of great interest to us all, for further conversation. *Know Your Own Mind* is full of examples drawn from 15 years of psychiatric and psychotherapeutic practice, and 41 years of life! I am indebted to those who have shared their experiences with me. It has allowed me to comprehend the real wonder of the mind in all its scope, depth and complexity. Whatever may divide us emotionally and mentally, we have far more in common.

Although I believe this book will be of interest to everyone, it is especially for those who have experienced emotional or mental distress or illness. Having shared your world for 15 years I am left with an overwhelming sense of your pain and your courage. You may have suffered stigma on top of everything else which you have had to overcome, but you have experienced something of which those who stigmatise are both ignorant and afraid. I hope that this book will hold out a hand to you and be a true friend in your need.

# PART 1

# WHAT DOES IT FEEL LIKE?
## An A-Z of Thoughts and Feelings, Psychological Symptoms, Complexes and Illnesses

# INTRODUCTION

This section of the book deals with the emotional and psychological experiences of life, both normal and pathological, happy and distressing.

In most examples there is some comparison of what may require serious consideration and perhaps treatment, and what may, perhaps surprisingly, be considered normal. I say perhaps surprisingly because in the Western world we have come to expect that our pains and distress can always be relieved by modern medicine. To understand that in psychological terms some pain and distress is not only normal but also essential to natural development can often seem surprising. It can also seem cruel to those in pain at the moment.

The basic skill in any practice of psychological or psychiatric work is to help the individual draw a realistic line between a normal response to life, something better to live through and learn from, and what is unbearable for the individual, who then needs help. The distinction made between *psychological* and *psychiatric* helps us define the correct position at which to draw a realistic line. Psychology is the study of normal behaviour of both humans and animals in a variety of settings. Clinical psychologists start with this basic training before completing a further period of time spent learning to assess and treat those whose behaviour has departed from this norm. Psychiatrists start as doctors, learning a medical 'illness' model to explain human distress, before completing a higher training in psychiatry. This helps them to view mental illness both from the viewpoint of that illness model of general medicine and with an understanding of human psychological development and the dynamic interaction between an individual, his or her family and society. Thus the psychological starts with the normal and the psychiatric with the abnormal or ill. In the field of mental health psychiatrists and psychologists work side by side, helping to define the boundaries between normality and abnormality and helping those whose experiences or behaviour fall onto the abnormal or unbearable side (see p.460–4 for more on mental health professionals).

This section will allow you to consider your feelings and experiences across a wide spectrum from normal to abnormal, and hopefully equip you to make a more accurate decision about your own psychological experiences and whether or not you require help. We have all been brought up to have a specific attitude towards our emotions: some families and social groups are much more willing to talk in emotional terms than others. Almost all of us to some degree resist demonstrating our most distressing emotions, because we wish to protect ourselves and others from our true vulnerability. We also have an in-built resistance to demonstrating those emotions which were most censored in our childhood: for boys this is often sadness and tears, for girls, anger and aggression. Too often these experiences end up being expressed in distorted ways, which results in their being diagnosed in adulthood rather than being understood in the context of the individual's life. Teaching a son not to cry does not protect him from sad events as an adult. If the event is big enough and sad enough his stiff upper lip will become a handicap to his coping, not a strength. Similarly, bringing up a daughter not to express anger or aggression does not mean that she is not going to experience events that leave her angry; rather, the need to express something will be squashed and the anger she experiences will be turned inwards into depression.

Many of us have been brought up to believe that too much expression of emotion is dangerous. There is, therefore, a stigma placed on those who either dare to express or cannot stop themselves from expressing strong feelings. We are frightened by such people, because we can feel that we, too, have such strong emotions hidden away and out of sight, in the way that our parents taught us was right and proper. We might think to ourselves 'well, I can cope', so why should others take their feelings so much more seriously and seek help? Often this leads us to view those who ask for help as morally weaker than ourselves. If a friend has a broken leg we can see and accept that she is weaker than we are at the moment, and we do not feel inclined to make moral judgements about that weakness. If another friend says that he is depressed it is so easy to jump to the conclusion that not only does this demonstrate moral weakness now but suggests a lifelong weakness in his character. We may be unable to forget and allow him to recover.

Such issues influence the way we talk to each other about our emotional experiences. The social norm is to appear psychologically stronger than we truly know ourselves to be. This façade limits our knowledge of what is normal or abnormal about our own experiences, because there is so little social 'truth' against which to compare ourselves.

A study in Manchester showed that at any one time a quarter of the adult population are in some form of distress, ranging from minor to major problems. Of those only half will consult their GPs. Whether or not that consultation occurs depends as much on the degree of social isolation the individual is experiencing as it does on the severity of the symptoms. Any emotional distress is worse when experienced in isolation. For those who are not alone the feedback they receive from family and friends about their symptoms will probably dictate whether they seek help or not. Some families will resist any suggestion of emotional or psychiatric illness within their ranks, and will 'protect' the individual from getting any help in order to foster their overall image of sanity and coping. Other families respond quickly to the first hint of distress, without allowing time for normal coping mechanisms to spring into action. What is considered normal varies to a considerable extent between families and between social and racial groups. The decision to consult the GP does not usually depend on the severity of the illness, and surveys consistently report high levels of equally ill or distressed people in the community who have never thought of bringing attention to themselves or their problems. Such stoicism may mean that they have suffered unnecessarily for years. It is also sad because we aim resources at the distress we can see in those who are willing to present themselves for help. Usually there are more than enough patients to eat up all the resources, but it means that those equally ill or distressed people who suffer in silence are having no impact on resource planning and distribution.

Of those who present the symptoms and signs of emotional distress to their GP about half will use physical rather than psychological words. This is because our emotional vocabulary is limited and we feel more comfortable talking about headaches, stomach pains and strained muscles than about our feelings. Amongst GPs there is also a preference for physical talk based on the fact that they may feel overwhelmed by and unable to be helpful about emotional problems. Hence out of these consultations comes the 'tip of the iceberg' of referrals to the specialists in mental health, referrals which have already been filtered by the perception of an individual, a family and the GP. This filtration usually means that those who are less assertive about themselves and their feelings often find themselves dismissed, which only feeds their basic assumption that they should probably not have bothered anyone in the first place.

This section is designed to help you place your experiences into context, so that you can judge whether or not you need help. Not all the feelings described are symptoms and signs of illness, but some are. Some pain and distress accompanies each developmental stage of our lives, but this should not mean that we have to suffer alone and unsupported through such times. Not everything can be understood or cured, but much unnecessary suffering persists because of the outdated notions about mental health treatments being unsuccessful and therefore not worth trying. Mental health has its fair share of success, so if you feel that you do need help, you should have access to it.

# A

## Absentmindedness

From time to time, and increasingly as we get older and more under stress or when we are tired, we forget to do something. Sometimes we forget something extremely important. A friend of mine, Liz, went shopping not long after the birth of her second child. As she was getting out of the car and unstrapping her toddler from his child seat she had the uncomfortable feeling that she had forgotten something, but she could not recall what it was. Only when half-way through her shopping, when confronted by rows of disposable nappies, did her mind suddenly register . . . 'Oh, goodness, the baby!'.

Her absentmindedness caused her considerable anxiety as she dashed back to her house, where thankfully she found the new baby still safely asleep in his cot.

Usually it is the trivial minutiae of life that we forget. Most of us have had the sensation of walking into a room and then not being able to remember what it is we wanted there. Absentmindedness can cause considerable anguish when people feel that a bad experience happened to themselves or others just because they forgot to do or say something. Very occasionally, of course, absentmindedness can cause chaos for a person or his or her family, but usually the feeling of responsibility for a bad event is exaggerated because of our guilt, anxiety or anger about that event (see **Anger, Anxiety, Guilt** and **Guilt Complex**).

Hannah was 38 when she came to see me. She said that it was only her absentmindedness that had led to her missing her normal exit from the motorway. This had, in turn, led to her taking a different route, on which she'd been involved in a serious accident in which a man was killed. She explained that she would never forgive herself for the moment when, due to lack of concentration, she absentmindedly carried on to the next exit (*see* **Concentration Difficulties**). She had never done it before, and could only remember normal episodes of absentmindedness prior to the accident, although since, she said, she could hardly remember the date or her telephone number.

Hannah's absentmindedness on the day of the accident was normal. It could have happened to any of us. Fate decreed the tragic sequence of events . . . a dog running across the road caused a car to swerve and drive straight into Hannah's car. The other driver was killed instantly. Tragedy often does result from a number of minor 'discrepancies' from normal behaviour, and then it is natural to think 'if only I had done what I normally do . . .', because each of us has a great psychological need to believe that by decision-making we can control fate and the unpredictable. It was clear that Hannah's memory problems since the accident had become more severe, and that her need to attribute blame to herself in a situation where she could not have done anything to avoid an accident was a part of her depressive reaction to the what had happened (*see* **Depression** and pp.375–7 on Life Event Explanations in Part Two).

It took several months of working through her experience of the accident before Hannah realised that she was not a guilty party but another victim: a psychological victim (*see* **Accident Neurosis** and **Working Through Pain**).

Another example of absentmindedness is when we lose the thread of our thoughts. A sentence that was clearly formed in our minds just a second or two earlier seems to vanish, leaving us open-mouthed and often feeling rather foolish. Again, this is usually a normal phenomenon, but occasionally it reflects an inner disturbance in our thinking. It may suggest fatigue, or be what was first described by the American doctor G.M. Beard in 1880 as the *neurasthenic* reaction (*see* **Neurasthenia**). Basically this refers to a reaction to an event or experience that overwhelms a person, so that he or she has very little energy left to do, say or feel anything. The fact that people's memories for unusual events, particularly traumatic ones, are often blurred and inaccurate, is probably a reflection of their sense of being emotionally overwhelmed.

Absentmindedness in its more extreme forms may suggest that the person is unduly anxious or has an underlying depression. In people who develop schizophrenia there is a tendency for them to have difficultly finishing their thoughts, and in the early days of the illness, before an accurate diagnosis can be made, this may present itself as a form of absentmindedness, which appears to 'disconnect' them from everyday life. They are sometimes described as being on the other side of a plate-glass window, watching the world. In this situation it is not unusual for family and friends to notice a difference and therefore the problem long before it is possible for a medical diagnosis to be made with any certainty. However we should remember that schizophrenia only occurs in 1 to 1.3 per cent of the population in the course of a lifetime, whereas almost all of us experience absentmindedness at times (*see* **Schizophrenia**).

Sometimes absentmindedness is our unconscious' way of letting our conscious mind have a clue about how we feel. Hence we forget those things that we are not particularly interested in, have not concentrated on, or, deep down, want to forget about. This can be embarrassing when consciously we are striving to believe the opposite is true. It means that our actions and our memories are at odds with what we want to believe about ourselves. This can be especially difficult when we absent-mindedly 'forget' an anniversary or an arranged meeting with a friend. Of course sometimes this is just the pressure of daily life driving such events out of our memories, but occasionally it is our unconscious reminding us that things are not always the way we like to pretend they are.

The tendency to be absentminded increases with age, and in

its most severe form causes large memory deficits (*see* **Dementia**).

If you are occasionally beset by absentmindedness, simple measures are often the best. Getting adequate sleep and not over-stressing your work or home life often make a considerable difference. However, if memory loss is a persistent problem, there are exercises you can use to work your mind back into shape (*see* **Amnesia**).

## Accident Neurosis

After an accident we feel shaken up. The intensity and duration of that feeling will be in some way related to the extent of the accident and its consequences for us. As a society we take a rather hard-hearted view of recovery in that we think that if a person seems physically well again, then the effects of the accident are over. In fact the psychological consequences of an accident often continue for a long time after physical healing is complete. Indeed, those who suffer greatest psychological damage from accidents have often not been physically injured at all.

There is a group of people for whom the accident marks the start of a 'career' centred around the treatment of on-going problems, some of which may have no organic basis, and the legal actions arising from the accident or its consequences. Accidents often involve loss, either of property or of an aspect of the self. Most importantly they rob us of our sense of the security and predictability in life, because they take us by surprise and frighten us. Those whose personality seems to change because of an accident have been particularly affected by whatever loss they perceive. Many people experience at least a passing depression after an accident because of the losses involved, but those who become entwined in an accident neurosis seem to become caught up in psychological protest about whatever has befallen them, and often cling to this protest because it keeps their sense of depression and helplessness at bay.

Rebecca was 24 when she was involved in a car accident. She had been driving around a country lane when a car came round the corner on the wrong side of the road and hit her car in such a way as to make it roll over into a ditch. She thinks that she lost consciousness momentarily as the car rolled over, but was then fully awake for the 30 minutes it took before help came along. When examined in casualty she complained of a stiff neck and was given a supportive collar after X-rays demonstrated no visible damage. Ten years later she is still in her collar and involved in lengthy legal action against the other driver. Despite advice from doctors and solicitors Rebecca has now constructed her whole life around visits to out-patient clinics, a variety of osteopaths and healers, solicitors and helping agencies.

Undoubtedly the accident changed her from a happy, out-going person to someone who is entirely preoccupied with her own suffering, having given up her work, abandoned her friends and distanced herself from her family. It is however her response to the trauma of the accident which seems to have been most damaging to her life, and in particular her sense of anger and grievance that it took 30 minutes before anyone came to her rescue.

For someone like Rebecca the accident can be seen as a precipitant to a destructive personality change. In her case it seemed as if the momentary loss of consciousness and her sense of helplessness and despair during those lonely 30 minutes of waiting combined to make her feel extremely vulnerable. During the immediate aftermath several friends suggested that she begin legal action 'in order to cheer herself up and put her back in control.' Anyone who has been involved in similar legal proceedings will know that these are unlikely consequences even if you are victorious. It might have been better advice to suggest that she changed nothing important for at least two years after the accident, in order to allow her sense of proportion, cruelly damaged by the accident, to regain its balance. Instead she made a number of major changes to her working and social life which added greatly to the psychological damage already caused by the accident, thus altering her sense of proportion in a more long-standing way.

People are often suggestible after accidents because of their increased vulnerability, and need help to contain their anxiety and sadness in ways that do not hurt themselves and their lives. It is difficult to know whether there is a particular personality which is more likely to respond to accidents in this mal-adaptive way. I have often thought that pessimists survive traumas rather well, perhaps because they spend their lives expecting things to go wrong and are therefore less surprised than the rest of us when they do! Some people seem susceptible to the intense physical care given them while they are recovering from their wounds, and become 'addicted' to that amount of looking after. Perhaps this represents an underlying dependency need that they were managing to keep in check before their accident. Others enjoy the publicity or attention and yearn for this to continue.

Related to this group who are precipitated by accidents are a group of people who respond to more general disappointments in life by becoming enveloped in litigation proceedings of various kinds. Again this often seems to be some sort of defence against an underlying depression, and suicide is not unusual among members of this group. They may have been somewhat paranoid about people prior to the upsetting event that triggered their resorting to legal methods. Such people often seem superficially arrogant and self-assured but are in fact hyper-sensitive to any slight; often they hide a sense of inferiority about their failure to meet their own super-high standards. They usually relate in a cold and hostile way to the world, believing strongly in the 'rational and objective' approach to everything, suspicious of the motives of others and unable to empathise with anyone else's point of view. Clearly, with this group it is important to separate those who are expressing a facet of their personality, whose ideas about their own grandeur and the world's attacks may be greatly over-valued but not delusional, and those who are presenting symptoms of a genuine illness, such as **paranoia** or **schizophrenia**. The first group are not usually helped by drugs or electro-convulsive therapy, whilst the second group may well be (*see* **Grandiose Behaviour, Overvalued Ideas**, and **Persecution Complex**, as well as Part Four).

Ideas become delusional when they are completely outside the reach of rational conversation or judgement. Such ideas commonly stem from real events, but are then woven into a complicated system of understanding, which is at odds with the individual's cultural and religious norms. Relatives and friends can be drawn into these systems because of the intensity with which they are presented (*see* **Delusions**).

## Acting Out

'Acting out' describes actions which arise from our unconscious minds, often of an aggressive or destructive nature to ourselves or others. Although we might rationalise such actions to an uninvolved observer, they will seem both out of character and inappropriate to the here-and-now.

For example, Petula, aged 32, became extremely angry with her male therapist during a therapy session but was unable, because of her dependency on his approval, to voice this to him. On her way home she decided to do some shopping, only to find herself shouting at two male shop assistants, an action completely out of character to her normal unassertive self.

It is usual for the acting out to occur after the situation which has upset us. The intensity of feeling passes into the unconscious area of the mind and slips out in our behaviour in another situation.

Paul consulted a psychiatrist after hitting his wife for the first time. As the story emerged it was clear that this acting out had been a response to an episode when his female boss had reprimanded him. Usually acting out occurs against those we consider weaker and more helpless than ourselves, as a deflection of feelings aroused in situations where we have felt less powerful. Those who have no one whom they consider weaker may then resort to acting out against themselves, either through obvious self-harm such as taking an overdose, cutting their wrists or even resorting to suicide, or in more covert ways such as faking an apparent 'accident' (*see* **Censorship** and **Suppressed Feelings**).

## Activity and Passivity

Much of our behaviour is dictated by instinct, and theorists have argued for many years about the nature of our instincts and their power over us. Socialisation, culture and our own particular childhood experiences determine how we express these inner drives, which are common not only to mankind but to all animals (*see* **Instinct for Mastery** and **Instinct for Survival**).

Activity and passivity represent an important dichotomy in our mental life necessary for achieving both self-mastery and survival. Activity is required if we are to pursue our emotional needs. However, many instincts, for instance the sexual drive, are not expressed in a straightforward way in any culture, but have been distorted by learning and example throughout childhood into behaviour which is permissible by society. For healthy mental life there needs to be a balance between activity and passivity, enough freedom to pursue the aims of our instincts so that we satisfy ourselves while still being able to contain ourselves sufficiently to satisfy the needs of social living.

Freud believed that the repressive Viennese society of his time, with its prohibitions against sexual enjoyment, particularly for women, caused much of the emotional distress that these women experienced during adult life. They had been taught that it was ladylike to be sexually passive, whatever their true nature. Certainly most cultures think there is some connection between female/passive and male/active, and give strong messages about this to children from an early age.

In an interesting experiment, a five-month-old child was dressed first in 'boy' clothes and then in those traditionally worn by baby girls, and the behaviour of a group of mothers with the baby videotaped. The 'boy' was given a great deal of stimulation, one of the women always holding 'him' and giving 'him' every encouragement to jump and pretend to walk. They also talked to him continuously. The 'girl', on the other hand, was only briefly played with, and then it was presumed 'she' was tired and 'she' was placed to rest in a cot in the corner, and given no further physical or verbal stimulation. When confronted with their different treatments of the same baby, the women all expressed amazement and concluded that the baby had in some way behaved differently and therefore encouraged their varying behaviour. What was apparent was how rapidly a child of this age conformed to their expectations of how active or passive it should be.

Such early experiences mould our behaviour for life. Enforced passivity for little girls often has the sad effect on the adult women that Freud first observed, namely that they have no experience of actively seeking the aims of their instincts and are therefore reduced to waiting passively for the world to give them what they desperately want. Their almost inevitable disappointment turns into a variety of psychiatric symptoms (*see* **Depression**, for example).

In some ways boys suffer from the reverse phenomena of being encouraged always to be in active pursuit of their aims. For many men whose personalities do not fit this 'action man' profile this can cause misery.

In total passivity we resemble the youngest baby, dependent and helpless. Occasionally this phenomenon is seen in psychiatric practice, most commonly in those diagnosed as having schizophrenia.

Paul was first thought to be schizophrenic when he was 19. His behaviour had become withdrawn, his personal hygiene had deteriorated and his academic abilities seemed to dwindle. It was a terrible time for Paul and his family, not only because he was obviously unwell but because no professional was willing to diagnose serious mental illness in the absence of any of the so-called 'positive' features of schizophrenia (*see* **Schizophrenia** and Part Three). A year later he began to express a loss of self, to the extent that he believed all his thoughts had been 'inserted' from outside himself and that all his feelings and actions were being controlled by someone else. He experienced himself as totally passive and helpless in what, to him, seemed a very frightening world. At this point he began treatment (*see* pp.451–7 on Drug Treatment in Part Four), and although he has never managed to get back to his original self he has made great strides in regaining his confidence and capability. In order to do this he had to recover his ability to be active.

## Adaptive Responses

Our ability to react to new situations with flexibility is an important component of human intelligence. Our personalities will to some extent dictate the range of flexibility we can show. Our ability to adapt will also depend on the models of adaptation offered us by parents and other important adult figures, and the nature of the event to which we have to respond.

During childhood each of us has to navigate a pathway through a series of developmental stages. Although each new step represents gains in terms of personal freedom and enriched experience it will also include losses in terms of our dependency needs. Children respond in a number of ways to this necessary growth, some of which may worry parents although they are in fact quite normal. For example, children can normally regress to earlier patterns of behaviour when they are feeling stressed. These adaptive responses, such as thumb-sucking when a child is weaned or when a new baby arrives in the family, are temporary. It is also developmentally normal for infants (aged 6 to 18 months) to experience anxiety when exposed to strangers, and for older children to experience anxiety about separation when it comes time for them to go to school. These responses represent the child's attempts to adapt to change, and disappear as the child discovers better ways of dealing with the changes, such as enjoying the advantages of his new-found freedoms.

It has been suggested that depression may be an adaptive reaction to an intolerable loss situation, making it psychologically possible to withdraw from the world which has hurt us, thus limiting further damage until we are sufficiently recovered to cope again. We usually need to move on to an understanding of the benefits of a change before our adaptation can become positive and healthy, whilst when we sense loss or lack of control our adaptation may be temporarily rather like that of a stressed child in that we regress (*see* **Depression**, **Grief** and **Regression**).

When Dorothy was widowed, aged 62, she withdrew from family and friends, left her part-time job, drew her curtains and ate and drank minimally. Her GP diagnosed that she was depressed because of the sudden loss of her husband, but recognised that it was an adaptive response which was likely to be temporary. As the months passed Dorothy became aware that her youngest daughter was struggling with her three young children and gradually came out of her shell, feeling that she was needed again. Dorothy had proved herself adaptable enough to recover, even though she still felt the loss with much sadness.

It becomes more difficult to react with flexibility as we get older, which is unfortunate because we often have to deal with more loss when we are old than at any other time of life. Those with obsessional personalities find it difficult to adapt at any time, and may restrict their lives so as to prevent the occurrence of anything likely to distress them in the first place (*see* **Obsessive Compulsive Illness**).

## Addiction

The World Health Organisation defines addiction as 'a behavioural pattern of drug use (including alcohol) characterised by overwhelming involvement with the drug, compulsive drug-seeking behaviour and a high tendency to relapse after withdrawal.' Any assessment needs to include some rating of the degree to which the life quality of the individual is affected by the drug.

One of the problems in defining, diagnosing and treating addiction is the discrepancy made between health hazard and legal availability of the drug in question. The National Commission on Marijuana and Drug Abuse defines five separate categories of abuse which may or may not then lead to addiction. They are as follows:

a) experimental use, stemming from curiosity about the drug;
b) socio-recreational use, resulting from peer-group pressure;
c) circumstantial/situational use, in order to cope with a specific situation or pressure;
d) intensified use arising from a perceived need or desire for the drug at least daily; and
e) compulsive use as a result of a psychological/physical addiction.

A distinction is made between substance abuse and substance dependence, the second requiring that the individual has built up tolerance for the substance and thus needs increasing doses to achieve the same effect.

The drugs used can be divided into categories depending on their actions, such as

● Depressants: barbiturates, methaqualone ('ludes') and minor tranquillizers such as diazepam (better known as Valium) and lorazepam (Ativan)
● Stimulants: amphetamines and cocaine
● Hallucinogens: LSD, psilocin (magic mushroom) and mescaline
● Indolealkylamines: DET and DMT
● Opiates: codeine, heroin, opium, methadone and morphine

Most people will deny addiction not only to others but also to themselves ('I have *not* got a problem') until they meet a social, legal or health crisis. Once the crisis has been overcome they are in great danger of returning to their habit, unchanged. Often life has to become extremely difficult before the individual is motivated to seek help to rid him- or herself of the habit.

Opinion is divided about whether there is always an underlying psychological or personality problem associated with abuse and as to whether treatment should be aimed at the underlying problem or the addiction. Realistically, once the criteria for dependency are met, there is no way to help the underlying problem without first tackling the addiction.

The criteria for dependency include an awareness that you are taking more of the substance or using it for longer periods of time than you had intended, attempting to get off the substance or wanting to reduce its impact on your life, being intoxicated when expected to meet work or family requirements, which often leads to these important activities being relinquished in favour of the habit, continued use of the substance even after you become fully aware of the problems it is causing, tolerance of larger and larger quantities of the substance, and experiencing withdrawal symptoms in its absence. (*See also* **Alcoholism**.)

## Aggression

It is surprisingly difficult to define aggression because it can take so many forms and be directed either inwards or outwards. This difficulty extends to the very origins of aggressive behaviour: is it an instinct to which we are all subject or does it result from frustrations and privations in life?

For many years Freud resisted the notion that aggression was an instinct with which we are born. When Alfred Adler first postulated in 1908 that there existed an inborn instinct of aggression Freud argued against it. In his increasing psychoanalytic practice, however, Freud became aware of a hostility in his patients that seemed directly contrary to their expressed desire to explore their psyches (*see* **Resistance**). Eventually, by 1920, he had begun using the term 'aggressive instinct'. For Freud mankind lived stretched out between a desire for life (the life instinct, Eros), and a desire for death (the death instinct, Thanatos). Freud saw the aggressive instinct as the outward expression of the death instinct, meaning that we turn our need to attack the self outwards, onto other people (*see* **Death**).

Melanie Klein took Freud's ideas further, suggesting that even the youngest child has powerfully aggressive instincts that seek to destroy his mother, to savage and attack her, while at the same time loving and needing her (*see* **Ambivalence**). Most theorists agree that aggression is closely linked to sexuality, a link which is demonstrated in both fantasising about and practising sado-masochism.

All of us are capable of aggression; circumstances dictate to a great extent how and when we express it. Of course it is easy to see the aggression in an act of violence such as rape or murder. It is sometimes much harder to identify and deal with other forms of aggression, for instance verbal aggression such as sarcasm, or aggression that is passive or negative: a person might infuriate others by apparently well-meaning actions or finding ways of avoiding doing something important.

The expression of aggression within certain limits is a normal part of mental life. There can be few close relationships that do not, at some point, contain expressions of aggression between partners, and certainly mothers will have witnessed aggressive rage in their small babies and extraordinarily aggressive outbursts in toddlers. The 'terrible twos' are well named: children of this age respond with aggression to the increasing limitations placed on their behaviour by parents on behalf of society.

In psychiatry and psychotherapy we are sometimes confronted with aggression that has gone well over normal cultural limits. It is a mistake, however, to think that all psychiatric patients are aggressive or dangerous. It is true that a small minority act out aggression towards others, most commonly towards family members or members of the psychiatric team attempting to care for them. The vast majority of psychiatric patients, however, hurt themselves because they have difficulties expressing their aggression directly or appropriately to those who have upset or hurt them, and therefore turn it inwards with devastating effects.

When judging the aggressiveness of others it is important to be honest about one's own aggression. Most of us harbour a desire to murder someone at least once in a lifetime. Our socialisation, our better nature and our knowledge that we will probably be punished all weigh against our acting out this desire.

When someone acts in an overtly and unacceptably aggressive way it is important first of all to establish whether there is an organic cause. Many substances, including alcohol and a variety of other drugs, precipitate outbursts of aggression. Head injuries, infections or tumours of the brain and epilepsy can all make aggressive otherwise gentle people. Treatment with corticosteroids (used for a variety of auto-allergic responses in the body, for example when a person's body threatens to reject a newly-transplanted kidney) can produced sudden outbursts of rage that are quite out of character. And certain people, particularly young men between the ages of 15 and 25, have a tendency towards more aggressive behaviour when they are in large groups.

The psychiatric illnesses most commonly associated with aggression are mania, schizophrenia and pathological jealousy, while in children the *hyperkinetic syndrome* (a medical term for extreme hyperactivity) is quite common. The vast majority of aggression seen in everyday practice, however, is of the kind that exists in all close relationships; it is just that it has become distorted in some way in its expression.

Kathy was a 28-year-old housewife, referred by a GP to a community psychiatric nurse (CPN) because of her 'aggressive' behaviour towards her husband. Each evening, just before he returned home from work, she would empty the kitchen waste-bin into a large, smelly heap on the kitchen floor. She could not explain her action logically, merely saying she felt 'compelled' to do it, despite the uproar it caused each evening. Richard was a quiet and at first sight inoffensive 30-year-old. He was however obsessional about cleanliness in the house and was outraged by Kathy's behaviour. Both Kathy and Richard said that their marriage was perfect, that they never normally argued and had never experienced any sense of aggression with each other before Kathy had started this unusual behaviour. Richard went to great lengths to describe how gentle and unaggressive his personality was (although during one interview with the CPN he disclosed that his hobby was standing with camera in hand on a bridge over the section of the M1 near his home, hoping to catch an accident in the making!). After spending an hour in Richard's company the CPN commented that Richard had made him feel very irritable.

As we got to know this couple better it became clear that Kathy too felt irritated and even murderous towards Richard, who insisted she clean the entire house to his standards each day. In the past he had even inspected her housework on his return home. The episodes with the bin not only allowed her to escape this inspection but were also an very accurate way of hurting Richard. It took weeks of marital therapy, however, before the couple could acknowledge that they had any problems. What started out as a referral for Kathy turned into help for the marriage and treatment for Richard's obsessional problems (*see* **Obsessive Compulsive Illness**). Kathy also needed help in becoming assertive in more straightforward ways. Their case is a good example of how it is always easier to spot the 'madness' in others, particularly those with whom we live, than in oneself.

Some people have more aggressive personalities than others. Perhaps some are born this way; certainly circumstance, most usually the example of violence when they are children, can make people aggressive adults. Some seem to remain unconditioned by social restrictions, believing themselves to be outside of any laws and quite uncaring of the feelings of others. These people are loosely labelled socio- or psychopaths. It is clear that in an organised society, where laws are clearly spelled out and enforced, such people form a tiny minority. Rather than think of ourselves as living in an aggressive society I sometimes think we should be amazed at how so many very different people can live in such close proximity with so little violence. In less organised societies the aggression that is in all of us has a chance to get out without fear of punishment. In looking around the world at any point in history we can see the sad global consequences.

In the acting out of aggression men, particularly young men, predominate. It is interesting that there has been so little research into this fact . . . is it hormonal or social, for instance? We simply do not know, and in many ways each society turns something of a blind eye to this fact. Statistically, for instance, young men stand a greater chance of being injured or even killed by each other when out at night, than young women stand of being injured at all. Newspapers tend to make much larger headlines about the women however, often with advice to stay home or have escorts . . . advice that is not offered to the young men. Women more commonly turn their aggression inwards. Perhaps this accounts for why we have so many more men than women in prison and so many more women than men as psychiatric patients. (*See also* **Mania**, **Othello Syndrome**, and **Schizophrenia**.)

# Agitation

Agitation (also known as restlessness or purposeless activity) is rarely seen as an individual symptom but rather as part of a total picture in a number of psychiatric problems. Most commonly it is associated with problems in the elderly.

Some depressions manifest themselves in agitation rather than lethargy, and although the drugs often used to treat depressions are meant to have a sedative effect, the elderly are particularly sensitive to medication and can become agitated.

In both Alzheimer's disease, a form of degeneration of brain cells, and arteriosclerotic dementia, where the brain cells die because of inadequate blood supplies (*see* **Dementia**), agitation is often an early symptom. Memory loss and an inability to be as efficient as one was in the past mean that daily life and routine become disrupted. This leads to agitation and behaviour which is often rather repetitive and yet secretive, as if the person knows something is wrong and is desperately attempting to hide it. Alongside these active attempts to get things right or back to normal, there is often a sense of perplexity and fleeting moments of depression and euphoria. This is distressing not only for the individual concerned, who at least in the early days of the illness knows that their faculties are slipping from them forever, but for his or her close relatives, who see the one they love losing intellectual and emotional ground day by day. Treatment and practical help for these illnesses are discussed in Part Four.

In young adults agitation is most commonly seen in the mothers of young babies; these mothers may develop sudden and unexpected psychotic illnesses. Recent studies suggest that as many as 5 in a 1000 new mothers are likely to have this problem. The agitation, interspersed with periods of confusion and visual or auditory hallucinations, usually becomes apparent within a month of childbirth. It is the agitation which sometimes makes families and carers so anxious for the well-being of the baby, although with treatment, support and advice these women make as good mothers as anyone else. In the acute stage of the illness, however, they do need constant attention, most particularly when they are handling the baby. Current opinion is that it is best for baby and mother to stay together even when the mother is extremely distressed and agitated, as long as constant supervision can be provided (*see* **Post-natal Depression**).

A more rare illness which results in agitation is known as Cushing's disease, in which the pituitary gland in the brain causes an over-secretion of cortisol into the bloodstream.

Although this is a hormonal disease, more than half of the people diagnosed have originally experienced psychiatric rather than physical problems. Sudden outbursts of agitation followed by withdrawal and lethargy are common. There are also many physical signs, most noticeably a change in facial features to what is typically described as a red, moon-shaped face. Often symptoms such as impotence, amenorrhoea (lack of periods) and loss of libido have alerted the patient to the presence of a problem prior to psychiatric referral. This is a treatable illness, and the agitation, along with possible depression, paranoia and hallucinations, rapidly disappear once treatment commences.

## Agoraphobia

Agoraphobia is a fear of open spaces, quite often meaning a fear of everywhere outside of the home. An agoraphobic avoids any situation which causes fear, anxiety or panic, retreating into the security (but also confinement) of what they perceive to be a safe living space (*see* **Anxiety** and **Panic Attacks**). This is a limiting life for the sufferer, and also places strains on other family members who have to conduct normal family activities such as shopping as well as be available to accompany the agoraphobic, who may venture out if accompanied. Agoraphobics know that their fears are irrational and are often angry at themselves for their limitations and desperate for someone to help them out of their 'trap'.

Agoraphobia is much more common in women than men (the ratio is 3:1), and often runs a chronic course over many years with minor alterations in severity. Many women experience a mild form of agoraphobia when they return home with a new baby. The first few trips into the world can seem frightening and may persuade a woman that she is 'safer' at home. The longer she allows herself to retreat in this way the more difficult it becomes to emerge again into the world (*see* **Flight into Illness**).

Many women would argue that there is good reason to be frightened of leaving your own front door, as there are daily reports of attacks and rapes, especially during the evening in the dark. Families are also strangely protective of women who are developing agoraphobia, perhaps reflecting that there are benefits to families in having mother trapped in the home by her own fears.

Madeline had been at home for 23 years, going out in the company of relatives, and had only sought help intermittently for the problem. It was only when her youngest daughter left home that Madeline began to feel that she had a problem that needed to be tackled. Her husband Bob was only superficially supportive, and whenever she made minimal progress, such as walking alone to the corner of their street, he would remind her of just how dangerous the world was. She, too, was ambivalent about wanting to be better, feeling that many demands would then be placed on her which she would be incapable of fulfilling. Eventually she joined a local self-help group which organised volunteers who had themselves conquered the problem to walk with her. Organised outings initially represented a great challenge to her, but after a few months Madeline found herself looking forward to these trips with her new-found friends.

Treatment normally consists of having a trained therapist come to the house and participate with the patient in activities outside of the house until the sufferer's anxiety decreases to bearable proportions. Some patients require psychotherapy, their fears being rooted in deeply-buried memories of early physical or sexual abuse; others can be helped by medication for any accompanying depression or obsessional symptoms. (*See also* **Depression** and **Obsessive Compulsive Illness**.)

## Alcoholism

The abuse of alcohol is a serious problem in much of the world. Only countries which operate a severe ban seem able to limit the social and industrial as well as the personal and family damage that abuse can bring. Most developed countries bear the enormous cost of accidents, crimes and days off work through illness resulting from problem drinking. Alcoholism is also an illness about which we tend to be socially discreet, rarely even confronting friends when we think or know they are drinking too much and often failing to take responsible decisions about letting people who we know are over the legal limit drive.

The World Health Organisation has recently adopted the term 'problem drinker', as this tends to be more acceptable to a person with the problem than the label 'alcoholic'. Our vision of alcoholics tends to be of the 'down-and-outs' of society rather than the housewife secretly drinking heavily during the day, or the businessman drinking too much at work-related events.

Much health education advice is now offered on the maximum safe doses of alcohol per week for both men and women, with 14 units per week for women and 21 units per week for men said to be safe doses (a unit being half a pint of beer, a glass of wine or a small measure of spirits). Consumption above this level on a regular basis opens the individual to the threats of physical, psychological or social consequences. The problem with these measures are that drinks within the home are rarely measured out in accurate doses, and it is therefore easy to fool oneself and others about one's true level of consumption.

Individuals become problem drinkers because of the amount of alcohol they drink, whether or not they experience problems immediately. Many escape problems for some years but are still within the 'problem' category. Most drink because of early habits learned in the home or because of social pressures. Some relieve social anxieties or other forms of psychological distress with alcohol, but this remedy is short-lived, because as soon as the effect of the drink wears off the person is likely to feel even more anxious or depressed. Thus the dose and rate of repeated doses of alcohol tends to rise.

As well as the amount of alcohol consumed, other danger signs include needing to drink during the day, taking alcohol to work or in the mornings, drinking much more than friends or colleagues in any situation, gulping drinks (particularly the first few of the day), feeling the need to lie about how much you are consuming or disguising it by hiding bottles, and becoming forgetful as a result of the abuse.

Alcohol is a toxin to the stomach, often causing indigestion, nausea and diarrhoea as well as triggering longer-lasting damage to the liver, pancreas, lungs, and vascular system (resulting in high blood-pressure and heart strain). Pregnant women who are heavy drinkers risk damaging the unborn foetus.

Socially, problem drinkers tend to have marital difficulties as spouses become unable to tolerate the drunken abuse, aggression, sentimentality and forgetfulness of the drinker. Many drinkers lose their jobs and/or their driving licences, or have accidents or become involved in crime. Alcohol is a depressive drug, and its effects lead to depressing personal lives of isolation and non-achievement, often littered with failed relationships. It should not be surprising then that drinkers often commit or attempt suicide.

Attempts at withdrawal without help and supervision can lead to *delirium tremens* (d.t.'s), causing the person to experience frightening hallucinations and making him or her restless, agitated and likely to have fits. Long-term abuse leads to deterioration of intellectual and emotional functioning. *Korsakov's syndrome* describes a condition in which almost all of one's ability to remember new material is lost, although memory of the past remains. This leads to the drinkers having to make up stories and information in order to cover the increasing gap in their memories. Dementia can also result from long-term alcohol abuse. (*See also* **Addiction** and **Amnesia**.)

# Alienation
*See* **Isolation**

# Ambivalence
People often find the co-existence of two directly opposite

feelings or opinions within themselves one of the most disturbing aspects of their mental life. It is perhaps sad to find that you hate the one you also love, or frightening to discover a wish to destroy something of great value to yourself. Theorists have however always considered this ambivalence central to human emotional experience.

Bleuler first used the word ambivalence in his studies on schizophrenia at the beginning of the 20th century. He made a distinction between emotional ambivalence, which he considered most important, and ambivalence affecting the intellect and will. Sigmund Freud and later Melanie Klein realised the importance of this dichotomy (*see* **Aggression**), and Karl Abraham incorporated the concept into his ideas on the development of our psyches.

Central to all their theories is the dichotomy between love and hate: love, according to Freudian theory, arising from our sexual instincts, while hate comes from the instinct to survive. Kleinian theory is based not only on the ambivalent love/hate of the baby for her mother, but also on the fact that the baby finds containing both feelings intolerable and therefore projects the painful dichotomy out of herself, constructing a 'good' mother whom she can love and a 'bad' mother whom she can hate. Such splitting and projection should, in the course of normal development, be gradually resolved until the growing child can bear to hold the ambivalence within herself, acknowledging both good and bad in mother and herself. Ambivalence is painful, however, even for adults, and therefore this developmental step is hard to achieve and often only partially accomplished. This means that although under normal circumstances the adult may take a balanced emotional view of a situation, stress of any sort can throw him or her back into splitting and projecting as a means of defence.

Derek is a computer analyst; his wife Pauline is a pharmacist. I first met Pauline when she became depressed within months of beginning what had seemed an idyllic marriage. Apparently, from the moment they returned from their honeymoon, Derek had criticised every aspect of Pauline's behaviour, something he had never done when they were courting. Pauline, trusting his judgement, had reacted to this by struggling to please him. Yet however hard she tried, nothing seemed to work.

Couples often seem to choose each other in an almost uncanny way so that their unconscious worlds interlock just as readily as their conscious ones do. Pauline was the third daughter of a couple desperate to have a son. It became clear in therapy that Pauline's mother had been depressed after her birth, which made her unresponsive to Pauline's needs. From her earliest days Pauline had learned to keep angry, destructive feelings to herself; if something was wrong with mother then it must be her fault for being a bad baby, she had reckoned. Despite this difficult beginning she had done well in life and seemed a happy well-adjusted young woman up until her marriage. At the first sign of trouble in the relationship, however, without stopping to wonder what was happening to Derek, she had switched back to that early model of believing the bad to be in herself.

Derek, on the other hand, saw his mother as all-bad. She nagged him throughout childhood, was always tired and never had time for her three children. He was still so angry with her in adulthood that he had not invited her to the wedding. Gradually Derek realised that from the moment the Registrar had turned to Pauline and said 'Congratulations, Mrs Stanford,' he had associated her with his mother, the other Mrs Stanford. The hate he felt for his mother had become displaced onto Pauline, and until he came to realise this there was nothing Pauline could ever do that would make him happy.

The couple worked at first individually and then together to readjust their feelings about themselves and each other. Derek's mother turned out to have been widowed and financially struggling with her three sons, and although she was far from perfect Derek began to appreciate how hard her life had been. Even more difficult was the realisation that he had at times made things between them very disagreeable. Pauline's mother on the other hand slipped from her pedestal, allowing Pauline to feel angry, for the first time, about her lack of mothering. In allowing themselves to have rather less black-and-white images of their mothers, they also found they could be more accepting of them. In our final session Pauline announced that she had managed to get angry with Derek 'when he was impossible'. Derek started to say that he was never impossible, but stopped halfway through, laughing.

The pain of ambivalence is so great that many people find 'symptoms' to disguise it. Obsessional symptoms, for instance, often disguise the split between wanting to damage and wanting to protect. Jenny, a 38-year-old mum of Jerry, 5 months, found herself having to wash his bottles so many times that her hands started to bleed. She said she was frightened of poisoning him. Her obsessional rituals with the bottles was her way of protecting him from the aggression she felt towards him (*see* **Obsessive Compulsive Illness**). Phobias project the hated, frightening part of self onto something or someone else.

The ambivalence experienced by schizophrenics is often distressing and incapacitating. They become so acutely aware of the dichotomy both within and outside themselves that life becomes impossible. Decisions cannot be made and no one, including oneself, can be trusted. It becomes clear talking with someone in this state why most of us turn a blind eye to the contradictions within us as often as possible. Contradictions are painful, and it is only when our way of coping with them causes us or someone else even more pain that we are motivated to look more closely at our split selves (*see* **Schizophrenia**).

## Amnesia

Memory suffers as a result of both psychological states of distress and organic damage to the brain. Amnesia is a failure of memory more serious than mere forgetfulness, and as memory consists of three stages – registering information, storing and then being able to retrieve the information – failure can occur at any or all of these stages.

If the brain is damaged by toxins such as alcohol there may be a phase of memory 'blackout' from which there is no recovery of memory even when the toxin has cleared from the body and despite attempts to trigger it. External observers may be unaware that the person is so inebriated that they are having a memory blackout but should be alerted by repetitions of the same story or evidence that important messages have not 'registered' (*see* **Alcoholism**). Sometimes this form of amnesia is fragmentary, so that part of the person's experience will be recalled later whilst the remainder is not remembered at all.

If the blood supply to the brain is interrupted transiently by a spasm of the arteries, or if the oxygen concentration in the blood that is going to the brain is decreased because of heart or lung problems, then memory may be the most obvious of the brain's functions to suffer. Such memory loss is usually total for the period of time of the insult to the brain tissue. Many people experience amnesia after fits and may be irritable during the post-fit stage, but have no memory of this later.

Head trauma, especially trauma leading to unconsciousness, may cause amnesia that may affect the memory of events before and/or after the trauma. Memory suffers in all forms of dementia, although once the deterioration is advanced most people do not seem to notice their own deficit and are therefore not unduly disturbed by it. In contrast people who suffer poor memory as a result of depression are often anxious about their inability to remember.

All forms of mental illness that cause disturbances in the way people think also affect the memory, thus memory can be impaired in cases of schizophrenia and manic depressive psychosis. Some psychological trauma is so overwhelming that it 'blanks out' the memory, although subsequent events may trigger these memories again.

When in *fugue*, that is, a state in which people can continue to function but are not registering any new information, people can travel away from home and assume new identities, without memory of their previous past. Once returned they have no memory of their period in fugue. Such an episode is usually precipitated by extreme stress and only lasts for a few hours. It is an unusual syndrome and distinct from what is known as malingering, which usually has obvious motives such as gain that can be made from the adopted memory failure. Occasionally people use the occurrence of fugue as a defence in violent crimes. Its use is considered contentious in psychiatry, with opinion divided as to whether it is possible for a person to do something entirely out of character without previous intent.

If character change is part of the fugue the new character is usually a less inhibited version of the old one. In cases of psychogenic amnesia people are less purposeful and more obviously confused than those in fugue. They have usually forgotten important personal information and may be remarkably unconcerned about their own plight. It is probably a defensive gesture by the brain, which might otherwise be overwhelmed by an event or piece of information. Recovery is usually rapid and complete once the original stress is removed.

## Anger

Anger is closely related to irritability and involves the build-up of tension during a latent phase between the unpleasant disruptive stimulus and the expressed angry response. In some personalities and in some psychological states the length of that latent phase is altered: repressed people may take days, weeks or even years between stimulus and response, whilst those with a manic-depressive illness can erupt apparently instantly, even at times spontaneously, without any obvious external stimuli.

Each of us is aware of what makes us angry, how we express that anger, and how long our 'fuse' or latent phase is. As we become adults and mature our latent phase normally becomes longer, but as we go into old age it frequently becomes shorter again.

In psychological and physiological terms anger is part of our survival instinct. However, as with all instincts, it can go into 'over-drive', making us react too impulsively, without rational thought and to our own detriment. As we became angry our body changes in accordance with our awareness that tension is building up. The physiological changes are very similar to those found in anxiety, in that the heart rate quickens, blood is redistributed from inner organs to our muscles, the small airways in the lungs (the *bronchioles*) dilate, and adrenaline is released into our bloodstream, along with more sugar, which is released from the liver. All this prepares us to fight if we are angry or to take flight if we are anxious, and is therefore commonly called the fight or flight mechanism (*see* **Instinct for Survival**).

The closely related nature of our physical response to anger and anxiety leads some people into confusion about which state they are experiencing. John was a 45-year-old executive who worried excessively about many small things. His anxiety was such that he regularly experienced panic attacks, usually about his work. One day he described to his therapy group a fear that the paperwork he had left on his desk might be lying over the electric wire to his computer. This in turn might spontaneously catch fire, and because it was his paperwork it would be his responsibility when the whole building burned down. Most of the group were incredulous as to the extent John would go to in order to find something to worry about, however one woman grasped the underlying difficulty and said to John 'wouldn't it be quicker just to blow the place up?'. At this John broke into an angry outburst about how unfairly the work was divided and how he had been repeatedly passed over for promotion despite his commitment to the firm over many years. He then got angry with the woman whose comment had led to the outburst, but even as he started to speak to her he began to feel overwhelmingly anxious again, starting to sweat and fearing that he might be having a heart attack because he could feel his heart thumping so loudly.

John had come from a poor family where his father had repeatedly urged him to be successful in order to avoid the humiliation of poverty. When in his 20s John's mother had told him, during a family argument, that he was a great disappointment to his father. Driving home after this episode he experienced his first panic attack. He described his feelings immediately prior to that experience as murderous rage combined with dejection and a great fear that his father would reject him. Since that time anxiety and anger had become confused for him, and he often reacted with anxiety when anger might have been more appropriate.

In the centre of the brain there is an area called the *thalamus*. Surrounding this are a number of centres apparently connected to a rage response. The more sophisticated, 'higher centres' of the brain inhibit these lower centres most of the time, but if the function of these 'higher centres' is in some way reduced or distorted, irritability, anger and rage can result.

Physical insults to the brain, injury, infection or epilepsy can act to decrease this inhibition, thus releasing the angry, raging response. Some practitioners believe that there is a variety of psychopathy, found in young men with angry, aggressive behaviour, which is associated with abnormal brain waves as measured on an electro-encephalograph. Others would argue that this is a personality trait, and not a physical condition.

Psychological conditions also predispose some people to become angry more rapidly than others and with less stimulus. In some cases the stimulus is actually imagined. An example of this is pathological jealousy when a partner believes his or her spouse to have been unfaithful despite all evidence to the contrary (*see* **Othello Syndrome**). In manic-depressive illnesses, particularly during a manic phase, euphoria can suddenly turn to fury, which may then be expressed externally as attacks on people or property or internally as an attack on oneself.

Circumstances also affect our levels of irritability, and lack of sleep, poor diet, little exercise and stress all make us more likely to 'blow-up'. It seems likely that all of us experience tension that mounts to anger sometimes. The way in which we respond to our internal distress depends on the messages we have received in childhood about open expression of 'negative' feelings and on our perception of whether anger is likely to meet with understanding, permission or punishment in the present. Men seem freer to express anger and irritability, this being partly because of social permission and even encouragement to do so.

Expressing anger may however also have a hormonal basis. Many women report feeling more angry at a particular time in their menstrual cycle, most commonly just pre-period. They often also feel very uncomfortable about their levels of anger, believing them to be wrong. Research has demonstrated, however, that even at their most irritable time of the month the majority of women are not as irritable as men are all the time. It may be that the outbursts of anger once a month act as a safety valve, allowing safe and limited expression that serves to protect women's overall mental health. (*See also* **Anxiety**, **Irritability**, **Pre-menstrual Syndrome** and **Repression**.)

## Anxiety

Anxiety to those who suffer it is probably the most painful of the psychological/physical states. It can be experienced in a variety of ways ranging from constant free-floating anxiety through specific anxiety-provoking situations and on to full-blown panic attacks (*see* **Panic Attacks**). Often the fear of becoming anxious becomes almost as painful and limiting as the anxiety itself. Most people go to great lengths to avoid whatever it is that causes them anxiety, and this avoidance becomes a rigid pattern, setting severe restraints on their normal functioning and enjoyment of life.

Anxiety can be experienced as either a physical or psychological state, but most normally presents itself as a combination of the two which feed each other in a vicious circle. Hence the initial experience of anxiety, whatever the cause, produces physical symptoms – increased levels of adrenaline circulate the bloodstream, thereby increasing the heart rate, often to the point of causing palpitations and making the blood vessels 'pound' in the head and causing a sensation of pressure on the chest. These physical symptoms are frightening in their own right, making the people who experience them believe they are going to die of a heart attack, brain disease or suffocation. This increases their psychological experience of anxiety, which in its turn makes the physical symptoms worse. The initial frightening experience, which may have been trivial and caused only low-level anxiety, thus leads to a crescendo of terrifying proportions. From that moment the first experience is associated with the crescendo, and by this route people become incapacitatingly anxious about things that to others can appear trivial.

Gut symptoms are also common in anxiety, giving rise to indigestion, nausea and vomiting. Chronically anxious people often suffer from stomach ulceration as the long-term consequences of their higher-than-normal production of gastric (stomach) acid, and their bowels may become 'unstable', affected by both constipation and diarrhoea in turn. Headaches that feel like tight bands around the forehead are also common.

Freud coined the term 'anxiety neurosis' to describe a state he found frequently amongst his women patients. He believed it to be the result of unreleased sexual tension. Interestingly, sexual functions are often affected by anxiety, with a loss of libido and in men an inability to maintain erection (*see* **Libido** and **Sexual Arousal Disorders**). When an emotion has such a profound effect on the cardio-vascular (heart and blood) system that it causes sweating, a loss of blood from the face, giddiness and dizziness or even fainting, it seems likely that its effect on sexual functioning must also be extreme. Freud's suggestion that the original anxiety was connected to a woman patient's fear of sexuality completed a circle of mind/body interaction so that it becomes impossible to say whether mind or body is dominant. The women may have become anxious about their physical response to sexual stimuli, and this anxiety prevented further sexual response; or perhaps more generalised anxiety may have made their sexual activity difficult or unenjoyable, leading to physical difficulties which then caused further anxiety.

Undoubtedly sexuality does cause some people extreme anxiety. I have, for example, seen a number of patients who developed asthma-type symptoms on their honeymoons. Many people still show up at a variety of out-patient clinics with a multitude of symptoms that are rooted in their anxiety about sex, perhaps proving Freud right in believing sex to be fundamentally important as a basis for anxiety.

There are other causes of anxiety, however, and amongst those most often disclosed are fears about violence, death and separation from a loved one. Many people experience being out of control as frightening, and flying can combine this fear with the fear of death, making airplanes a source of anxiety for many people.

Suzanne, a 26-year-old teacher, came to see me feeling guilty about her masturbation fantasies and wanting to check up whether or not she was normal. Late at night, Suzanne, who lived alone, would become frightened of the dark and of her perceived separation from the rest of humanity, and of the possibility of attack from the outside. Even when she got to sleep she would be disturbed by violent, frightening nightmares which would either make her wake sweating and anxious or feeling sexually aroused. This latter experience had triggered an 'experiment' when she had masturbated with the violent, anxiety-producing imagery of her nightmares as a conscious fantasy. She was amazed to discover that not only did this prove physically satisfying to her but that she experienced none of her usual anxieties that night and fell into a peaceful sleep immediately thereafter.

Such episodes make a clear connection between anxiety on the one hand and sexual satisfaction on the other, and are quite common. Like Suzanne, those who make the connection often feel a sense of guilt, as if they have stumbled on a disturbing facet of human experience. The guilt seems to spring from the idea of combining sex, aggression (usually only fantasised) and anxiety in a potentially satisfying way instead of keeping them rigorously apart as we normally consciously try to do. This triad possibly represents our earliest emotions of physically intimate love for our mother combined with the rage and aggression we feel towards her and our extreme anxiety that we might kill or injure the one we love and need. It seems possible therefore that whether or not sexuality is the underlying cause of anxiety, passionate arousal and orgasm may be a 'self-help' cure for it.

Certainly anxiety is physically connected with anger (*see* **Anger**); for some people the two are indistinguishable. Becoming angry with someone also threatens separation from that person, and if the object of the anger is an important and loved person, then the experience of becoming angry may well make us anxious as well as physically angry. Hence anxiety may hide anger and anger mask anxiety. Watch a mother who has lost, sought and then found a child. The anxiety of the separation often expresses itself as anger towards the child for getting lost. I was certainly grateful to learn early in my practice of psychiatry that the most dangerous patient is a frightened one. This is not only true in mental institutions but in society at large.

Because anxiety can present in a wide range of symptoms, both physical and psychological, its source may be identified as almost any facet of life. A person's response pattern to the pain of anxiety may also be varied, ranging from a chronic experience to a lifetime devoted to avoiding the event with which the original anxiety was connected. Each person needs individual assessment of his or her perception of what it is like.

It is helpful to distinguish between normal, healthy anxiety or fear, which serves a protective function in our lives, and that anxiety that is overwhelming and engenders a reaction that is out of proportion to the stimulus. Normal anxiety is often the result of an abnormally stressful situation: taking exams and going to job interviews being two of the most common situations in which we all experience some anxiety, and, as long as it is not too severe, this kind of anxiety probably improves our performance. Pathological anxiety, on the other hand, occurs in situations where the stimuli are either absent or not so great as to explain the intense feelings provoked.

People who suffer this form of anxiety know that their fears are irrational and yet cannot control them. The young and old are especially vulnerable: young adolescents who are newly exposed to the rigours of the world, have little experience against which to judge what happens to them and often they have a shifting sense of who they are, leading to considerable anxiety. The elderly, for their part, need established routine and familiar surroundings in order to feel safe, and any alteration may produce great anxiety. Loneliness and death often preoccupy them, and life offers few distractions away from their frightening thoughts. There are also those people who seem unduly anxious from early childhood. Some are constitutionally anxious, others are reared in 'anxiety-producing households' where violence and unpredictable adult responses mean that the growing child never experiences safety.

Alongside the physical components of anxiety, people describe feeling 'tense', a state that is often reflected in the pains they experience in various muscle groups (particularly the neck and back muscles) and their inability to concentrate. They may feel tired from lack of sleep because they have been lying awake worrying or awakened repeatedly by nightmares. It is quite common for people to feel depressed about their problems, which adds further to their anxiety. (*See also* **Depression** and pp.433–50 on Psychological Treatments and Self-help Groups in Part Four.)

## Apathy

Apathy, a general lack of interest in things that are normally considered interesting, extending sometimes to a complete lack of emotion, is a symptom of many psychological/psychiatric problems. It often appears as if the person has simply 'switched off' from involvement with life. Individuals experiencing this describe feeling distant, detached and unconcerned about themselves or others.

We all experience apathy in its milder forms from time to time. We have all felt like saying 'I don't give a damn' when we have experienced some kind of frustration. It is as if we 'blow a fuse' after exerting ourselves, and things that we felt were important enough to work at, argue about and even fight over suddenly lose all importance. We cease to care.

In its more extreme forms apathy is more disturbing for others than for the sufferer. The sufferer, who has reached his or her limit and 'turned off', is protected by the apathy. Often a symptom of depression, apathy can however represent an end point, the sufferer ceasing to feel depressed because he or she has placed all feelings in cold storage. There may have been a history of prolonged depression preceding the apathy, a depression that has been ignored until the person's mind can no longer stand the pain and finally shuts down in order to protect itself. As the apathy recedes during treatment sufferers have to face their depression again on the way back to normality. It is at this point, as energy returns alongside the original problems and pains, that people are most at risk of killing themselves, something they would not have had the resources or concern to do when apathetic (*see* **Depression**).

Apathy is common in old age, and may be complicated by bad diet resulting from an apathetic attitude to shopping, cooking and eating alone, which then makes the apathy worse through malnutrition and as a consequence of the sufferer feeling cold, lonely and bored. Not only does the underlying depression need treatment, but there is also a need for common-sense forms of caring in such a situation.

It is also usual for people who have experienced major or minor trauma to go through a phase of not caring. A friend who has recently been in a serious car crash commented that although she was usually scared of flying she was facing an imminent holiday flight 'without concern'. 'I don't care if I crash,' was her feeling. It is important to warn people to be extra careful of themselves when they experience apathy; it is all too easy to have repeated minor accidents because they are not paying sufficient attention. If I know patients are driving home after a particularly difficult psychotherapy session which may have temporarily 'fused' their capacity for concern about themselves, I always remind them to take care.

Major trauma can leave people with profound apathy, making them unresponsive to their loved ones. It is often difficult to know how long such a situation will last, and can be hard for family and friends to tolerate. Apathy is particularly difficult for children who do not understand why a loving mum or dad should suddenly 'turn off'. However extreme the trauma, the vast majority of people do seem to recover eventually, although it may take many years (*see* **Post-traumatic Stress Disorder**).

Since the 1950s much attention has been given to the apathy that develops in long-term hospital patients. What is called *institutionalisation* covers an apathetic attitude to any form of responsibility, personal or social, which arises when a patient is placed in an environment that robs him or her of the right or need to make decisions. All over the Western world considerable efforts have been made to rehabilitate patients who have suffered in this way, and many patients previously considered 'hopeless' now lead more fulfilling lives within their communities. There remains however a small number of patients for whom rehabilitation does not seem to work, and it is impossible to know whether this is a result of their illness in the setting of their personality or whether some effects of institutionalisation are irreversible for some people. Much care and consideration is now given to young people who develop illnesses previously considered chronic, so as to prevent such hospital-produced apathy. Sadly, however, apathy does seem to be a central problem for many young schizophrenics, however enlightened their care (*see* **Institutionalisation**).

# Arteriosclerotic Dementia
*See* **Dementia**

# Attempted Suicide
*See* **Suicide** and **Suicide Attempts**

# Autism

This rare disorder affects boys more commonly than girls and is usually although not always associated with mental impairment. The children affected cannot socialise normally, seeming to prefer the predictability of objects over relationships with other humans. They become distressed when objects with which they are familiar, for example furniture, are moved. Their responses to people and the environment strike everyone as 'odd', and they often have behavioural problems, including aggressive outbursts.

Mothers often suspect that their child has a problem before it is possible to make a definite diagnosis. The problems in relating start in the early days of life when an infant's relationships are often confined to those with his mother and father. Parents often harbour their misgivings, however, thinking that they are in some way to blame, and many months or even years may pass before they seek help.

The outcome is not favourable, with most autistic children needing long-term care, often outside the home. A few possess special creative or mathematical talents, and can therefore become self-supporting financially, but they usually continue to require help and must continue to live in a quiet, routine-based atmosphere.

# B

## Bedwetting

The ability to control our bladder and bowel functions is an important part of development, occurring in stages and normally complete by the age of 3 to 4 years. Daytime control tends to come before night control, and most children learn bowel control more easily. Hence bedwetting (known medically as *Enuresis*) represents a delay in the last of the hurdles to full control.

A number of factors are important in determining when a child will be dry at night. Most important is the genetic (inherited) make-up of the child. It requires a certain degree of physiological and neurological development to be able to control these functions, and in some families this development is delayed; thus a family history of bedwetting is common. It is possible to condition a baby to pass urine on the pot at a very early stage, but this behaviour, which is only a response to an outside stimulus such as the feel of the pot, is soon lost. In order to achieve true control the growing toddler needs to understand what is expected and must wish to have control.

Because control is such a complex mixture of neurological readiness (the nerves telling you your bladder is full and the nerves which allow you to pass urine need to connect in a meaningful way) and psychological willingness, the path to total control can be difficult.

It is all too easy for toilet training to become something of a battleground between parent and child, the parent feeling that the quality of their parenting is going to be judged by the degree of their child's control. Also, as bedwetting does tend to be genetic to a certain extent, one or both parents may have had unhappy experiences themselves as bedwetters, making it difficult for them to be detached and rational about their child's difficulties. Analysts believe this to be a crucial time, with the child taking her first steps to self-control and mastery of her own body; hence it is anathema if the parents attempt to take control of the training. The child does however need to know what is expected of her, and it is hard for parents to convey their expectations without at least a hint of removing the very control the child is struggling to master. It is important that the control is the child's and not the parents', and yet equally important for the parent to give positive rewarding responses to improvements in the child. It is easy to see what a tightrope parents and children walk towards control.

Assessment of the problem needs to take all these features into account. The child and parents need encouragement to talk about the pattern of bedwetting without feeling foolish or uncomfortable. The self-esteem of the child may be at risk, especially if she has been the object of ridicule or punishment, and the parents may feel under considerable stress. Common-sense measures such as not drinking for a few hours before bedtime and waking the child at the parents' bedtime often improve the situation. If these methods fail there is a device called 'the pad and bell', which conditions the child, over a period of several weeks or months, to respond to the signal of a full bladder. The pad is placed under the child in bed, and when urine is absorbed by the pad it completes an electrical circuit which rings a bell and wakens the child. Eventually this repeated pattern causes the child to awaken once the bladder is full. Occasionally, if prolonged bedwetting has not responded to any of these measures, small doses of drugs such as imipramine (an anti-depressant) can be used.

In a well-adjusted child bedwetting is usually developmental and will occur less frequently as the child grows older. If it has become a bad habit then the simple remedies work best.

Occasionally, however, children are brought in for treatment for bedwetting when the problems of both the child and the family are more complex.

Nathaniel had been bedwetting for three months when his mother and father decided that there was something wrong with him. He had been dry at night since he was 3 years old, but had suddenly started wetting the bed at age 6. His GP confirmed that there was no physical explanation.

In our four sessions together I talked with his family about the atmosphere at home. Both parents agreed that it had been strained recently as they had had a series of arguments leading up to a decision to separate. This was however financially impossible at present, and they had decided to continue to live together even though each still felt hurt and betrayed by the other. They had tried to protect Nathaniel from this tension, and yet even as they spoke about it he stopped playing in the far corner of the room and moved closer to them, obviously interested in and anxious about their conversation.

While it was difficult for his parents to give him any reassuring messages since they themselves did not know what the outcome of their problems was going to be, the therapist suggested that they could at least acknowledge that there were problems and stress to Nathaniel that they were grown-up ones, and that whatever was decided his mum and dad would always love and care for him. After this session the bedwetting stopped.

Whatever measures may be suggested specifically for the bedwetter it is helpful for families to have family therapy to sort out their problems. What is important in this situation is that the child does not become the family scapegoat, responsible for all problems, but that the family as a whole take responsibility.

## Bipolar Illness
*See* **Manic-Depressive Psychosis**

# Borderline States
*See* **Personality Disorder**

# Bowel Control

Most of the children who have problems with bowel control (*Encopresis*) are disturbed. Some come from chaotic homes where standards of personal cleanliness are low, others soil themselves under stress, often chronic family stress, or as a result of over-control, leading to constipation and then overflow.

Gaining bowel control is an important step in psychological development. Freud postulated three crucial phases in development: the oral, anal-sadistic, and phallic. The middle stage lasts from ages 2 to 4, and involves the first struggle for the child between activity and passivity. Actively the child desires to void the faeces, partly as a sadistic, destructive act and partly out of a desire to give his mother a 'present'. Passively the retention causes the child anal-erotic feelings and also allows expression of control, often in an aggressive, sadistic way against mother. Hence lack of bowel control is often found in children who cannot express their aggression or sadism directly to mother, perhaps because of her own over-controlled standards, and instead use this indirect route to express their anger.

Freud also suggested that there were character traits which resulted from people negotiating their way to physical control but never resolving the psychological issues that abound in this phase. Such people tend to be obsessionally tidy and ordered in their lives, obstinate, and over-careful with their money. Interestingly, many people with such traits are also very preoccupied with their bowel movements, which suggests that Freud was right to make this developmental link.

# Brain Tumour

Although not common, when they do occur brain tumours tend

to show up in young adult or middle-age life and to produce psychological symptoms before they produce physical ones. We do not know what causes the *meninges* (coverings) or the supportive tissue of the brain to grow into tumours, although a number of brain tumours are secondary to tumours elsewhere in the body, such as in the breast or lung. Because the brain is enclosed in the bony confines of the skull there is little room for the tumour to expand, thus once it and its surrounding inflammation begin to grow the remainder of the brain rapidly becomes squashed. This leads to a clouding of conscious awareness, sometimes making the sufferer change rapidly from being fully awake to being delirious. This may be accompanied by a headache which gets worse as full consciousness is restored.

As the brain's function is affected increasingly by the pressure being exerted on it, a form of dementia may appear that seems strikingly at odds with the youth and general good physical appearance of the person. Hallucinations and delusions may also occur and, although the person's mood is usually rather flat or facile, people sometimes experience depression and/or anxiety.

When neurological and other physical symptoms are lacking until late in the illness it may take a great deal of suspicion on the part of the diagnostician for him or her to be able to spot a tumour in one of the 'silent' areas of the brain.

Fiona was admitted to a psychiatric ward in a general hospital with what appeared to be an atypical depression. Her behaviour was childlike and dependent, and she claimed that 'like Alice' she had become 'very small indeed.' Her family reported that she had always been a person who leaned on others emotionally, and that a younger and much-loved brother had recently died, perhaps explaining Fiona's emotional regression. A physical examination revealed no abnormalities, and she was treated for several weeks with anti-depressants.

Fiona deteriorated, gradually becoming less and less interested in other people or her surroundings (*see* **Apathy**). One of the ward sisters took a three-week break; on her return she could not help but notice Fiona's deterioration, whereas other staff had not noticed her gradual downhill path. This provoked the team into rethinking their diagnosis and to ordering a number of investigations. Although an X-ray of the skull demonstrated nothing abnormal (only tumours which have calcified, that is, ones in which calcium has been deposited, have radio-opaque areas and therefore appear on X-rays), the team had become convinced that they were dealing with something organic, and proceeded with more detailed psychological studies of Fiona's intellectual functioning. It became clear that the deterioration in her memory and intelligence must have a more sinister basis than depression, and eventually a frontal lobe tumour was demonstrated by special X-rays capable of taking pictures as though they were slicing through brain tissue. Fiona had an urgent operation to remove the tumour and is still receiving radiotherapy. She has recovered some of her intellectual abilities and has returned home, feeling and behaving more normally.

# Breakdown
*See* **Emotional Breakdown**

# C

## Castration Complex

According to psychoanalytic theory the phallic stage of development (from ages 3 to 5) consists of a desire for the parent of the opposite sex and feelings of rivalry with the same-sex parent (*see* **Electra Complex** and **Oedipus Complex**). For little boys the rivalry with father also carries with it the fear of father's retaliation. Boys have already experienced loss of part of the self in the form of being weaned from the breast, which they had previously presumed was a part of themselves, and in parting with their faeces, another element of the self. Knowing such loss is possible, therefore, they fear that father's retaliation will be in the form of castration.

In order to resolve this dilemma the boy needs to work through to an identification with father, and it is because of the fear of castration that he abandons his incestuous desire for mother and achieves an identification with the male world. These conflicts re-emerge in adolescence when physical changes make the genitals the centre of concern again. During this later phase the boy can transfer the desire for mother to a more general desire for a woman, once more safeguarding himself in his relationship with father. However a sense of competition commonly persists between male family members at this stage.

Freud struggled to see how such a theory could be extended to girls. Children, in seeking to explain the sexual differences between girls and boys, are said to assume that the girls have been castrated. Clearly if they already believe themselves to have been castrated, the threat of castration cannot apply. Indeed

Freud believed that girls felt inferior because they lacked a penis and suffered from envy when they compared themselves with boys (*see* **Penis Envy**). According to Freud a girl's the desire for her father and competition with her mother is resolved by a desire to give her father a baby, thus instilling her with a desire for future conception. In this theory the baby is seen as a penis substitute.

Most modern theorists would see this theory as a predominantly male attitude towards development. Undoubtedly some girls/women envy men, however as a patient said to me 'my brothers had all the love, all the education, all the encouragement, none of the restrictions or responsibilities . . .I envy them all of that much more than I've ever thought of envying their penises.' I think this is probably a response that many women would echo.

Freud's theory also gives little weight to notions of uterine envy. The power to give life is great indeed, and therefore it seems unlikely that babies are a substitute for anything, and much more likely that boys are the ones who need to find a substitute source of power and attention once they realise they cannot give birth (*see* **Womb Envy**). If this is the case then it might seem reasonable to assume that the hostility boys feel towards their penis is not generated by father but by themselves: if they could pull it off, they could be women and give birth. Certainly in some psychotic states men have colourful delusions about their penis shrinking or disappearing into their body, and some disturbed men actually try to cut their penis off. This desire to be a woman is seen most strongly in male transsexuals, who feel that they are women trapped inside men's bodies. They will go to great lengths, including surgery, to achieve castration.

Freud also thought that since girls believed themselves to be 'lacking' and at the same time free from any fear of castration they could not develop the same super-ego (sense of inner control) as boys, and were therefore weaker morally. In this theory it is the fear that the father will castrate them that makes boys more likely to conform. In the experience of many analysts this notion has always been a puzzle, because it is apparent in therapy that women have severely self-punishing super-egos, whilst men's super-egos often seem more self-forgiving. It is probably true, however, to say that whilst women will conform to 'keep the peace' to a much greater extent than will men, they are also more non-conformist. Perhaps not having to worry about being castrated is a psychological advantage, after all.

## Censorship

In the Freudian model of the mind, we have a *conscious*, thinking mind readily available to us, a *pre-conscious* that contains dimly-remembered things, thoughts that are just out of reach, and material that is about to surface into consciousness, and an *unconscious* that is like the bottom of the iceberg (very big and out of sight). Much of the material in the unconscious has been actively repressed by our defence mechanisms because it is in some way frightening or unacceptable to our conscious, rational selves (*see* **Unconscious, Conscious and Pre-conscious Minds**).

Obviously there needs to be a 'gate-keeping' function between these layers to keep them separate; this function is carried out by the super-ego and known as censorship. The super-ego is built into our minds through personal and social experience. What is acceptable in one culture or religion may be unacceptable in another, and the growing child has to internalise these social norms if he or she is are going to fit into the culture and time.

In this way the super-ego can function as a personal censor of our experiences, memories and instinctual urges. It dictates what stays unconscious and what is allowed into pre-conscious or conscious thought. For some people it is not enough to censor only their own internal worlds; in order to feel comfortable they have to extend that censorship to those with whom they live, or in extreme cases to their entire culture or religion.

Life without our internal censor would be hopelessly chaotic, but life with someone else's internal censor in force over us can be equally bad. It has been suggested that relationships work best if the partners have similar censors, and that the greater the discrepancy the greater will be the problems of understanding or appreciating one another. This may cause problems in two-culture marriages, for instance, when the censors are bound to be different.

Janice's husband Omer was Iranian. The longer they lived together the more they discovered that their understanding of what was reasonable in a relationship was different. When they argued it felt, in Janice's words, like 'hitting a brick wall'. Each knew what his or her censor would allow and each was horrified to discover that the other's censor had totally different points of reference. Because the super-ego is so fundamental, built as it is into our minds, it can be a challenging and even frightening experience to have someone close to you disagree with it.

Janice believed it was acceptable to air all feelings within a marriage, even the angry, hostile ones. She had been brought up with this idea firmly embedded into her super-ego by her expressive parents. Omer, on the other hand, had never seen a woman in his close family openly lose her temper with a male relative, and believed that only bad women did such a thing. The concept of internal censors was useful for this couple in their attempts to understand one another. An ability to understand and appreciate other cultures often has the welcome side-effect of making us less judgemental, and loosening some of the more rigid socio-religious ties of our own censor (*see* **Conflict**).

# Cerebral Tumour
*See* **Brain Tumour**

# Childhood Sexual Abuse
Freud discovered that many of his female patients remembered

and had been damaged by sexual abuse from male relatives or friends of their families. For a year he wrote and talked about this until pressure from his colleagues persuaded him to rethink his discovery. He decided that, as children, these patients had fantasised about sexual activity and were, in adult life, relating these fantasies, not fact.

This confusion between fact and fantasy in the minds of carers remained for many years with people choosing to disbelieve what children said in order to maintain our social belief that children do not get sexually abused. Sadly, this belief is not true. Over the last twenty years we have been struggling to come to terms with the bare facts: children do get sexually abused; they have great difficulty drawing attention to their plight; and they still receive mixed or negative reactions from adults when they try to seek help.

The increasing publicity in recent years about childhood sexual abuse has revived for many people the memories of past abuse and encouraged them to seek help to overcome the damage done to them. In psychiatry and psychotherapy, it is now relatively common for a patient to relate an abusive past whatever their present symptoms.

The damage done to the developing personality of the child depends on the child's age, the person or people involved, the degree of violence and threat used, and the physical consequences of the abuse, such as infection, pregnancy and abortion. Personally I believe that all childhood abuse is damaging in some way; only the extent of the damage varies.

Most people have difficulty believing that anyone would sexually abuse babies and yet examples of abuse, including full penetration with horrific physical damage have been recorded in babies of only three or four months. At a time when the developing ego needs love and predictability the baby meets betrayal and pain. Not surprisingly such physical damage also damages the foundations of the personality leaving the adult incapable of loving, intimate relationships in adulthood, and with no sense of trust or security in life.

Abuse during the early years of life becomes embedded within the development of the child, becoming the child's 'norm' for life. This separates them from the remainder of their families and from any possibility of friendships. They often live in fear that they will be discovered, thinking that they are unclean, contaminated and disgusting, and that everyone can 'see' this badness in them. Above all they believe themselves to be guilty for what is happening and often love and identify with the parent who is abusing, hurting and frightening them. Thus they suffer emotional damage not simply from the abuse but also from the resulting separation from any other possible sources of love or rescue.

As the child grows and develops into a more conscious and thinking person so the abuse causes them to have to construct explanations for why it is happening to them. Such explanations almost always involve the child believing in their own fundamental badness, and a desire to protect the abusing parent whilst hating the other parent who they see as failing to love and help them. The conflict is established between fear and revulsion of the abuse on the one hand, and loving the abusing parent, who is often perceived as the good parent, on the other.

Conflicts of these sorts are too powerful for children to maintain and areas of their minds develop 'splits' so that different feelings can remain separated. Such splits may include a denial of the abuse which causes it to slide into their unconscious mind, out of sight of their conscious memory. Thus they 'forget' until something in later life reminds them.

If the degree to which these splits have developed is extensive the adult personality will be unstable, with different events and people in effect relating to different split-off aspects of the same person. Such a person has the terrifying experience of not being able to predict how they will react or who they are from day to day, sometimes from minute to minute.

The psychiatric and psychological effects of abuse are wide ranging and it seems likely that childhood abuse is so damaging that it makes whatever illness the individual was originally vulnerable to much more likely to occur under relatively minor stresses in adult life. Depression and anxiety are frequent consequences of abuse, as are anorexia, obsessional illnesses, personality problems and relationship, particularly sexual relationship, difficulties. (*See* **Anxiety**, **Depression**, **Eating Disorders**, **Obsessive Compulsive Illness**, **Sexual Arousal Disorders** and **Sexuality**.) The person is often either too ashamed to talk of the abuse or has consciously forgotten it: the symptoms then seem puzzling and without foundation. If they can build a more trusting relationship with a key carer then it becomes possible to risk exposing themselves. Carers have to be careful not to explode with fury towards the abuser, which is all too easy when hearing these tales, because the person will still have the conflict between fearing and yet loving the abuser within themselves and often still wish to protect those who have so disastrously betrayed them.

Much can be healed by exploration, acceptance, relinquishing guilt and sharing of pain. Confidential help lines, self-help groups and women's counselling services have all made good contributions to helping the abused not only survive but become whole again. However, occasionally I have met individuals who seem shattered beyond repair from what has happened. It may be possible to survive physically after repeated 'performances' for your Dad's paedophilic group, for instance, but the mind cannot survive except as many unconnected fragments only capable of limping through a disturbed and unhappy adulthood. Much like rape, childhood sexual abuse is rarely just about sex, indeed it may have remarkably little to do with sex. Instead it is about power and aggression, domination, control and humiliation. For children to experience and internalise such qualities is a toxic start to any life. (*See also* **Paedophilia**.)

## Compromising

We have probably all experienced the sense of relief we get when an argument or problem is resolved by an agreeable compromise. It is often a good way of sorting out an external conflict. Similarly, when our mind is taxed with internal conflict it looks for a compromise.

Internal conflicts exist between the material we have relegated to our unconscious mind which wishes to resurface and the defence systems we have established in order to keep the material out of conscious sight. Such material might be memories or instinctual urges.

The unconscious contains a great deal of our early life experience (most people cannot consciously remember much before the ages of 5 to 7 years, yet a great deal happens during those first years) and also any experience that is unbearable to remember, any emotion that we refuse to accept we feel consciously. This material is held at bay by a wide variety of defence mechanisms which we operate unconsciously. Thus it is not only the material but the fact that we have hidden it from our conscious minds that is outside of our conscious knowledge.

Freud suggested that we form symptoms as a compromise between the repressed material which wishes to make the leap into consciousness and the defence systems which are determined to keep it under control. In this way symptoms act as a warning to our conscious minds that an underlying conflict is active in our unconscious minds. In psychotherapy we meet a spectrum of symptoms. Some symptoms are connected primarily with resurfacing repressed material, and others seem centred on defence systems; but the majority of symptoms seem to represent a compromise between the forbidden and the forbidder.

Pauline is a 35-year-old hairdresser who obsessionally turns off taps at home hundreds of times a day, although while she is at work she does not worry about the taps there at all. During the course of individual therapy it became clear that her marriage (which she'd described previously as perfect) was traumatic for her. She harboured murderous feelings towards her husband, but had never let herself consciously acknowledge them. She defended herself from seeing her hate by a reaction formation, that is, she told herself and others the complete opposite of what was true about her feelings. Thus she was able to say she loved her husband and was very happy in a perfect marriage. As she began to realise how much she used reaction formation as a defence she began to question her obsessional symptom with the taps. 'I think', she said, in a flash of insight, 'that I really want to drown him and so I go around protecting him by making sure the water is turned off.' This demonstrates how clever the brain can be at finding a symptom which does constitute something of a compromise between the forbidden wish, in this case the wish to kill her husband, and the defence system, which in this case led her to 'protect' her husband in a way that satisfied her super-ego. (*See also* **Defence Mechanisms** and **Obsessive Compulsive Illness**.)

## Compulsion to Repeat
*See* **Repetition Compulsion**

## Concentration Difficulties

It is difficult to concentrate if we are preoccupied with things from either our internal world, consisting of recurrent memories that distract us, or from our external world in the shape of problems that we cannot seem to solve and which begin to overwhelm our ability to concentrate on anything else. We are also more likely to be distracted from things which we have reasons for not wanting to concentrate on too much, either because they bore us or have some special, painful significance for us (*see* **Repression**).

Such difficulties in concentration become extreme when someone is either depressed or anxious. People then report being unable to concentrate even on things that they previously enjoyed, and their work often suffers because of the limits on their ability to think (*see* **Anxiety** and **Depression**).

Sophie was a 23-year-old legal secretary who'd become

depressed after she'd had an abortion. Her depression was strongly coloured by anxieties about her health and particularly about whether she would be able to have future children. She became unable to concentrate at work, even filing suddenly seemed beyond her, and her main hobby of reading became impossible: she would find that she would get to the end of a page and be unable to explain to herself what she had just read. Friends kept telling her to 'pull herself together', which made her feel worse, and she began to feel as if her whole life was slipping away from her. Luckily this reaction was relatively short-lived in its extreme phase, but she discovered in the three years afterwards that around the anniversary of the abortion she would find herself preoccupied with her health in ways that made it hard to concentrate on her present life. She began to understand that she was grieving for the aborted child and that her internal preoccupation was a normal part of the reaction to loss, and this understanding gradually eased both her sense of guilt and her inner certainty that she would be punished by death or infertility for what she had done.

Some forms of schizophrenia also begin with difficulties in concentration. These types of schizophrenia occur most frequently in bright boys in late adolescence, and are often initially dismissed as fatigue, overwork, anxiety about exams, or puberty. Such adolescents tend to grow into rather vague, dreamy adults who will sadly not fulfil their original potential. Their inability to concentrate leads them to find it hard to formulate plans or carry through any work project, their relationships become chaotic and unsustainable and they have a tendency to sink into unskilled jobs or unemployment (*see* **Schizophrenia**).

# Conflict

None of us manages to live very long before finding ourselves in some sort of conflict. We are born with powerful instincts: to survive, to master our environment, to fulfil ourselves sexually and to procreate (*see* **Instinct for Mastery** and **Instinct for Survival**). These instincts are curbed, however, first by our mothers and families and then increasingly by the wider society. This repression of the outward expression of our basic nature means that the conflict changes from an external one, between ourselves and the outside world, to an internal conflict between our instincts and our super-ego (which is our internal policeman), representing the dictates of our parents and our society.

There are repeated shifts in the advice given to parents about the extent of repression to administer and whether or not it is good or bad to actively repress a child's urges, and if it is good, how it should be achieved. Fundamentally, however, man is a social animal and has to learn enough control to function effectively within society. That control is bound to be in some conflict with his more basic inner urges.

The analytic idea of neurosis is based in an understanding of this internal conflict, which for some individuals becomes extreme (*see* **Neurosis**). Karen Horney, a neo-Freudian who moved to the USA in the early 1930s, wrote widely about the extent to which our culture influences our attitudes in ways that we may only be semi-conscious of, if at all. In this way our internal policeman has taken on board the message of our society without us ever giving conscious thought to whether or not we really want to live by these rules. We may be totally unaware of the influence and consequences of these self-imposed rules on ourselves as individuals.

Travel or meeting foreigners often gives us a glimpse of the fact that not everyone behaves as we do, and it is easy to find a clash of super-egos between differing cultures, each believing that it is right (*see* **Censorship**). Karen Horney suggested that it is not having a controlling super-ego that necessarily makes us neurotic but that the extent to which those internal rules are held will determine how we cope psychologically with life. If the internal rules are held rigidly (as a result of the individual's anxieties about breaking them), this will render the person unable to bend psychologically with the problems of everyday life. For such people controlling their inner instincts is their foremost consideration; they cannot allow any hint of internal conflict to emerge, and so their instincts have to be squashed out of sight. Using a range of defence mechanisms in order to accomplish this can however become a serious problem for them.

Horney talked of four main defences used in the conflict solution, namely: *'eclipsing'* part of the problem, either by pretending it does not exist or super-imposing other pseudo-problems on it to cover the underlying problem which is somehow too bad for us to face; *isolating* the self from others so that nobody will see the inner 'bad' part we so fear; *idealising* the self as a protection against the 'bad' parts; or *externalising* conflict by projecting the parts of ourselves that we do not like onto someone else, thus enabling argument with these parts from a point safely removed from ourselves.

The relationship we have with our society should be in flux; this makes mental health easier than does a rigid view of how things should be. Since much of our conflict with society is internalised and unconscious we may be unaware of how strongly we feel about issues until something major happens in life. Eric Fromm, another neo-Freudian, commented on how we had to come to terms with three basic conflicts, namely the fact that we are born and die without choice; that we have only a limited time in which to achieve whatever we wish; and that our abilities cannot stretch beyond our time or culture. These truths cause individuals much psychic pain, and it is only by maintaining a degree of flexibility within ourselves and our culture that the conflict of wishing both to be an individual and a part of society can remain bearable.

# Consciousness
*See* **Unconscious, Conscious and Pre-conscious Minds**

# D

## Daydreaming

Daydreaming is a normal part of childhood experience. Adults, too, tend to have episodes of it, particularly if their present life is difficult and they find relief in sinking into another, easier world in their imagination. Occasionally however this mechanism of escaping reality overwhelms a person's ability to hold on to any sense of reality, and the world of the daydream begins to seem more real than the actual external world, all boundaries between the two ceasing to exist.

Steven is a 27-year-old who was diagnosed as schizophrenic when he was 21. He has spent the last year lying in bed believing that his thinking and writing are of crucial importance to the world. In fact he has not written anything that makes sense to that world: his importance lies within the world of his daydreams, which fill his waking hours.

Daydreams tend to have a different character to the dreams we have when we sleep. In our sleep-time dreams our unconscious world takes over, presenting us with what tends to be rather chaotic versions of our lives, coloured by past memories and strongly flavoured with our present emotional state. Daydreams represent a much more conscious attempt at deluding ourselves into believing that our lives or ourselves are better than they really are.

## Death

Each of us has to come to terms with the inevitability of death, our own and that of those we love. The neo-Freudian psychologist Erich Fromm pointed to this need to recognise life/death as one of the great existential dichotomies of our lives. Somewhat more revolutionary was Freud's idea that we have a death instinct (Thanatos), a drive towards the inorganic state and disintegration, co-existing within us in direct opposition to our life instinct (Eros). This death instinct inserts itself into every aspect of our lives, becoming aggression when projected outwards onto others, or sadism when mixed up with our libido or sexual instinct. Melanie Klein agreed with the central importance of the concept of a death instinct, believing that babies are born with it and immediately project it out as aggression vented towards their mothers. The resulting anxiety about hurting the mother then causes the baby to 'split' the mother into a 'good', nurturing mother who can be loved and a 'bad', ungiving mother who can safely be hated (*see* **Aggression**).

Mid-life is often the time when people come to terms with death, perhaps becoming preoccupied with thoughts of it during the process of acceptance. Such preoccupation may be precipitated by the death of their own parents, leaving them 'next in line', as it were, or by the death of a friend, suddenly making mortality real for them. Obsessional personalities commonly ruminate excessively about death alongside such questions as the meaning of life.

In many ways we are all preoccupied with death. Certainly our present ideas of what constitutes news is closely related to such a preoccupation, with death usually considered much more newsworthy than birth. Most of us feel uncomfortable about the extent to which death can fascinate us, but this preoccupation can be seen as an attempt to exert some control over or gain some knowledge about our own death.

# Defence Mechanisms

We employ a number of mechanisms to defend ourselves from

undue anxiety, which might result from the tension between our desire for pleasure (driven by our instinctual drives for survival, sex, and procreation) and our need to conform to the realities and constraints of life.

Sigmund Freud, his daughter Anna Freud and Melanie Klein have all contributed to our understanding of the diversity of such mechanisms, which are often remnants of a particular stage of development that we have retained into adult life.

Melanie Klein spoke of the most primitive of these defence mechanisms used against anxiety, employed by the infant but also retained by adults, such as splitting into a good and a separate bad person, idea, situation, etc. and projecting parts of ourselves onto others, who may or may not respond by acting as if they were that part of ourselves.

Nicola believes herself to be a non-angry person and, indeed, she never loses her temper. Whenever her tutor, Peter, is with her, however, he experiences flashes of rage which seem to have nothing to do with his own life, but to be in some way a response to what Nicola projects towards him. If asked Nicola would say that she sees that Peter is the kind of man who has to fight to keep control of his rage: she can recognise in him what she is unable to bear in herself.

Equal and opposite to projection is introjection, in which the ego sucks in some aspect of another which it feels it needs. Depending on our personality or upbringing we are just as capable of sucking in the bad or unhealthy aspects of another as we are of adopting more positive attributes. This is similar to identification, in which we associate ourselves with an aspect of another, but when we use introjection as a defence we are probably unaware that we have adopted a part of another, experiencing it as if it were truly a part of ourselves. Sometimes grieving spouses come to realise that what they had considered aspects of their own personality for many years have, in fact, been introjected aspects of their partners' personalities. The death of the partner will therefore mean the loss of that part, long experienced as an aspect of the self, hence the expression often used that 'a part of me has died with him.'

Melanie Klein also talked about the need that some adults retain from childhood to exercise an omnipotent control over things or other people in order to quell their anxieties about loss of control. We may idealise or denigrate people or situations in order to keep our anxieties about the uncertainties of life and relationships at bay. Alternatively, if someone threatens to overwhelm us with aggression we may make the psychological leap necessary to identify with the aggressor and his or her strength rather than feel weak and vulnerable. Such mechanisms prevent us from being able to make rational decisions about the nature of many of our relationships and may also mean that we swing from one extreme, such as love, to the other, hate, as a result of apparently trivial provocations.

Much of our psychological nature that may be anxiety-provoking is repressed 'out of sight' of our conscious mind into the dark and unseen depths of our unconscious. If adult life feels too serious, if reality threatens our sense of self, we can regress back to an earlier phase of development and hope that others will take up the reins on our behalf (*see* **Censorship, Regression, Repression**, and **Unconscious, Conscious and Pre-conscious Minds**).

It is not unusual for people to want 'mothering' when under strain, indeed we all survive stress better if there is someone to spoil us a little at the time. Some people, however, regress back to an earlier stage and get 'stuck' there, unable to take the care which is offered as a support for their return to adult life. Others even though involved in close relationships live in such emotional deprivation that they have to become sick or mad in order to get any sympathy or care, which makes them regress further under stress than they would probably have needed to if they were part of a more loving or caring relationship. It is a sad comment on the impoverished nature of many adult relationships that so many people are admitted to hospital with psychological and physical problems when really all they need is some tender loving care. Hospital care is often a bitter disappointment to such people, organised as it is not so much as a caring retreat but as an invasive curative environment.

Other forms of defence mechanisms include reaction formation, in which we convince ourselves that we feel or believe the reverse of what is truly buried in our unconscious mind (*see* **Compromising**). Many adolescents fear the bisexual or homosexual aspects of their personalities, an anxiety which is often particularly poignant just before they have consummated any sexual activity at all. As a defence against those fears they swing to the other extreme and overemphasise their heterosexual nature and their disgust of any other form of sexuality. For some this over-reaction to the sexual choice of others remains into adulthood, often denoting an on-going anxiety about their own sexuality (*see* **Sexuality**). The person who fears that he or she may be lacking in spirituality may adopt religion with outward fervour. Jung believed that organised religion was, in itself, a defence against individual spirituality.

Our anxieties can also be controlled by isolating thoughts, feelings and memories so that no cross-referencing, contrasting or comparing can take place. This protects us from having to deal with the rather grey areas of reality with all their paradoxes and confusions. Similarly we can unconsciously 'undo' thoughts, gestures, words or actions and then deny that they ever took place, thereby releasing ourselves from guilt or anxiety about their consequences. This tendency to rewrite history is not limited to individuals, but is often attractive to nations or whole races, too (*see* **Guilt** and **Suppressed Feelings**).

Instincts that may cause anxiety if expressed externally, such as aggression, may be turned inwards against the self. The person who leaves home angry after an argument and drives dangerously fast to work is a case in point. As in this example there is a tendency for such defences to divert the aggression onto others by mistake, so that others who are totally uninvolved in the original incident become the innocent targets of misplaced hostility. More actively, feelings can be displaced from a close and important person such a child or spouse onto someone 'less important' psychologically, such as a colleague. Such displacement can also occur in the reverse direction, as when people feel safer expressing hostility at home than at work (*see* **Anxiety** and **Conflict**).

Probably the most common of all defence mechanisms, which most of us use to some extent every day, is denial. Unconsciously we choose to be blind to aspects of ourselves and others that would otherwise provoke anxiety and confusion; denial allows us to achieve this selective blindness. Many relationships come to an abrupt end because something occurs that bursts through the denial, allowing us to see aspects of a previously loved or admired person in a totally different light.

Defence mechanisms are essential to our healthy emotional functioning. At times however they may get out of control and become more of a problem than whatever conflict they are supposed to be protecting us from. At that point some form of therapy is often helpful in order to identify the mechanism being used and to find alternative ways of coping. As long ago as 1943 the psychologist Edward Bibring talked of 'working off' mechanisms, that is, intellectually-controlled notions that could be employed to release a person from the destructive over-use of unconscious defence mechanisms.

## Delirium

Delirium is a disturbance in our level of consciousness. When we are fully awake and alert we are completely conscious, and respond to situations with the full force of our intellect and experience. The ability to do so resides in what are known as the higher centres of the brain. These centres are particularly vulnerable to physical insult, such as an injury, an infection, high fever or some form of metabolic disturbance, and consciousness can then become clouded. The extent of that clouding is determined both by the extent of the injury and the person's age, the young and the elderly being most susceptible.

At the point when consciousness is clouded to such an extent that the patient does not know which day or time of day it is or where he or she is, we describe this as delirium.

John was 25 and previously healthy. Then suddenly one Monday he began to feel restless, somewhat irritable and unable to concentrate at work. Initially he put this down to an argument with his girlfriend, but by the end of the week he found himself unable to concentrate even if he made a great effort. He could hardly remember what had happened during the week, and on the Friday evening expressed concern about his condition to his roommate Brian. Brian went out for the evening, but when he returned just after midnight he found John pacing around the flat, unable to sleep and clearly disturbed. He did not seem to be able to have a conversation, could not remember simple words and appeared to be seeing things on the walls. At first it seemed as if he might be drunk, but luckily Brian remembered their earlier conversation, and thinking back over the week realised that there had been a real deterioration in John's appearance and behaviour.

Once hospitalised John sank into a deeper state of delirium, hardly talking or responding at all. He was diagnosed as having kidney (renal) failure. This illness results in high levels in the blood of uremia, a substance normally excreted by the kidneys. Often such physical problems first present themselves through psychological or emotional disturbance, irritability, tiredness and apathy, leading the patient to think, as did John, that these symptoms are merely emotional responses to an argument. It is more likely, however, that the argument occurred because of his increasing irritability and not the other way round. His girlfriend Paula visited John throughout his hospital stay and agreed with this alternative explanation for their argument.

John's symptoms were classic of the gradual nature of the onset of delirium. First he experienced a mild clouding of consciousness, making it hard to concentrate, and felt generally irritable and low; then he began having problems with his memory, and everything seemed somewhat unreal. As he sank into delirium on the Friday evening, his restlessness became extreme and he began to have illusions (the patterns on the wallpaper seemed to form themselves into dancing animals) and hallucinations (he saw floating devils sneering at him for being foolish). Such symptoms usually become worse at night.

Many illnesses can cause delirium. It is always a symptom that should be taken seriously, although it does not always require admission to hospital. It is common for small children suffering from fever to have hallucinations, become restless and ramble on in a way that is very frightening both for themselves and their parents. Usually the child's temperature drops and in the morning he or she cannot remember what happened. Many people have similar experiences as they recover from operations.

Delirium demonstrates just how sophisticated and yet delicate our brains are, needing a perfect environment to function normally. Because the brain is so sensitive, disturbance to its environment is often demonstrated psychologically before any physical symptoms are evident.

## Delusional Jealousy
*See* **Othello Syndrome**

## Delusions

Human beings are symbolic creatures; the ability to symbolise our thoughts and feelings begins in mid-childhood and marks the development of our mode of thought from a concrete to a more abstract and creative one. Cultures and religions perceive symbols that are normal for their society at a given time. We accept symbolism that is familiar and reassuring in our lives. For those who develop some forms of mental illness, however, the symbolism they attribute to everyday happenings or objects is often frightening, and they lose the ability to know that such thinking is merely symbolic. Despite feeling puzzled they accept their symbolism as reality. Delusions are such perceptions of life, which take real happenings or objects as their starting point and then give them symbolic meaning that is not in keeping with the cultural or religious expectations of the individual. What starts as a single, sudden misinterpretation can rapidly become more generalised so that all that happens subsequently is taken into the delusional system and made 'sense' of in that way.

It is usually rapidly apparent to the individual who experiences delusions that the rest of the world does not share his or her interpretation of events. Delusions are however unshakeable; the individual knows that everyone else is wrong. Delusions can also be 'used' by those experiencing the schizophrenic phenomenon of passivity (that is, inertia applied by so-called external forces experienced by the patient as a loss of self) or emotional lability to explain and give structure to their chaotic experience of life. In this context the delusion is a desperate attempt to make sense of frightening phenomena, and thus less serious than what is called a primary delusion arising unexpectedly in an otherwise healthy person. Delusions may be based on external objects or events, or on thoughts and ideas within the individual.

Julie, a 19-year-old art student, saw a picture at an exhibition and suddenly 'knew' that it meant that the world would end that Friday. She became determined to warn as many people as possible. By Wednesday everything that was happening around her seemed to validate her original perception. On Thursday she told me that she believed that she was a prominent religious figure whose identity must remain secret as there were potentially hostile agents all around who might kill her. She was convinced that she had been sent to save us all. During Friday she carried out a variety of rituals, all of which had symbolic meaning for her. Julie actively believed that she was in the process of saving us all, and that the world would end if she was prevented from acting in this way. At the end of the day she believed that her actions had saved us and became more quiet and happy, although of course still deluded about what had happened.

Dorothy was 73 and believed that her neighbours were trying

to gas her. She pointed at the socket on their shared wall, saying that the gas came out through the holes during the night. Although she could not see or smell the gas, and was suffering no ill-effects from it, she believed in her theory with total conviction.

Delusions can occur in a wide variety of illnesses and drug-induced states. Damage to the brain, trauma or infection, dementias and states that alter blood biochemistry such as renal (kidney) or hepatic (liver) failure can all produce delusional states. Delusions are a central symptom of schizophrenia and appear in other psychotic illnesses. In puerperal psychosis (the psychotic illness that can affect a woman soon after she has given birth) the delusions are often of a persecutory or guilt-ridden nature. In psychotic depressions the person is often convinced that he or she is guilty of something unforgivable. When delusions occur within a relationship anger and violence often follow, particularly when they are connected with alcohol abuse (*see* **Alcoholism**). A 'special sign' may convince a husband that his wife is having an affair, and no amount of evidence to the contrary will shake that belief (*see* **Othello Syndrome**). A woman may come to believe that a particular man who has a prominent role in the community, perhaps her doctor or vicar, is secretly in love with her; everything he then does is woven into her delusional perception of him.

Occasionally people act on their delusional beliefs. Usually this is relatively harmless, as in Julie's 'world saving' rituals. In the case of those who feel guilt-ridden, however, the result may be suicide since they believe so completely in their guilt. The jealous deluded husband is especially dangerous to his wife; statistics suggest that a sizable number of them – perhaps as high as 10 to 15 per cent – attempt murder at some stage. The presence of delusions is therefore an important and serious sign that a person needs help (probably drug treatment and a stay in hospital), and should not be ignored.

# Dementia

Dementia is a progressive disease resulting from cell loss of brain tissues. It is irreversible and at the present time unhelped by treatment. Between 40 and 60 out of every 1000 people over 65 suffer from dementia, and the likelihood of its occurrence increases with age. There are two major types of dementia, *senile* and *arteriosclerotic*.

Senile dementia appears to run in some families, demonstrating that there is an inherited tendency towards this form of degeneration of brain tissue. Symptoms do not usually begin to appear until after a person reaches the age of 70; and the disease is more common among women. It is marked by a gradual inability to remember recent events or experiences, although often the person is still able to recall the past in infinite detail. This symptom goes hand in hand with an overall disintegration of the personality. Relatives often find themselves thinking that mum or dad is aging more quickly than before. Gradually it becomes clear that the person has little interest in life and is no longer responding emotionally to life events (*see* **Apathy**).

At some point, usually between two and five years after the initial memory problems, a sudden deterioration occurs, perhaps representing the point at which the person can no longer make any attempt to cover up his or her difficulties and gives up. Control over the bladder and bowels goes and the sufferer may end up in a distressing state if help is not rapidly forthcoming. This stage of senile dementia can be heartbreaking for both the individual and his or her family. Sometimes the sufferer's children are criticised for being 'unwilling' to help their parent, but I wonder how many are not so much unwilling as unable to bear seeing the person they have loved and respected for so many years reduced to a helpless state.

Arteriosclerotic dementia follows a different course, and is more commonly found in men. It occurs somewhat earlier in life, when the person is in his or her 60s or early 70s, although it sometimes strikes when a person is still in his or her 40s. About half of the people who suffer this illness have high blood-pressure, and actual damage to the brain cells is secondary to the damage caused to the blood supply to those cells. Because of this there tends to be a step-like pattern to this illness, each step connected to a stroke. True dementia may not occur until after a number of such incidents, since the damage done by each stroke tends to be patchy, affecting only the particular area of the brain whose blood supply was impaired. This means that patients often retain an awareness of their increasing difficulties until late in the illness, which in turn makes them depressed or emotionally labile. Often they retain elements of good judgement and islands of memory amidst the gradual deterioration and disintegration of their minds. Suicide attempts are common at this stage.

Much work has been done in recent years to detect and treat those with high blood-pressure early in their illness so that these problems will not arise later in life. After a vascular accident brain function may be temporarily damaged but still able to recover, the cells involved having been short of oxygen for a while but not actually hurt irreversibly. Usually however there will be some residual damage even after recovery; and this damage increases with each subsequent incident. Prevention is therefore much better than any hope for cure, and any medical advice offered on diet, life style and exercise should be taken seriously.

Treatment varies according to the underlying cause. The vast majority of people with dementia remain at home, although sadly this is often because as a society we lack adequate facilities with which to care for them. Those who do get admitted for treatment tend to be those who become aggressive or noisy and need sedation, or those who lack relatives who can care for them. Some improvement in functioning can be achieved in the short term by retraining the patient in both social and self-help skills, but what is really needed is tender loving care, which can sometimes be demanding and sad work for the carers involved.

In many ways it is difficult to get an accurate picture of what dementia feels like for the patient. The change to personality and mental ability is global, so talking to the individual about his or her experience may not provide accurate information, and also the description might change from one moment to the next. For instance depression is a common reaction to an awareness of decreasing intellectual capacity, yet that depression can alternate with high spirits, noisy outbursts and even euphoria.

Ted was 64 when he had his first stroke. This was followed by three others in rapid succession, leaving him with limited mobility, slurred speech and memory loss. He had always been an active man, who worked on his allotment at weekends, umpired for school football matches until he was in his late 50s and delighted in reading and playing card games. He had retired from his work as an accountant when he was 60 in order to enjoy his other interests.

I first met Ted when he was admitted to a psychiatric hospital after a failed suicide attempt. He had tried to drown himself and was brought immediately from the river to the hospital by the police who had saved him. Despite it only being some 30 minutes since the attempt Ted was singing and delighted with himself by the time I met him. He regaled me with stories of wading ashore during the Normandy landings, memories no doubt revived by this episode, and seemed to have completely forgotten the despair which had driven him to his earlier actions. Three days later, during another lengthy war memory that was vivid in detail, Ted began to cry, saying that he felt useless: 'Couldn't even do a proper job of killing myself!', and that he wanted to die in order to put an end to his suffering and that of his family.

These mood swings continued unaffected by any treatment for a number of months, until Ted suffered a fifth stroke that damaged his brain still further, leaving him 'flat', without any obvious emotion. After this it was impossible to talk to him about his feelings; the word seemed to have lost its meaning for him.

When dementia is caused by gradual brain cell death, as in

senile dementia, the sufferer may not be aware of decreasing faculties for many months, even years, although outsiders may begin to notice symptoms. It can be cruel to test the abilities of such patients, because during the test they suddenly may become aware of how much they have deteriorated, and the knowledge of such lost ability may bring about great despair or outrage. If the sufferers are aware of their deficiencies most try to cover them up, making themselves lists so that they do not forget things so easily, or making up stories to cover omissions. It is difficult, if not impossible, to talk to them about how they feel about losing some of their intellectual ability, since they deny that these losses have occurred. Often by the time they do accept the truth they are past being able to put words to feelings, even past having any feelings, relating in only a bland, rather flat way to the world.

It is easier to know how sad and distressing this illness is for relatives and carers. They will experience many oppressive feelings, although they may also be made to feel better by being able to arrange or give good care to the sufferer. Often the family members are left feeling useless and at the same time angry; they may also be consumed by a resurgence of all the feelings they have had in the past for the person. They may find themselves longing for the death of the sufferer so that the misery can end, although this then makes them feel guilty. Many children back off from involvement as their mum or dad sinks further into deterioration, feeling that they are no longer recognised and therefore no longer important. Carers must be given our help and support, whether they are paid or voluntary.

There are occasional moments of joy amidst the sad progress of dementia. I remember an old lady called Amy, whose husband came every afternoon to walk her round the grounds of the hospital. They would walk in silence, Amy being incapable of sensible conversation, and they could not walk far. Amy's husband always looked at her with such love and devotion, turning a blind eye to her incontinence and considerable mental deficiencies. When asked how he coped he would say that he simply remembered the young Amy he had fallen in love with 55 years earlier. One evening after he had left Amy said to me, 'I don't know who he is, but he is a very nice man.' Despite her apparent flatness of mood, his kindness had got through and meant something to her. Relatives who feel unimportant and unrecognised can take comfort in this simple truth as Amy expressed it.

## Denial

Denial is one of our defence mechanisms. Defence mechanisms act to keep any material we do not wish to have in our conscious minds safely locked away in our unconscious. Such material consists of memories of both experiences and our emotional response to these events. Denial is an active process but also an unconscious one: when we protect ourselves from that which we do not wish or cannot bear to remember we do it automatically, without conscious thought. Thus we remember neither the memory nor the fact that we have buried it. For this reason it is also much easier to see other people operating this defence mechanism than to recognise it in ourselves.

Nigel, a 28-year-old plumber, had never had a girlfriend. He claimed that this was because he was shy, and joined a social skills group in order to overcome this problem. As the group progressed, however, Nigel became depressed and tearful. Eventually he became angry with the other members of the group, saying that they were 'hurting' him. This experience led him to seek individual therapy, because he felt so confused and agitated. In taking a careful case history over a period of some weeks the therapist, also a young man, began to feel that Nigel was trying to seduce him. This led him to ask about any homosexual experiences Nigel might have had. Nigel claimed not to remember any such experiences, saying that he had never 'fancied' a man. A few days later however Nigel announced that he had had a dream the night before in which he seduced several younger men. He had awakened feeling sexually aroused but also anxious and guilty. Exploring this dream with his therapist Nigel commented that it had felt as though a memory was being 'tickled', but he had no conscious idea of what the memory was.

Over many weeks and after several similar dreams Nigel began to talk more and more about his school experience, particularly focusing on a period when he was about 8 years old and had been sent to prep school. Although he spoke mostly about the tension headaches he suffered from at that age, headaches which interfered with his education, both Nigel and the therapist were aware that something was being hidden. On one occasion the therapist said 'I think you are frightened that I will catch you saying or doing something that you think is very naughty.' Initially Nigel protested this angrily, but then he said that he could suddenly remember waiting outside one of the school master's offices. He thought he was waiting to be punished, but he could not remember for what.

A gradual unveiling of painful memories such as this is common in therapy, the patient's denial gradually giving way in the face of active attempts to understand what is hidden behind it. In Nigel's case the memories that eventually emerged were of feeling sexually aroused by being beaten, of having a love/hate relationship with the master concerned, whose threats of punishment Nigel had also found sexually stimulating, and underneath all this an abiding fear that he would always remain attracted to men. He believed further that any sexual activity with a woman would in some way expose his true and 'terrible' secret nature and had therefore avoided it although he also longed for it. This memory caused him considerable anguish and anger, and it was clear that the 8-year-old child had been unable to cope with the experience at all, having nothing to judge it against and no way of knowing whether such feelings were normal or permissible. Such was the boy's pain and confusion that his mind had tried to erase the memory by denying that anything had ever happened, and although Nigel's social behaviour was totally dictated by the experience the memory had remained unavailable to his conscious mind.

We all use denial to some extent. It can even be useful at times: without it we might be constantly overwhelmed by the past and unable to get on with the present. It is only when we deny something which continues nevertheless to affect our lives detrimentally that we need to unbury the past by shaking off our denial.

It is also possible to use denial to cope with present reality which we might otherwise find unbearable. Many people with serious illnesses deny this fact to themselves in order to get through each day, taking them one at a time. Likewise many people who exist in difficult and damaging relationships on which they are nevertheless dependent, will deny the extent of the difficulties so that they do not have to give up the relationship. In addition, at times of social hardship there can be a collective denial of just how bad things are, which serves to unite people and focuses their thoughts on a better tomorrow rather than the suffering of today (*see* **Defence Mechanisms**).

## Depersonalisation

During a particularly unpleasant examination I once found myself no longer sitting opposite the difficult examiner but floating to the ceiling. The room, table, examiner – all seemed small and distant, and although we continued talking, it all seemed of little or no interest to me. Moments before I had been extremely anxious, but once on the ceiling I found that emotion had left me; I felt serene and quite unlike anything I had felt ever before. It seemed to me as if my head was very large but filled with clear water, whilst my body had shrunk, enabling me to float.

This was a depersonalisation experience, and it happened under conditions of extreme anxiety. Such experiences are common in those who suffer regularly from anxiety states, particularly those who are phobic, when circumstances have forced them into the anxiety-provoking situation they normally go to great lengths to avoid (*see* **Derealisation**). Depersonalisation is also common in situations where you would expect to experience extreme anxiety, particularly when either your life is in danger or where circumstances are about to overwhelm you psychologically. Several clients I have seen since the Hungerford massacre of 1987, for instance, have told me they experienced depersonalisation during the shooting, and it is commonly described by those who survive car accidents. Near-death experiences also seem to be very similar to depersonalisation.

Others may not realise that the person they are with is experiencing depersonalisation, especially if they are only briefly in his or her presence. However, if the state continues they would begin to notice that the depersonalised person was 'cut off' and, if answering at all, was only doing so 'automatically'. Most commonly, depersonalised people do not relate to others at all.

It is not clear what causes depersonalisation, although it is undoubtedly associated with levels of anxiety the individual finds unbearable. It appears to be an in-built safeguard for our minds: when they are about to go into some sort of overload, they can instead refocus consciousness in a more limited area, away from whatever is causing the anxiety. This enables us to survive psychologically in situations where we might otherwise 'blow a fuse'. It is occasionally seen in other psychiatric illnesses (*see* **Depression** and **Schizophrenia**), but this is much more rare than its occurrence in association with anxiety (*see* **Anxiety**).

# Depression

There are many events in a normal life that make us sad. Some of these events, particularly loss, cause mourning, an extreme form of normal sadness. Depression on the other hand is a rather abnormal sadness, and although often arising as a direct consequence of a sad life event it is an over-reaction to whatever has happened. Sometimes what precipitates depression is not obvious, and sometimes it seems as if there is no precipitant.

This observation has led to considerable research into what causes depression. One theory is that there may exist a metabolic change that will explain the feelings from which depressed people suffer. Certainly some drugs that affect chemical substances in the brain have been administered to good effect in those with depression.

It has been suggested that there are at least two forms of depression: one clearly psychological, a response (albeit an over-response) to a loss event, and one clearly biochemical, caused by unknown factors but remedied by drugs. This has led to a specific interest into whether the depressed person has primarily 'biological' symptoms, such as difficulty sleeping and eating, constipation, or retarded movements, or 'psychological' symptoms, such as a distressed mood, feelings of unworthiness, disinterest in life and suicidal thoughts. It is thought that those with 'biological' depression recover better with anti-depressants, whilst those with 'psychological' depression improve with counselling and psychotherapy.

In real life, however, things are seldom so clear-cut, and depression remains something of a mystery in terms of its cause. What is clear is that depression in children is much more common than we as adults might like to acknowledge. Children's feelings are extremely labile, and pre-school children can swing from delight, euphoria and perfect happiness into misery, despair and depression in an instant. For some people this lability lasts into adulthood.

Melanie Klein described what she called the 'depressive position', in which infants aged approximately 6 months begin to have an awareness that the good, loving, available mother and the bad, absent, ungiving mother are not two separate beings, as previously perceived, but one. This causes intense anguish for the baby, who has projected much hostility and sadism onto the bad mother, secure in the belief that the good mother, on whom he is dependent, is separate and therefore safe from these attacks. Developmentally the baby has to struggle with the issue of ambivalence, the good and bad in everything, including his own emotions (*see* **Ambivalence**).

As the baby grows, several experiences make this struggle more bearable. Firstly, he learns all the time to cope with his aggressive, sadistic feelings by containing and neutralising them for himself instead of having to project them onto mother. This process is a lengthy one. (Most of us go on blaming our mothers for a very long time and the blame is often merely a reflection of our aggressive fury that our mothers are not perfect but simply human.) Next the baby learns about 'repairing' feelings, and by his responses and his healthy growing gives his mother much pleasure. By gaining external validation that mother has survived his fantasised attack and loves him despite it, the baby can repair the split-off bits of himself and become more comfortable with his own range of ambivalent feelings. This need to make amends, however, is closely connected to feelings of guilt (*see* **Guilt** and **Guilt Complex**). Finally, the baby's relationship with his mother becomes less intense as he becomes a social person with an ever-increasing social circle made up of his father, grandparents, siblings, playmates and friends. This lessens the intensity of the baby's feelings and makes them more manageable.

Although this process begins at 6 months it goes on throughout our lives, each resolution being constantly reworked as new events challenge us. Undoubtedly some people move further along this developmental spectrum than others and are therefore better equipped to deal with life's ups and downs, while others remain very vulnerable to hurtful events.

Sad childhood events that are buried away instead of being dealt with cause the person to have a peculiar vulnerability to similar events that occur later in life (*see* **Emotional Breakdown** and **Denial**). Some events are too sad for children to deal with adequately, and almost always will have to be worked on at some point in adulthood, when a new loss triggers off the sadness about an old loss. This is often true for women who lose their mothers before their early teens and do not grieve at the time but become depressed with the birth of their own children, as if the memory of mother is triggered by the experience of mothering (*see* **Post-natal Depression**).

Whatever the cause or developmental basis for depression it is undoubtedly a painful experience, often starting with apathy and lethargy, feelings which the individual may try hard to resist. At this point he or she may not be consciously aware of being depressed, but may feel worthless, guilty, haunted and suicidal. In fact many of those who commit suicide are people who have not been diagnosed as depressed, and sometimes have not even been recognised as depressed by those closest to them.

Gradually, depressed feelings become more evident and physical symptoms appear. Trouble sleeping is the most common complaint, including an inability to get to sleep, terrible, frightening dreams that wake the sleeper in a state of anxiety, and waking early feeling unrefreshed but unable to get back to sleep. That early morning time, when if feels as if the whole world is asleep and you are alone, is often the worst time of day. In addition the appetite may be affected, accompanied by weight loss or gain. Some people believe they do not deserve feeding, others try to comfort themselves by overeating or drinking heavily (*see* **Alcoholism** and **Eating Disorders**). Often their entire digestive tract feels as if it has given up; this is accompanied by constipation. Their posture may seem to droop, their movements become sluggish and their faces adopt a mask-like flatness. Tearfulness often disappears as the depression deepens. All these feelings can fluctuate during the day, lightening in the evening. Underneath it all the person's mind is functioning as well as ever, and if he or she can bear to be tested his or her intellect will be found to be intact, although usually the patient will show no energy for or interest in the test nor its results. Delusional feelings of being dirty, smelly or contaminating are common, as well as a total negation of anything good about the self or life.

In some people this feeling alternates with a form of mania, overactivity, and jollity, which often seems rather false to the observer. When in this phase the depressed person will deny completely that there is anything wrong (*see* **Manic-Depressive Psychosis**).

Clearly such an overwhelming emotional experience as depression has effects on the individual's relationships, particularly as sexual interest is diminished or lost and the depressed person becomes more and more preoccupied with his or her own self, work and hobbies. Parenting is particularly difficult when depressed, and it has been said that the most unlucky start in life is to have a depressed mother.

A depressed person may or may not seek help depending on his or her perception of emotional illness, the intensity of the distress as balanced against any fear of being stigmatised as neurotic or unstable, and whether he or she feels anyone can be of help. Relatives and friends can play a part in letting the person believe that he or she is worth helping and then finding help that is appropriate not only to the form of illness but for the individual's personality. Some people do far better by joining a self-help group, for instance, than by handing over control and going into hospital for more physical forms of treatment.

On the other hand, it has to be remembered that depression is sometimes a fatal illness, not only to the sufferer who may take his or her own life, but also to any close relatives whom the depressed person, believing they will suffer if left behind, may murder. This means that sometimes the more extreme measures of hospitalisation, drugs and ECT (electro-convulsive therapy) are clearly called for. Hospital can be a welcome reprieve to the person who has been trying to maintain 'face' and survive the outside world, and offers in addition a break from his or her relationships, which may only be adding to the sense of strain.

## Derealisation

This experience is often associated with depersonalisation. Just as depersonalisation makes the self feel unreal, so derealisation makes the outside world seem unreal.

People who are depressed sometimes experience the world as having 'stopped'; anxious individuals see the world as if at the end of a telescope. Usually such experiences are fleeting and the individual is aware that his or her perception is in some way abnormal throughout the experience, although often he or she is unable to just snap out of it, but must wait for it to pass (*see* **Depersonalisation**).

## Destructive Instincts

Andrew was 11 and his friend Paul 8 when they began to play in a cruel and destructive way with animals. Initially they 'experimented' with frogs in a nearby wood, but as they grew bolder they also hurt cats and pet rabbits. Their 'game' ended when Paul's father caught them torturing a friend's rabbit. Andrew was completely unrepentant, saying that it had all been a 'laugh' and that grown-ups made a fuss about nothing. Paul, however, was tearful and shocked by how angry his father was. It was clear that he had not realised that what they had been doing was bad in any way. The encouragement of the older boy had lead him to believe it was an acceptable form of behaviour, whilst Andrew knew that if caught they would be punished, even though he thought it ridiculous that anyone should care about animals so much.

At some point in childhood most children do something that is deliberately destructive, sometimes openly to see what reaction they will get and sometimes more surreptitiously. Between the ages of 2 and 4 are often seen as 'negative' years, during which the child is frequently at odds with her environment and will have sudden swings of mood into temper tantrums. At this age children are struggling with their destructive instincts, which Freud postulated were an outward expression of our basic self-destructive instincts. Other theorists have suggested that aggressive outbursts are the result of the degree of frustration experienced by the child. Certainly children learn quickly from those around them, and if the family norm is to express angry or hostile feelings in an uncontrolled manner, they will use that model for themselves and openly express whatever hostility they feel.

Paul was basically a normal child from a family that controlled aggressive feelings and set realistic boundaries on his behaviour. Hence his shocked and sad reaction to being caught acting destructively. Andrew was a very different child, having caused anxiety at school since he was 5 because of his unpleasant and callous attitude to others, particularly those in authority. He came from a home where the mother was rarely and the father often drunk and abusive. Nobody had set limits on his behaviour at any point in his life, so he could not tolerate any attempts made at frustrating his instincts.

It is usually easy to spot the difference between children who are passing through a destructive stage and those who are stuck at that stage, and easy to see which families are coherent enough to set boundaries on the behaviour of their children, thus teaching them to manage frustration at an early age.

Learning to cope with our destructive instincts, whether they arise from a turning outward of our self-destructive feelings or as a response to frustration, is one of the major tasks of development. Those who turn them inward often develop neurotic-type symptoms and syndromes; their inability to cope with destructive impulses therefore hurts themselves. The psychopathic personality has similar problems dealing with destructive instincts but turns them outward instead, thereby making society suffer. Personality varies along many spectrums, and when this psychopathic version of dealing with destructive instincts is combined with a cold, unsympathetic and distant personality, the danger to society becomes great. What is clear from history and experiments is that most 'normal' people can be trained into expressing considerable destructiveness to both property and human life. Thus the restraints we learn as children to our natural destructiveness can be unlearnt in adulthood if circumstances encourage it.

# Difficulties Concentrating
*See* **Concentration Difficulties**

# Disorientation

In order to be totally orientated we need to know where we are in time and space – that is, we need to know the day of the month of the year, have a rough idea of the time or part of the day it is, and also know where we are. Most of the time we know these things without having to think very hard about them, but diseases which damage the brain can rob us of this normally effortless knowledge, leaving us disorientated.

The brain functions as a whole organ, and can therefore sustain some damage before deficits in our functioning become obvious, as one part works to overcome a loss in another. If there is focal damage, however, a particular ability may be lost while other equally complex mental activities remain unaffected.

Our brain is made up of two halves. They are mirror images of one another, but one side, or *hemisphere*, is dominant. If you are right-handed your left hemisphere will be dominant, and any damage to the left hemisphere will produce greater difficulties than would damage to the right. Each half of the brain is divided into a number of lobes which serve different functions. These are connected by pathways of nervous tissue, along which passes types of electrical excitations. The two hemispheres are connected by a crescent-shaped body called the *corpus callosum*.

In psychiatry disorientation is most commonly met with in patients who are suffering from senile dementia or Alzheimer's disease, in which there is generalised damage to brain tissue (*see* **Dementia**). Problems can also be encountered as a result of brain injuries after an accident, infection or tumour. When questioned the patient cannot remember his or her address or date of birth. They are uncertain about the date, the year, or even the time of day they ate their last meal. Such questioning needs to be handled with care, as stimulating the patient's awareness of this loss of ability can produce catastrophic emotional results. It is usually late in illness that we forget who we are, perhaps an indication of just how important it is to our psychological survival that we remember this basic information.

It is difficult and sometimes infuriating to look after a disorientated person. Emily was 75 when her 78-year-old husband Albert began to show signs of serious disorientation. Emily had guessed for some months that all was not well, because Albert had seemed increasingly forgetful and disinterested. She kept her worries to herself, however, until he got lost on a shopping expedition and returned home accompanied by the police. Albert denied that there was any problem, saying that he had merely taken a detour. The police said that he had been wandering aimlessly around the town, clearly lost despite the fact that he had lived there all his life.

Albert became increasingly restless and although determined to go on walks got lost on each occasion, making Emily feel that she had to accompany him everywhere. This became exhausting for her, which increased her intolerance for a variety of difficulties his illness caused their relationship. Albert insisted she was not feeding him, as he could not remember their last meal, and that she was stealing from him when really it was just that he could not remember where he'd left things. Eventually worn down by this process and by her despair about what was happening to her much-loved husband, Emily began to hit Albert when he annoyed her. This was only discovered when their daughter visited from Australia and was alarmed to find her father not only clearly suffering from dementia but covered in bruises as well. Both Albert and Emily needed help, Albert in the form of practical care and protection and Emily an understanding and ability to forgive herself for what had happened.

# Dreams

When we sleep deeply we dream, a fact acknowledged to the

outside world by the fact that our eyes move rapidly from side to side under our closed eyelids (this is known as *rapid eye movement*, or REM sleep). Dreams often 'disappear' as we awaken, rather as if they are dissolving as we regain consciousness. Remembering dreams can be a useful way of gaining an insight into the unconscious world; Freud called dreaming 'the golden pathway to the unconscious'. If you want to analyse your dreams it is useful to keep a pad and pencil by your bedside, since the best way to capture as full a description of the dream as possible is to record it the moment you wake up.

Dreams represent certain wishes, anxieties or experiences which cannot be consciously acknowledged but which the mind needs to display in some way. This latent content of the dream is distorted by what Freud called 'dream-work' so as to make it into a story, the manifest content of the dream, which we remember on waking. The story is produced by mechanisms that condense material, often connecting things in unlikely ways, and displace feelings from one person or thing onto another, representing the wishes of the dreamer in a narrative and then revising the whole into a more or less coherent experience. Dreams can consist of recent experiences, childhood experiences and bodily sensations, all of which are coloured by the emotional state of the dreamer.

Psychoanalysis often uses the interpretation of dreams as a way of helping individuals to understand themselves more fully. There is no universal truth when interpreting dreams; they mean whatever the individual concerned believes they mean. There are some dreams that seem common, however – for instance the dream of being chased. It is probably not possible to analyse a dream completely; some of its meaning will remain unclear however hard you try to understand what it represents, and looked at in retrospect a dream will often seem to mean different things than you had originally thought. Despite this, dreams often do provide us with valuable clues if we are willing to learn from them.

Nightmares are dreams in which we experience terrifying

material, often including sensations such as that of being chased, hunted or trapped, or disturbing visual images such as monsters. People often wake up feeling anxious, and usually at the point in the nightmare when they are about to be caught, killed or made to face whatever is terrifying them.

Jonathan, a 23-year-old medical student, went to a student counsellor because of a recurrent dream in which his parents were killed in a car accident. It was a vivid and detailed dream, and Jonathan had seriously considered 'warning' his parents, as if the dream were a premonition. The counsellor explained to Jonathan that the dream belonged to him, it was a story about himself for himself. Perhaps, the counsellor suggested, it was a warning to Jonathan rather than to his parents. As Jonathan reflected on this possibility more details of the dream fell into place, because his parents were in *his* car and not their own, on a journey he often undertook. Jonathan was in his final year of medical school and had recently done a placement with a geriatric team. This was a placement that he had enjoyed greatly, feeling that it might represent his career choice in future. Amongst the patients he had got to know were several who had died during his placement, and there were two people in particular whom he remembered with fondness and whose deaths had caused him sadness. But in his circle of friends it was not the done thing either to become fond of patients or to have feelings about them, especially if they were likely to die, and he had therefore kept his sadness hidden.

Talking about his dream Jonathan remembered that it was on his car journey to and from the hospital that he thought about these feelings most, and that this was the journey, albeit distorted, of his dream. His feelings about the patients had been displaced onto his parents, with whom he had rather a love/hate relationship, both wishing them dead and yet fearing that they would die. He also remembered an incident when he was 8 when he had run away from school and remained undiscovered in a local playground overnight. His parents, of course, had been extremely frightened about what might have happened to him, and so when he was found they were both relieved and angry with him. He remembered his father shouting 'you might have been the death of us', a thought which had frightened him as he took it as fact that a child's behaviour could kill the child's parents.

It would have been easy to leave the dream at this point, when much material had emerged that could provide the focus for the work of the counselling session. In a moment of inspiration, however, and remembering Jonathan's emotional idea that his dream was a premonition, the counsellor suggested that Jonathan had his car checked. During the subsequent service the car's brake fluid was discovered to have a leak. The mechanic could not understand why Jonathan had not noticed the gradual decrease in the effectiveness of his brakes. But Jonathan had been emotionally preoccupied with the death of his patients for several weeks, and only unconsciously had noticed the danger posed by his car.

## Drowsiness

Drowsiness is a feeling familiar to most people, usually occurring just before we fall asleep. Its presence only becomes pathological when a person is more drowsy than usual and at unusual times of the day, or is continually drowsy. This may be associated with damage to the brain as a result of a head injury or disease, or by a change in the biochemical balance of the body which blurs the brain function, such as taking various drugs, running a temperature, having low blood sugar, liver or kidney disease, or after an epileptic fit.

# E

## Eating Disorders: Anorexia Nervosa, Bulimia, Obesity

The first relationship of our lives centres around the experience of being hungry, being dependent on others for the relief of that hunger, being fed and being satisfied. Although it has been clearly demonstrated that emotional love is as important a contribution to a baby's survival as feeding, food is crucial of course. Surprisingly, many new mothers find feeding their babies more difficult than expected. Babies can be ambivalent about what they want, how much or when. Mothers may also misread signals and think the baby is crying because he is hungry, when he really just wants company or sleep. Food may then become a substitute for other forms of love. There is also a power-battle centred on food which affects many mother/baby relationships: the baby dislikes his dependency and wishes to control the food, whilst the mother feels she should have control of the situation. This struggle has been the topic of many a baby-care argument, such as whether babies should be fed four-hourly or on demand. Weaning is another time of potential discord between mother and baby, and the negotiation often feels like a failure to both sides. Watching one-year-olds play with food gives much insight into how ambivalent they are about it, wanting to put it on the floor as much as in their mouths, wanting to play with, control and dominate it.

Perhaps it should come as no surprise then that at the moment that children emerge from adolescence into adulthood those early preoccupations come back, and food is once again the centre of attention. This is particularly true for girls, probably because so much media attention is given to slimness. Present fashion would tell women that they should be almost stick-like whatever their true shape might be. Thus more than half of the female population will admit to a life-long awareness of 'needing' to diet. Many teenage girls turn that into action, slimming becoming a heated competition within their peer groups. Being fat, or even just slightly overweight, means less social acceptability and therefore there is great pressure on them to maintain or decrease their weight. For most girls this is merely a phase, which loses its intensity as they grow into women and find their identity, which includes acceptance of their shape even if they harbour life-long regrets about their imperfection. For some, however, the slimming stage becomes an addiction that they cannot shake off.

It is difficult to know why some girls (and a very few boys) develop anorexia, a state in which their diet is so inadequate as to push them via a spiral of ever-decreasing weight to the point of severe ill health. It is true that most of these girls come from upper-middle-class backgrounds and are often bright and pushy people with a need to succeed. In my experience they are often angry, rather prickly people who are trying to fight 'the system' whilst also maintaining deep dependence upon it. They can induce feelings of angry impotence in those who try to help them. They are also sad, often protecting themselves from the full brunt of their depressive feelings by inducing the 'high' that starvation brings. Thus they see the efforts of others to feed them as painful.

Anorexics also often have extremely low self-esteem, particularly when they judge themselves as sexual beings. Below a certain weight a woman's periods stop, and many anorexics find that gaining the weight that restarts periods is the hardest step of all. Being a fully operational woman frightens them. This is commonly the result of some form of sexual abuse, either in childhood or as a young woman. In these cases incest or rape are often the starting point of what can then be seen as a protest starvation. Involved in all their behaviour is a flirtation with death, although most do not state that they wish to die. Starvation brings biochemical changes in the body, making them unrealistically happy, energetic and hopeful, and cutting them off from an awareness of how ill they have become.

Bulimia, often combined with anorexia, means forced vomiting as part of a weight-control or weight-loss pattern. This is often combined with bingeing, so that a whole fridge full of food might be consumed in a gastronomic orgy, followed by self-recrimination, feelings of self-disgust and self-hatred that can only be alleviated by vomiting. Because our gastric contents include acid, which is vomited up with the food, bulimia induces more rapid and dangerous biochemical changes to the body.

Obesity, too, can be life-threatening. Some cases do seem to have an inherited basis, with people's metabolism for burning food varying greatly. Many people eat for comfort and when stressed. Heavy consumption of alcohol also produces rapid weight gain.

The eating disorders which bring people to the attention of doctors are the extremes at the end of a continuous spectrum. Most women inhabit places on that spectrum with which they are not totally happy. Such self-criticism is probably a result of women's bodies being objectified, becoming things to look at rather than live in. Pornography continues to display bodies in a way that humiliates and allows envy and hate to be expressed as if it were admiration. Women are often amazed and upset by how readily all men feel they have a right to comment on any woman's body, not in terms of whether it suits her or not but in terms of how much arousal it causes them. Men's bodies do not receive such attention, and therefore men usually feel much less critical about their weight and shape. Whatever the particular cause for an eating disorder, it is important to see it as a symptom of the underlying and serious social illness, which individual sufferers express for us all. (*See also* **Greed**.)

# Egotism
*See* **Narcissism**

# Elation

Most of us have experienced feeling 'high', sometimes in connection with happy or exciting events and sometimes spontaneously. The feeling of elation is intense, pleasurable and usually short-lived.

Elation often has a rather different quality when it occurs in the context of mental illness. Although people diagnosed as schizophrenic commonly have a flat emotional experience, they are sometimes subject to mood swings between the poles of depression and elation. In this context, although 'high', the person often has difficulty experiencing the feeling as pleasurable, and may not be able to express it verbally at all. Those who cannot express their elation in words might become more agitated, or they might show much more restless activity than usual, as if the energy of the elation has to be let out somehow. In other forms of mania the individual may demonstrate the reverse reaction, becoming so preoccupied with their rapid stream of thoughts that they lie speechless and immobile for lengthy periods, with just an elated look on their faces.

Elation is an internal, private experience; manic activity is its outward demonstration. Elation can be normal, mania is not. Elation is not usually contagious; on the other hand, when in contact with someone who is manic it is hard not to smile and be 'infected' by their exhilaration. (*See also* **Manic-Depressive Psychosis** and **Schizophrenia**.)

# Electra Complex

This term, introduced by C.G. Jung, a one-time colleague of Freud who later established an independent psychological theory, was meant to describe the female equivalent of the male Oedipus complex as discussed by Freud (*see* **Oedipus Complex**).

Each of these complexes describe the child's rivalry with the parent of the same sex for the parent of the opposite sex. This developmental phase, seen as closely linked to the 'phallic' stage (occurring between the ages of 3 to 5 years, according to Freudian theory) and to the 'depressive' position, which helps people become whole beings (according to Kleinian theory and occurring at around the ages of 3 to 9 months) is extremely complicated, and will vary greatly for girls and boys and across different cultures.

Initially Freud thought that his theory was equally valid for both girls and boys. Later he rethought much of what he had originally written about women, perhaps most importantly taking the essential and unique closeness with mother as the daughter's clear starting point in life, something which he had failed to see as significant until late into his work. In spite of Freud's rethinking, however, for him the central understanding of sexual development in humans was always predominantly phallic, or penis-centred. In his theory the little girl is aware of her lack of a penis, and feels inadequate and punished (castrated), and angry and resentful towards her mother (who she also perceives as castrated) and therefore needs to 'compensate' herself during her voyage through the female Oedipus complex; that is, the Electra complex. This compensation comes in the form of appealing to her father and fantasising that she will have his babies. For Freud these fantasy babies magically equal the missing penis in the daughter's psyche, enabling her to grow up and take her 'rightful' place in the adult world.

Melanie Klein felt that children were born with an inner knowledge of their bodies, and that young infants fantasise about parts of their anatomy which they may not yet have the manual dexterity to explore. This theory allows for a much earlier complex that involves some form of sexual awakening and acknowledgement. It also seems likely from this standpoint that girls might respect and like their own anatomy every bit as much as little boys like their own – certainly the incidence of masturbation in young children is much the same for both sexes, although the parents' reaction may be very different when it is manifested.

Some concept of a developmental stage involving sexuality is important for at least two major aspects of the psyche. First the sexual development of a child is a crucial part of his or her journey to adulthood, and, as with many phases, early psychological foundations need to be laid which can then be 'followed up' and reworked in adolescence and early adult life. Some adults do not become psychologically sexual no matter how much their bodies develop physically, because they have not worked through the Oedipus or Electra phase. Secondly, it is during this phase that we choose and then become fixed on an 'object' choice for our sexuality. Not only does this include whether future partners will be of the opposite or same sex, but manifestations of sexual perversion have their roots in this object choice. Alongside these two aspects, the incorporating of a sexual self within a full understanding of a developed psyche has repercussions for every aspect of functioning.

Much has been written about the competition between daughter and mother, in what is commonly regarded as the most heated, ambivalent and passionate relationship of many women's lives. For a daughter to compete with her mother or even to hate her as a rival for father's attention also means cutting herself off psychologically from the nurturing part of the person on whom she has been totally dependent since birth. Undoubtedly many adult woman do seem to have cut themselves off from any hope of being cared for and only see themselves as carers, often in a way that is competitive not only with their mothers but with all women. To see this as a normal or positive part of female psychological development would seem to many modern feminist psychotherapists a rather negative view. Yet, originally, the daughter maintaining closeness and uniting with her mother, against her father, was seen as a negative Electra complex. It is difficult to know how much the words positive and negative describe the outcome for the individual or for society – we know, for instance, that women who maintain an ability to be close to their mothers *and* other women, have better mental health than those who cut themselves off from the 'female group' in their search for heterosexual unity.

How much the Electra complex is a function of social norms and experiences rather than inner normal psychological drives would seem questionable. Why should 4- to 5-year-old girls suddenly desire their father's attention at the cost of cutting themselves off from the main provider (usually) of their needs, their mother? This seems particularly strange in the light of the fact that many women will say that they hardly knew their fathers during childhood. The 'cut off' is additionally complex in that the girl seems to go from dependence on her mother to meeting the dependency needs of her father and by extension of other men, that is, brothers and then partners: making the switch not only from mother to father, but also from cared-for to care-giver.

Sometimes the girl switches from her mother as part of an unresolved battle between them, a battle which dominates many mother/daughter relationships throughout their lives. If the daughter cannot fuse the images of good and bad mother into one acceptable person she will remain full of rage at the ungratifying bad mother, rage that may push her away despite her need for the good mother. Unlike a son, who cannot identify with his mother, the daughter can and needs to identify in order to have a functional model of what being a woman means. That model is, of course, heavily overlaid with social sex-stereotyping, including the socially accepted norm that a woman needs a man to take care of her in the big wide world. Thus in her rage and confusion with her mother she is rescued by social convention, which begins to suggest to her that what she really needs is a 'prince', not a mother. This suggestion may be the guiding light which turns her attentions to her father, even if he is an absent or shadowy figure in her life. However, this is the point when the discrepancy between what is psychological and what is social becomes so difficult to elucidate. Is it competition with her mother and envy over her mother's position in the family that turns the little girl into a carer, or does the little girl discover that the 'prince' will care for her socially, in worldly-wise ways quite different from the 'inner-world' caring she received from her mother? The price for that worldly care is that the little girl has to become, like her mother, a carer for the inner worlds.

If such a psychological jump has been made in the furious confusion of the relationship with her mother, much will remain unresolved. The good/bad split will not be healed, and the little girl will grow into a woman particularly liable to disillusionment and depression. She will probably not have received enough from her mother, having cut herself off too early in life, and will impose upon herself impossibly high standards of womanhood, motherhood and what makes a good wife. She will restrict or prevent herself from having close female friends, and will almost always suffer disillusionment in her relationships with men – all of this because her inner world seeks more of the good mother and less of the hurly-burly of a heterosexual relationship.

If there is a healthy Electra complex which needs resolution, how does it come about? Certainly girls need and enjoy contact with their fathers. It is a special relationship in which the girl should be able to blossom into womanhood, without fear that her father will abuse or ignore her. Undoubtedly there is an element of competition with the mother in the daughter's relationship with father, although a mature mother, confident of herself and her role, will have no need to engage in that competition, enabling her daughter to moderate competitive feelings as she grows and develops. This allows a new and more mature closeness to develop between mother and daughter, resulting in a healthy and positive identification for both women.

It is normal for there to be a degree of sexuality in the father/daughter relationship, with the daughter feeling free and safe to flirt and her father expressing his approval of her femaleness without intruding into it. Every society has an incest taboo so that this special closeness can be a healthy and not distorted relationship. Such a taboo is central to lifting our social behaviour above the level of immediate gratification of needs to a more complex social interaction. There is obviously a delicate balance between action that helps the daughter develop as a sexually active woman who appreciates herself and that leading to abuse, either in the form of physical intimacy or a void in the responses of her father. Sadly many fathers do not respect this taboo, despite its deep roots stretching back to the very beginning of civilisation. (*See also* **Childhood Sexual Abuse**.)

Here again, social norms and psychological development are closely entwined, a daughter's sexuality being perceived differently from that of a son. Society itself is confused about how it expects its female members to develop sexually, and those societies which are most adamant are usually highly restrictive against any female expression of sexuality. What is clear is that mixed messages are given to girls as they grow up, so that they often perceive their sexuality as belonging to someone else, first to their father and then to their husband. This confusion about 'ownership' of an essential part of another human being leads many incestuous fathers into acting out on a physical level what has always been meant as a symbolic ownership. Even with those fathers who do not act out physically, however, it is the daughter's sexuality in its virgin state that fathers are classically meant to be giving to their sons-in-law during the Judaeo-Christian ceremonies of marriage. It would seem to me that for a daughter/father/mother triangle to completely resolve itself each of the three participants needs to feel that they have possession of their own sexuality, but this would put them into conflict with any culture that believes that men, by virtue of marriage, own women and children.

So-called 'normal' development for girls into heterosexuality implies then a dependence on men which is merely the displaced and unresolved dependence of the mother/daughter relationship and thus still experienced at the level of a young child, added to which is the ability to allow others to own her sexuality and, by extension, her body. Such development into heterosexuality is fraught with dangers that are at most only partially to do with a girl's psychological make-up and her experiences with her mother and father. It is uncertain how much the concept of an Electra complex can help us in our understanding of this complex issue.

Perhaps fathering needs to be a much more active process, so that from birth the daughter is able to learn to love/hate the father in an accepting way alongside the love/hate relationship with mother. She could then make a conscious object choice for her future desires and affections based on a more complete understanding of herself and others, which could run alongside her unconscious choice based on psychological pressures and fantasy. Having some sense of freedom of choice and freedom of action, whatever one's individual resolution, must also be important for psychological health.

In psychotherapy, as in life, it is not unusual to come up against what seems to be a brick wall. The impact of time, culture, religion, philosophy, scientific notions and concepts of normality on an individual are awesome and usually limiting. There is a high cost to any individual who dares cross the wall, because she will then find herself at odds with the remainder of society. For many women struggling through the complexities of sexual psychological development in a confused society (sounding so simple when described as the Electra complex) climbing the wall feels like the only option, whatever the costs. Paradoxically, the result of a more liberal view of women's sexuality is that it has led women to choosing to maintain closeness with other women alongside their other choices about intimacy with men. Perhaps within this freedom of choice lies the answer to what a successfully resolved Electra complex might consist of, that is, an understanding that a woman has to make sense of her relationship with her mother before true intimacy with her father, and thereby with men, is possible.

# Emotional Breakdown

People often describe themselves as having had a 'nervous breakdown' when they have experienced psychological or psychiatric distress. It can mean almost anything from a brief disturbance in their functioning to a total collapse. It is a phrase used to express the seriousness of what has transpired, emphasising the overwhelming nature of some of our more unpleasant emotions and psychological experiences. It also suggests a mechanical cause, rather like a car breaking down, and this relieves the individual from the burden of guilt that many experience when they allow their feelings temporarily to run wild. Sadly there is still a great deal of stigma attached to psychiatric illness. When people disclose that they are depressed, for example, they are often told to 'pull themselves together', and moral judgements are frequently made against people who 'cannot control themselves'. Thus to infer that something physical 'broke down' in your head is felt to be more acceptable.

Sometimes the breakdown is clearly associated with a life event, such as a loss or a trauma (*see* pp.375–7 on Life Event Explanations in Part Two). We all have certain vulnerabilities, some in-built and part of the personality we were born with, others acquired through our lifetime experiences. These vulnerabilities not only dictate what event is specifically upsetting to us but also how we then 'break down'. Thus some people will become depressed and others anxious after a trauma (*see* **Post-traumatic Stress Disorder**).

We also learn early in life what sort of 'illness behaviour' is expected of us. If children receive a message that they are not allowed to be psychologically distressed, they will learn to use physical symptoms to express that distress. If they grow up in a family where a parent frequently collapses under minor stresses they will internalise this as their own 'norm' for later life.

As a culture we tend to frown on 'breaking down' as if it

reveals unacceptable weakness in an individual. The mind cannot cope unendingly with whatever is thrown at it, however, and just as a bone will break if unduly stressed, so too can our psyches 'snap'. And just as a bone takes time and rest to heal, so too does the mind after trauma. Some of our expectations about the speed of recovery of our emotions are totally unrealistic. Thus being 'strong', going back to work the day after your mother's funeral, for instance, may be building a flaw into your psyche that even minor problems in the future will suddenly uncover. Emotions need time to be assessed, experienced, survived and then integrated into our total perception of ourselves and our world. If we do not allow ourselves this time we are in danger of over-loading our psyches to the point of eventual collapse.

Adults tend to be particularly dismissive about the emotions of children, or will attempt to protect them in ways that deny the children's feelings. Although children may appear to survive and even be relatively unaware of major life events they are taking it all into themselves. The emotions will surface at some point in life, often distorted and intensified by the years of enforced silence. Thus breakdown can be a totally unexpected experience in what appears to be a normal adult life.

Paul was 26 when he attempted suicide. He was a high achiever with an apparently happy relationship with his girlfriend Susan. He had however become depressed, irritable, and unwilling to get up or do anything for some weeks after the death of Susan's father, a man he hardly knew. Rather than be there to support Susan, he had collapsed, feeling hopeless and guilty. In this state he had convinced himself that she would be better off if he were dead. Luckily the attempt failed, and he could begin to work on why this death had affected him so profoundly. He had not consciously made the link between this death and the death of his own father, when he was 12. His unconscious mind, however, had responded in the way he had felt prevented from doing 14 years earlier.

Paul had been at boarding school from the age of 7. On the

day of his father's death, from a sudden, unexpected heart attack, a teacher had come into the class and, in front of everyone, told him his father had died and then left. Nothing further was said or done him until his mother visited ten days later. He never saw his father's body nor attended a funeral, and so the event took on an unreal quality for him. He could not openly grieve; his environment did not permit it and his inner world could not grasp the reality of having lost his father. So the emotions were bottled up deep inside of him, and to all those around him he was considered to have coped wonderfully well. When Susan's father died however a door opened inside his mind, allowing those previously unacceptable feelings out. For the first time he experienced the loss of his father as real. Gradually he could experience the grief that the 12-year-old was denied, greatly helped by Susan's very natural grieving for her own father. Together they spent many hours talking, laughing and crying about their mutual loss, and gradually Paul began to integrate both his memories of his father and the loss into a new and more secure view of himself.

# Encopresis
*See* **Bowel Control**

# Enuresis
*See* **Bedwetting**

# Envy

Envy is often confused with jealousy. They are however distinct emotions, which occur within different relationships. Envy is targeted at one other person: you envy something he or she possesses, whether it is a personality attribute or a material possession. It is a destructive feeling which makes you want to destroy the possession rather than have it for yourself. Jealousy occurs within triangular relationships, when you are jealous of the relationship between two others, and wish to claim one of the partners for yourself (*see* **Jealousy**).

The importance of envy as a hostile, destructive emotion which undermines love was first noted by Melanie Klein, who analysed young children as well as adults. She hypothesised that the strength of envy arises because it is an extremely primitive emotion, experienced by the infant in her earliest days, at her mother's breast. Envy is an angry feeling, encountered when we perceive, accurately or not, that someone else has and is enjoying something which we desire. The anger makes us want to destroy whatever it is that we think they have. At the breast the baby finds not only love, satisfaction and comfort but also frustration and a sense of deprivation. The constant goodness and protection experienced by the foetus can never be recaptured. Melanie Klein believed that the infant felt that the breast sometimes kept its goodness and comfort to itself, and envied the breast that ability.

Whether or not you accept this hypothesis, it does seem true that breast-feeding arouses strong and often hostile impulses in people. The infant may be envied for the goodness and love she is receiving and the mother may be envied for being able to provide those resources. In order to protect us from the discomfort of those envious feelings, society has a disinclination to allow any form of 'public' breast-feeding: it is felt generally that it ought to be a private business despite the fact that a small infant can need feeding often and for long periods of each day, so that by making it private we isolate the mother from the affectionate and companionable environment that she needs in order to mother well.

There is also a resistance to breast-feeding felt by a large proportion of mothers. Even those who leave hospital feeding happily tend to discontinue and resort to bottle-feeds surprisingly rapidly. I say surprisingly because bottle-feeding is more expensive and requires much more organisation, preparation, heating and equipment than does breast-feeding.

Most mothers will say they want to breast-feed but feel that something stops them. Breast-feeding represents the most primitive form of giving love and goodness to another person. The baby receives this in a wordless but powerfully emotional way. Many mothers find this high emotional charge confusing and distressing, not realising that the interchange of love and hate, reflected in Kleinian terms as envy for goodness alongside gratitude for it, is the normal and healthy developmental experience for the baby. Using a bottle allows for the intensity of emotions to be displaced onto an object and therefore less actively projected straight at mother.

In adult life the experience of envy is often connected with destructive actions. Jimmy had joined the Royal Navy when he was 18. Five years later he decided that he wanted a vasectomy. The surgeon was reluctant to perform the operation on someone so young and as yet without children, and suggested that Jimmy attend a counselling session. Jimmy was adamant that he would never want children; as the eldest of six he felt that he had had a hard life from the very beginning, having to 'get everything for myself . . .nobody has ever given me anything.' He could remember the births and early infancy of his three youngest siblings, all girls, and said that he had hated them 'from birth'.

It was clear from his tone that Jimmy experienced intense rage whenever he thought of his family, and he declared again that he had no intention of 'repeating Dad's mistakes'. It was equally clear, however, that Jimmy was a sad and lonely man, isolated even within the comradeship of his ship. He agreed, with ill-grace, to return, and see me for further counselling before he made a definite decision. As the sessions progressed he became rude and hostile towards me, saying, 'You are stopping me having what I want; you have no right to play God in my life!' He could not see the caring or protective concern that I shared with the surgeon, and could only experience us as hostile parent figures who had something, in this case the power, which he wanted and envied in us. When I pointed this out to him he became agitated, and for a moment I thought he might hit me. Instead he started to cry. At first it seemed as if the tears were having to fight their way out, and then suddenly it seemed that two decades' worth of tears were being unleashed.

He talked about how he had envied his sisters, who had had 'everything they wanted from Mum and are still close to her'. Although he had chosen to leave home and join the Navy he had experienced it as another rejection. 'Who is rejecting whom?' I asked. He described how much he hated his mother and had wanted to get away 'before I did her some harm'. I said that just before he had cried I had felt that he might harm me, and that perhaps his destructive rage was connected to his sadness. It became obvious that his relationships with women since leaving home had always had an edge of hostility. He described fantasies of hurting them, 'especially their breasts', when having intercourse.

It would have taken a long time in analysis to help Jimmy through such a weight of unresolved envy. In fact he did go ahead with his vasectomy, paying for the operation as a private patient, and triumphantly announcing that he had 'beaten' me and the NHS. Years later, when in one of my group therapy sessions a male patient who had also had a vasectomy before having any children was addressed by another male member of the group, who said, 'You know the saying "cutting off your nose to spite your face"?, well, you've cut off your balls to spite your mother', I thought of Jimmy, and wondered what had happened to him.

It may be the element of envy in male/female relationships that leads us to talk about the war of the sexes. As we can only be one or the other, male or female, there is always an aspect of life which we cannot have, cannot experience. Small children often play at being the other sex, little girls trying to pee standing up, little boys with pillows stuffed up their jumpers saying that they are going to have babies. Growing up means we have to relinquish the hope of being both sexes, but we may still envy the capacities of the other sex. If we accept the Kleinian hypothesis that envy starts at mother's breast it seems likely that men may come to envy women rather more intensely and primitively than women do men. Even if women do have penis envy (*see* **Penis Envy**), their experience of it may not occur until they are 3 or 4 years old, whereas 'breast envy' is a primary experience.

Many women feel that their mother was a bad mother, that is, a bad breast. This means that they do not have to envy the goodness in her or feel gratitude towards her for that goodness. They can grow to have breasts and be mothers themselves; by competing with mother they can lessen the discomfort of envy still further. Boys on the other hand grow to discover that they will not have the feeding breast themselves, and therefore remain always in a state of hostile envy as well as blissful love towards the breast as an object (hence the 'Page-3' and soft-porn phenomena). Much of the aggression that men demonstrate towards women may result from their envy of them. Women tend to act out their envy of men in a more passively aggressive way, likening them to children in order to deny their strength and power, or mimicking them to demonstrate that a woman can be the best man of all, a suggestion often made about former Prime Minister Margaret Thatcher, for instance. Expressing aggression passively is a common trait among people who experience themselves as both angry and powerless, thereby making straightforward aggression too dangerous and leading them to express their aggression by more covert means (*see* **Activity and Passivity** and **Aggression**).

## Epilepsy

Primary epilepsy has always been of interest to those who study the brain's functions because of its ability to produce momentary dysfunction in an otherwise normal brain (in secondary epilepsy on the other hand the fit results from and is centred on an organic abnormality within the brain, such as a tumour). An epileptic fit consists of a large electrical discharge within the brain which lacks any of the modifications and controls that electrical discharges usually have; this discharge causes movements, sensations and behaviour of many sorts. The fit may be limited to an area of the brain and its functions (partial epilepsy) or may be generalised.

The majority of people with epilepsy have their first fit before the age of 20 (this figure does not, however, count the infants who suffer fits as a direct result of having a high temperature, since they are not particularly liable to have any further fits). In the UK approximately 5 people in 1,000 are affected. Research suggests that there is some tendency towards inheriting a lower resistance to having fits, but insults to the brain at birth are also known to produce a high incidence of fits, which partially explains the common association between intellectual impairment and epilepsy.

Most of those who suffer from epilepsy manage to live lives that are only somewhat restricted (for example, they may not be able to drive) but which are none the less successful and fulfilling. Medication can reduce the danger of further fits substantially, and many sufferers come to recognise the warning signs of a fit and can take steps to protect themselves from injury. Epilepsy can however result in the frightening and often public loss of self-control which may make the person increasingly uncomfortable in social situations or even in close relationships.

There is some evidence that repeated, poorly controlled epilepsy may alter a person's personality, and that people so affected become aggressive. Most epileptics experience some mood change before the fit, experiencing either irritability or depression, both of which are usually relieved by the fit. Outdated research which suggested a link between psychopathy, crime and epilepsy has now been discredited.

As a society we are ill-informed about epilepsy, often finding it shocking and something we would prefer not to be exposed to rather than an illness. The sufferers often receive surprisingly little support either within their family or from colleagues, employers or friends. By its nature epilepsy is intermittent and unpredictable, meaning that the person is well and normal for long periods of time. Nevertheless there is the mistaken tendency to think of sufferers as permanently disabled because of the limits the illness and medication place on them.

## Eroticism

Eros was the God of love, and Freud borrowed his name to signify the life instinct, one of two basic instincts (the other being Thanatos, the death instinct) central to his psychoanalytical theory. In this sense, then, eroticism means that which is connected with the making of life, and perhaps also with the feeling of life, of being alive. Freud knew that to speak of Eros and of life instinct was rather more easy than speaking of sexuality and libido in the anti-sexual culture of 19th-century Vienna. Even today, sexual activity that is conducted with contraception (and is therefore not procreative) is frowned upon as a perversion by at least one major religion. Indeed, in psychiatric terminology perversion is often seen as that which involves sexual activity but reaches some form of climax and satisfaction prior to intercourse. But while preservation of the species may be the underlying psychological motivation for sexuality, within an individual it is the libido that provides the energy for the expression of this psychological need.

Since Freud, all psychoanalytical thinking has included some concept of the development of the libido, which is present from birth. The small baby feeding makes noises of great physical satisfaction that express the infantile level of organisation of the libido, and lead, in their satisfying adult version, to the oral delights of kissing and eating, and also of feeding others. It is typical of this development that the satisfaction can be more generalised and can grow to include the concept of giving to others, so that satisfying others becomes a part of the total experience of satisfaction for the self. This development seems to me to be a crucial part of the libido coming to the service of our life-giving instincts, as when we reach the point in adulthood when giving life to others is a part of our own satisfaction and when we no longer need only the individual intense sexual satisfaction that our libido can give us directly. Retaining some aspect of the libido for the self remains important, however; sexual satisfaction is a healthy expression of Eros, in that we revel in the experience of life and the feeling of being very much alive.

The relationship between libido and Eros grows during the 'anal phase' of development, as the child struggles to master control of her sphincters. During this phase of development associations with power and control are made of our basic sexuality; these may later be expressed in our adult eroticism. In the third phase of infant development the child focuses on her genitals, finding stimulation exciting. In this phase new prohibitions may well be administered by parents and other adult sources; these prohibitions become the basis for any shame or guilt we may feel about our own eroticism.

Within psychiatric diagnosis eroticism may be increased or decreased, the libidinal energy becoming exaggerated or extinguished. The expression of eroticism will depend on the developmental experiences of the individual, and the extent of their expression will depend of the availability of the libidinal energy. Therefore manic patients often have enormous reservoirs of libido which they act out in a variety of erotic forms. Some of these forms belong to their own development, but they are also at risk of being adopted by others who will 'plug in' to the libidinal reservoirs to serve themselves rather than the person who is manic. Depressed people tend to feel lacking in libido, which in turn makes them unable to hold on to the life-giving and life-enjoying instinct.

Eroticism can also be a deliberate act of making something which is fundamentally neither sexual nor life-giving look as if it contained these values in order to excite us and stimulate us into wanting it. Advertising is based on such notions. Washing powder can be sold if the housewife looks to be having an affair with her washing machine. The nation holds its collective breath for the next sexualised experience achieved over instant coffee. Even political parties, cars or weaponry can be sold as objects of sexual excitement, and though we all know intellectually that what we are being sold is not sexual, imagery can be used that catches us up in the excitement so that we cease to question the true value of the object. The scope of exciting imagery is enormous, and varies between individuals and cultures. It is based in the relationship that has grown up between our life instinct and our libido, and because that relationship develops over the length and breadth of our childhood experiences it is connected in our brains with an almost limitless number of other possible objects and almost all areas of the body, so that even internal organs can come to possess erotic connations for us.

In some sense it is always a matter of opinion as to where each of us draws the line between what is perverse and what is erotic. The position of that line can change dramatically depending on our personal development, social norms and experiences within relationships. Clearly, the majority of people within almost every culture no longer believe that the only true experience of eroticism is that which is directly connected to conception. We may have come to this conclusion, collectively and unconsciously, not because of any new sexual openness but because world over-crowding has become a bigger threat to humanity than the failure to reproduce sufficiently. Thus finding other outlets for our libido has become important in the service of our life instinct. Western culture seems to have made dramatic moves towards believing that what takes place between two equally consenting adults can be viewed as erotic and acceptable, while any sexual activity (including intercourse leading to conception) which is forced on one person by another, for the satisfaction of only one of the pair or only part of a group, is a perversion (and a crime in many cases) and therefore not socially acceptable. Such definitions sound safe enough, yet within the arena of sexual activity there is always a degree of coercion, collusion and seduction. Aspects of power, dominance and control cannot be clearly separated, especially when much sexual activity occurs within the socially acceptable environs of marriage. We also use eroticism to give some relationships greater value than others, for instance, one sexual partner usually feels some innate right to come 'first' in his or her partner's life. This means that sexuality is also closely linked into the feelings of dependence we experience within closest relationships. To imagine that adults have 'free' choice within sexuality when so much else is wrapped up in our erotic expression is probably naive.

Pauline was 38 when she was admitted to the psychiatric ward of a hospital suffering from a severe anxiety state. She had no previous history of any form of ill health. She was married to Bill, who was 45; Bill had three children and Pauline one from previous marriages, and together they had one child, Simon, who was 6.

For several weeks the sudden emotional distress which Pauline had experienced seemed inexplicable. The whole family agreed that their lives were happy and that nothing of any note had happened. The doctors involved with Pauline became increasingly worried that something serious, such as a brain tumour, had altered her behaviour, but one of our more experienced nurses said that she thought that Bill was reluctant to leave Pauline alone to talk to us. 'He is over-involved', was her comment. This nurse made a special effort to be available for Pauline to talk to in the evenings after her family had left, and gave her clear messages that if something was worrying her it was safe to talk about it. One evening Pauline told her that she had returned home early one evening to discover Bill standing in the kitchen dressed in her clothes. 'It was as though he was pretending to be me,' she said, 'I was terrified.' This terror had not been eased when Bill, after initially laughing off the incident, said that he had enjoyed cross-dressing for many years, and that now she knew about it saw no reason why they couldn't enjoy it together.

Cross-dressing, or transvestism, is not uncommon. Women can wear trousers freely, and in some cultures and at some times men are also encouraged to wear kilts or long, flowing, rather feminine robes. Such dressing is not usually used for the purpose of sexual arousal, however, although it does undoubtedly give satisfaction to some. In transvestism the purpose of wearing women's clothes is that it is arousing, often much more arousing than any other form of sexual expression. Boys around the ages of 3 to 5 frequently enjoy dressing up in their mother's clothes, and may even start to 'steal' underclothes from mum as an object of excitement. Such behaviour seems to be a complex mixture of being erotically aware of mum as their love object and also wanting to identify with her and be a love object themselves (*see* **Perversion**).

Bill reported that he had first started cross-dressing after his first wife disappeared with a neighbour, leaving him with the three small children. He had felt lonely and abandoned, and had turned to this behaviour because it made him feel both satisfied and safe. He was able to both arouse and mother himself. He had stopped cross-dressing when he had met Pauline, but recently he had felt increasingly inclined to revert to it, most particularly since Simon had started to make comments that suggested he was going through a stage of erotic attachment to his mother.

Bill could not envisage relinquishing the behaviour that had satisfied him for so long; Pauline felt despair and disgust at his behaviour, but she also felt that she could not abandon him, partly because of her own need for security, partly because she had experienced single parenthood and did not wish to return to that difficult state, and partly because there was much true affection between them and she recognised Bill's need for a family as well. She had therefore felt trapped and had 'used' hospital as a breathing space in the midst of her terror, hoping that something might save her from having to make a decision where she felt that she could not win.

Such conflicts within relationships are not uncommon, and what passes for mutual acceptance is often nothing of the sort, but rather a disturbing disequilibrium maintained by other needs and forces. Bill's reluctance to give up his erotic behaviour is also not unusual, that form of eroticism having become more important and more satisfying to him than anything else. For the partner, choosing to live with such a scenario can never be easy or totally comfortable, however much 'free' choice he or she may have.

## Excitation

It is a sad life which is not experienced as exciting some of the time. Physiologically, however, excitation is closely linked with anxiety, and sometimes individuals have difficulty recognising which state they are in (*see* **Anxiety**). This is reflected in the design of fairground rides and horror movies, which deliberately excite by threatening to frighten us. Early experiences as well as basic personality traits decide how much we can tolerate and even enjoy anxiety. Often as people grow into middle age they feel ready to settle for a slightly less exciting life in the interests of also experiencing less anxiety. This is why young people often feel that their elders are rather 'boring'.

Much excitation is embedded within our understanding and experience of sexuality. Social activities are often perceived as more exciting if a potential sexual partner is present, for instance, and much that creates excitement can be seen to be objects of a displacement of our sexual energy into other creative, life-inspiring pursuits, such as the arts. A friend of mine recently commented that he was aware of just how exciting I found people, but that he had always preferred mountains!

Children are more easily excited than adults, but they also have more difficulty controlling that sense of excitement, which can then spill over into rage, tears or restlessness. For some people suffering from the more serious psychiatric phenomena such as schizophrenia, manic depression or dementia that same excitement coupled with little or no control is also evident (*see* **Dementia**, **Manic Depressive Psychosis** and **Schizophrenia**). There is some evidence that such states are not separate but form part of a continuum resulting from the more or less impaired development of a small but important area of the temporal lobe of the brain. This means that the increasing sense of control most of us gain over becoming excited is not as well developed in these sufferers, making them more sensitive to becoming over-excited if sufficient stimulus is applied. This has in turn led to theory that you are more likely to become ill if you have both the in-built vulnerability and a family in which high levels of emotion are commonly expressed, causing you over-excitement.

The excitation demonstrated in illness can be a disturbing spectacle, and in its acute phase requires a high degree of nursing and medical skill to manage. A calm, controlled and containing environment, within which there is limited expression of emotion until the phase of excitement has passed, is very important. Drug treatment has revolutionised treatment for patients who previously were locked away in the pain and sadness of their over-excitement, sometimes for many years. Environment is just as important as medication, however, and we need to be careful not always to resort to drugs as the alternative. Sadly, provision for sufferers within the NHS has never been good; they are not the sort of people who can easily make their own case for humane treatment, but instead often frighten and disturb others. They are then in danger of being put 'out of sight' and forgotten.

Paul was a greengrocer's assistant after leaving school; he had been the sort of adolescent the school described as nice but quiet, and seemed to have no friends by the time he was 17. His paternal uncle had been diagnosed as manic depressive when aged 22, and his father had suffered from depression 'on and off' throughout his life. During his 18th year Paul experienced a number of difficulties at work which left him feeling criticised. His mother had also started making noises about it being time for him to leave home, something which worried him a great deal.

One Tuesday morning just after opening the shop Paul seemed to lose control, becoming over-excited to the point of shouting at customers that they 'didn't know their fruit from their vegetables' and juggling the merchandise, an exercise that rapidly deteriorated into throwing fruit all over the place in his rage at not being able to juggle properly. Although other staff tried to restrain and reason with him, he seemed oblivious to anything they could say. Eventually he ran off into the high street and proceeded to cause chaos to the morning rush-hour traffic. The police took him to the police station and immediately called the police surgeon who then contacted the duty psychiatrist. When examined it was clear that Paul was highly excited and also deluded, in that he believed himself to have been transported from home to a distant planet by blue Martians (the police) because he was a special being who knew more about fruit than any other living being (*see* **Delusions**).

Later in the week it also became clear that Paul was experiencing distressing hallucinations during which he would hear voices criticising him because he was not good enough at his job. During these experiences his excitement would disappear and he would become tearful. Paul responded well to treatment, became stabilised on injected medicine and returned to work. He is now 24 and has maintained his improvement, although he needed friendly and supportive accommodation away (but not too far) from home as part of his rehabilitation to a normal life.

Over-excitation can be recognised because it is at best only loosely connected to what is really happening. The manic person may be entertaining for a few minutes but will rapidly come to seem boring as it becomes apparent that his or her excitement is not related to what is transpiring in the environment or within your relationship. Such excitement can easily spill over into rage, hostility, criticism of others or tears, reactions any mother will recognise as the everyday experience of her toddler.

# Experience of Satisfaction

The experience of being satisfied is not given much room in the average textbook on psychiatry or psychotherapy, yet it seems to me to be an essentially healthy experience at all times of life, from birth till death, which when absent has far-reaching consequences for the person's emotional well-being.

A newborn baby achieves satisfaction in being fed and held. The baby also has a need to relate to others, which when successfully achieved produces feelings of satisfaction. Failure to have enough satisfaction, or if that satisfaction is intermittent, unpredictable and not in response to the baby's needs, leads to a basic inability to trust in later life. As the months pass, the baby gains satisfaction from her mobility and from exploring the people and places around her. In the second year she gains major satisfactions from taking control over her body functions and feeling powerful. Failure to gain satisfaction in these phases can lead to a person becoming psychologically 'cut off' from his or her body, a 'head only', and being scared or disinterested in explorations of all sorts and unwilling to form relationships. Power and control become the focus of many difficulties for those who do not experience the satisfaction of gaining these aptitudes.

As the weight of social injunctions begins to limit the child so the need to be able to achieve satisfaction needs to be balanced by the understanding that needs cannot be met in anti-social or unacceptable ways. This is a delicate but essential balancing act to master for future mental health. It seems increasingly possible that some people inherit a weakness which limits the extent, one way or another, to which they can adapt their needs to the established social injunctions. Such an inheritance is probably, at most, only a vulnerability, so that the experiences of the child etch themselves dramatically on the original template and the experiences of adulthood act constantly to challenge or preserve psychological well-being.

Learning provides wide new fields for satisfaction, as the child conquers reading and writing, painting, counting and scientific endeavours. Increasingly the infant gains a sense of mastery over his world, making it a place where there is more satisfaction than anxiety (*see* **Instinct for Mastery**). During mid-adolescence the great potential satisfaction of sexual behaviour becomes a central focus, often continuing as a prime mode of expressing need and gaining satisfaction throughout adult life. However, sexuality is profoundly affected by all previous experiences of satisfaction: only if those phases have been successfully survived will the arena of sexuality bring lasting satisfaction.

An important part of the experience of satisfaction is the complementary sense of helplessness and dependence, that is, we need to be able to hand ourselves over to the delights that will satisfy us, be they from another human being or a major work of art. Such a transaction mirrors the early infantile dependence on the satisfying, good-enough mother. That satisfaction heals the inner tension associated with a need. When the need is fulfilled, then the individual is satisfied. Whatever satisfies us remains as a memory which we can evoke at future times. We therefore develop a sense of desire for that which we remember has satisfied us in the past.

The sense of having had satisfying experiences and being able to predict that there will be similar experiences in the future is an important part of a healthy life. Despair can overwhelm us when life seems empty of satisfaction. An inability to control the search for satisfaction can equally cause despair in both ourselves and others. Often a sign of recovery from depression is when someone can make a plan with the expectation that he or she will receive satisfaction from it, and a sign of impending illness when someone fails to gain satisfaction from events that he or she previously found fulfilling.

# Extroversion
*See* **Introversion and Extroversion**

# F

## Failure of Memory
*See* **Amnesia**

## Fear of Castration
*See* **Castration Complex**

## Fear of Persecution
*See* **Persecution Complex**

## Feelings of Guilt
*See* **Guilt** and **Guilt Complex**

## Fetishism
*See* **Perversion**

## Fixation
This term describes the attachment of libidinal (that is, sexual) energy to a particular phase of an infant's development. Although such a fixated stage may then be repressed out of consciousness and into the unconscious, it remains stuck none the less, so that when incidents in adult life trigger off memories the individual regresses back to the phase of development at which he or she got 'stuck'.

This happens to everyone to a greater or lesser extent. Freud postulated that certain individuals were particularly 'adhesive', perhaps to certain developmental stages. It is easy to see that such personal 'stickiness' might be an inherited phenomenon or may be learnt from parents who got stuck at the same stage. Most probably it represents both. If the ability to progress from one developmental step to another is limited in some individuals or families, then clearly the chances of energy becoming fixated at that stage is increased. Because such a phenomenon is then repressed into the unconscious world, we can continue our developmental steps in our conscious minds as if all were well; only under stress will the potential psychological weakness be exposed. During childhood specific traumatic situations or long-standing stresses may equally cause a fixation.

Nigel was 23 when he was admitted to hospital for an emergency appendectomy. During the week of his recovery nursing staff noted that he seemed depressed to a much greater extent than they expected in such patients. He had also been incontinent several times and was demanding attention all the time. I was asked to assess Nigel's mental state before his discharge because the staff feared that he might be suicidal.

During the course of our conversation several things became clear. First the staff were right and Nigel was low in spirits beyond what is normally seen in post-operative patients. Secondly, this was not Nigel's only experience of being hospitalised as an emergency. When he was 22 months old he had developed meningitis. He had no conscious memory of his four-week stay in hospital but said that his mother had repeatedly talked about her distress at leaving him alone, and how she would hear him screaming for her as she walked away at the end of her visits. She also said that over the four weeks he had ceased to scream and had become 'horribly' quiet, refusing even to look at her during visits.

I asked Nigel how he imagined that little boy had felt. He became tearful and said that he must have felt lonely, frightened, sad and angry all at once. Then I pointed out that those were the feelings he was experiencing now. The trauma of the early experience had fixated some of his libidinal energy at the stage of development of a 22-month-old baby. Re-living the experience as a 23-year-old had not only brought back the feelings of the event but also the behaviour – the incontinence and the need to demand attention – associated with that phase of development. Once Nigel had seen the connection he asked for a few sessions of counselling with his mother to talk over his earlier experience. This proved a moving and healing time for both of them.

Sometimes such regressions back to a fixated earlier phase are benign; they heal without intervention as the precipitating cause of stress decreases. Most people who are ill, for instance, experience some regression back to an earlier mode of behaviour in which others are allowed to care for them. In some people, however, regression can become malignant, set firm and immovable no matter what happens. The psychotherapist Michael Balint used the terms benign and malignant when describing those suitable or unsuitable for psychotherapy. Clearly if someone is inclined towards malignant regressions back to fixated points of development then it is probably more healthy not to encourage him or her to regress at all. Quite what makes the difference between the benign or malignant nature of regressions may well be connected to the events which led to the fixation in the first place. Those events which are both exciting and traumatic seem more likely to fixate in a way that makes regression back to such points malignant.

Melanie is now 42 and has had an illness leading to increasing difficulties with her vision over the past three years. Although she knows that she will maintain some of her sight, her illness has undoubtedly altered her life. When she first fell ill she was frightened and regressed back to the infantile level of wanting help and attention from all the staff who treated her. Although this seemed appropriate in the short term, this behaviour continued beyond physical treatment and beyond repeated explanations from the staff that all that could be done for her was being done. She was undoubtedly sad and distressed; she experienced a pressing need for attention and 'support', often for hours a day, from the out-patient staff. Yet at the same time she was angry and dismissive, and would repudiate any help she was offered, so that workers quickly became exhausted of giving her their time only to be told at the end of it that they were useless in helping her.

It was clear that Melanie was excited by her new-found position as well as frightened of her illness. She gave a clear history of sexual abuse as a young girl, abuse which she experienced with a similar combination of excitement and fear, helplessness and yet powerful control over the desires of an adult, need for attention and yet fury at the kind of attention she was being given. Even after many hours of talking about these experiences and their similarities with her present experience, Melanie cannot give up on the behaviour to which she has malignantly regressed. The original fixation occurred within the context of excitement as well as trauma, making it almost impossible to shift at this late stage.

## Flashbacks

Flashbacks are disturbing experiences that occur after traumatic events. The imagery of the event becomes 'burnt' onto the memory of the survivor and repeats itself, like a snapshot or video, without warning or prompting on the part of the individual. Such pictures often contain horrific material which causes a panicky feeling and a sense of being trapped by the traumatic event, unable to escape it because it is 'inside' the sufferer.

Flashbacks usually lessen in frequency and intensity and then disappear after a period of days or weeks. If they continue for more than a few weeks, however, it may be necessary for the person to seek help in actively 'debriefing' their original experience. Flashbacks form the most distressing part of post-traumatic stress disorder, and also occur after sexual abuse and rape, car accidents and witnessed violence. For some people even seeing a frightening image on the television may be enough to start a brief series of such flashbacks. Active debriefing immediately after the incident can help to stop the process by which these flashbacks become perpetuated (*see* **Post-traumatic Stress Disorder**).

Since they are visual memories they may be evoked by specific situations which evoke the memory. Thus sexual activity after a rape may be visually re-experienced with flashbacks of the rapist rather than the loved partner.

Alec had been driving along the motorway in the early hours of the morning and had been the first on the scene of an accident. The first he knew of it was when he very nearly ran over a body which had been thrown from the crashed vehicle. At the time he behaved in a way we would all hope to in the circumstances: he called an ambulance and the police from the nearest phone and then parked his car with hazard lights flashing so as alert and stop any oncoming vehicles; he then checked each of the people lying across the road. All but one were dead, and the one who appeared to be alive was seriously injured, unconscious but moaning.

Afterwards Alec experienced sensations of fear whenever he was driving; he also often felt like bursting into tears and was irritable with his family. Most disturbing, though, was a series of flashbacks in which he would see again the whole scene of himself walking, as if in slow-motion, between the bodies on the road. The flashback was accompanied by moaning sounds, and would be so vivid that he would think momentarily that it really was all happening again. It took several 'debriefing' sessions in which Alec described his experiences over and over before these flashbacks ceased.

## Flight into Health

Just as our psyches sometimes rescue us from inner conflict by a flight into illness (*see* **Flight into Illness**), so too can our psyches recognise when that flight is too costly. At that point a decision, conscious or unconscious, is made to get better again and relinquish all symptoms. In this way our psychological perceptions of illness, health and the care we receive makes a major impact on the timing of our illnesses and return to health. It is often noted that the patients who fear dependence and get angry when looked after, although rather difficult to deal with in the short term, often get better much more quickly than those who enjoy the care.

I have seen patients who although seemingly deeply disturbed, deluded and hallucinating, tolerate only a day or two of a psychiatric ward on which there are patients who are clearly more disturbed. At some level these people must recognise that they are not going to get as much care as they wanted or needed and have made a choice, probably unconsciously, to either get worse or get better. Similarly, those who are in therapy as the result of having taken an overdose, apparently because life felt overwhelming at the time, often fail to keep follow-up appointments: their flights into illness being brought to a rapid end by a flight into health.

The trouble with both flight mechanisms is that they remove the individual's attention from the real problem or conflict, replacing it with a false dilemma which is more easily solved or has to be solved by someone else. For the person who takes an overdose there is often an underlying question along the lines of 'does anyone care for me enough? Probably not . . . so I won't care for myself and then I'll see what reaction that produces.' Usually there is some life event that has produced the uncertainty and pain; perhaps a real rejection or a fear of rejection. The overdose then poses the question to loved ones, neighbours and of course, hospital staff, who respond appropriately to save the life, although they may at the same time seem shockingly uncaring, because self-destruction disturbs most people, making them feel angry towards the attempted suicide rather than understanding. Hence the individual gets the answer he or she feared; his or her life may have been saved but nobody does seem to care very much. This is too painful to be considered and therefore there is a flight towards health. Sadly, none of this answers the cry for love and attention, things we all need sometimes and which are, for many people, in genuinely short supply.

During the early weeks in various forms of therapy, individuals begin to see that therapy is not just about being supported and emotionally looked after but can also be painfully confronting. Patients who are really looking to change themselves engage at this point in a relationship with the therapist, known as a 'working alliance'. A small percentage, however, suddenly decide that they are better and no longer need help. If the therapist is inexperienced such patients seem remarkably rewarding as they stay briefly, are positive towards both therapy and the therapist, and then announce themselves 'better'. Experience has shown, however, that such people are taking flight into health and away from the pain of their underlying conflicts. This may bury those conflicts but does not heal them, and in future such individuals are vulnerable to further psychological troubles. Each of us uses the mechanisms of flight into illness and health as a kind of timing device that allows us to switch from what we can and cannot cope with in both our inner and outer worlds.

## Flight into Illness

When there is a conflict of interest between our inner and outer worlds we experience psychological pain and tension. Sometimes this becomes unbearable, and it is at this point that symptoms of illness can 'rescue' us, by channelling the energy generated around the conflict down a different pathway. We can 'choose' illness at many different levels of consciousness and unconsciousness, although I have been taught to think that those who most overtly choose illness may well be the sickest of all.

Many of us will have had the experience of feeling over-tired and stressed just before succumbing to an infectious illness, a cold or flu, which makes us retire to bed for a few days, giving us no choice but to take the rest we desperately need. In this sense the illness has been a rescuing event, allowing us to take flight from the relentless pressures that previously threatened us. Society is much more forgiving if we take flight into physical illness than if we fly into psychological illness. Most of us believe that it is 'not our fault' to be physically ill, but a sign of moral weakness to admit to depression or anxiety. Most GPs agree, however, that at least 50 per cent of the patients that come to them with physical complaints are under psychological stress which they are often clearly trying to avoid or deny.

A wide variety of symptoms can provide relief from inner conflict, and once the symptoms are produced they begin to manufacture 'secondary gains' from our environments. Such gains may be simply a matter of gaining some tender loving care for a few days, having a rest or getting the attention of a loved one who was previously preoccupied with other matters. They may allow a complete retreat from the pressures of adult life and offer the prospect of a life that although more limited and dependent may feel safer and less troublesome to the individual.

Michelle is a 35-year-old woman who developed agoraphobia at the age of 23, just after the birth of her first child, Tracy. Over the last 12 years she has never felt able to leave the house on her own, experiencing overwhelming anxiety whenever she has tried to do so. During the course of this terrible symptom she has felt various emotions. Sometimes she is depressed but mostly she is calm and untroubled, that is, so long as no one suggests that she change at all. As soon as that suggestion is made she quickly becomes angry and tearful, saying that no one understands just how terrible an illness she has. She has had many courses of anti-depressants and several attempts at behaviour modification, all to no avail.

It is clear that Michelle's original illness was a flight from something that caused her painful acute anxiety, a symptom which then reappears as soon as she is challenged to re-involve herself with the outside world. It is also clear that over the years she has developed a position of total power within the family network which can now only function around her, taking her needs as their central decision-making focus. Such a powerful position adds extra protection against her experiences of anxiety and makes her even less willing to relinquish the symptom, even though it is limiting her life to a great extent (*see* **Agoraphobia**).

Michelle was not keen to enter psychotherapy, but Tracy's emerging adolescence had begun to affect the balance of power at home and Michelle had also become aware of envying Tracy's increasing freedoms in the outside world. Such realisations moved her to acknowledge that something (not necessarily herself) would have to change. Thus she came into therapy hoping that we could change the family back to a position in which she felt comfortable again, and therefore was furious with me when I insisted that she had to manage to get to sessions in the centre of Southampton, by bus. I suggested she join the local agoraphobic self-help group so that they could provide volunteers to accompany her, at least to begin with; this removed the burden of having to be involved from the family but it also allowed Michelle to make contacts outside of the family for the first time in years.

In many ways Michelle's view of and anger with me as the non-caring therapist was strangely helpful. Her family had been unendingly understanding and that had not helped her free herself. When I pointed this out, it provoked a long conversation about the nature of personal freedom. She had been the youngest of a family of four girls, very much allowed to be the baby of the family and restricted from developing much sense of exploration of the world or relationships outside of the family. The vision of the world which her childhood had left was always restricted, and her agoraphobia had made remarkably little difference to the life she was leading in comparison with the life she thought her mother had led. 'Mum only went out to do the shopping, pick up the kids and run errands for us all,' was a comment she made early in therapy. 'So, going out was not a particularly satisfying experience, then?' I asked. Michelle seemed rather amazed by the use of words such as satisfying or freedom, as if she had had no expectation of such occurrences in her life.

After a year in therapy Michelle had made several friends in the self-help group, and this had led to her making her first non-family outings for many years. 'When was the last time you went out with someone other than your husband or mother?' I asked. She looked startled and very uncomfortable at the question. Several sessions later she asked how confidential therapy was – was I reporting any of what was said back to her mother or husband? This reflected just how little sense of worth as an independent adult she had of herself. When I reassured her that whatever was said stayed between us, she told me the story of an affair she had had at work, not long after her marriage. 'It was the most exciting thing that ever happened to me,' she confided, and indeed, I had never seen her as animated as she was while she told the story. When I asked what had happened, however, she became sad and tense. 'He left me, refused to even see me,' she said, 'when I told him I was pregnant.'

Michelle had thus never known for sure whose daughter Tracy was, and had during the first few months of Tracy's life been terrified to take her out in case she met friends who would recognise that the child was not her husband's. Such was the anxiety that swept over her when she even thought about taking Tracy out for a walk that she had taken to staying at home and seeing only close family. 'It's funny,' she said, 'but I had forgotten what was on my mind during those early months, I could only remember the pain of the anxiety.'

As our sessions together moved on from this revelation Michelle spoke more and more of how confused and painful her feelings towards Tracy had been. On the one hand she had always wanted a little girl and was delighted and proud. The circumstances of Tracy's conception, however, and the difficulties during her birth as well as her own emotional responses when she realised that she was no longer the pampered baby of her family but instead the mother who now had to produce the pampering, had caused her considerable pain and anger. The symptoms of agoraphobia had provided a perfect 'hiding' place into which she had gratefully taken flight. This is not to say that the symptoms, the experience and the distress were unreal, quite the contrary, they were terribly real, as were their consequences: the 12 'lost' years. However, until Michelle could understand both the primary and secondary gains of her flight into illness she could not feel any true desire to change the situation, and any form of help was bound to fail.

Sometimes secondary gain is financial; it has long been noted that people take longer to heal if insurance claims or legal action of some form is hanging over their heads. In this sense secondary gain is often aimed at self-preservation, the person's psyche having decided to accept the symptom as an integral part of the self in order to achieve some good out of an otherwise distressing experience.

## Frigidity

*See* **Sexual Arousal Disorders**

## Frustration

Life, for all of us, has its share of frustrations. This is true from our earliest weeks, when the parenting we receive will never be a completely perfect 'fit' to our needs, however hard our parents try to make it so. Learning to tolerate frustration is an important part of our development (*see* **Experience of Satisfaction**). Some people seem to have a much greater tolerance than others, often demonstrated from an early age. The models we are set as to how our parents and other important figures in our lives manage when frustrated may provide us with images we mirror, and the age at which we are exposed to frustration and its amount determine our capacity to cope. For each infant there is an optimum amount of frustration for each developmental stage: too little or too much will mean difficulties coping later on when inevitable frustrations of adult life occur.

Frustration implies that a basic instinctual need has not been met, although often we sublimate (that is, transfer) those needs into other activities; if these fail as well our frustration is increased. Frustration can be an internal phenomenon in that we prevent ourselves achieving the thing we most desire, or an external phenomenon, in that the world or important people in the world refuse to fulfil our desires. It is painful to be frustrated; people often use descriptions like 'it made me boil over', 'I could feel my blood-pressure rising', or 'I thought I would explode' to explain the sense of the enormous build-up of energy that cannot be released along the chosen and desired pathway.

Instinctually the needs to survive, procreate and be sexual are those most likely to be frustrated. Survival within a complex civilisation may be sublimated into almost anything – even into the need to be at a crucial meeting on time when you are stuck in the middle of a traffic jam! The need to have children is for many a pressing yet frustrated urge. Infertility clinics know the degree of frustration couples suffer and the lengths they will go to in order to fulfil their desires. And for many the need to express their sexuality is thwarted, either by inner dictates or by outer circumstance (*see* **Instinct for Survival** and **Sexuality**).

The potential we all have for self-denial is great, and sometimes mid-life crises are precipitated by people suddenly realising what it is that they have been denying themselves for years, wanting to recapture it, but finding that it is too late.

Pamela became a nun when she was 22 and lived happily for many years within her order. When in her late 30s she developed high blood-pressure, which her GP suspected had a psychological basis. She referred her to me with a note commenting 'This is one angry nun!' Certainly Pamela was pent-up, but it was soon clear that her sense of boiling over was more to do with frustration than anger, although she sometimes expressed it angrily. Psychotherapy is by its nature and design a frustrating business. The complete attention of your therapist is only yours for specific and limited hours of the day or week, and progress is a slow business. All therapists are less than perfect, and certainly with Pamela I was slow to catch on to what she was trying to tell herself and me.

She told me about a dream in which she had seen someone who looked like her, but was not her, living a completely different life, with a husband and children. 'This woman,' she said, with great embarrassment, 'was wanton'. 'Do you mean that she enjoyed sex?' I asked. She nodded, clearly in great misery about this display from her inner world.

'I think that a part of yourself is trying to communicate with you. It is desperate to get out. But for the moment you are too frightened by it to have a conversation, a negotiation with it,' I commented. 'Can one part of you talk to another part?' she enquired, 'Isn't that a rather mad idea?' (I have for a long time appreciated what a luxury it is to be a psychotherapist, and to be allowed, even expected, to be rather mad at times.) 'Are you afraid of going mad?' I prompted. She nodded. 'My mother was mad sometimes. I was very frightened by it as a child. She once threatened to kill us all.' 'When was that?' I asked. 'It was the day my periods started.'

There followed a story of sexual repression throughout her life, with evidence that Pamela truly expected to die if she allowed herself to be sexual. This had presented her with an impossible choice: either her instinct for survival or her sexuality had to be frustrated. She had chosen, unconsciously, to deny herself sexuality by choosing 'a higher calling'. However, when she was 34 and in the course of acting as a teacher she had met a man to whom she had been greatly attracted. Although she had rapidly got herself transferred so as to be distant from him, her sexual feelings were aroused and she could no longer ignore them. They were literally 'boiling over' in her bloodstream.

We spent many weeks gently exploring the 'other Pamela' who threatened the security of her life and yet promised gratification. Gradually she began to see that she could not return to her old self, simply because she had now met the frustrated self. The Mother Superior at her convent was helpful in allowing Pamela to see that she should make an honest choice for herself while remaining in keeping with her vows. Pamela realised that the new her was not the one who had made the vows, and with much sadness left the Order. There was a time of grieving for all the love, hope and comfort she had found there, alongside a burning anger that she had in some way wasted her life, but she used her considerable psychological resources to build a new life, and after much debate risked a relationship with a man. Although not an instant or complete success, she came to therapy some weeks later and reported that at least her blood-pressure was normal these days!

## Fugue
*See* **Amnesia**

# G

## Grandiose Behaviour

Our behaviour is governed by social convention; therefore what is normal and appropriate for one person in a particular situation will be abnormal for another. There is obviously a degree of judgement, of subjectivity involved in deciding what is or is not grandiose. Behaviour is only the outward show of our thoughts and belief systems about ourselves and our environment, and therefore it is possible for someone to fit in socially while still harbouring grandiose thoughts about him- or herself.

I wonder if we don't all at least fantasise about being rich, famous, powerful, clever, beautiful or royal. Certain functions allow us to 'dress up', just as children do, and to act 'as if' for a while. Some roles in life allow us to adopt certain grandiose mannerisms at moments. Royalty is the extreme example of this, and yet we all know that such figures are 'normal' beneath the mannerisms and we assume that they are not so taken in by their roles that they presume them to extend to their persons. My young life was spent as an Army child, and I was always fascinated by the difference between the pomp and circumstance of 'official' occasions, when the grown-ups often acted in rather grandiose ways of dress and behaviour, and our behind-the-scenes life of constant travel and often extremely uncomfortable circumstances.

The important distinction to make in order to keep our incipient grandiosity in check is between that which is role-associated, fantasy, or 'as if' behaviour and that which we come to believe is true about ourselves. I know several doctors, for instance, who believe they possess almost miraculous powers of life-saving, quite over and above the evidence of their skills. They have adopted their role as doctor as their total persona, forgetting all the other facets of their personality in the process, thereby becoming grandiose.

The realities of life – the ironing that needs to be done, the children who need looking after, the toilets that want unblocking, etc. – remind most of us continually that we are not special people, but merely fulfil special and privileged roles for a part of our lives.

In psychiatry there are a number of illnesses that cause people to become grandiose in their ideas and behaviour. They may adopt titles or names of famous people, truly believing themselves to be these people in a way that will not admit any argument. In this sense they are deluded about their real selves (*see* **Delusions**). They may act as if they were these people, and become outraged when 'the public' refuses to recognise them. They can be high-handed in any discussion, believing everyone but themselves to be stupid, or they may even refuse to talk to 'lesser beings'. In the course of schizophrenia many patients learn to keep these grandiose delusions to themselves, so that it is only in the course of conversation that you come to realise there are areas they refuse to talk about, or the mention of which makes them agitated and restless (*see* **Schizophrenia**). For manic patients such self-restraint is more difficult, as it is for those who become grandiose as a result of alcohol abuse or early dementia. The frontal part of the brain seems to be an area associated with our awareness of 'appropriateness', and if there is a tumour or other organic lesion there the person's behaviour may well become strangely grandiose (*see* **Alcoholism**, **Dementia**, and **Manic Depressive Psychosis**).

When we are young we adopt grandiose thoughts as a way of protecting ourselves from recognising how small and dependent we are, and, at least from the world's point of view, how unimportant. As our sense of self grows and we begin to establish ourselves as adults the need for that psychological protection diminishes and we can begin to replace it with real achievements. During adolescence people often display remarkably grandiose thoughts: they have all the answers, and display amazement (and can be very rude) over just 'how wrong' their parents' generation have been. This element of grandiosity is necessary, however, to their feeling able to embark on their hazardous voyage into their own lives. It is important for parents to be able to allow their children to make their own mistakes, without feeling this makes them failures. Children as well as the rest of us need to know that we can make mistakes and still be loved. The more we know this, the less we need to make ourselves grandiose.

## Greed

In Kleinian theory greed is closely related to envy. The envious person can never be satisfied and is in that sense perpetually greedy. To feel greedy is to feel insatiable far beyond true biological needs and also beyond that which can realistically be expected. Both envy and greed are destructive emotions. When the baby envies the goodness of the breast he wishes to spoil or destroy it; when the baby feels greed at the breast he wants to empty it completely. The difference lies in whether the baby projects his own sense of badness outwards, in envy and the wish to spoil, or whether he introjects (pulls in) the destructiveness, as in greed. These feelings are moderated in the baby by 'good enough' mothering, that is, when the mother demonstrates her capacity to withstand and survive the baby's attack. This requires the mother to be secure enough in her own sense of goodness not to need a constant flow of love from the baby. When mothering is applied to the baby in response to the mother's needs rather than as an empathic response to the baby's needs, feelings of envy and greed cannot become moderated and instead come to be major parts of the individual's personality (*see* **Envy**).

Women with bulimia (a compulsive need to vomit after eating) often go on a tremendous binge of overeating prior to their vomiting. This is the acting out of their unresolved greed. It is not uncommon for bulimics to eat everything in the fridge, for instance, before being overwhelmed with feelings of guilt and badness. They have introjected these feelings into themselves at the same time as they have physically ingested their food (*see* **Eating Disorders**).

Women often have a deep-seated fear of their own greed, and develop a tendency to over-control as a protection from it. Many women describe their need never to ask for help or emotional support, because they feel that if they did ask it would open the floodgates to an overwhelming, greedy need which would then lead to them being rejected. Mothers who feel this way often have difficulties feeding their daughters, being unable to judge what is reasonable in the daughter's demands.

We usually ascribe negative connotations to the concept of greed and most particularly to demonstrations of greed in women, who are meant to be social givers rather than takers. Thus individuals who do experience strong pulls of greediness often go to desperate measures to hide their behaviour. As greed is basically a destructive emotion, whatever is sucked in during our experiences of greed then feels bad to us. If it is related to an early infantile need to assume the bad from mother, in order to keep her good and perfect in our eyes, we may then find that any experience of the bad in others leaves us feeling greedy. We may represent that to ourselves as a physical (usually oral) need to take in food, but at the level of fantasy we are hoovering up the anger or hostility in the relationships around us, and the food, far from comforting us, leaves us with a bad taste in our mouths. In this way greed can be differentiated from 'comfort eating', in which the individual turns to food after a relationship difficulty and is soothed by it. Clearly such experiences are related closely to our experiences of being fed as an infant and to the chaotic fantasy world we inhabited while we were relating to the breast or bottle.

# Grief

During the course of life we all lose people who are important to us: parents, spouses, children and friends. It is natural for this loss to provoke intense feelings, yet it is often difficult for people to find ways of expressing these feelings or of knowing whether or not they are normal. In the Western world we seem to have lost formalised or ritualised mourning behaviour and as yet found no replacement. We also live in greater isolation from our extended family, and increased geographic mobility often makes us distant from our friends as well. Thus when we are bereaved there may be no one to whom we can turn to for comfort in our distress.

The intensity of the distress, its timing in relation to the actual loss and the way in which it is expressed are dependent on a number of interwoven factors. Clearly our relationship to the person who dies is central to our experience of bereavement. If the relationship involved a heavy degree of dependence in either direction, or if it was a particularly ambivalent and heated relationship, we are more likely to suffer prolonged and intense feelings of sadness, anger and despair. Marriages within which there have been unshared power and decision-making, few expressions of feelings and conflicts left unresolved may leave the remaining spouse with an unbearable weight of emotion.

Widows seem to experience more distress than do widowers, and mothers more distress at the loss of their children than fathers. This may reflect women's greater investment in relationships. Widowers tend to remarry rapidly without any apparent conflict about making a new relationship within the context of grieving for an old one. To the outsider this can easily look as if the widower is merely replacing an employee, that wives are replaceable in the practical sense of the man's feeling that he needs looking after, and that such practicalities weigh more heavily than the emotional experience of having lost a wife. Widows, although often feeling lonely and in need of companionship, remarry much less frequently, partly because of the lack of available men of a similar age (because of their higher death rate at each age) and partly because of what appears to be a more intense emotional commitment to the lost spouse. This commitment may have social as well as emotional roots, women still expected to be more dependent financially and perhaps having less investment outside of the family which they could balance against their grief.

As our lives are usually constructed around our key relationships, our basic assumptions about life, ourselves and our roles are also focused within these relationships. When a focal person is lost from the network of relationships we are affected directly by that loss and also indirectly by the consequences of that loss on every other person in the network. Thus a grandmother who loses a grandchild may grieve thrice over, once for the lost grandchild, once for the effects of that loss on herself, and then once again for the pain she has to witness in her son or daughter.

It is normal to fear that a major loss would overwhelm us. In fact our defence mechanisms spring into action to defend us against being overwhelmed. In the immediate aftermath of tragic news people often feel numb, shocked, becoming suddenly very organised and 'sensible' while they arrange the funeral. There may be moments when the reality of the loss comes crashing through the defences. One man described this to me as similar to the big waves that crashed through the sea walls during the 1990 storms: he felt he had to rebuild his defences rapidly after each such wave in order to remain protected enough to cope. Our defences usually do hold so that we can cope, minute to minute, hour to hour and day to day (*see* **Defence Mechanisms**).

As time passes so there are moments when the loss is felt acutely. Something happens, often a trivial component of life which nonetheless carries meaning 'under the defences', and we experience the sadness, despair and aching emptiness. In a life of other relationships and roles the loss is experienced in this gradual way and alongside each moment of grief there comes a new structuring of life which gives each aspect new meaning, allowing us to carry on and redevelop hope and trust in our lives. If the lost relationship represents the largest 'investment' of emotional energy in our lives we may find ourselves lonely, isolated and cut off from other purposes or sources of support. It is clearly much more difficult to rebuild a life from this position, and not uncommonly a survivor feels that to rebuild is to 'desert' or 'abandon' the lost relative or friend, feelings which provide further obstacles to overcoming the loss (*see* **Guilt Complex**).

In the immediate aftermath of tragedy our minds find ways of comforting us. Some people experience hallucinations of the lost person, experiencing momentarily an image of him or her sitting in a favourite chair or pottering in a much-loved garden. Defences may allow us to block out or deny our loss, particularly if there are other important things or relationships to 'get on with'. Mothers often report that they are 'saved' from overwhelming grief after the death of a child because other children continue to make demands on and need them. Such demands can, however, feel terribly unfair to a person whose defences will not allow this much denial. Bereaved spouses may also continue, holding their grief in check, if there are young children to look after. Loss causes grief, however, and it cannot be expected magically to go away because it is inconvenient. When it has been squashed down out of sight it may re-surface years later, either when we experience another loss or when the relationship in which the grief has been 'buried' changes, for example when the children grow up and leave home, thereby exposing the underlying grief (*see* **Denial**).

Buried grief can erupt in ways other than sadness. Many people experience grief in an angry way. For most people anger plays some part in the mourning process, often felt against the doctor or hospital that has 'failed' to save their relative, or towards the event or illness. This can lead to the creative use of that anger as people fight to ensure that others do not suffer similarly. Sometimes the anger is free-floating, ready to attach itself to the most minor inconvenience as an excuse for its expression. When grief is buried the anger may erupt without warning, without provocation, like the explosion of a volcano whose pressure has become too great to suppress any more. Sadly this explosive grief is often expressed at the very people whom the individual is trying most to protect by burying their grief in the first place: children, relatives and friends.

Natalie was 32 when her husband Thomas was killed in a car crash. Their three children were under 5 at the time and so, with the help of grandmothers and two sisters, Natalie had little choice but to cope. For the first two months she surprised herself with how well she was coping, and began to wonder if she had ever loved or needed Thomas as much as she had thought she did. Such thoughts made her feel guilty, and to compensate she worked even harder to look after her family. Of course the children were all distressed at the loss of their father, although the youngest two could not express this verbally. Each in turn suffered nightmares, crying, and temper tantrums, and would frequently say they 'hated' mummy who they believed had 'lost' their dad. Natalie was the central figure in their lives, so it is easy to understand why their grief and its accompanying anger should be expressed towards her. Their feelings served to combine with Natalie's own sense of being a 'bad wife', however; and on top of this, the rest of the family, who had been so keen for Natalie to 'cope for the sake of the children', became openly critical about just how well she was coping.

Natalie knew that her coping was a thin facade, and would spend hours crying whenever she was alone, particularly at night. She was also aware of how rapidly she lost her patience with the children: this added to her guilt. A wall had been constructed by this time between herself and the other members of the family, one of whom now sought the advice of a social worker about whether Natalie was 'fit' to look after all three children. The social worker suggested that I come with her to meet the family. She said it was unusual to be asked to check on a parent who was 'over-coping', and she guessed that much was going on in the family that was 'undercover'.

In order to be as unintrusive as possible we set up an appointment for Natalie to come and see us rather than visit her at home. Her mother-in-law Sophie, mother Marion and one sister, Claudia, were also present. She arrived with all three children, clearly angry about the appointment – an anger she expressed in terms of the difficulties in getting all three children ready for a morning appointment. When her mother-in-law said that she would have been willing to help, Natalie told her it was her fault that they were there in the first place. There was an extraordinary amount of noise in the room as the children squabbled and cried and all the adults except for Natalie tried to have their say. In an attempt to cut through the noise I asked Natalie whether it was always such chaos when the family got together. Natalie nodded, and 4-year-old Amanda, who had a protective arm around her mother, said 'Yes, it's terrible!' It became clear that this was exactly how this family arranged itself and behaved all the time, and that all the help offered to Natalie was heavily tinged by this excited competition between Sophie, Marion and Claudia.

I commented that families have to have predictable order to run smoothly, and that Sophie, Marion and Claudia needed to negotiate about how much time they could spare to help Natalie. Natalie, as the parent, must have the authority to then decide how much help to accept and when and where to accept it. 'She needs us!' the three of them cried in unison.

I said that I was sure that was true, but that what she needed most was structure and positive support with the practicalities of life, and that the emotional expression of all their combined grief needed to be separated from these practicalities. In order to demonstrate this point we set up four further meetings at which a designated adult would care for the children while the other three took the time to talk about the loss of Thomas and how their grief was affecting them. These meetings allowed each woman to expose the angry/sad feelings that she had and the way in which the competition to care for and control the children had to some extent hidden that grief. Natalie was able, in the absence of the children, to say just how much she was grieving privately. Sophie became tearful at this and said that she had come to assume that Natalie had never really loved Thomas, and that this has made her angry and resentful about her son's death. This exchange allowed the women to return to their previously supportive relationship. Claudia talked of her envy of Natalie's life prior to Thomas' death, and how guilty she now felt, and Marion said that her grief for both Natalie and the children was so great that she felt unable to cope in any way except by burying herself in practical details.

A further meeting with the children was much calmer than our first. Feelings of sadness were more evident, but there was also more sharing and more support between the adults, while the children seemed less tense and tearful. A further meeting six months later revealed that Natalie had experienced surges of sadness after our meetings which the family felt to be appropriate; they had therefore responded in a helpful way to her requests for help. Now that Natalie felt stronger Sophie seemed in low spirits, and the family were gathering around her in order to support her. The lack of men in this family was noticeable. Both Natalie's father and father-in-law had died several years before Thomas' death, and her one brother was abroad throughout the immediate aftermath of the loss. Thomas had held a crucial and central position within the family for this reason, and it was easy to see in retrospect why his sudden death had precipitated the whole family into chaos. An external source of reference is often helpful when a whole family feels itself 'lost' in grief in this way. Sometimes one family member can play this role, at other times several members take turns at being the 'reflective' one. It is perhaps sad that so many families fragment in times of grief instead of finding strength together.

Grief, with its phases of numbness, sadness and anger, is an experience which almost every human being has to deal with during life. The acute experience can last for several years, as if we have to let the circle of anniversaries go around two or three times before we can hope that the pain will diminish. The despair and anger often come in waves, precipitated by events which remind us of what we have lost. Each of us will experience this in different ways, the healing will take longer in some than others, dependent on the nature of the relationship which has been lost, the manner of its loss and our own understanding of ourselves and grief. There is some suggestion from research that those who try to control and suppress grief initially may suffer the consequences longer as a result (*see* **Suppressed Feelings**).

What is clear is that as a community we have very little in the way of rituals to contain grief, and that our expectations about people 'pulling themselves together' are usually based on what is socially convenient rather than being a realistic appraisal of what the individual needs to feel and do in order to complete the mourning process. In this sense we are cruel to ourselves and each other. The healing of grief only occurs over lengthy periods of time, and friendly patience is needed in our support of those who have been bereaved.

## Guilt

We feel guilt when we think, feel, say or do something which our super-ego (our inner policeman) tells us is against the rules. Most of us are taught a set of 'inner rules' in our earliest years, which reflect our parents' attitudes (and sometimes those of our grandparents too) as well as society's values. Since we learn these guidelines at such a young age they become incorporated into our understanding of ourselves and the way we value and judge ourselves as good or bad, successful or worthless (*see* **Guilt Complex**).

The degree to which we take in the rules and make them part of our psychological make-up, and the degree to which we accept responsibility for what we do and what happens to us, varies from person to person. Some people experience little or no guilt in their lives, believing that whenever they do something which they might judge as wrong, they have in fact been forced into that action and that it is therefore not their fault. Others are haunted by guilt for anything and everything, taking responsibility and feeling bad about the whole world's sins as well as their own. There is a healthy balance: in order to feel in control of our lives we need to feel a degree of responsibility, and in order to live within our family and our society we need to follow the base-line rules that are acceptable to others.

If we find ourselves hating the ones we love we experience a deep and disturbing guilt, which we try to suppress out of sight (*see* **Suppressed Feelings**). Melanie Klein brought our attention to the fact that babies experience hostility and hatred towards mother as well as love. She also suggested that in the fantasy world of the baby that hate and envy is acted out, so that the mother is attacked and damaged. Also in the baby's fantasy is the ability to repair the mother, but this does not entirely make up for the destruction fantasy, destruction of the most loved and desired object. The baby experiences guilt about her attack, and if the mother cannot be reassuringly strong enough to cope with it the baby's fantasies of destruction grow unchecked (*see* **Aggression**, **Envy**, and **Greed**).

As the infant grows she develops rivalries with both parents for the attentions of the other, which involve a sense of competition and a desire to 'beat' and even kill the rival. The child may also feel envious of brothers and sisters, again with destructive fantasies, which some small children act on until disciplined by an adult. Thus the attacking feelings and fantasies remain and are experienced primarily towards those who are most loved and needed. This causes anxiety and guilt in the growing child (*see* **Anxiety**, **Electra Complex**, and **Oedipus Complex**).

Alice, 45, was the third of five children and described her life as a long attempt to be 'good enough' for the important people around her: initially her parents and then her husband and children. She constantly sought their reassurance that she was loved and lovable, feeling herself to go 'down like a pricked balloon' if praise she had hoped for was not forthcoming. She told me that she had an inferiority complex because she secretly knew herself to be a bad person and felt that she had spent her life successfully hiding that fact. She lived in the increasing fear, however, that her secret would be released, and this fear had become so intense in recent years that she thought she might 'burst' with badness.

Her inner 'badness' had become particularly intense when her husband confessed to having had an affair. She said it was puzzling because it was she who had felt guilty, not him. 'I felt it must be my fault for not making him happy,' she reasoned. I commented that she had spent a lifetime trying to make people happy and that, perhaps, she was fed up with it. She tried to laugh this comment away, but agreed that she felt guilty as soon as she thought about not making everyone happy. 'I have to be the life and soul of my family,' she said. 'Why?' I asked, 'What would you do if you were not making them happy?' 'I'd feel terribly guilty.' It felt to me like a never-ending circle.

Gradually Alice came to realise that failure to make another person happy was not explanation enough for the ominous weight of guilt she experienced. 'Why, it's more like I've committed a murder,' she exclaimed. 'Perhaps, in your mind, you have,' I suggested. Many people, maybe all, experience a desire to kill or hurt their nearest and dearest at times. Most do not act on those feelings, and many deny them as soon as they are felt, precisely because of the guilt such emotions stirs up. Alice began to talk about her murderous feelings towards all her family members. Towards the end of the session she complained of feeling 'sick with guilt'. I pointed out that she had only talked of murder, that this was a means of relieving the pressure of the emotion, and quite different from committing murder. The following session she arrived late and seemed ill at ease. 'I think you are waiting for me to reject you now that I've seen your inner badness,' I suggested. 'Yes,' she agreed, and added that she had spent a miserable week feeling guilty and depressed. 'I feel I need to make amends, buy you a present or something to make you feel better. Then you could like me again.'

The guilt, hostility and need to make amends were all experiences that were familiar to Alice in all her relationships. Gradually, during the course of therapy, she saw that I did not end up damaged when she was angry with me. Taking strength from that she was able to become angry with her husband, who also survived her verbal attack. She was genuinely surprised at the vitality we demonstrated in the face of her attack, because her childhood fantasy of destruction was still active. Seeing that we survived made her feel less guilty about being murderously angry.

## Guilt Complex

For those with a guilt complex, the experience of feeling guilty about large areas of their lives becomes all-pervasive (*see* **Guilt**).

Sara was 31 when she became seriously depressed after the birth of her second child. She described it as 'a black envelope' in which she was living, and although she felt continually sad the most distressing experience for her was her sense of overwhelming guilt. She felt guilty as a mother – not just the normal experience of guilt that all mothers will recognise, but guilty over every facet of her mothering, keeping her awake at nights and making her tearful during the day. She felt guilty as a wife, guilty about her home and also guilty that she has stopped being successful in the outside world for the time being, and for not earning any money. The word guilt seemed to occur in every sentence she spoke.

Sara had been the eldest of four children. She remembered a 'busy' childhood: when she was still only 8 she had taken responsibility for the youngest two, who were then aged 4 and 2. She remembered being frequently frightened by her mother's rages. Whenever anything went wrong in the home or with the family it was clear that her mother had managed to make it Sara's fault. Sara had accepted this, feeling instinctively protective of her mother and wanting to 'take the badness from her'. She said that the experience of being guilty was familiar to her because she had been a 'bad and irresponsible' child and had made her mother's life 'a misery'.

I had to miss the eleventh session of our therapy together because I had a cold. Sara interpreted this as her fault. She explained to me that she had felt guilty about my being ill because she had been so demanding in our previous session. 'I think I must have worn you out,' she said, near to tears and very apologetic. I suggested that this experience was like her experiences with her mother. 'I wonder if I would be allowed to have a cold without it being your fault?' I questioned. Sara looked puzzled by this and said, with the first hint of anger that I had heard from her, 'I don't understand you.'

'I'm suggesting that it is my responsibility to look after myself, just as it was your mother's adult responsibility to look after herself. Your sense of guilt takes that away from us.' Sara went on, apparently ignoring this comment and diving instead into a long and clearly aggrieved story about an ungrateful neighbour for whom she had done a great deal. 'Perhaps you think I'm ungrateful for not wanting your guilt about my illness', I suggested at the end of the session. 'I just don't think you understand me,' she threw over her shoulder as she left the room.

Sara was ten minutes late for our next session and came in covered in guilt and apology. 'When you're angry with me for not understanding, it seems quite reasonable that you might want to be late, to punish me,' I said, once again refusing to accept her guilt. We had a number of exchanges of this sort over the next ten sessions. Gradually Sara became openly angry with me for being the bad, ungrateful and misunderstanding therapist. She missed the session after her angry explosion at me, and when I asked her about this she said 'I presumed you would not be here.' 'Why?' I asked. 'I thought I had hurt you,' she said. 'Did you think you had damaged me with your anger?' 'I felt guilty . . .' 'Is this how it felt with your mother?' 'I couldn't be angry with her. She would have killed me.' 'Or perhaps, in your fantasy world,' I suggested, 'you might have been frightened of killing her?'

There followed a long exploration of the anger which Sara had harboured against her mother and which seemed to have been rekindled by the birth of her daughter. Because the anger remained unexpressed it had to find a psychological escape route. Sara turned anger into guilt in every situation. Over the following weeks Sara made a conscious effort to use the word anger whenever she would have normally used the word guilt, and gradually the story of her life began to make more sense. 'I'm not the saint that I had hoped I was,' she said towards the end of therapy, 'I wonder if all the saints felt as depressed and guilty as I did.'

This was an interesting comment because it reveals that our understanding of what is sinful is closely linked to our religious beliefs. Although merely social values – a fact clearly demonstrated by the variety of different sins according to the different religions – they carry the weight of our gods with them and are therefore even more tangled up in our make-up than the more explicitly social rules. In the Judaeo-Christian and Islamic religions the concept of original sin is prevalent. Although this sin is a comment on all of mankind, it is clearly established as being Eve's fault. This has had serious psychological repercussions throughout history for women, who experience more guilt, particularly in relationships with their nearest and dearest, than do men. Women are often held responsible for the success of a man and of their marriage. If either fail, it is common for the woman to experience more guilt than the man.

Women are also frequently held to be responsible for men's behaviour, both sexual and violent. Men believe their behaviour can be the woman's 'fault', and women, so well-programmed for guilt, often accept this presumption. Certainly as mothers, women commonly experience guilt when they fall from perfection (as we all do) to just being good enough. Fathers very rarely even question their capacity for fathering or the quality of the fathering they provide, let alone feel guilty about it. Guilt is a constricting emotion: it can act as a container for all that is wrong within the members of a family. Thus a guilt-ridden mother and wife can become something of an emotional dustbin for many of the more uncomfortable feelings of those around her. Guilt can also be a strongly controlling experience, whereas allowing other family members responsibility for their own feelings and actions may feel dangerously like being out of control, particularly when the woman of the family knows that society will be judging and blaming her if anything goes wrong.

It is often useful when feeling guilty to ask yourself 'What would I be feeling now, if I didn't feel guilty?' and 'Does this guilt really belong to me?' Of all the emotions we experience, guilt can be the most wasteful of time and energy, and needs therefore to be examined and explored whenever it appears, rather than simply accepted.

# H

## Hallucinations

Hallucinations are experiences within our minds, triggered by internal rather than external stimuli and yet perceived by one of our senses as coming from outside us. It is possible to hallucinate with any of our senses, although auditory (heard) and visual (seen) hallucinations are most common.

Auditory hallucinations are experienced as voices or sounds; sometimes these are critical or carry messages; sometimes they take musical form. The individuals affected totally believe that what they are hearing is real, that there is an outside source of their experience, even when others try to tell them this is not so. It can be a very disturbing experience, especially when the voices are critical or hostile. Auditory hallucinations may be linked with visual ones, thus confirming for the individuals that the source is outside themselves.

Hallucinations can on the other hand be pleasant and even comforting, and people experiencing them will sometimes converse with the voices they hear for hours at a time. They may not be able to report on the conversation, however, as the voices can be indistinct, use made-up words (*neologisms*) or even speak in what appears to the individual to be a foreign language. The senses of taste, smell and touch can also be affected by hallucinations; the first two commonly associated with a paranoid understanding of the person's surroundings and fears of being poisoned or gassed and the third frequently experienced as uncomfortable, frightening or painful.

Hallucinations occur in many illnesses and are usually

associated with a change in the person's state of consciousness. With a high fever, for instance, hallucinations can occur
as the patient slips into a clouding of his or her conscious
mind. In schizophrenia the mind seems clear and yet the
experience of hallucinations, usually auditory, is often central
for the patient, whose voices may direct every action and move
him or her to recite every thought our loud. Indeed it is rare
for a schizophrenic illness not to include some experience of
hallucination, and for some diagnostic criteria, auditory
hallucinations are seen as a prime symptom (*see*
**Schizophrenia**).

There are many other causes of hallucinations: diseases that
affect the chemical balance in the blood, such as renal (kidney)
or hepatitic (liver) disease, sensory or sleep deprivation, vitamin
deficiencies, various forms of brain disease or metabolic
disorder, or epilepsy. Hallucinations also occur in post-partum
psychosis, an illness seen in the mother over the early weeks after
child-birth, and in dementia, as well as in various forms of self-
poisoning with alcohol or drugs (*see* **Alcoholism**, **Dementia**,
**Epilepsy**, and **Post-natal Depression**).

There is no general agreed explanation for the occurrence of
hallucinations. Clearly a lessening of conscious control over the
brain plays some role – people sometimes talk about such
experiences as being like dreaming while still awake. The
difference between reality and the fantasies of our inner world
is one we learn as children. Babies cannot distinguish between
the two, and even small children sometimes find the boundary
hard to define.

Much research in schizophrenia is aimed at discovering
which chemical is doing what to which part of the brain during
the illness. Everything that happens in the brain has to be
mediated by the neuro(electrical)-chemical system between
nerve cells, and therefore it would seem reasonable to assume
that a primary disturbance in that system will produce
experiences not unlike those that result from ingesting various
disturbing chemicals such as drugs or alcohol. We know that

drugs that are classed as major tranquillisers have a healing effect on hallucinations. Thus the vulnerability towards experiencing hallucinations may be greater in some individuals; their neuro-chemical balance may be more delicate and therefore more easily disturbed. That balance may be essential to maintaining the boundary between reality and fantasy. The content of the hallucination is specific to and personal for each individual, however; the voices may be familiar to the patient, and they often say what the patient secretly believes to be true.

# Hate

Hate is perhaps the strongest of our destructive emotions; it is the opposite side of the coin to love, and often co-exists with love in a relationship. Kleinian theory accounts for this juxtapositioning of apparently contradictory emotions in later life by looking at the early emotional life of the baby at the breast (*see* **Aggression**). Freud postulated a death instinct (Thanatos), inherent and inwardly destructive, a force equal and opposite to the life instinct (Eros). Klein agreed with this as a starting point, emphasising the anxiety that the baby experiences alongside the fear of death and annihilation that is part of his own chaotic inner world. Part of the way to cope with such anxiety is to project a portion of the destructive impulse out onto the first familiar object in the outside world, that is, the mother's breast. Thus the baby enters his first relationship already involved in the heated mixture of love and hate, need and fear, which so often characterises later relationships of any intensity.

In early infancy the baby splits love and hate, projecting them out onto what is perceived as two different mothers, the good and the bad. As the baby grows, if development is normal, he comes to realise that there is only one mother, whom he both loves and hates. As the baby's dependency decreases and he experiences himself as stronger and more separate, the intensity of these feelings diminish, thereby lessening the feelings of anxiety. Freud suggested that the remainder of the baby's original destructive impulse becomes attached to the libidinal (sexual) instinct, thereby creating the connection between aggression and sexuality, and allowing the growing individual to discharge powerfully negative feelings safely as sexual energy. Many couples will testify to the passion that is aroused by a fierce argument, passion which can be utilised as a creative and bonding energy in the relationship in the form of sexual activity rather than as a destructive force expressed in hate and fury (*see* **Aggression**, **Eroticism**, and **Sexuality**).

Clearly this is a complex developmental pathway, and while the growing child needs to experience a wide range of emotions fully she must also learn to handle these emotions safely, for her own sake as well as that of others. Those who become stuck at certain points on the pathway will experience recurrent difficulties in their close relationships (*see* **Fixation** and **Repetition Compulsion**). For those who grow up without learning to expect strong feelings of hate in connection with loving and sexual ones, adult relationships can be disillusioning and disappointing. For those who are taught from an early age to repress all feelings of hateful hostility, close relationships will prove a stress on their defence systems which will have to work overtime holding negative feelings in check.

Perhaps most destructive is the individual who has never made the emotional connection between good and bad, love and hate, but continues to believe in a complete split between the two. Such a belief is often based on a splitting between parents, one of whom is seen as all-bad and the other all-good. This often colours individuals' perception of all men and women, and leads them to relate to people who in some way fit their belief system so that it is constantly strengthened. In some relationships they even manage to manipulate their partners' behaviour until it does fit in with their expectations. This means that they never achieve true intimacy or a sense of attachment to another whole person, but rather relate to selected parts of others depending on their allotted role within their belief system. Such relationships are unstable, dependent as they are on the partners' willingness to play out their supposed roles. Deviation from the role will often produce rage in the individuals.

Mary-Anne came into therapy when she was 32, saying that she thought she was going mad. She described feelings of being out of control which she likened to events in films she had seen where humans were taken over by aliens and then made to act out the aliens' wishes. Who was her alien? She did not know consciously, although immediately after saying this she went on to talk about her happy marriage. Jonathan was three years her junior, a successful businessman who had swept Mary-Anne off her feet by falling in love with her and insisting they marry immediately. Such impulsive behaviour was out of character for her, but the intensity of Jonathan's love made her banish any anxieties in the short term.

Their relationship was 'blissful' – as long as Mary-Anne was the woman Jonathan wished her to be. Any sign that she was a separate individual with plans and beliefs different to his own, however, threw him into such a rage that she soon learned to moderate her own behaviour to fit in with his expectations. He had developed a strong dislike of all her female friends within months of their marriage, and would denigrate them to her while applauding her in comparison. She was his good object and they were all bad objects. This behaviour then extended to her family, with whom she had previously been close. Loss of this closeness had made her sad, and her sadness had enraged Jonathan: his perfect woman was never sad. The initial thrill of being a totally, obsessively-loved person soon diminished, and although Mary-Anne still talked about her perfect marriage it was in tones of fear and desperation rather than happiness.

During the course of therapy she began to acknowledge the unreal nature of her relationship with Jonathan, based as it was in his fantasy world. This led her to challenge his views of life and of herself more persistently. Just as suddenly as he had decided she was perfect and that he wanted her, he decided overnight that she was bad, mad, and disgusting, and left the supposed perfect marriage without a backwards glance. Mary-Anne was both saddened and relieved at this turn of events. She described sensations of emptiness, and needed to work through the reasons why she had allowed herself to be pulled into a world so different to her own in search of love. Within weeks Jonathan went on to form another intense relationship which followed a pattern similar to that of his marriage with Mary-Anne: once again believing initially that he had found the perfect love object, only to reject her absolutely when he discovered the other side of the coin.

To experience hate of the one we also love is deeply distressing to most of us (*see* **Guilt**). Many relationships survive through a lessening of the intensity of both love and hate as the years pass by, so that feelings are more mellow and less passionate. Sometimes the hate is turned into contempt and bitterness which rumbles just beneath the surface, souring the relationship but allowing it to continue. If we have learned from our childhood experiences that close attachments produce a complex mixture of feelings, we will have more realistic expectations of the range of emotions that adult ties will bring. A partner cannot heal our childhood pain, adult love cannot fill the emotional hole that is left by deprivation in childhood, and all relationships are imperfect. To hate your chosen partner, your parents, your children and your friends in moderation is normal. Learning ways of holding that uncomfortable feeling and discharging it safely, without destruction to yourself or others, is one of the most important responsibilities of adulthood.

# Headache

Aches and pains are warnings that something is wrong, the human equivalent of an alarm system. Headache is a common symptom associated with a variety of illnesses, both physical and psychological. Unless they are frequent most of us tend to ignore headaches or to just treat them with aspirin, rather than wonder about their cause. The experience of being 'wound up' by a busy or difficult day often leads to increasing headache as the day progresses. This is muscular tension, and if we stopped and looked at ourselves we would probably find that we were tense throughout our body even though it was only our head that was actually causing us pain. The headache in this case is a sign that we should stop, take a rest or a meal, and relax.

Headaches can take on a variety of characteristics, from the sensation of a tight band around the forehead that is so typical of tension headaches, to a dull throbbing, or a piercing pain. Usually headaches are a relatively benign symptom of stress, but occasionally they are associated with other, more serious emotional and physical illnesses. Women can experience headache as part of PMS (Pre-menstrual Syndrome), during which they retain more body water than usual and therefore feel bloated and clumsy (*see* **Pre-Menstrual Syndrome**). Other changes of the water/salts (electrolytes) balance, for instance the dehydration associated with a hangover, or salt loss after excessive sweating, can also cause unpleasant headaches.

Any form of head injury can cause long-lasting headaches. Concussion after a blow to the head, even an apparently trivial blow, can cause headaches for weeks after the event. Some infections, particularly those of the brain and its coverings (the *meninges*) cause throbbing headaches, recognisable by the fact that if you try to place your chin on your chest the pain becomes severe where the meninges in your neck are being stretched by this activity. Any increase in pressure in the brain, from infection, high blood-pressure (hypertension) or a tumour or broken blood vessel in the brain, growing and occupying space, will cause an headache that increases in its intensity.

Perhaps because it is such a common symptom of so many disorders it is hard to diagnose which are the headaches with the more serious underlying pathology. Certainly headaches that last for more than a few hours, that continually return despite basic treatments, that seem worse on waking or that seem quite unconnected with stress or any other identifiable illness should be investigated. Most turn out to be harmless.

With modern X-ray techniques most areas of the brain can be seen clearly without there being any need to open the skull. Therefore a rapid diagnosis can be made once the level of suspicion about the nature of the headache is raised. In psychiatric practice much care is taken to make sure that the occasional physical illness is not passed off as psychological. This is most at risk of happening when the individual's symptoms are non-specific or the illness is taking an unusual course. In order to minimise such mistakes each patient admitted to a psychiatric hospital has a full physical examination as well as a psychological one. They are also 'screened' with a number of blood and X-ray tests if there is any doubt about their physical well-being.

Common sense is often the best headache cure. Used as a warning, the headache can be seen as telling us to slow down and re-arrange the more stressful aspects of our lives. Its appearance clearly spells out that too much has happened to us in a short space of time and that we need to take a little more care of ourselves.

## Helplessness

We all begin life in a state of helplessness. We are unable to make co-ordinated movements of any kind and are therefore totally dependent on the source of care and nurturing, most usually our mother, who protects us in our helplessness. We tend to assume that this source of our salvation is omnipotent, which it is in comparison with our own helplessness, and via our relationship with mother we develop our template for all future relationships as well as coming to know ourselves. Thus the experience of helplessness is universal and pervasive; it is also frightening. The world seems like a terrifying place if you are helpless to defend yourself. As we grow and develop a sense of mastery over ourselves and our environment, our fear diminishes (*see* **Instinct for Mastery**). If we have received empathic mothering we will have had the experiences of satisfaction and safety to put alongside the more frightening experience of raw helplessness. This will have allowed us to build a basic trust in our surroundings and in other people (*see* **Experience of Satisfaction**). Becoming helpless again at some point in life is often a person's deepest fear.

Circumstances during childhood or in adult life can make an individual feel helpless again; such experiences are usually accompanied by feelings of depression and/or anxiety in response to the helplessness. Overwhelming catastrophes in which the individual not only fears for his or her life but also realises there is nothing he or she can do to alter the situation bring back a sense of helplessness. Many of the descriptions that people give of surviving such incidences include a 'key' moment at which the reality of their helplessness hit them. This is often experienced as the opening of a door to memories of terrifying helplessness experienced earlier in their lives. Post-traumatic stress syndrome often incorporates a new sense of helplessness with a profound disquiet at the random nature of fate, prompting the typical question 'Why did I survive when someone standing next to me did not?', the underlying thought being that the person realises just how close he or she came to not surviving (*see* **Post-traumatic Stress Disorder**).

Helplessness can also be 'relearned' in adult life under certain conditions. As helplessness is such a universal experience we are all continually (and unconsciously) checking just how much control we have in our lives, in order to reassure ourselves. Sometimes the fear of being overwhelmed by our own sense of helplessness means that we have also to test our power and control over others in order to be reassured. If we come to realise that nothing that we do, say or think makes any difference to what then happens to us, then we are in a position in which we will relearn that we are helpless. Such circumstances sometimes happen to whole populations, for instance those under dictatorships or in the face of appalling and overwhelming social conditions. Psychologically such an experience can also occur in a relationship with a rigid and obsessional person whose need to control is so dominant that he or she has to reduce his or her partner to helplessness. However hard the affected partner tries to manoeuvre back into a position of some power the other will be able once again to reduce him or her to powerlessness.

Hermoine is 62; she told me at our first meeting that she had been depressed ever since returning from her honeymoon 40 years earlier. She said that she had spent many years being secretly angry with herself for being 'such a baby' when she enjoyed such a good a life with her family. Her description of that good life sounded very much like a gilded cage, and when we began to explore which areas of her life allowed her to exercise authority or decision-making we discovered there were none.

Her husband Patrick had accompanied her to the interview with a printed list of her symptoms, including the times and dates when she had experienced them. I asked him what he made of the situation and he confidently told me, in a stage whisper clearly audible to Hermoine, that she was really 'just a child' whom he had always had to look after. I pointed out that she had lived both independently and successfully for three years prior to marriage and that her 'childlike' status seemed to have returned with the marriage. He was very upset by this statement and said, 'But I wanted to look after her properly.' Sadly his need to look after her concealed a need to control and dominate that had, for all practical purposes, left Hermoine helpless throughout her marriage, something she had rapidly recognised psychologically but did not understand intellectually until we talked about it. Making it conscious meant that it had to be talked about and that she and Patrick had decisions to make about their future.

Few people would willingly accept helplessness for such a long period of time. Most only accept it and its psychological effects when they believe there to be no alternative. Some, however, experience the depression without thinking about whether or not they have a comfortable degree of power and control over their lives. People who have little expectation that they will play a decisive part in their own affairs are particularly at risk of making relationships with others who will dominate them in this way. As a growing child Hermoine had been under the total control of a domineering mother. Her three years of freedom seemed like a reaction against that childhood, but unsurprisingly she had then chosen a husband who psychologically resembled her mother. When she once again found herself dominated she did not have enough experience of being an individual to question her lack of control. There has been a suggestion that the rate of depression in women (twice that of men) is connected with their social helplessness, and that this is particularly true within marriage where male power is still strong.

## Homicide
*See* **Murder**

## Hostility
*See* **Anger** and **Rage**

## Hypochondriasis

A hypochondriac worries about his or her physical well-being unrealistically. Anxieties about their health frequently lead hypochondriacs to consult a large variety of experts, who are often tempted or persuaded into lengthy, unnecessary investigations, the normal healthy results of which do nothing to calm the hypochondriacs' fears. Many constantly 'scan' their own bodies searching for the first indications of disease and misperceiving normal healthy bodily functions as signs of illness. The preoccupation with illness may become so severe that everything else in life takes second place, and work and relationships suffer. Those with such health anxieties often feel offended and angry about any suggestion that their complaints may have a psychological rather than biological explanation, and are unlikely to welcome referral to a psychiatrist.

Those prone to anxiety and depression, particularly those with an obsessive-compulsive personality, are also prone to hypochondriasis, and if you ask them how they are feeling you must be prepared for a long, detailed answer. There is a danger of 'crying wolf' for such people, as the doctors involved in their care may fail to notice the onset of real disease in amongst their many other complaints (*see* **Obsessive Compulsive Illness**).

It is not clear whether people inherit a tendency to worry about their bodies or whether they learn this maladaptive way of expressing needs and getting attention in childhood. Many are excessively self-concerned in all aspects of their lives, but equally others are kind and considerate people when not so preoccupied. Such people are common in all forms of physical medicine and will only consent to see a psychiatrist or psychotherapist who will take their physical complaints seriously as the starting point of any discussion. It is sometimes possible for the analyst to form an alliance with them by a detailed and sympathetic attention to their symptoms, which then allows them to trust enough to explore the other troubling aspects of their lives; generally, however, hypochondriacs avoid this help and the hypochondriasis therefore remains a chronically disabling condition.

# Hysteria

The notion that some symptoms are hysterical in origin is as old as Hippocrates. During the 19th century the term hysteria become more closely defined by Charcot and Janet, two scientists working in neurology who were to have such a great impact on the young Freud. They saw hysteria as a reaction to an external event, which mimicked organic disease, for example, paralysis, but which was produced by a pathway of suggestion (either from others or from within the self). A common example of this in the Victorian era was the 'swoon', a way in which a woman could avoid a difficult emotional situation, since fainting was not ascribed any consequence or social blame. Thus society 'suggested' that swooning was normal, even endemic, amongst the female population.

Freud saw hysteria as a definite clinical entity which required, in each case, a specific diagnosis of what had caused the 'trigger' event. British psychiatry began to take the view that any symptom for which adequate psychological motivation could be discovered must then be hysterical. There were difficulties with this approach, namely that what some of us may accept as motivation others might query, and that in some cases which seem clearly hysterical it is impossible to discover the motivation behind the symptom.

Thus the definition of what truly can be seen as hysterical has changed and continues to change; it is a subjective decision. Individuals who experience hysteria will initially feel that their symptoms are physical in origin and will resist the idea that these might be psychologically-based. They may well be offended by any suggestion of this sort. However, alongside displaying what are normally considered frightening or at least worrying physical symptoms, such people display an enviable calm which reflects a 'dissociation' between themselves and their symptoms. This is the first clue that the symptoms represent something for the patients, hiding their true complaint and anxiety.

The patients may also choose to present the symptoms with dramatic flair, either through verbal gymnastics or by physically lashing about or doubling up, but there is always a quality in this presentation which begins to alert others to the 'play-acting'. Such people are not 'putting it on', rather the functioning of their central nervous system has become more chaotic and excitable, resembling the central nervous system organisation of someone very young or very old rather than that of a mature adult.

If the cases of patients who have been diagnosed as hysterical are followed up over the long term they are frequently seen to develop more serious mental illnesses, such as a psychotic or manic depressive illness (*see* **Manic Depressive Psychosis**).

For many years it was thought that certain personalities, perhaps those which were by nature more flamboyant or extroverted, would be more likely to develop hysterical reactions. All research has shown this to be untrue, however, and hysterical reactions found to be widely distributed across all personality types. Women, more frequently than men, have been diagnosed as hysterical; in some ways this very term allowed their symptoms to be dismissed. One early theory even suggested that the uterus was the seat of hysteria, and that this organ would 'wander around' the bodies of some women, thereby producing symptoms.

In Freudian theory such 'breakdowns' of the central nervous system are stimulated by external and often sexual or potentially sexual events, which lead to the person displaying a range of neurological symptoms. Because they have learned during their childhood that sexual feelings must, at all costs, be repressed, any sexual stimulation is experienced as over-stimulation, and can produce hysteria. There is the suggestion that the tendency as an adult towards hysterical reactions may be rooted in sexual over-stimulation experienced as a child; that is, some form of abuse. This does not explain, however, why such reactions are more unusual today than they were in Freud's time, when sexual repression was greater but sexual abuse at least as common. More up-to-date research would suggest that there may in some people be a vulnerability for experiencing hysterical reactions if the circumstances that stress or excite them arise, and that such reactions are not, therefore, directly related to sexual repression or sexual stimulation, although these may form a part of a more complex jigsaw.

Victoria was a 45-year-old church-goer of many years, a devout Christian who had devoted her life to her family and to a wide range of volunteer activities for those less fortunate than herself. She had a strict code of moral ethics to which she had always attached great value and from which she had apparently never deviated. She had been a virgin when she married, and she and her husband valued faithfulness as the cornerstone of their marriage. Victoria was admitted to a psychiatric hospital after two weeks of investigation on a neurological ward for a sudden paralysis from the waist down. From the first it was clear that Victoria was strangely undisturbed by this symptom, even though her husband and family were frightened and distressed for her. When I first met her it was as if we were at a tea party, chatting together, even though she was sitting in her newly-acquired wheelchair.

A technique called *abreaction* sometimes helps such people to talk about the things that would normally be completely concealed. It involves injecting tranquillisers into a vein and encouraging the patient to talk about whatever seems important. During our several sessions using this method it became clear that Victoria had become enamoured of their new, young vicar. She was under no illusions about the nature of their relationship or his feelings for her, but had felt so shocked by her own reactions to his presence, both psychological and physical, that she quite literally had been bowled over. She felt a deep sense of shame and repugnance, considering herself dirty and disloyal and, having repressed sexual feelings for many years, had no way of venting these distressing experiences. Her central nervous system seemed to have gone into 'overload' as a response.

Victoria responded well to help and became able to talk about her feelings without the use of tranquillisers. The staff were then able to help her feel more positive about her reaction, along the lines of 'This was the only way out that someone as good as yourself could find.' She was relieved to find that all her feelings were more manageable and less frightening having talked about them, and even managed to reveal the problem to the vicar, who responded with gentle acceptance that such things happen to us all, 'because we are God's children'. This afforded her great relief.

The most dramatic cure I ever saw was of another case of hysterical paralysis, this time in a 24-year-old following the death of her father. Her sister came to visit one day and simply said 'The dirty old man did it to you too, did he?' whereupon her paralysis evaporated to be followed by an outpouring from both sisters of terrible sexual abuse suffered during childhood at the hands of their now deceased father.

Symptoms such as paralysis are called 'conversion hysteria', where one problem, a psychological one, is converted into another, physical one. These may sometimes be transient reactions lasting just a few hours or days when we might present a symptom with more excitement and drama than normal. This is probably common-place as a response to stress and may be protective, allowing us sympathy for a small physical problem and some release from the stress for a brief period of time. It may also be contagious because of the element of suggestibility that exists in hysterical reactions. If someone at work has a few days off with a bad back, for instance, there may be an outbreak of such problems, only some of which will ever to be demonstrated as being organic in origin.

In understanding hysterical reactions it is important to know that it is the unconscious mind which is overriding the individual's conscious decision-making process, and will almost certainly be doing so for good reasons psychologically – thus hysteria is not, nor should be, a dismissive diagnosis. Similarly, symptoms that cannot easily be understood or that are at the fringe of or even beyond our knowledge have a tendency to attract the label 'hysterical', when it might be more true to say that we simply do not know what is causing them.

Freud attached similar theories to 'anxiety hysteria', known more commonly today as phobias. In this state, anxiety about one thing is converted into anxiety about something else which may seem more acceptable. For instance, most people find it easier to talk about fear of flying rather than fear of death, although clearly the two are closely linked (*see* **Anxiety** and **Death**).

Because hysterical reactions depend upon the response of an overloaded central nervous system, anything which disrupts that system, such as mental subnormality which has delayed or stopped normal development, concussion, or any organic disease or injury to the brain, may make a reaction more common. Any assessment of a hysterical reaction needs to take the individual and his or her life story, as well as the state of his or her general physical health, into account. There should be no blame attached to these reactions, the individual is not making the symptoms up, at least not consciously, and at any rate such symptoms are the result of real and genuine distress.

# I

## Idealisation

Our perception of ourselves and others is usually distorted to some extent by our own needs. When we fall in love, for instance, we need to believe that the person we love is in some way better than all others. This involves raising them onto an emotional pedestal, and the height and permanence of that pedestal will depend more on our need to idealise them than on any of their characteristics. In this way idealisation is a narcissistic process, arising from our love of self, which then transfers itself to another.

Our ability to idealise lies in our ability to split good from bad and project aspects of one or the other into our perceptions of those around us. There is also a reverse process whereby we can re-introject (take back in) the ideal object which has been in some way transformed by the transaction. Thus the baby may perceive all good in her mother, but that perception carries with it envy and hostility. If the mother can hold the complete projection and allow the baby to re-introject the good, whilst modifying the bad, she is left with a sense of goodness about herself.

It is an important part of psychological development that the baby comes to re-introject the goodness and thus is able to identify with the good, loving mother and see herself as a good, loving baby. This leads to a more stable sense of self. For those babies who persist in idealising the good mother, the sense of goodness remains external to their sense of self, leaving their developing psyches more unstable and anxious. The baby also experiences strong destructive and persecutory feelings, and idealising her mother is one way of protecting mother in the baby's mind from her own destructive capacity. The need to continue idealisation is always closely related to the need to keep hostile feelings under control. As the child grows her need to see goodness in things may become more generalised, and then idealisation lessens her ability to discriminate and select what she really wants from relationships or life generally.

Peter, 36, was on the point of his second divorce before seeking treatment for a depression which had recurred many times in his adult life. He expressed extreme loathing for his wife, Julia, and felt the depression to be due to the fact that she had let him down. He also described his first wife as persistently persecuting him and ruining his life with her unreasonable demands. It was soon clear that Peter had idealised both of these women during the early days of his relationship with them. This was in parallel to his vision of his mother, whom he also idealised unrealistically.

Part of Peter's recurrent sadness was based in his belief that all that was good lay outside himself and within women. His only hope of possessing goodness was therefore to find it in heterosexual relationships, and yet, repeatedly, the women in whom he invested so heavily disappointed him. Gradually he began to acknowledge his feelings of envy towards his mother and both wives. In order to moderate his envy he had to come to see that they were only normal people, although he raged about the unfairness of this. Later he began to see that it was not they who had fooled him about their natures, but he who had fooled himself by idealising them. He also began to experience a desire to persecute them, which he expressed in violent language to his (female) therapist. As he became more persecutory in his imagination, his view of the persecution from his first wife changed. He saw that much of what he had previously imagined to be persecution from her had, in fact, been set up by himself. Peter's depression gave way to bouts of anxiety connected to his experience of himself as a man who was hostile to women. This was totally at odds with his previous vision of himself as someone who 'adored' women.

There are many examples of idealisation in fiction and in the structures of our belief systems about life. Advertising often plays on our underlying hope that an ideal can be reached, and most religion is based on investing a figure 'above' ourselves with ideal qualities. Motherhood is often raised to an idealised pedestal, the image of the Madonna and Child being a very potent one. It would seem as if we all retain from childhood the need to idealise some aspect of our lives, but it is healthy to remember, as Peter discovered, that the other side of the idealisation coin is persecution, and that we lift people up in order to save them from our own savage need to destroy them (*see* **Aggression**, **Envy** and **Hate**).

## Identification with Persecutors

The development of our personality depends on our ability to identify with the character traits of those around us, most notably, during our early years, our parents and siblings. Identification involves an internalising of our perception of ourself and others, so that we do not merely imitate what we see, but instead psychologically become what is seen. We retain the capacity to identify ourselves with aspects of others throughout our lives, although the degree to which we practise this varies greatly from person to person. The internalised traits with which we have identified may be contradict each other, and this leads to one part of our personality being 'at war' with another. If the discrepancy is large considerable confusion about our true identity or nature can arise.

Pauline, 23, had been raised by her mother only until she was 8. Her mother was a gentle woman who believed her daughter to be a very feminine and basically good child. Pauline had identified with the good mother and internalised a good and nurturing view of herself. The introduction of a stepfather meant that the mother/daughter dyad was changed. Her mother suddenly demonstrated a sharp tongue and considerable bitterness with life, and the stepfather seemed to take over the role of being the good and reasonable person in the house. Pauline then identified with the waspish mother, and relatives commented that the 'good little girl had gone sour'.

In early adult life Pauline had had a series of relationships that started well, with the loving part of her personality, but which rapidly deteriorated as she became bitter and disillusioned. She realised that she was the one who made this dramatic change, and felt pain and confusion about which woman she really was. A period of counselling allowed her to view the two very different aspects of her mother with which she had identified and then internalised, and to see them as more compatible: it was possible to be both nice and nasty within one relationship. With less pressure on her to keep these two aspects separate, she discovered that each could moderate the other, making an on-going relationship a more realistic possibility.

It was Anna Freud who first suggested that we feel a particular form of identification with those who threaten us. At times of complete helplessness the anxiety associated with an outside threat to our well-being is so intense that we need defence mechanisms to survive (*see* **Helplessness**). One such mechanism is identification with the aggressive force or person threatening us. This identification decreases our sense of helplessness. It is probably this mechanism which explains why children who are the victims of aggression so often grow up into adults who are aggressive towards children. This is an example of identification in retrospect.

Sometimes the identification accompanies the fear and precedes the actual violence; in extreme cases leading to the victim's role-reversal into that of the attacker. In instances of aggression that include sexual attack the victim may identify with the guilty part of the attacker. This is particularly common as a response to incest where the child often carries the adult's sense of guilt having identified with that aspect of her parent in order to preserve a loving image of him or her.

In recent years there has been much research into the form of identification known as the Stockholm Syndrome (named for the incident in the early 1970s when a group of hostages were taken to Stockholm upon their rescue to be 'debriefed'). This is the experience whereby those taken hostage discover that they develop strong alliances with their persecutors, often including an identification with the beliefs of the group holding them, beliefs which they then rapidly internalise. Such identification can lead to a form of total psychological submission, whereby the persecutors are seen as saviours; real salvation by the outside world may then pose a severe psychological threat to the hostage.

## Impotence
*See* **Sexual Arousal Disorders**

## Incest
*See* **Childhood Sexual Abuse, Paedophilia**

## Inferiority Complex

Daniella was a successful 34-year-old lawyer when I first met her. Hers was a story of striving for high achievement and, on the whole, reaching the goals she had set for herself. Yet she came to therapy feeling inferior to all of her friends and relations. 'They have something which I seem unable to gain,' she commented, but when I asked what that was she could not answer.

Adler, the father of Individual Psychology, saw this sense of inferiority as central to much human effort. He postulated that people who sense that they are inferior have to compensate, and often over-compensate by way of outward achievement. For some this seems to be a winning (if slightly precarious) solution to their underlying feelings of inferiority, but for many it only provides a superficial disguise behind which they suffer in silence. These people tend to develop an 'impostor syndrome', where on the one hand they maintain high-flying careers or excel in some way while on the other live in fear that someone is going to spot them for the 'fraud' they secretly believe themselves to be.

Adler felt that we develop a sense of inferiority in childhood, and that it is based on a physical deficiency, for example some sort of handicap, or in a psychological perception that we are in some way deficient, which may be real or imagined. He is suggesting that from an early age we judge ourselves, and those important to us judge us, against some 'norm' or perhaps 'perfect' model and then spot our 'mistakes'.

On this basis it is perhaps not so surprising that many of us sometimes experience a sense of being inferior. For most this only clouds a period of our lives or certain contained situations, but for others it colours their entire perception of themselves.

Freud felt that inferiority was not as central a theme as Adler proposed it to be, but still believed it to be a childhood response to 'injuries' to our self-esteem. Such injuries might be real, such as the loss of a parent due to death, divorce, or psychological difficulties in the parent, or they might be imaginary. The loss he postulated that children felt most deeply was that contained within a fear of castration, and the organ he regarded as most obviously inferior was the clitoris (*see* **Castration Complex**). Nowadays many would feel that the susceptibility of women both to experience and express inferiority is more of a social than a physical phenomenon, which men are able to hide more adequately because of their heavy investment in the external world.

Daniella's inferiority seemed rooted in her family's belief that girls were inferior. This had been reflected in their attitudes and behaviour throughout her life, and to some extent her achievements were a way of 'putting the family in their place and proving herself'. She could not change their attitudes, and because she still needed their love and approval – things she had never been freely given – of herself as a woman, she was still enmeshed within their value judgements as to what was inferior and what superior. The problem surfaced because she had become depressed after the breakdown of an important relationship. It is not unusual for such worrying feelings to drive much of our lives but only come to light and be recognised when we become depressed. In this way periods of depression can become useful times in which to work through such issues.

Feelings of sexual inferiority can lead to an abundance of sexual activity with a variety of (often disappointing) partners, in an attempt to disprove our inner conviction that we are failures. It can also lead to boastful claims about non-existent conquests, and, perhaps most frightening of all, to forms of pathological jealousy, where one partner's fear of inferiority is psychologically transformed into a belief that his or her partner is unfaithful, despite evidence to the contrary. Such a belief can reach delusional proportions and even, in its most extreme form, lead to murder. This is sometimes known as the Othello Syndrome, named after Shakespeare's famous hero (*see* **Othello Syndrome**).

It has also been suggested that the greater your sense of inferiority the more susceptible you may be to becoming paranoid when exposed to circumstances that alter normal psychological functioning, for example stress or physical illness.

## Inhibition

The concept of inhibition, or inhibitory processes that limit or contain our more excitable impulses, is both analytical and neurophysiological. Freud and Pavlov worked at much the same time yet came to very different understandings of how the human mind functions. For Freud our inborn instincts provided energy which formed the basis of psychological development. Pavlov, the physiologist famous for his experiments which made dogs produce saliva at the ringing of a bell, suggested that all our behaviour could be explained as conditioned and unconditioned responses to stimuli. The dogs' unconditioned response to food was to salivate. When Pavlov combined their experience of food with the sound of a bell, he managed to condition the dogs to salivate when they heard the bell ringing, even when no food was forthcoming. This was a conditioned, that is, a learned response. The brain can be divided into more or less primitive parts: unconditioned responses come from the more primitive areas, while a conditioned response, which requires the ability to learn, involves more refined areas of the brain.

In both theories there is also a 'control' loop. Freud saw that the more dangerous aspects of our instincts were repressed by our experiences as children (*see* **Repression** and **Suppressed Feelings**). This repression led to inhibitions in our thinking, feeling and behaviour. This hypothesis was later expanded. Klein talked of the inhibitions she recognised in the children with whom she worked: depending on the nature of the repression and the developmental period in which it occurred, different aspects of the child's emotional and intellectual growth were inhibited.

For his part, Pavlov theorised that inhibitory responses to stimuli, and particularly to over-stimulation, were a protective network designed to stop the brain becoming overloaded. He saw that the entire range of behaviour which we, and indeed all animals, demonstrate depends on the careful balancing between excitatory and inhibitory responses to internal and external stimuli. Because he recognised that there were wide variations between individuals he described a number of different parameters of excitation and inhibition, the force of these processes, their equilibrium and their mobility, and a number of different combinations that existed to make up recognisable personality groups. Thus he suggested that people could be divided into four main personality groups: the mildly inhibitory and the strongly excitable, and the lively or quietly equilibrated.

Although the two theories are often seen as contradictory and mutually exclusive, with the benefit of 80 years of hindsight it would seem that they confirm each other, although perhaps at different levels of description and with different views of mankind. It is clear from both that inhibitions are extremely important in controlling and containing our mental activity, whether we view them scientifically, as electrical responses to stimuli within a cell-by-cell view of our brains or, in an analytical attempt to understand man's thinking and activity, as the end-product of repressing our inborn instincts. Without inhibitions our mental process would be like a national electricity service without any form of control or fuse system. We would be incapable of sustained movement, intent, thought, enjoyment or achievement. However, inhibitions can become too severe, and they then move from defending us against our own over-stimulation to withholding from us the potential to respond effectively to events.

Within psychiatric and psychotherapeutic practice we see the end-product of both over- and under-control. Some people experience both extremes, alternating in a frightening and distressing way. In schizophrenia and manic depressive psychosis the inhibitions towards overt and inappropriate (for the adult world) sexual behaviour are often temporarily lost in the overactivity of the brain. In dementia, as the higher centres of the brain begin to loose their grasp, inhibitions towards many forms of anti-social behaviour, including violence, may appear to dissolve. In depression a person often appears to be labouring under his or her inhibitions against any form of spontaneous expression. In physical illness too we may lose our inhibitions and behave very differently to the way we would normally expect ourselves to. In these instances an illness is having a definite effect on our inhibitory system, either a physical effect on our nervous system as per Pavlovian theory, or a regressive effect, taking us back to a more childlike and therefore less inhibited existence, as per analytical theory. Such changes in levels of inhibition can cause great distress and remorse during recovery. Staff working with such patients need to recognise the effect of the illness and not assume they are seeing the normal personality under these conditions.

This is often an issue for women after they have given birth.

Labour is an extreme physical event, often causing great pain and fatigue, conducted at a time of both high anxiety and excitement and with the added complication that the lives, physical and emotional, of two, not just one human beings are at stake. Despite all this, most births in the Western world are presently' conducted' by staff who are not only strangers to the woman involved but who may well change shifts several times during her experience. Women in labour frequently behave in an uninhibited way that is out of character for them. Normally stoic women scream, quiet women become demanding, shy women tell jokes. Their normal psychological boundaries are temporarily less active because of both the increasing readiness to be psychologically available to their new baby and because of the extreme physical nature of labour. Sadly women often feel they have 'failed' in retrospect because they sense they have disclosed some unacceptable aspect of themselves. They were not brave enough, clever enough, good enough. Staff are also sometimes guilty of 'judging' the woman in the delivery room by the same social standards they might use when meeting someone at a party. Clearly this is inappropriate, and there are right times, particularly under stress or during illness, when we need to be less inhibited about our feelings and needs, allowing ourselves to be more childlike and dependent without fear that this will be judged adversely.

Pavlov and generations of psychologists since have also commented on the more or less inhibited nature of people, offering us a number of descriptive understandings of different personality groups based on the degree to which they are inhibited. Sociologists and educationalists have also studied this from the perspective of what inhibition does to individuals and societies – what level of inhibition is optimal for the self, the family, and the social group? It has been noted repeatedly that girls, more advanced than boys in their intellectual development until their early mid-teens, quite suddenly drop behind them at this stage. Is it just that their interest strays to other things which seem more important than education? But if this is so, why don't boys also show decreased intellectual interest as their sexuality blooms? Klein suggested that the intellectual spontaneity and curiosity of our children can be inhibited before the latent phase, between the ages of 7 and 11. Such built-in inhibition may only become obvious when it is later activated by external events such as exams, which naturally increase anxiety levels. (*See also* **Dementia, Depression, Manic Depressive Psychosis, Post-natal Depression,** and **Schizophrenia.**)

# Insecurity

The term 'feeling insecure' is used commonly in everyday language. Most people have some idea of what insecurity feels like, having experienced it at one time or another for themselves. Generally it means that we feel less rooted in our environment, less certain about ourselves, our plans and the future, and more anxious about the outcome of any undertaking (*see* **Anxiety**). It is a painful feeling which accompanies most upheavals and transitions in life. Some people experience a permanent form of insecurity, which stems from their own low self-esteem or from major upheavals experienced early in life from which they have never truly recovered. In order to cope with such a painful sense of themselves they often have to organise their lives thoroughly so that they feel in control of everything around them. This goes some way to compensate for the fact that they fear losing control all the time.

Our sense of security lies in a complex network of experiences, relationships and environmental factors. Children are particularly susceptible to change, although they often appear to cope, at least in the short term, rather better than adults. If they feel secure in their relationships with parents, grandparents and siblings, children can withstand greater change than if they already have psychological reasons for doubting if they are loved, or if important others can be trusted. In adult life, too, our ability to withstand whatever happens depends on the initial sense of security we developed as children, as well as on our present-day relationships and circumstances. Most of us experience days or weeks when we wonder if we are loved, if anyone cares, if anything we do really matters or even if the world is going to survive. Of course such feelings leave us feeling insecure. Usually they indicate that something is going on in our lives, not necessarily a bad thing, but something that is disrupting our normal understanding of how things should be. Sometimes these feelings point towards anxieties over an important relationship, a sense that all is not well; sometimes people start feeling insecure just when everything begins to look fine, on the basis that 'this can't last' or 'I'll have to pay for this happiness.'

Some of our sense of security is an illusion to protect us from the fact that not only will all those we love some day die, but we will as well. It is hard for the human mind to make sense of that fact and use it in a helpful, creative way for the individual during the life he or she has. It is particularly hard when death is sudden and unexpected, and not in the general pattern of things, for instance when younger members of a family die before older ones. Deaths of children cause vibrations in the psyche of whole families which can even outlast the generations which actually experienced the deaths and cause new patterns of child-care and parenting in future generations. Families develop their own myths in an attempt to structure such events, and these myths help to quell the insecurity aroused by death.

Almost all religions contain some notion of a life after death which allows for a greater sense of security while we are alive as well as promising an eternal future. Such institutionalised security becomes extremely important to whole nations after disasters or wars, when only the comfort of believing that death (and by extension life) is not meaningless allows us to continue to build and rebuild. The shock waves that spread through the country after a major disaster affect everyone, not only those directly involved. The names of such incidents become part of each of our life experiences, and so powerful that they will never be forgotten, denting permanently our sense of security. Very few people had any anxiety about cross-channel ferries before the Zeebrugge accident. Many of us who had travelled in this way could easily identify with those on board. Many of us continue to travel by ferry, but not without at least a passing thought that it is no longer as secure as we once thought it was.

Of course there are many benefits from rapid world-wide news coverage, but psychologically it also threatens any sense of global security we manage to construct for ourselves, as well as constantly re-awakening our fears about ourselves and our families. A sense of security demands that we keep events in proportion to our own lives. This can be particularly difficult for those in the 'caring' professions who, by the very nature of their work, tend to be continually exposed to those whose lives have been turned upside-down. It is easy in such a working atmosphere to forget how normal, safe and organised most of the world is at any one time. It has only recently been recognised that those who help at disasters are as much in need of psychological support during the aftermath as are those who were directly concerned. This support most often needs to take the form of a debriefing: who was doing what when such-and-such happened? They will also need to know who survived, what caused the disaster and how it can be prevented from re-occurring. Such emotional needs are very similar to the ones felt by those immediately involved, who may also have the added burden of injury and bereavement (*see* **Post-traumatic Stress Disorder**).

The more unlikely the event the greater the shock to our sense of security. I have worked among some of the people who experienced the Hungerford shooting of August 1987. One comment made over and over again was 'How could it happen here?', and indeed, driving through this quiet and beautiful English village it is easy to experience that disbelief, that sense of another brick falling from our wall of security. If such an incident happened in Beruit, the sense of grieving and trauma might be as great, but the sense of losing what had previously been experienced as safe would not exist to the same degree.

The anxieties aroused by a sense of insecurity can be great. Colette was 26 when her house was burgled during the night while she slept. Although grateful to have slept through the experience, she found that she could no longer relax enough to go to sleep 'in case something terrible happens and I don't know about it'. These entirely normal feelings were a reaction to her sudden loss of the security of her house boundaries. Gradually, over some months, she rebuilt her own inner vision of security.

Norman was 56 when he was knocked over by a bus and broke his leg. Although the leg healed Norman found he could not walk on it further than his own front door. 'My leg is not strong enough for the outside world yet,' is how he experienced his loss of a sense of security about his own body. The time to recover a sense of security varies depending on how secure the person was before the trauma and how great and unexpected the trauma was. A bone is an extremely simple part of the body, yet once broken it can take months to heal before we can put any stress on it again. Part of our psyche, which is what a sense of security is, is an infinitely more complex and sophisticated piece of ourselves. When disrupted or broken we must expect it to take months or even years to heal, be patient with ourselves and others, and try to avoid repeated stresses during the healing process.

Those who suffer most when their security is shattered are those who experienced similarly shattering experiences as a child. For them the nightmare of childhood is revived and experienced alongside whatever adult trauma has befallen them. Thus a sexual attack on an adult woman who has experienced sexual abuse as a child compounds both abuses and deals an even more extreme blow to her psyche than either form of abuse alone might have done.

Our environment also affects our sense of security. At a personal level, socio-economic conditions clearly play a major role in proving our internalised vision of security, or lack thereof, an accurate depiction of our real experience of the world. We also live at a time when not only might we deliberately destroy our world with nuclear weapons if we so choose, but seem in great danger of destroying it by accident or negligence. All these factors contribute to a sense of insecurity, of how temporary we are, and of how potentially temporary our world is. When we place these elements alongside the insecurities which arise from within, from our own inner knowledge of ourselves, it is hardly surprising that insecurity is a commonly known and understood experience.

# Insight

The word insight means to look into oneself and see clearly. It is used in a way that reflects this meaning while at the same time has different connotations for psychotherapy and psychiatry. In psychiatric terms insight is related to a person's view of him- or herself as ill or well. It is used to describe those who cannot judge for themselves whether they are at risk from their illness because they cannot believe themselves to be ill or have to problems. In psychotherapy insight conveys the end-point of psychological work on a particular issue, at which point you experience the sensation, almost physical, of knowing something about yourself that you had not previously realised. This may be anything from a small detail to a massive understanding of how you came to be the person you are. Once known it cannot become 'unknown', although sometimes it is such a stunning experience that it takes time to see it clearly; it is as if it is emerging from a thick mist, so that you may catch sight of it and instantly recognise that it is important for you and yet you cannot quite grasp it immediately. Sometimes it is an instantaneous experience. Insight does not necessarily change our behaviour, but it provides us with a new vision of ourselves which may allow us to change if that is what we wish to do, whereas previously and hard as we might have tried we were still too 'stuck' in old patterns to try something new (*see* **Fixation** and **Repetition Compulsion**).

Ray, a 32-year-old plumber, had a long history of depression that recurred every spring and kept him away from work for several months each year. He entered group therapy after a variety of other treatments failed to produce long-term results. Despite talking through a detailed history of his life during several psychiatric assessments there appeared to be no obvious reason why his depression should always return in the spring. Ray joined the group in September, the group members were familiar with a gentle and helpful fellow-member and were taken aback by the dramatic change in Ray when late February rolled around. 'You actually seem to have shrunk,' commented one member, while another said she felt close to tears just sitting by him. He said that this was his normal pattern and that once again he was off work and not sleeping or eating well.

The group worked hard at trying to elicit what was wrong but were increasingly put off by Ray's snarled and hostile replies. 'It's all useless, everything fails with me. No one can understand.' The woman who had commented on her own tearfulness said that he seemed like a hurt animal in a corner, fighting when he really needed to let someone in to care for him. Ray continued with his aggressive defence, however. Although he appeared to be achieving little in the group, I became increasingly aware of how much time he was taking up, not allowing others to work but not allowing them to help him, either. As a group leader you sometimes experience the group as a small family of children of various ages, all with their own needs and ways of making demands. I commented to Ray that I felt as if he was only allowing me to have just the one child, himself, during his sadness. 'Are you calling me selfish?' he shouted. 'Well, I think you are being selfish,' said one of the other men in the group. 'No, I didn't mean you are selfish,' I said quickly, 'just that somehow it is important for you to be the only one, and I wondered why.'

Ray started to cry, with the hottest, most angry tears I think I have ever seen – they almost seemed to come out of his eyes in puffs of steam rather than water. 'My mother always said I was selfish, being an only child.' After a long pause and more crying he added 'but I wasn't an only child.' Ray had been born six months after his 2-year-old sister Yvonne had drowned in an accident. This was no revelation, we had all known this about Ray for a long time, and he had said repeatedly, and believed, I am sure, that because the death had occurred before he had even been born it had had little effect on him. Another group member commented that whether it had affected Ray or not it must have had an enormous effect on his mother. At this Ray once again started to shout. 'Her – she was all right, she was always communicating with my sister in the front room.' At this the group were stunned into silence, not least of all Ray, who seemed almost unable to believe what he had just heard himself saying.

The story of the long grieving of Ray's mother, with seances almost nightly in the house until he was at least school age, and of a dead sister's birthday recalled with more attention than his own, had been buried deep in Ray's unconscious, far too painful to remember consciously. He had always claimed to love his mother, and indeed had a close adult relationship with her. He admired the way she had coped with life, and it was just too difficult for him to hold that view of her alongside the view that he'd had of her while he was still a tiny infant, when she was distressed and often acting wildly in her grief (*see* **Ambivalence** and **Idealisation**).

Having expressed most of his anger in the group he felt it was safe to try to talk to his mother about his feelings and particularly the on-going puzzle of why they were worse in the spring. Ray's sister, Yvonne, had been born on February 26th and had died during a birthday outing two years later. The end of February was the peak time of trauma in the household for many years, and Ray had internalised this in his understanding of himself. At some level he believed that it was right and that everyone was depressed at that time of year. Once he knew the background to these feelings, he was able to work on the many grievances of his childhood. The following spring those members of the group who remembered the Ray of the previous year waited in some trepidation as February progressed. He admitted on several occasions to feeling low, but always added, 'but I know what it is about now, which makes it a totally different experience'.

Insight, for Ray, had been a painful process of discovery, meaning that he spent the best part of a year feeling regularly distressed, angry or tearful. Six years on, however, his February depressions have ceased.

Katy-Anne was diagnosed as lacking insight by a psychiatrist. She was discovered in a tree in a local park, half-naked, dropping rubbish on the heads of those who passed underneath. When questioned she claimed that she was 'on the side of good and fighting all evil', and that there was nothing wrong with what she was doing, nor did she believe herself to be in any way distressed or ill. She promised not to behave like this again and was released from police custody, but less than an hour later was found completely naked and about to jump into the river. She said that the voices were telling her what to do and that it was wrong of the police to interfere (*see* **Hallucinations**). Once again she denied any illness or distress, even though she might well have come to harm in the river.

When people behave like this they are said to lack insight into their true psychological state in such a way that is likely to endanger them. Under provisions of the Mental Health Act it is possible to arrange admission to a psychiatric hospital for observation and/or treatment when people are in this state. Similarly if their illness looks as if it might endanger others, for instance if they are severely depressed and say that they feel it would be helpful to kill their family as well as themselves, and are clearly beyond recognising that this is an unusual statement, provision can be made to admit them even though they do not believe themselves to be ill. The Mental Health Act is discussed later in this book (*see* Appendix B), but it is important to note here that in and of itself lacking insight into the severity of an illness, of whatever sort, is not enough to justify compulsory admission, and every effort is made to encourage people to make free choices about what sort of help they will accept. Sometimes, while themselves lacking insight, patients will trust their doctors, nurses, or families to make the decision for them, without any need for legal coercion. Many patients, when they regain insight, are grateful for the intervention and say that they would wish it to be repeated if ever they were in a similar position in future.

## Insomnia

The amount of sleep we need varies from person to person, and from one period of our lives to another. Babies and small children mostly want to sleep more often, although perhaps for shorter periods of time, than do adults. Adolescents appear to need an enormous amount of sleep, but once into early adulthood people often manage on less than 8 hours a night without ill effects. When we reach middle age we often need more sleep, yet older people in their the late 60s and 70s find they need little sleep once again. The amount of sleep our bodies and minds need may be different to the amount of sleep we think we ought to have.

As with eating, our sleep patterns tend to have to fit in with social expectations. Most people are expected to sleep at night, going to bed between 10 p.m. and midnight and waking up between 6 and 8 a.m. having had 8 hours of sleep. Such a pattern fits in with schooling and most, although not all, work. It is also presupposed in much of our social life. It fits in with the schedules of the cinema, theatre, concerts and restaurants, and TV. It is a pattern that suits the majority of people reasonably well for much of their lives. If the freedom existed, however, some of us would adopt a different sleeping pattern. Those who like to go to sleep early and rise early often find that they have to decide between their favourite sleep pattern and a social life. For those who would naturally like to stay up later but then also rise later the choice of occupation usually provides a limiting factor. External factors, such as noise, discomfort, cold, heat and hunger can also make it difficult to have our chosen sleep routine.

There are also the many thousands of people who work in shifts to consider. Their sleeping pattern is disrupted regularly, as is that of all the parents of young children, who probably consider themselves lucky if they get a single good night's sleep.

Given these 'normal' disruptions of our sleep it is perhaps surprising that so many of us sleep well for such long periods of our lives. Sleep deprivation affects our ability to concentrate, particularly for lengthy tasks during which our concentration will drop off more quickly than usual, and our emotional ability to withstand stress. When we are tired small upsets that we would normally take in our stride become enormously upsetting, maybe leading to tears or anger. Being awake when everyone else is asleep, for whatever reason, is also an upsetting experience, especially if it is a persistent problem, and being unable to go to sleep when tired makes people feel hopeless and despairing.

Our sleep pattern is a barometer to our emotional and psychological well-being. Not only is it essential for maintaining emotional equilibrium that you have regular sleep in the right amounts at the times that are right for you, but if that equilibrium is unsettled for any other reason, it is often the sleep pattern which is the first thing to be affected. Anxiety, whatever its cause, may make it difficult to get to sleep. This is painfully true for those who fear the dark or who feel especially alone at night. Even when they do get to sleep, terrifying nightmares may disturb anxious people further, waking them and leaving them close to panic and unable to contemplate sleep again, even though they become progressively exhausted (*see* **Agitation** and **Anxiety**).

As we drop off to sleep there are a number of common, and slightly disconcerting, experiences associated with our losing consciousness. One of the most common is the sensation of falling through the bed into a bottomless hole. The time of going to sleep may also be a time when the anxious person has pseudo-hallucinatory experiences of hearing, seeing or smelling something worrying or frightening. This makes him or her increasingly resistant to the idea of closing his or her eyes and trying to go to sleep, although yearning to be asleep.

Depression often causes sleep problems. If you are preoccupied with a problem, going to sleep becomes difficult. Many people who are depressed are not consciously aware of their problems, however, and can go to sleep relatively easily, only to wake up in the early hours of the morning. Sometimes a dream or nightmare wakes them, but often they find themselves repetitively awake at 3 or 4 a.m. without knowing why they have woken up. Such waking is often accompanied by overwhelming feelings of hopelessness, loneliness and despair at having to face another long day ahead. Sleep is only restored to normality when the underlying depression has lifted (*see* **Depression**).

Sleep loss is, in itself, depressing, and can become part of a vicious circle of symptoms. If you are having difficulty getting to sleep because you are preoccupied, it often helps to get up, write your problems out on a piece of paper and then write alongside them some possible action that you can take the next day. Even if the answer is 'can't do anything', it can be surprisingly comforting to recognise that fact, and people often report going back to bed and sleep once their problems have been written down in this way.

A good preparation for bed includes no stimulating drinks, a warm bath, a comfortable room and no external irritants. If you are having difficulties getting to sleep there is also no point in going to bed until you are tired. Lying awake and restless will only increase your sense of frustration.

For those who wake early it sometimes helps to redefine the problem. Your brain is waking you up for a purpose. In the remainder of the day you may feel lethargic and unable to do anything, yet here is your mind telling you that it is ready for action in the middle of the night. For many years it has been the teaching in psychiatry that early waking is a main symptom of an 'inner' depression caused by changes to the brain chemistry, rather than an 'outer' depression caused by life events. Certainly there seems some connection between this symptom and the symptoms that are likely to respond to anti-depressant medication, suggesting that there is a true imbalance which needs righting before improvement can occur. However, despite much research, the nature of that imbalance remains a mystery, as does the fact that while all the other symptoms of depression are about a slowing down or even stopping of various intellectual and emotional functions, this symptom seems to indicate a brain that is unable to rest. This may be because the inhibitory system to the brain which 'turns it off' for sleep is underactive alongside all the rest of the underactivity of depression.

Depressed patients often say they feel most alert and therefore most depressed at this early time of day. This is particularly true if they stay in bed attempting to sleep or if they feel lonely. The pain of depression is so horrible that most people would love to be able to sleep many more hours than normal rather than less. The early hours need not be wasted, however, even if they are painful. The alertness may make this the only time when those who are depressed can concentrate enough to read, write or watch television (or a video). Once the day starts the inertia may take over again. It may also be the only time when they can think about their lives and the potential problems to which they are presently turning a blind eye. Even those depressions which seem based in an inner chemical disturbance may well be a warning signal that something in life is not well and needs rethinking. Depression robs people of the ability to think about or plan their lives, but sometimes the wakefulness of the early hours gives them opportunity for new insights. Writing a brief autobiography as a way of focusing the mind on your own life experience may help to unearth what is troubling you.

Lack of sleep is a problem that occurs in schizophrenia, manic states, manic depressive psychosis and dementia. Generally the underlying illness needs treatment before the sleep pattern can be restored (*see* **Dementia**, **Mania**, **Manic Depressive Psychosis**, and **Schizophrenia**).

Parents are particularly sensitive about their children's sleeping patterns because these have such an important effect on the quality of their own lives. Difficulty going to sleep, or constantly waking and demanding parental attention, are often features reflecting the mixed messages the parents are giving the infant about what is expected of him. Although the sleep pattern of the child may be deplored, the parents, either singularly or together, may also be encouraging it without realising that they are giving both messages. As mentioned earlier the normal sleep pattern is, to some extent, a habit which is trained or forced on all of us. If children are to grow up within the family norms and later the social norms of sleep, they need regular clear messages about the boundaries of acceptable behaviour. Obviously these boundaries have to be flexible enough to allow for the child's age and any illnesses.

Sleepwalking can occur at any age, although is more common amongst children. It is for the most part insignificant, so long as the child is protected from accident. Nightmares are also common in children, particularly around the ages 3 to 5, when the child is learning to represent good and evil and various forms of conflict symbolically. The images offered to children, both through fairy stories and TV, are really quite frightening, and tend to return in the form of 'monsters' in their dreams and nightmares. Reassurance and comfort are usually all that is required to calm the child.

'Night terrors' are rather more disturbing in that the child appears to be awake but is in fact still in the twilight world of the nightmare and cannot therefore be comforted. After a period of time the child falls back into complete sleep, and unlike a normal nightmare experience will later have no recollection of the event at all. Some people believe this to be a form of epilepsy which passes away as the child grows. Others see night terrors as an indication that something is wrong in the life of the child which needs attention. Any persistent sleep problem in a child would probably benefit from some discussion with a professional person outside of the family (*see* **Dreams**).

Disturbances of sleep, although worrying and upsetting, usually do no long-term damage to the individual. For those who have persistent insomnia, particularly that involving early waking, and who seem to those around them unusually worried about this symptom, it is important to consider their safety. It is notoriously difficult to predict who will commit suicide, but prolonged early morning waking in someone who is preoccupied, restless and distressed, certainly should raise peoples' awareness to the severity of that person's plight. Specialist help should be enlisted to determine the extent and intensity of the problem.

## Instinct for Mastery

As infants we have to learn to control our movements and our sphincters, so that we can make co-ordinated muscular activity in order to explore our world and to achieve a release from nappies to the desired independence of free toileting (*see* **Bowel Control**). Analysts have suggested that babies are born with an instinct to master which provides the energy for these momentous early developments. Freud thought of the instinct to master as a primitive drive which preceded any ability to feel concern for others, and that it was therefore the basis for infantile cruelty when directed externally. If unmodified in adulthood, the need to have complete dominance in a relationship can often result in that form of cruelty we think of as 'having no pity'. When adults are released from normal social expectations and even encouraged to be 'master' of everyone, cruelty often results. Thus the instinct which drives our early learning to master ourselves can become sinister when outwardly directed towards others.

Adler also talked of the importance of achieving power and believing in our own power during both childhood development and also in finding fulfilment in adult life. From early childhood mankind demonstrates a need to master the environment, and struggles relentlessly with external reality in the attempt to make it more and more of what is desired. Some people use their instinct for mastery inwardly and feel more deeply the need to have control over themselves than the need to dominate their external world.

The language we use to describe this instinct has a masculine flavour: we talk of mastering rather than mistressing. Boys usually receive more encouragement to dominate the external world in a masterful way, while girls are generally encouraged to use their instinct for mastery more in terms of being in control of themselves and their behaviour. Part of being masterful for men used to be seen as being able to control a wife and children, and greater emphasis was placed on that in assessing a man's power than on how well he controlled or mastered himself or his own body. Some of the cruelty which men still inflict on women may reside in this external (and to some extent socially encouraged) use of their instinct to master. If women use it externally in relationships it is more likely to be with their children than their partners.

Inability to use this mastery can leave individuals adrift in life, with a sense of being out of control of everything including themselves and their bodies. However, emotional development needs to have modified the primary instinct so that awareness and concern for others can be reflected in our actions, if the retaining of the instinct to master is not to sour adult relationships. This instinct rapidly becomes connected with sexual instincts during development, providing the energy for the sadistic impulses which want to degrade, humiliate and hurt the object of sexual desire. Because of this much of the cruelty which can arise from the unmodified instinct for mastery in adulthood has a sexual and perverted element to it (*see* **Activity and Passivity**, **Eroticism** and **Sado-Masochism**).

While still in his 20s Alan committed a series of rapes; finally he was caught and sentenced to 8 years in gaol. Some of this time was spent at a prison run on the principle of group therapy which attempts to help men like Alan find the basis of and a cure for their behaviour. His need to be dominant in relationships was changed in prison because there were no women present. However there were some women therapists and visitors, and this allowed staff, and eventually Alan, to see that his need to be masterful with women was extreme. He fitted Melanie Klein's description of 'excessive protestations of masculinity', in that alongside this need to dominate he was also contemptuous of women, believing them to be stupid.

Alan's attacks on women had been extremely sadistic and he described the pleasure he'd felt inflicting pain and fear on his victims. He had no concern for them as people, indeed, at the beginning of his treatment he could not perceive them as real people at all. He had not been able to make a 'safe' relationship with his mother during his pre-school years, and expressed rage towards her. She had worked as a prostitute for much of his infancy, on occasions utilising his presence as a 'little waiter' for her customers. He had seen sexual intercourse on a number of occasions and had always connected it with violence and attacks rather than loving and concern.

Most boys between the ages of 3 and 5 need to pass through a femininity phase, according to Klein. Because they fear castration, boys then learn to protest against the feminine role: 'little girls are stupid', and to re-identify with their fathers (*see* **Castration Complex**). For Alan there was no father with whom he could identify, and therefore he became 'stuck' in the phase where he had to assume an excessive protest against femininity, directed initially at mother and then at all women. At the same time his sexuality was awakened in a precocious manner. Attacking women sexually was the only way he had of asserting his masculinity, and his instinct for mastery had become injected into this solution, adding a further dimension of cruelty and lack of concern.

# Instinct for Survival

Within everyone's fundamental make-up is a range of behaviours, the energy for which arises from a need to survive. The baby knows, at some level, that she needs to eat to survive. Instinctively she turns her head to the breast, intuitively knowing that is where food and therefore life resides. As we grow, numerous other activities become important to our survival: our senses of vision, hearing, smell and touch are all crucial if we are to live in safety. We also need to develop co-ordination of our muscles and an ability to control our sphincters. If any of this development fails we are less likely to survive.

Our basic instincts continually push us towards survival as a primary goal in life. Freud suggested that equal and opposite to this is a death instinct, in an effort to explain why our behaviour is often a strange mixture of self-preservation on the one hand and kamikaze recklessness on the other (*see* **Death**). Infants seem to vary in the extent to which they carefully preserve themselves, and other instincts, most particularly the sexual ones, are often at odds with the instincts that would keep us as individuals safe. Freud thought that this represented the fact that self-preserving instincts were based in reality while sexual instincts were based in the pleasure-seeking and fantasy-bound realms of our minds (*see* **Eroticism**). There is also a real conflict to be observed between the survival of an individual and the survival, via sexual behaviour, of a species.

The instinct for survival, so strong in the newborn infant, often re-emerges strongly in adults during times of threat or hardship. There are many descriptions of people caught in situations where death seemed inevitable who appear to have cheated it simply through an inner determination to survive. In physical illness some people seem able to re-engage their absolute determination to survive, even when doctors have thought there was no further hope, and there are a number of descriptions of near-death experience where people feel they have made a decision not to die which they were then able to put into effect.

The balance we achieve between our survival versus the survival of our species or race, culture or religion varies between individuals and depending on external circumstance. For many the survival of a particular way of life becomes symbolically the same as their own physical survival, but it may be our sexual and competitive instincts which lead us into confrontational war-type situations where our basic self-preserving instincts would stay well clear. For women the decision to become pregnant clearly marks some crossing from the totally self-preservative towards species preservation, and, of course, is the result of a previous decision in favour of sexuality. The joke about whether there is life after motherhood is only half humorous. Women often report that their own instinct for survival changes, at least in the short term, once they have children, the survival of their children becoming instinctually more important than their own. Pregnancy and labour were until recently major causes of death for women throughout the world, and there remain circumstances in which maternity is still a great threat to life and health.

If we do live on a spectrum between an instinct for life on the one hand and death on the other, it would seem probable that our healthy position on that spectrum changes according to our age. Thus babies would be expected to be most determinedly on the life instinct end of the spectrum, while increasing age would make us more preoccupied with and perhaps more welcoming of death. I have seen some patients who seem to have 'swapped places' on the spectrum with important others in their lives. Take for instance Claudia, who made several serious attempts at suicide when in her late teens and early twenties. She had come out as a lesbian when she was 18 years old and had been thrown out of the house by her mother with the words 'You'll be the death of me.' During analysis she remembered this phrase as one that her mother had frequently used throughout her childhood as a reprimand. She also had dreams that her presence in the analyst's room would be toxic enough to kill the analyst.

Her mother had been ill during her pregnancy and had indeed nearly died during Claudia's birth. This story, in full gory detail, had been told many times, and Claudia felt an enormous burden of guilt for almost killing her mother. Every time her mother used her favourite sentence, this guilt was reactivated. The suicide attempts seemed to represent an attempt to give mother her life back. Eventually she went home. Her mother responded with some warmth but also with the inevitable 'You'll be the death of me.' This time, though, Claudia challenged her, replying 'I think children are *meant* to be the death of their parents in some way.' This statement surprised Claudia as much as her mother, but seemed to shift their positions on the life/death spectrum dramatically. Claudia was able to invest in her life in a way that reflected her new-found belief that it was all right to be self-preserving even at the expense of your mother, and her mother was also able, at last, to come to terms with her sense of there having been no life after motherhood, and see that responsibility for that lay with herself rather than blaming Claudia for it.

## Institutionalisation

We are all subject to institutionalisation to some extent. We have to learn to live within the large 'institution' of our society with its expectations of us and our behaviour. On a smaller scale, many work in companies, businesses or large social concerns such as the NHS or Social Services. Such workplaces undoubtedly institutionalise some of our reactions and values, at least during working hours. Being in a professional group exerts pressures to conform which may mean that the style of the individual undergoes changes until it suits the 'institution' of that group. The vast majority of us do however go home to a place where we can relax, change our clothes, attitudes and expectations, and, to a greater or lesser extent, control what we do and how we do it.

For those individuals who live within institutions there is no such place which is free from external rules and expectations. Everything is ordered according to the needs of the institution, and even with the best intentions towards patient care, the needs of institutions are often at odds with an individual's needs. Within our own homes we have very different, special relationships of intensity and meaning with family members. Friends and colleagues can never be as close, even if our relationships with them are just as important and perhaps more comfortable. Within an institution such intense close relationships are against the fundamental rules. Indeed one of the benefits of 'asylum' is often said to be the lack of demanding relationships, which allows the vulnerable individual some peace of mind. Despite being against the rules, however, intense relationships do exist – between patients, between staff, and between staff and patients, but these tend to be covert, negatively regarded even to the point of punishment, and not lent credibility or importance.

Life within an institution runs in an organised way, which is, mostly, predictable and stable. Change, if and when it does occur, is rarely discussed with patients, merely enforced, often without explanation. Patients are expected to get up, do whatever is ordained, eat, socialise and sleep in a pre-set pattern. Even staff within institutions often feel individually helpless. The institution is far larger than the individual.

Children growing up within institutions are known to suffer long-standing damage because of both the rigidity of the structure which is applied impersonally and also because of a lack of close meaningful relationships that are predictably stable. The psychiatrist and psychoanalyst John Bowlby explored the psychology of disturbed adolescents and produced his theories of maternal deprivation. He concluded that such children, often raised in orphanages, lacked a central important person to whom they could relate. This experience produced severe disturbances in their developing psyches, including an inability to relate closely to others throughout their lives. Later writers have greatly modified his theories, and it is now generally agreed that it is not being deprived of maternal love particularly which is damaging, but of being denied predictable love and environmental stability from some source. Institutions, by their design and nature, are not able to provide predictable love: the staff are there because they are paid to be there, however dedicated they may be, and regularly change shifts, or even leave as a result of further training or promotion. An institution can provide some degree of environmental stability, however, and this should not be underrated.

Since the 1960s attention has been given to the effects of long-term institutionalisation for those originally diagnosed as mentally ill or mentally impaired to such an extent as to make them unable to live in the outside world. Attention was first drawn to the possibility that institutions were in themselves damaging to patients during the 1950s, when a number of group psychotherapists began to work with such patients. Their reports suggested that if you take responsibility, control and power to organise away from individuals they forget how to use these aspects of themselves, and helplessly sink into conformity with the institution. Thus some of the indicators of their inability to manage in the outside world, for example their inability to use money appropriately, organise their personal hygiene, make plans and also their lack of interest in the world were seen to be results of the care they had received rather than their illnesses.

It took major breakthroughs in medication, most particularly the discovery of chlorpromazine, before 'open door' policies began to gain respect. Drug therapy allows people to regain a sense of control over their mental life, making their feelings and behaviour more predictable and less frightening to themselves and others. Gradually it became accepted government policy to house the long-term ill within the community to as great an extent as possible. In order to achieve this with those who had already suffered the effects of institutionalisation a new speciality, rehabilitation, was developed in the field of psychiatry.

For a time there was a real hope that there would be no further need for long-term institutions, and much pioneering work was done towards what all the workers hoped would be a much better deal for patients. Undoubtedly the move away from institutionalisation was a great breakthrough for the many people who now live more fulfilling and relaxed lives in the community than they could ever have achieved in a hospital. However, communities do not necessarily open their arms to the thousands of patients being resettled out of hospital. Mental illness still causes fear in most people, and the thought of a hostel or group home in your road might make you think very differently about community care. Certainly there is often local uproar and every attempt made to prevent property being acquired for the mentally ill.

Many mentally ill people are themselves initially unhappy about the idea of community care. Nobody asks whether they wish to be resettled and so, to that extent, this 'breakthrough' was merely another institutionalised decision. Many become 'converts' however once they realise the benefits, but a considerable minority do not like the outside world and continue to yearn for the security of their old institution. Others find the move so stressful that they relapse into illness once more.

Over the years there has been time to consider the consequences of community care alongside the consequences of institutionalisation. There has been a reassessment of the true needs of the patients and a growing awareness that there will always be people who are too emotionally vulnerable to survive except in a structured institution. This group is much smaller than we thought it was in the 1950s, and if new treatments become available its size may again shrink.

Community care needs considerable financial input to make it an attractive alternative to institutionalisation. All too often it has been seen as a cheap option, and patients have been released into circumstances that reduce their enjoyment of life rather than enhance it. Within an institution much recreation, work opportunity, protected socialising and outings can be arranged. Often the mentally ill in the community lose these aspects of their lives. In order to have control over the fine detail of what they eat, how they spend their money and where they spend their time, they may have to relinquish the factors most of us would consider essential to happiness. It is a difficult choice.

The nature of the illnesses which require some form of institutional treatment tend to make people apathetic, disinterested, without initiative and lacking in relationships with individuals or even with society. Institutionalisation can make these symptoms worse by robbing the individuals of any vestige of power or control. In such circumstances they eventually become submissive, too. These patients have difficulty fighting for what they need, and many have difficulty even thinking about what they need. The staff responsible for their care therefore are often placed in the position of feeling like parents of young children rather than carers of adults. However vulnerable, it is important to see patients in a way that reflects a compromise between their true age and the limits of their abilities to take responsibility for themselves. If they are adults then they must be treated as such to the limits of their capabilities, rather than to the limits of the institution's tolerance.

Awareness of this need is growing constantly within the field of mental health. Nurses and doctors dealing with patients are trained with different expectations and understandings than they were previously, and every attempt is made to allow individuals dignity and hope. Most people working in this field would agree, however, that we still have a long way to go before being able to provide the right degree of environmental security on the one hand and normality on the other for this group of patients. Progress in this area will also require that society as a whole, that 'caring community', develops new understandings of mental illness, and that the State is willing to invest hard cash in enhancing these patients' quality of life.

# Intellectualisation

We all use our intellect to master the world, both external and internal. Within ourselves we are at various times aware or unaware of strong emotions and fantasies. We of course have instincts that would if not controlled drive us to behave in ways which we know, intellectually, are not socially acceptable. Often our upbringing and experience has led us to believe that our emotions and fantasies are similarly unacceptable. They demand, however, some form of expression since we cannot contain them for ever.

For the most part then intellectualisation is a useful defence, allowing us limited expression of those aspects of ourselves we think would shock or hurt if expressed directly. Thus a woman faced with her partner's infidelity may discuss the relative merits of faithfulness and 'free' love, rather than reveal the true depth of her hostility. Such a defence allows the relationship to continue, which may be more important to both parties than an honest expression of feelings. In a grander way we have developed an intellectual understanding of our universe in order to defend against feeling insignificant and insecure in ourselves. Margaret, a 35-year-old university lecturer, commented after the hurricane that hit Britain in 1988 that she was amazed to find that understanding how such winds developed did not prevent her in the least from feeling awe-inspired when they arrived. In a sense the hurricane had blown away her intellectualisation, revealing a childlike wonder about the world.

Our world, particularly the 20th-century Western world, puts a high value on all that is intellectual, rating it above that which is 'merely' emotional. However, much that is carried out with supposed intellectual understanding and decision-making can also be seen to be an external representation of the inner emotional world of the individual or group. To understand what drives politicians, for instance, it would probably be as useful to look at their background, parents and upbringing as to listen to their intellectualisations about their policies. Such a perspective would probably be dismissed as irrelevant or unfair, however, intellectualisation having allowed for a split between what is thought and what is felt.

Generally men value intellect even more than do women, and are often dismissive of the emotional perspective women feel more free to have about an issue. Throughout my medical career I have regularly sat through case conferences listening to male doctors discuss people and their problems in an 'objective' and intellectual way without any recourse to thinking emotionally about what ails the patients or how their illness might affect them and their relatives. The extent to which intellectual medicine has been given supremacy over what might be thought of as emotional medicine is extraordinary, and doctors who dare to think in emotional terms are often relegated to the bottom of the league.

In psychotherapy and analysis intellectualisation is seen as a defence which gets in the way of psychological work. In this way it is similar to rationalisation, in which a sensible, but untrue, version of events and motivations is offered: 'I must' or 'I ought' is said instead of 'I want' or 'I am driven to'. Both of these modes of defence are important in moulding what form of assistance is offered to people when they are ill or distressed. It may be psychologically impossible for the doctor to say 'I don't know' or 'I can't do anything', leading him or her to take a rational or intellectual approach in spite of the fact that he or she knows, at some level, that such an approach is useless and possibly damaging. The old adage 'first of all do no harm' is often forgotten in the enthusiasm to solve intellectual problems which are contained within the bodies and lives of individuals. Acceptance of such help contains the mirror-image defence of believing that we know enough as rational beings to avoid death, pain and despair if we try hard enough (*see* **Defence Mechanisms**, **Grandiose Behaviour** and **Rationalisation**).

# Intelligence
It is hard to define exactly what is meant by intelligence but most

definitions agree that it is the capacity in humans which allows for a degree of biological adaptation to ever-changing circumstances. It allows us not only to learn but to also put that learning to a useful and creative function in the service of further survival of the self and the species. This basic biological definition is rather different to the generally accepted notions of intelligence, which often refer to the educational levels reached by an individual. This latter, educational concept includes memory, attention span and complete use of all the senses, as well as a variety of social and family factors, all of which are separate to an individual's intelligence.

Intelligence can be measured by tests such as those requiring the individual to take certain items of information and transform them into more complex answers to questions. All these tests, however, require of the examinee a moderate command of language and often cultural understanding as well in order to be able to make sense of the information given and questions asked. Despite these limitations tests are sometimes useful in assessing an individual's true capacity; and repeated testing can be helpful in pointing out losses or gains in intellectual ability over the course of a disease.

Within a community intelligence is distributed in a curve, with the majority of the population being in the middle of that curve with average or moderate intelligence. As you get to the ends of the spectrum, indicating high and low intelligence, the numbers of people involved get smaller. At the low end of the spectrum there is a slightly larger number than at the high end because there are a number of disease processes which limit or stop the intellectual development of an individual, often at an early stage of life. Intelligence develops as we grow and learn, although our innate capacity for that growth is there from birth. Thus those individuals who suffer from genetic and/or metabolic disorders increase the numbers at the lowest end of the scale because these diseases have robbed them of their capacity to develop from the outset. With genetic disorders the limitations often stem from the moment of conception; in metabolic disorders the damage may occur in the first few months of life.

Increasingly we are becoming aware of the range of environmental dangers to the unborn child. Such knowledge should enable us to reduce the numbers of children whose intelligence is compromised so early in their lives. We are also becoming more sophisticated in diagnosing genetic problems in the unborn child at a stage when the mother if she wishes can still legally abort the foetus if damage is evident. For many parents such advances represent a liberation from the anxieties and suffering of previous generations, however they do also confer responsibilities and a need to make decisions which other parents find too taxing. Many mothers-to-be find that the advice on their diet and against smoking and drinking alcohol while pregnant adds to their burdens, making them feel guilty if they are unable to follow it. Those who advise parents in matters such as these must exercise caution against believing they know what the right decision is. However much the advice offered is sensible, mothers must be allowed to temper perfection with reality.

Throughout childhood, as intelligence is developing, the brain may be exposed to risks such as infection, trauma or poor nutrition (*see* **Brain Tumour**). Mental illness can occur alongside defects in intelligence but there is no definite relationship between the two. There is some suggestion that intelligence may be higher than average in those suffering from manic depressive psychosis and lower than average in those suffering from epilepsy (*see* **Epilepsy** and **Manic Depressive Psychosis**). Debate about personality disorders in the mentally subnormal have raged for many years; it is now generally thought that although there is little direct connection between the two, having a low intelligence may make it harder for an individual to both fit into society and cover up that inability. Those in the high intelligence group are probably similarly subject to difficulties 'fitting in' because by definition they are not 'normal'. It is certainly true that high intelligence alone will not guarantee an individual success in life, and many bright people struggle with relationship difficulties throughout their lives.

Inadequate education means that the individual is not encouraged to use the intellectual capacity he or she was born with. On the other hand, parents often invest large sums of money in their children's education in an attempt to raise their intellectual capacity, and although this may produce better educated children in terms of general knowledge and exam results, it probably has, at best, only short-term results for the child's intellectual ability. Motivating a child to like learning or to have a strong desire to succeed in life is probably more likely to enhance his capacity for utilising whatever intellect he possesses. Vitamin supplements have also been linked with increasing children's school performance.

Children with limited intelligence can often develop further than originally predicted because of enormous commitments of time and energy on the part of their parents and teachers. It is hard to judge when the limits of such encouragement have been reached, and attempts to over-stretch such a child may result in his feeling frustrated and acting out with violent outbursts.

Undoubtedly the constitution we were born with, our genetic pattern and the environmental circumstances of our mother's pregnancy and our birth set real limits on what we can or cannot achieve intellectually. However, these limits represent a range which the circumstances of our life and our personalities can influence greatly.

## Introversion and Extroversion

The term *introversion* first appeared in the work of Jung, although it was rapidly taken up by other analysts, including Freud, and then later by psychologists looking for parameters with which to describe the range of normal human behaviour. Thus was *extroversion* coined to represent the opposite end of the spectrum.

In its original form introversion meant the removal of energy (libido) from external objects and the re-investment of that energy within the self. Extroversion, as its opposite, therefore meant the continuing investment of personal energy in outside objects and people.

Analytical theory suggests that if the child experiences external reality as too frustrating she will withdraw her attempts to relate externally and instead re-invest that energy into her own fantasy world. Thus we might surmise that extroverts have found external reality more rewarding, or at least less frustrating, than have introverts. Introversion and extroversion also seem to be strongly inherited characteristics, however, and therefore the environment may make only minor alterations to the child's pre-existing tendency towards one or the other.

As the name suggests, introverts tend to be quiet and self-absorbed. Their pleasures derive from fulfilling internal wishes and desires and they find solitude easy to bear. They are able to maintain interpersonal relationships only with some difficulty, as they are more used to withholding aspects of themselves rather than sharing themselves with others. Their relationship with their own inner reality is more important to them than any outer relationship, which means that they are capable of hanging onto their own belief and value systems against enormous external pressures. Extroverts are more socially able than introverts because they use far more of their available energy in relationships in the outer world. Their pleasures stem from this external relating, and they need sharing relationships with a lot of interaction in order to feel truly satisfied. This need to be in constant relationship with the outer world means that they are more vulnerable to pressures from that world than are introverts.

Most people fall somewhere in the middle of this spectrum and demonstrate personality characteristics of both aspects at different times of their lives and in different relationships. Some are more 'stuck' at one end or the other; either extreme can cause serious problems in relationships.

Opposites are commonly said to attract and there does seem to be a tendency for introverts to marry extroverts. Such relationships can allow both individuals stability, the introvert using the extrovert as its link to the outside world, while the extrovert gets a containing, limiting sense of security from the introvert. There is an in-built weakness in such relationships, however, which becomes more pronounced under stress or when the individuals are extreme in their introversion or extroversion. Introverts will thus find extroverts demanding, noisy and exhausting, while extroverts commonly experience introverts as selfish and ungiving. Clearly such perceptions of each other would put any relationship under strain.

Mary and Josie had been friends since university, a friendship based on Mary's stable and quiet sense of self, which Josie with her traumatic love-life came to depend on, and Josie's sense of fun and 'making things happen', which gave an added and welcome spark to Mary's otherwise rather humdrum lifestyle.

Ten years after they had completed their education they decided to go on holiday together, with their four children. This was the first time they had lived together since college, and rapidly proved disastrous. Mary felt uneasy about the effects of Josie's emotional 'fireworks' on all the children, and Josie found Mary boring. Within three days their arguments started to demonstrate the degree of disillusionment both felt with their friendship. It was only after a year of non-communication that they returned to their old warm and more accepting relationship with each other, but at a safe geographical distance.

# Involuntary Movements

The nervous system controls our muscles and has both a conscious and unconscious element. For instance, when we walk we make a conscious decision to move in a certain direction. Meanwhile, however, we are unconscious of the fact that our nervous system then integrates the movements of many muscles and sensations of our legs and joints, so that the movement of walking is smooth and accurate. Sometimes our muscles move without any conscious instruction from ourselves in an unexpected way. This is called involuntary movement, and may be a generalised sensation of restlessness or a precise movement of a specific part of the body, which may be repeated. Children are generally more restless physically than adults, and this is why they are more subject to involuntary movements, such as 'tics'. If the brain becomes damaged by infection or other disease, involuntary movements become increasingly likely.

Many people experience the occasional twitch without there being any sinister significance. However, if the movement is persistent it may well be a signal that something is wrong. Children under pressure or who are lonely or constantly criticised seem vulnerable to such purposeless movements, usually in the face or neck, which have their origins in the mid-brain. The children cannot help themselves, and if they try to make a conscious effort to stop the movements they will feel generally restless and anxious. The incidence of the movements tends to lessen as the children grow; it is more difficult to know whether the associated emotional problems also disappear or merely go 'underground', waiting to surface years later when the now-grown-up child becomes stressed. Referral to a child guidance unit or a psychologist may be appropriate if the movements persist and are causing the child anxiety or making him liable to teasing and bullying at school.

In adults such repeated movements herald more serious disorders. Parkinson's Disease may first demonstrate itself in tics. The person's face takes on a rigid, often sad, countenance, and voluntary movement becomes increasingly difficult while involuntary movements increase. Characteristically the involuntary movements often occur after a voluntary action has been attempted. So an attempt at walking may end in the person's feeling unable to stop moving. Movements become jerky and weak, and this ever-growing prison of involuntary movement is often associated with psychological features that closely parallel the physical. Thus the person may reiterate words or expressions again and again, meaninglessly, or may echo whatever is said to him or her compulsively. Not surprisingly this disease often leads to depression and suicide. There are drugs which control the symptoms to some extent, although the success of these is variable and may lessen as the disease progresses. Recent reports of transplanted fetal brain cells to replace the patient's damaged ones, although highly controversial, have brought hope to previously despairing sufferers (*see* **Depression** and **Suicide**).

Parkinsonism is the name given to a syndrome which mirrors Parkinson's Disease but which has its origins in previous illness or drug treatment. Encephalitis (infection of the brain tissue) may lead on to Parkinsonism. In the past the major childhood diseases such as measles, German measles (rubella), mumps and chicken-pox could all produce encephalitis and its ensuing problems. Vaccination has made great inroads into decreasing the rate at which such diseases occur, although sadly there are still some cases each year. Other viruses can also produce a similar picture; the AIDS virus is a recent case in point. Such illnesses are difficult to treat and are often fatal.

Huntingdon's Chorea, named after the American doctor who gave the classic, although not the first, description of the illness, is an inherited disease. Because it is carried by a dominant gene, an affected individual can expect about half of his or her children to inherit the illness. Symptoms usually appear when the patient is in his or her late 30s or early 40s, although they may start as early as the 20s or as late as the 60s. Men and women are equally affected, although some research suggests that the symptoms start earlier in women. The involuntary movements, usually of face and neck, are often preceded by psychiatric problems and a change of character. Once the degeneration of the brain tissue commences it is progressive; the involuntary movements become increasingly disorganised and the patient begins to dement. As the thinking becomes more confused, apathy and inertia set in. This is a cruel and eventually fatal disease which causes anguish to the affected families (*see* **Apathy** and **Dementia**). Early diagnosis at least allows individuals to make an informed decision over whether they wish to risk to future generations. The rate of suicide in affected families is high, among both those affected by the gene and the other family members who have to live with the anxiety and sadness, even if they are themselves spared the illness (*see* **Suicide**).

Involuntary movements can also be produced as a side-effect of drug therapy. The major tranquillisers such as chlorpromazine can produce a reversible form of Parkinsonism, usually within the first month of treatment, or tardive dyskinesia, which is only reversible in some people. Tardive dyskinesia can take a number of forms, involving the muscles of the mouth, the face, the trunk or the arms and legs.

# Irritability

Who has not been irritable at some point? It is a normal phenomenon, often associated either with frustration or fatigue. Adults have a tendency to become irritated with their children because children, particularly infants, are a major cause of both fatigue and frustration. Most adults know that, whatever they are trying to do or think about, their small children will find a way of interrupting them, and most people find this form of frustration makes them irritable. Many of us have a time of day at which we are particularly irritable, and women report a greater sense of irritability at some points of their menstrual cycle. Normal irritation has a 'build-up' or latent phase during which we are increasingly aware of mounting irritation. If we do not take steps to defuse it and the irritating stimulus persists, our irritation mounts to the point of explosion. This is probably a normal and healthy response to frustrations and fatigue, as this mounting irritation also gives us a renewed sense of energy and enables us to overcome problems. Regular sleep, a healthy diet and a period of time each day, however brief, when you can do what you wish without interruption or frustration all go a long way to minimising the 'unnecessary' irritations of life.

Abnormal irritability has a more explosive nature, often with little or no build-up and with minimal or absent external stimulus. All those illnesses that have an effect on brain tissue – trauma or infection, tumour or progressive disease – produce increased irritability. This is because irritation is the watered-down remnant in man of what is described as the 'rage' reaction in animals. We need the sophisticated 'higher' centres of our brain to inhibit that more primitive response, and when these centres are disorganised by illness they are less capable of suitable inhibition (*see* **Inhibition** and **Rage**).

Within the realm of psychiatry those with manic depressive syndromes are often extremely irritable, and are prone to arguments that seem ridiculous to an uninvolved observer. Any emotional problems that disrupt sleep also make the individual more likely to be irritable, and 'illnesses' that cause increasing frustration in the form of, say, legal battles over being dismissed from work on the grounds of the illness or seeking compensation for it are almost certain to cause added irritation (*see* **Manic Depressive Psychosis**).

It is normally reported that the tendency to increased irritability is a character trait found more frequently in men. I suspect, however, that this has to do with two factors. First, women have strong social prohibitions against expressing irritation while men are almost expected to be more irritable. Second, men are more likely to express their irritability towards other adults, so that it is noted and commented upon. Women, because they usually spend greater amounts of time with children, are more likely to express irritation towards their children, often when they are alone with them. It therefore remains unrecorded. People who are constantly with children often develop a form of acceptance towards their more frustrating aspects, and it is interesting to see how often women protect men from the excesses of children in social situations, presumably to avoid their irritable outbursts.

Women often suffer from guilt because their irritability with their children is secret. A sure sign of genuine friendship between women is when they will lose their tempers with their children in front of each other. Because it is so often secretive, mothers feel that they may be much worse at mothering than anyone else, and fear exposing their irritation lest they be condemned for it (*see* **Guilt**).

Beryl is a 25-year-old mother of three pre-school-aged children. She sought my help because of guilt feelings about her 'violent temper' towards these children. She was fearful of exposing this to me, thinking that I might be so shocked by what she said that I would immediately take her children into care. Her 'violent temper' consisted of shouting at them once or twice a week, and occasionally restricting them to their bedrooms for short periods of time. She counted the number of times she had smacked each one, so desperate did she feel about each smack. Having listened to her 'confession' I then asked about aspects of her life such as fatigue and frustration. She acknowledged that she had not had a complete night's sleep since the eldest, now 4, was born, and that she felt constantly interrupted and intruded on by one or other of them. She also said that they filled her life to such an extent that she had lost touch with her former women friends and now mixed entirely with other young mums, all of whom she felt managed better than she did. When I suggested that maybe they were covering up their irritation just like she did, she was amazed.

It is clear in Beryl's case that her experience of increasing frustration had external origins, and that if anything she was rather over-controlled about it, setting herself unrealistically high standards in the circumstances. I set her some 'homework': to go back and attempt an honest conversation with some of the other mums of her acquaintance. She had no need of further appointments, but sent a lovely card saying that she had discovered a number of similarly irritable mums who 'confessed' and now met several times a week to relate stories about their frustrations in ways that made all the others laugh! The children's book *Tales of a Fourth-Grade Nothing* by Judy Blume is another 'cure' I've discovered: it is a delightful tale of the irritations of an 8-year-old with his 2-year-old brother who does everything up to and including eat his turtle. A quick read is guaranteed to put irritation into perspective.

## Isolation

Isolation can be an external or internal way of life. Often external isolation is a reflection of the internal world of a person, but in the case of older people, whose friends may die or who find they cannot go visiting as they once could, the isolation is unwelcome and imposed on them from without. Most of our understanding of mankind is that we are social animals who both need and like to live in groups. The amount of this need is variable, but so great is the average need for interaction that the majority would find social isolation a form of torture. We are born into a relationship with another, first our mothers, but rapidly including other important family members. Most of us feel most comfortable, fulfilled and able to grow emotionally when we are in relationships. Thus, even when relationships are experienced as painful or demanding, there is a recurring need to re-invest in them.

Social interaction does require however that we expose ourselves to at least some extent to the whims and perceptions of others. This is a dangerous process, which we modify by choosing increasingly to mix with those who are similar to us, so that we are questioned as little as possible and accepted as much as possible. At an early age we establish a structural way of understanding our world which consists of personal, family and cultural constructions. Each structure is unique to the individual although it may strongly resemble that of other family members or cultural groupings. Our need to have this understanding as a basic element of our perception reflects our need to impose some certainty and control on a world which we fear. The structure we impose, however, also limits the flexibility of our perceptions. The more inflexible the structure and the more 'alien' our surroundings the more we experience a need to isolate ourselves. This is the psychological basis, for example, of the immigrant's wish to live within a community of immigrants: it is a defence against the alien world he or she has chosen or been forced to live in.

There are some individuals who not only fear that their stability is at risk if exposed to outside influences but who also fear inner contamination from ideas they have, actions they take, or emotions they experience. In our early childhood we maintain splits between various developing aspects of ourselves because we have not yet acquire the necessary psychological maturity to accept that we have to live with contradictions within our own structural understandings. These contradictions can cover wide ranges of experiences, for example love and hate felt within one relationship (*see* **Ambivalence**). Some people never take the developmental step towards an integrated sense of self, maintaining instead a split or isolation between various aspects of themselves. Such inner splits make it difficult to relate to others with any flexibility, and consequently people with them tend to establish lives that are 'cut-off' from interaction. They may distance themselves from their families in early adult life, make only fleeting attachments to friends or colleagues, never marry or have children, and generally live on the edge of the social group, preferring their own company and wanting little or no excitement or external stimuli. There is no direct link between such personalities and mental illness, although people like these tend to be more obsessional by nature, and their social isolation may make them more vulnerable to emotional problems.

Anna was a 34 and single, and had worked for 16 years at a job clearly below her intellectual abilities. Her home life was characterised by a series of rituals – the way she washed, cleaned the house, and prepared food, what she was willing to eat, and also the way in which she constructed her thoughts. After each thought she would count to ten, in order not to 'contaminate' her next thought. She was quietly happy with her life, without family or friends, until she developed multiple sclerosis. Her increasing disability meant that she had to find ways of communicating with the people who were attempting to help her. She found this communication almost unbearable and complained to her home help that, 'You want conversation to run like a river, everything all mixed up, while I prefer not to make connections between things, but to maintain each in a clean space in my mind.' The home help pointed out that this made conversation almost impossible, and Anna agreed, saying that she preferred to read anyway. Anna was trapped between her personality's need to maintain isolation both within and without herself, and the conflicting needs imposed by her illness.

The turnover of Anna's home helpers was consistently high, with each one only able to stand her isolation for a short while. Although it was possible to help Anna explore her construction of life she remained, until her death, rigidly isolated.

It is very difficult to live with an isolated personality. Partners often become depressed, anxious or overwhelmingly angry, while the isolated individual seems quietly content. It is important for a partner to recognise that such an attitude is in the basic structure of the individual and not meant as a personal attack. Even with understanding and much love, however, such relationships tend to be one-sided, and the more flexible partner often has to leave in order to maintain his or her own sanity.

# J

## Jealousy

Jealousy differs from envy in that it involves three people rather than two. In envy we wish to destroy something good that another person has and we have not. In jealousy we perceive a relationship between two others and yearn to be a part of it by replacing one of the partners. Thus while envy is a primitive emotion initially felt at the mother's breast (*see* **Envy**), jealousy is experienced at a later stage of development, when we begin to compete with the parent of the same sex for the attentions of the parent of the opposite sex (*see* **Electra Complex** and **Oedipus Complex**). Associated with this sense of jealousy are feelings of hatred and murderous rage towards the 'opponent'. During development further relationships with brothers and sisters and a peer group occur, which begin to diffuse the original intensity of the experience of jealousy, although most of us retain remnants of the feeling, which are reactivated during our adult emotional and sexual relationships.

At times jealousy assumes dangerous proportions. This is more likely to occur if one adult is betrayed by another within a supposedly committed relationship. While it might be logical to expect our anguish and fury to be directed towards the betrayer it is often jealousy of and competition with the rival which forms the major focus of our rage and murderous feelings. At other times the betrayal itself may be imagined, perhaps stemming from our feeling that love always ends in betrayal, a feeling that originates in our own life experience. In these situations the accused partner cannot convince the jealous one of his or her faithfulness no matter how hard he or she tries, the imagined betrayal and resulting jealousy having reached delusional proportions (*see* **Othello Syndrome**). Such a problem is commonly associated with repeated alcohol abuse on the part of the jealous partner (*see* **Alcoholism**). These situations represent a decided level of danger to the partner accused, whether the betrayal is real or imagined. Domestic violence and murder are often the outcome, and if such partnerships are referred for professional advice it is usual for the counsellor to stress the dangers of jealousy and the benefits of a trial separation, in an attempt to reduce the intensity of the emotions involved.

In some countries the conviction of those found guilty of murder under circumstances the society believes to be 'inevitable' and even justifiable is modified to a reduced or even suspended prison sentence. These so-called 'crimes of passion' are treated very differently to other murder cases, perhaps because many of us have experienced murderous rage towards loved ones. However 'normal' such jealousy murders may be, it is clear that the adult acts in a way that allows the feelings of a 4-year-old to take over, and in so doing clearly demonstrates an under-controlled aspect of his or her personality which may well render him or her dangerous in future emotional relationships. The effects that drugs and alcohol have on reducing control cannot be underestimated.

# K

## Korsakov's Syndrome
*See* Alcoholism

# L

## Learning Difficulties

There can be few things more disturbing to parents than the suspicion that their child is 'backward' intellectually or developmentally. They may have a general feeling that their child is not reaching the milestones of development at normal times, or that a specific area of development seems delayed or abnormal. In some children any problem is diagnosed early, even immediately at birth if the backwardness is part of a total syndrome known to be connected with mental handicap; in others disorders manage to escape detection for months or even years, until the stress of exposure to education that is above their abilities begins to show. Quite often the diagnosis is a slow process made up of initial suspicion on the part of the parents followed by a period when they keep their anxieties to themselves as they search for more clues and hope that they are wrong. Gradually, as they accept what they are seeing, they become more willing to seek help.

In Britain at least 10 children in 1,000 will suffer difficulties with their intellectual development (the figures being higher for boys and in rural areas), having levels of intelligence that make it challenging or impossible for them to develop and adapt as they grow. But many others have specific learning difficulties within the context of an adequate intelligence.

Some children become backward as a result of an illness, either genetic or environmental, that occurs during their mother's pregnancy or in their early life. Recently a great deal of attention has been paid to improving ante-natal care in the hopes of preventing damage to the foetus. Some 55 per cent of those with severe mental handicaps and 23 per cent of those with mild mental handicaps have suffered from a problem before birth. Of these, more than half have a chromosomal defect. Every cell in the body contains chromosomes which carry the genetic material from one generation to the next, and the most common defect is a fault in chromosome 21, causing Down's Syndrome. Exposure to radiation (either environmental or diagnostic) and infections account for the majority of the remaining cases, the most common infections being toxoplasmosis (caused by a parasitic infection which is transmitted from the mother to the foetus), rubella (German measles), cytomegalovirus (a viral infection), herpes, and, recently attracting media attention, listeria. In the case of toxoplasmosis and cytomegalovirus the mother may be unaware that she is infected because both are symptomless, or have symptoms that are only transitory and therefore not recognised for what they are. Drugs given to the mother and her alcohol intake can also contribute to damaging the developing foetus.

Around the time of the birth (the peri-natal period) the placenta may cease to function effectively, reducing the blood supply to the foetus, or there may be a lack of oxygen reaching the baby if there are problems with the birth. After birth the baby's brain is vulnerable to any insult, be it traumatic, metabolic (some babies are given too much salt, because some milk powders are made up in double or triple strength) or infectious. Malnutrition also causes retarded development.

A person's experience of backwardness is highly variable. Each has his or her own personality with which to meet any limitations. The response of family and the wider community can also help or hinder an individual in achieving maximum fulfilment. People who are backward in their development often feel frustrated by their limitations, especially when they see what others of the same age can do or when they are pushed too hard to achieve beyond what is comfortable. Other disorders, such as epilepsy and a variety of psychiatric syndromes, seem to be more common in those with mental handicaps, adding to their problems. Throughout their lives they have an increased risk of illnesses of all sorts, although strides forward in medicine and standard of living conditions have dramatically increased their life expectancy.

People with a mental handicap may have trouble communicating their problems and may feel very frustrated because of their difficulty in forming ideas, verbally expressing those ideas, speaking or listening, or having a restricted understanding of both the subject under discussion and its larger context.

For the most part those with a mental handicap should be treated as a part of the community, with access to all the facilities that we would normally expect them to need at a given age, although some of these facilities may require modification in order to be suitable: schooling, for example, should be aimed at a level which is helpfully challenging rather than threatening and discouraging. (*See* Appendix A.)

# Libido

Libido describes the energy with which our love instincts are inspired. Sexuality is often the outward expression of that energy. To achieve an external sexual expression of this energy, a complex sequence of events, both psychological and physical, needs to occur. The results are often seen socially as 'a performance', as if the individual is being rated either by others or him- or herself in this expression of physical and emotional need. Perhaps we should not be surprised, therefore, that utilising libido and being sexual is, for many adults, not as easy or enjoyable as it might be.

There is a wide variation in the intensity of an individual's libidinal energy as well as in the object upon which it might focus. There are many situations in which it is normal to experience a loss of or decrease in libido. Fatigue, fear and anxiety, sadness, lack of factual knowledge about sexual matters, the 'wrong' partner, preoccupations such as worry about contracting a sexual disease or becoming pregnant, and external factors such as discomfort will weigh against enjoyable sexual activity.

Given the complex neurological basis for sexuality any illness which attacks the neurones involved will make it more difficult to achieve arousal. This can be a problem particularly in the case of some hormonal illnesses and in diabetes. The vast majority of people who have problems expressing libido however do not have a physical illness but rather are expressing their inner psychological difficulties with sexuality via the outer difficulty of physical expression of that sexuality. Terms such as impotence for men, meaning an inability to have or maintain an erection, and frigidity for women, meaning an inability to enjoy sexual activity, have tended to be replaced by more clinical terms in recent years in an attempt to avoid any sense of social stigma that so often pervades those who cannot feel free to express themselves sexually (*see* **Sexual Arousal Disorders**). In the space of a hundred years we changed from being a society marked by high sexual repression to a society where sexuality is seen as paramount. The people who now come seeking help with sexual difficulties might well have considered themselves normal in Victorian days.

The basis for loving and enjoying another person has to be a love and enjoyment of ourselves. The experimentation of adolescence, both alone in masturbation, and together with other adolescents, allows for an increasing knowledge of what pleases us, both in the physical terms of where and how we enjoy being touched and in the more inward aspect of the sexual fantasies that excite us most. The thrill of 'petting' is often lost by adults in a relationship to the detriment of the sexual enjoyment of both. For those who have already received strong warnings against sexuality during childhood, or who have either witnessed sexual violence or been a part of sexual activity themselves during childhood, the normal explorations of adolescence cannot go ahead and they enter adulthood with their childlike visions of sexuality intact. This usually means that sexuality is seen as dangerous and/or disgusting, although this may paradoxically be experienced alongside a great need for sexual activity. The survivors of childhood sexual abuse often experience guilt at the enjoyment they felt as well as disgust and fear about the nature of the sexual acts forced upon them.

During adolescence girls tend to receive more prohibitive warnings against sexual exploration than boys, despite the fact that their need for experimenting with ways of sexual expression is just as great. They are often made to feel that the expression of sexuality is entirely their responsibility, as if boys cannot be expected to attempt any control over their own libidinal desires. This expectation of female responsibility and guilt, plus fears of pregnancy, make it more difficult for women to grow into healthy sexual expression than it is for men. The fears, condemnations, guilt and responsibility can continue to exert their influence throughout a woman's life, an experience which would almost certainly then distort whatever image of sexuality she gives to her daughters. Alongside this emotional experience of sexuality, she may still be expected to 'perform' regular sexual activity with her husband or boyfriend, as a duty. This is often experienced as further abuse, making it even more unlikely that she will find enjoyment from her own sexuality.

For men there is anticipatory anxiety connected to their sexual 'performance' which can overwhelm their desire. Once they experience themselves as having failed, the anxiety becomes worse, increasing the likelihood of further problems. The strength of libido is often enough to overcome any sense of anxiety, and for most men the problems are relatively short-lived, at least until they reach their 60s or 70s. For a small group of men, however, loss of libido becomes a persistent problem. Sometimes this is associated with a generalised anxiety state or depression. These emotions can however also arise as a consequence of feeling repeatedly sexually inadequate. Reassurance, love and patience are often quoted as being important attributes for the partner to express. Alongside this, however, the man may need to explore his own inner world. If he is attempting to express sexuality with a woman when his main focus of desire is men, he is likely to be repeatedly unsuccessful. Men who experience disgust at women's bodies alongside their desire for them, or who over-idealise women, cannot express themselves until they have come to some understanding of their attitudes.

Our sexuality does not develop in an emotional vacuum but is instead touched by all the other childhood emotional experiences we have. These remain attached to arousal and enjoyment in our minds, causing sexual fantasies of a wide variety. Some people experience difficulty enjoying sex without fantasy, some even need to act the fantasy out in life. This becomes a problem when the fantasy is not shared by the partner, or causes him or her to feel upset or revolted. Sado-masochism is often connected with sexual arousal, with fantasies often having an edge of aggression or implied suffering. Within the bounds of fantasy such experiences may help the individual to 'diffuse' these feelings, leaving him or her feeling more peaceful and less aggressive as a result, however such fantasies are clearly dangerous when acted out, either with or without the consent of the partner. Failure to achieve arousal may be connected with the fact that sado-masochistic thoughts are aroused at the same time as the sexual arousal, and distress and frighten the individual enough to halt the sexual arousal (*see* **Masochism**).

Loss of libido can usually be understood in the context of an individual's development and current situation. Treatments can aim to explore these with the individual (and sometimes his or her partner) so that the problems become more comprehensible. This is often enough to reduce anxiety and distress sufficiently for the problem to evaporate. Other treatment can focus on reteaching sexuality as if reliving the adolescent experience of graduated exploration and discovery. For those who have never truly learned to 'let go' and express themselves via sexuality this is often a great success. For most people the experience of adult sexuality needs to contain a sense of communication with another person, the mechanics of sexuality, however satisfying in the instant, not really felt as the whole experience. In a relationship where violence, mistrust, dislike or even hate are the order of the day it is unlikely that that sense of communication can be established. Therefore 'curing' the relationship is often the most crucial part of helping the sexual relationship to improve.

At the other end of the spectrum, boredom within a relationship can decrease the libido, many people reporting that the thrill of the chase and of seduction is what enhances their sexuality. For these people a long-term committed relationship rapidly decreases their libido. The day-to-day details of living with someone can rapidly dampen libido. Marriage, supposedly meant to contain the sexuality of individuals in a safe context, all too often is experienced as extinguishing it. Sometimes a simple ban on any actual intercourse for a period of time, while sexual exploration and arousal are encouraged, can re-establish the sense of libidinal desire previously missing. This may be the reason why periods of absence or abstinence are said to improve relationships.

For many people the expression of their libidinal energy is not experienced as an important need. Whether this represents an initially low level of libido as a feature of their personality or whether it is the outward sign of massive early repression of their sexuality, these people are usually happiest in relationships that are based more on companionship. A good 'match' of levels of libido between couples could save much unhappiness in relationships. Expressing libido is not, after all, a compulsory adult activity, but always a matter of choice.

## Loneliness
*See* **Isolation**

## Love
Given that falling in love and being in love are important themes

in the lives of many, if not all, people, it is surprising that relatively little about love appears in psychoanalytic or psychiatric writings. Love means different things to each of us. It is not a universally similar experience, but rather a complex sequence of emotions. Most people will describe love in terms that reflect pain as well as happiness. Many try to avoid love, feeling that it is 'too dangerous' or 'too time-consuming'. Others seek out love, hoping that it will cure all that ails them. The questions of what it is and where to find it remain elusive, however.

Freud talked in terms of reaching a 'normal' attitude in love, meaning that the person had successfully negotiated three developmental phases – the oral, anal and sexual – and had resolved the Oedipus conflict, that is, had found a workable solution to the sense of competition with the parent of the same sex. This resolution enabled him or her to combine the earliest feelings of love and affection with sexuality, an important combination to achieve before reaching adolescence, according to Freud, as this is when our sexuality is organised in a way that serves the life instinct and the desire to reproduce. The final combination of affection, sexuality and procreation do epitomise the socially acceptable view of love relationships, but Freud's theory has been criticised on the grounds that it explains social norms and ideals rather than the true experiences of individuals.

Klein looks at the emergence of love in the baby's relationship with his mother. She argues that the baby will love his mother when his needs are satisfied. Alongside the sense of satisfaction there will also be a growing sense of security in the predictability of the mother's presence whenever she is needed, and thus a growing sense of trust in the world and in relationships. Love, therefore, for those who had this good experience of mothering, always has undertones of security and trust. For those whose parenting did not make them feel secure, however, the need for love will always be tinged with insecurity and lack of trust. It is generally agreed in psychoanalysis that it is necessary to have the capacity to love oneself before being able to go one step further and trust in the love of another.

It took work by the British analyst Ian Suttie, author of *The Origins of Love and Hate*, to focus on a more instinctual ability to both give and receive love from the earliest days of our life. Love in these terms is seen as of central importance, the baby reflecting his mother's love but also having his own early inner sense of love. The baby looks to the mother as if her face were a mirror of his own face. If he experiences love in this interaction, that love becomes a part of the baby, and can, in turn, be reflected back to the world. This interaction also inspires the baby with the belief that he is lovable as well as loving.

During further development we begin to understand that the mother who makes us feel loved and loving is the same person as the mother who makes us feel unloved and hateful. This discovery is often referred to as 'the depressive position' in childhood. The depressive position is a developmental phase usually occurring from the age of six months; its length varies but it is the period during which we have to abandon our hopes of a perfect, all-loving relationship in which we will experience the other and ourselves as totally good, and settle instead for the fact that all relationships are two-sided, love and hate, like and dislike, enjoyment and pain, togetherness and separateness (*see* **Aggression**, **Ambivalence**, and **Conflict**). This step in our comprehension of ourselves and others allows us to gain a greater sense of separation and independence from others. It allows us to bear the agony of our loved ones' anger and hate while, at the same time, giving us the freedom to experience these emotions in close relationships without fearing catastrophe. It is a difficult and painful developmental step, thus labelled depressive. However, for those who do not begin the long pathway through this discovery in early childhood, the whole of their lives is bound to be experienced as disillusioning and disappointing.

In adult life we take much of the energy that was invested in our relationships with our parents and re-invest it in loving relationships with our peers and then our own children. Such relationships often start out with the early childhood hope for perfection. We can be extraordinarily blind to the faults of our partners and children for a while, because we 'split off' the bad part just as we split our mothers into good and bad mother in the early days of infancy. Reality soon wins the day, however, and faults become apparent. Those who have already experienced this and survived it during childhood are not as surprised or depressed by this discovery as those who have not managed to resolve this developmental step.

Love and dependence are related. When we first experience loving and being loved, we are still extremely dependent on our mothers. The sense of being held by a trusted person remains important to each of us throughout our lives, especially during times of stress. However as we grow we need to develop a sense of separateness and a lessening in our dependence on others, both physically and emotionally. It is often difficult to negotiate the amount of dependence which is bearable in adult loving relationships and, as times change and different stresses are applied to each partner, the degree of necessary dependence changes. This requires that the negotiation is flexible. In the context of adult love, the notion of mature dependence is helpful in understanding that we all need someone on whom we can feel safe enough to lean at times. That is not a childish or immature need, but understandable and universally experienced as we try to cope with life's difficulties. However we also need to feel strong enough for others to sometimes lean on us, for them to be able to trust our strength and coping abilities, and we need to develop the capacity to be alone without feeling lonely. That capacity to bear separateness alongside an enjoyment of intimacy allows for flexibility within adult love.

The adult experience of love is entwined in social expectations about whom we should love and how and where we should love them. Given that love is fundamental to our development and heavily invested in our views on survival, societies of all sorts have felt the need to regulate the expression of love. One universal form of regulation is marriage. Thus love and marriage go together in our thoughts as well as the words of the old song. Until recently the structure of marriage was rarely questioned. It was the most important building block of society and therefore above question. Love, in order to be safe, needed to be contained. However, the marriage contract attempts to combine emotional, social, sexual, parental and financial commitments all in one deal, and only achieves this by failing to spell out exactly what is involved. Within the contract, emotional love is the energy required, but, as many people discover, there is no contract that can contain this most primitive emotion. The reverse of love is hate; to experience envy of someone you love can be common, because by loving them you place an image of what is good into them; as the relationship becomes less stable, that investment of all that was good can easily become enviable. Many experience an all-consuming greed for the love of their partner, 'the all-or-nothing syndrome'.

The marriage contract attempts to make socially practical use of the energy of love. It allows 'stable' sexual and parental bonding between men and women. Any other form of expressing love is either relegated to second place, for instance the love experienced between friends, or seen as 'abnormal', for instance homosexual love. All societies enforce the primacy of the marriage bond with enormous force, but whom does it benefit? In 1988 Anthony Clare surveyed the practice of marriage around the world for a television series; he concluded that it was for the benefit of men. He was surprised by this finding, explaining that we are told that marriage is designed primarily for the protection of mothers and children.

Perhaps we should not be surprised that the dominant accepted adult relationship benefits the group which has for generations been dominant. As the laws of society change so those who are not socially dominant have a tendency to vote with their feet. Thus the divorce laws of the late 1960s, which allowed women to keep custody of their children after divorce, opened the doors to ever-increasing petitions from women wanting to escape from marriage. Recent figures have suggested that up to 25 per cent of women are choosing to parent alone from the point of conception. Many others choose single parenthood as the better emotional option later in the process. So great is the social need to reinforce the primacy of the family unit that single parents are represented as social failures rather than studied as interesting examples of the growing separation between the experience of adult love and that of marriage, between the emotion and the contract. An embittered male patient who recently lost a custody case reflected to me that 'men love women, women love their children and children love their hamsters!'

Psychologically we may have come to a point of social development that will allow us to separate the various facets of love – the emotional, the sexual, and the reproductive – and begin to find ways of relating which trust these emotions enough to contain them less and accept and appreciate them more. The need to receive and give love is a central and undeniable human desire. It can never be the pure and totally 'happy ever after' experience of romantic fiction, or at least it cannot be like that for very long. But when we acknowledge the confusing mixture that emerges from our development, love can still make the world go round.

# M

## Mania

Individuals in a manic state will get out of bed early, full of energy and *joie de vivre* – quite different to the despair they will wake with when in a depressed state. Throughout the day they will race at tasks, impatient about the slowness of everyone else. For the lucky ones the results will be a productive reflection of their energy, but for most the outcome will reveal the emptiness of their manic enthusiasm, with work done in a haphazard fashion, often causing problems for fellow-workers and relatives.

Jonathan and Pamela moved into a new house, fully fitted and decorated, in 1986. Within three years Jonathan had had two manic attacks lasting several months each during which he had undertaken massive restructuring of their kitchen, bathroom and living area. Despite his enthusiasm about these tasks and his belief that he was increasing the value of their property, the house rapidly began to resemble a bomb site in which it was eventually impossible to live.

During mania individuals may show a superficial jokiness and seem briefly like good company. However the slightest obstacle or disagreement will reveal their irritability and inability to cope. Sometimes the behaviour will seem childlike and 'naughty'. This too can briefly seem enchanting or funny, although it rapidly becomes irritating. Talk may be rapid and difficult to interrupt; dialogue is impossible. Their thoughts may seem to be only loosely connected with each other as one topic gives way to the next, although the individuals believe that they are inspired and that what they say is of the utmost importance.

A certain degree of mania can serve some people well. There are probably a number of successful and famous manic personalities in every era. For most, however, it is a destructive state as a result of which they are likely to lose jobs and relationships, run up debts and destroy their possessions.

In old age the symptoms may be similar, but there is a lack of energy which makes the manic facade an obviously sad state. Analysts have postulated that mania is a defence against depression at all ages, and certainly stressful events which might distress or depress the majority of us are often the precipitant for a manic attack in a susceptible person. This susceptibility may be genetic, that is, the tendency for it may run in families. Alternatively children may 'learn' a manic defence to their problems by watching their parents' behaviour. Children often demonstrate manic states when under any stress, and most parents are familiar with the need to defuse or calm situations before they get out of hand. In adult life many retain the ability to summon humour to protect against depression, which may be the successfully modified version of childhood mania (*see* **Defence Mechanisms** and **Elation**).

The hypomanic personality is often a high-flyer, utilising the flow of energy and ideas to his or her advantage. If these people do fail it is most probably because of their irritability at the slightest foible in others or the least slowdown or setback, or because there is always the possibility that they will sink into profound depression when thwarted (*see* **Irritability**). The vast amount of energy demonstrated by such people may be a form of modified anger, and when creative outlets are lacking the energy reasserts itself as anger and aggression. Such people make taxing partners, needing constant mollifying in order to feel secure and lots of action in life to maintain their interest and enthusiasm. For those who have little or no outlet for their anger and aggression a hypomanic episode may be like a volcanic eruption, releasing all their tension and high emotion in one great burst (*see* **Aggression** and **Anger**).

Mary was a senior teacher who had combined a successful

career with bringing up four children. During her 50s she discovered she did not have the same reserves of energy as before, and this depressed her. The signs of aging seemed to her to be a condemnation of her entire life, as if she would have remained young if she had been as good as she had believed herself to be. Eventually her depression led to early retirement, a position she sought with superficial enthusiasm. The bitterness and resentment about her life, her marriage and her children mounted as her life seemed increasingly empty and meaningless to her. She expressed this in a display of childlike behaviour, demanding attention from the family and reacting with irritation or anger when she gained it. She began to dress in very short skirts and ankle socks, while at the same time getting herself elected to various voluntary committees and behaving in a domineering way once elected. All the energy which had once served her so well now seemed to have gone sour and to be out of her control.

Mary was able to begin to talk about the resentments of the past 20 years, and to put into proportion her achievements and failures. This process meant that her mood swung unpredictably from high to low and back again, but gradually it began to even out. Mary needed to find outlets where her forcefulness could be appreciated, but in order to achieve this her energy had to be back under her control. She gained this equilibrium by attending a psychotherapy group, having dismissed drug therapy. Many others do however benefit from drugs used to calm them down when they are in the extreme state of mania or hypomania and these treatments are discussed in Part Four.

The term manic-depressive describes those who experience sharp mood swings in both directions which seem unrelated to external precipitants. Such personalities are at some risk of developing manic-depressive psychosis under stress; often these are creative people (*see* **Manic Depressive Psychosis**). Some degree of mood swing is not unusual, and many women experience them in connection with their menstrual cycle or with the change of the seasons. Most of us seem to have 'in-built' rhythms of life and are therefore bound to feel more energetic at some times than at others. Within reason such swings may well enrich life, allowing the individual many different emotional perspectives and an inner flexibility. Response to physical illness may well resemble manic-depressive swings, as well as the more familiar depressive reaction particularly after having an infection or surgery. Whether this is a physically based response or a psychological one is often difficult to judge, and as the mind and body are so closely interlinked as to act as one it is probably a false dichotomy. Many people wish to be reassured that their mood swings are physical, however, feeling that if they are 'only' psychological they will not be taken as seriously.

## Manic-Depressive Psychosis

This is primarily a disorder of the feelings in which the person's mood is subject to wild swings from mania to depression, without the presence of obvious external precipitants great enough to warrant the severity of the swings. For some people one state or the other is their most usual response to stress, its mirror-image state only rarely triggered, while for others their lives resemble an emotional switchback railway with little equilibrium between swings. This is a serious and disabling problem because it renders living an organised life, following a career, or pursuing relationships or goals impossible.

The depression is often severe, with pronounced physical symptoms such as difficulty sleeping and eating, as well as an overwhelming sense of hopelessness. Suicide is an ever-present possibility when life appears to be this black (*see* **Suicide**). These feelings may persist for months and be resistant to any form of treatment. Mania is a rarer manifestation of distress and often occurs in more circumscribed episodes in which the person wears him- or herself out, but does a lot of damage to the economic or social aspects of life in the process: this means that the following depression is well-founded in the ruins of his or her life. Both the depression and the mania have a rather infectious quality about them, although because the mania is a defence against the depression it is also brittle and can degenerate into anger and hostility in the face of any confrontation. When manic the person's speech may be rapid and exuberant and the person may flit from idea to idea with only the loosest of connections. Physical activity may be excessive, leading to exhaustion and dehydration. Relatives often also look exhausted by the time the person seeks help.

In recent years the drug lithium has been used as a mood stabiliser and has afforded some relief to those most likely to experience profound mood changes. Psychotherapy and analysis can sometimes help the more motivated patient who is curious to understand him- or herself. The extreme mood swings resemble the normal state of infants, who go from tears to laughter, from happiness to fury in the blink of an eye. Such lability usually disappears from the child's emotional repertoire as a response to the overall control required by socialisation and particularly entry to school. There seems to be an inherited difficulty in establishing this emotional control in childhood, although environmental factors in the child's upbringing connected to the establishing of personal boundaries on behaviour and feelings also play their part in producing these troubled adults.

## Masochism
*See* **Sado-Masochism**

## Mastery, Instinct for
*See* **Instinct for Mastery**

## Melancholy
The term *melancholia* is of historical interest, having been used

since the time of the ancient Greeks to cover a wide range of depressive illnesses. The Greeks believed melancholy was the result of an excess of black bile. For some people with a chronic unrelievable depression the term still seems appropriate, conveying as it does some of the hopelessness of the illness.

There are a small group of people, usually women, for whom mid-life becomes an insurmountable problem, often because of a combination of cruel external events and an inner inability to change enough to accommodate new ideas on life and one's purpose in it. These people often appear to be sinking into their unhappiness, remaining submerged for some years (psychiatrists used to teach that two years was the average) and sometimes for ever. Their helpers and carers often also become despondent about change or improvement, and the patients' lives are often unenviable or unattractive and therefore do not encourage recovery or hold out any hopes of rewarding lifestyles to be had in the event of recovery.

Erik Erikson describes the final developmental stage of adult life as the despair/integrity phase. For those who have succeeded in meeting the challenges of life to their own satisfaction and who become increasingly comfortable with themselves as time goes on, death becomes less fearful, almost a welcome end to a life well done. This represents the final integration of many aspects of the self into a whole. For those who have failed themselves, however, aging can produce despair instead, often associated with a morbid fear of death and a preoccupation with all things unhappy. Such people often slide into a melancholic state as they age. This makes them unattractive company and so social isolation and loneliness add to their problems and their bitterness (*see* **Isolation**).

# Memory Problems
*See* **Amnesia**

# Mourning
*See* **Grief**

# Munchausen's Syndrome

People with this syndrome, named after the Baron famous for his tall tales, travel around the country presenting themselves to hospital casualty departments with complex stories of ill health that appear to warrant surgical intervention. Frequently their stomachs are criss-crossed with scars from previous operations. They tend to have no permanent relationships and to invent entire life stories for themselves which staff only become suspicious about after a while. This reflects their ability to concoct and relate believable, although usually rather over-exciting pasts for themselves. Once caught out they move on to the next health district and start again.

To a lesser extent many people use fictitious illnesses to gain love, care or power in relationships (*see* **Flight into Illness**, **Helplessness**, and **Hypochondriasis**). When taken to extremes individuals can fake many signs and symptoms, making differential diagnosis difficult.

Mary was a 23-year-old student nurse who complained to the staff doctor of blood in her urine. A lengthy series of investigations proved nothing, but there was undoubtedly blood in the urine samples she provided. A nursing friend became suspicious when she saw that Mary often had pinpricks in her fingertips. When confronted Mary denied that she had fabricated her symptom, but the blood in her urine stopped thereafter.

More seriously, some people resort to injecting themselves with drugs or toxins to produce symptoms and can make themselves very ill in their pursuit of attention.

# Murder

Murder is the intentional killing of another human being. It occurs most commonly within families as a result of intense emotional strife, often connected to some form of disinhibition, either through drug or alcohol abuse or some form of mental disorder which alters the person's understanding of life. The availability of a suitable weapon also influences the consequence of emotional tension between spouses, or between parents and children: thus in the USA, where the constitution allows for each person to carry a gun by right, murder is much more frequent than in the UK where such weapons are strictly (although not always successfully) controlled.

People who are prone to violent reactions when frustrated or angry and those who experience envy or jealousy, particularly in the context of sexual relationships, are more likely to commit murder; and men are at least six times as likely to kill as women. The carefully planned murder of the detective novel and the murder of strangers are equally rare, and the police look immediately to the close family in the majority of murder cases. Occasionally people with serious mental illness, in which they are deluded about the intentions of another, or those who hallucinate voices telling them to kill, do commit murder, however the notion that people with mental illness are usually more dangerous than the rest of us is statistically untrue.

Parents who murder children tend to fall into one of two groups. In the first group the parent, often the father, is uncontrolled in his expression of anger; he may also abuse drugs and/or alcohol. In a phase during which his tolerance to frustration is lowered a baby or child's behaviour may be enough to trigger rage leading to violence; this is seldom a deliberate attempt at murder, but the child, being physically fragile, is always at great risk of death in such outbursts. The parent may be immature and seek to blame the 'bad' baby who frustrated him rather than acknowledge his own blame. This is very different to the parents who fear that they may kill their children when tired and enraged in the middle of the night, and who suffer terrible pangs of guilt for even having the thought.

In the second group, more often the mother, there is some

pre-formed intention, which may not always be entirely conscious, to kill the child, often in order to attract attention to her own despair or neediness. Such mothers have unusual personalities and have often suffered severe emotional, physical or sexual abuse themselves and see their babies as extensions of themselves rather than as separate beings.

People who are severely depressed may decide that life is so bad that alongside plans for suicide they will 'rescue' those they love from life by killing them.

Most people experience an urge to kill at some point in their lives. In situations of social chaos this urge may become more generalised and random, whereas organised societies tend to focus such an urge on our nearest and dearest. There is a great difference between the thought and the deed, the fantasy and the intention, however, and this is reflected in the fact that despite much relationship strife, apparent from divorce statistics, for instance, the incidence of murder is not high. Most normal people cannot suspend their underlying inhibitions against murder simply to express rage or act for gain, and are only capable of killing if they or their loved ones are seriously threatened (*see* **Alcoholism**, **Depression**, **Envy** and **Jealousy**).

## Mutism

Occasionally people with schizophrenia are totally silent as part of an overall picture of immobility (*see* **Schizophrenia**). A child may elect not to speak as a signal of extreme distress, usually in response to a loss such as the death of a parent or a threatened or actual separation, for example when hospital treatment of the child is necessary.

Claire was hospitalised for an operation on her ears when she was five, just after the birth of a brother. The presence of the new baby made visiting more difficult for her mother, and her father was in the Merchant Navy and therefore absent. Nursing staff noticed that Claire had become 'quiet' on her third day in hospital but only concluded that she was mute five days later.

By that time she was not speaking to her mother, who became distraught and rapidly angry with her for 'messing around'. Claire seemed 'cut off' from her mother's outbursts, as if indifferent to her surroundings. Gentle persistence at communication was eventually rewarded by Claire nodding or shaking her head: Yes, she was upset; no, she could not talk about it; no, she did not know why she was upset; yes, she thought it might have something to do with being lonely; and so on, until two weeks later she recovered her voice in a flood of tears.

# N

## Narcissism

The myth of Narcissus is described in Ovid's work *Metamorphosis*. A young man who spurns with contempt those who love him falls in love with his own reflection in a pond as a punishment from the goddess of divine retribution for his treatment of others. It describes the emptiness and eventual tragedy of self-love to the exclusion of all others. Narcissus can never grasp his own reflection and eventually kills himself.

The theme of narcissistic self-love was taken up by analysts in the first decade of the 20th century to describe the perversion of considering one's own self a sex object. It was also seen as a developmental stage of establishing self-esteem, characterised by a greater investment in the self than in any other object or person. Freud pointed out that each of us starts with two sexual objects, our mothers and ourselves. We have a finite amount of libidinal or sexual energy which has to be invested in either self or others, and the more energy we invest in one, the less we have available for the other. During development our initial investment in the self is gradually transformed until we have an inner sense of an ideal we can strive towards; the closer we get to that ideal the more our self-esteem is enhanced.

Melanie Klein felt that relationships are always central to our psychological development, and that it is in our omnipotent fantasies about our roles in relationships as children that we most actively portray our basic narcissism. The stage of childhood when we still believe the world revolves around us demonstrates this narcissism most clearly.

Analysts such as John Bowlby have suggested that we use the

omnipotence in our narcissistic selves to proceed with the battle between dependency on our parents on the one hand and our desire to be separate and 'free' on the other.

What is clear from all these theories, in common with all the steps in our psychological development, is that when things go well and we develop without traumatic interruption our primary sense of narcissism can be transformed into a part of our adult selves which is healthy in that it allows us to be people who like and respect ourselves and others. When interrupted the person gets 'stuck' at a particular stage of development so that narcissism is still expressed in a non-transformed way even as an adult, causing that person and all around him or her much pain, frustration and non-fulfilment. The baby needs her narcissism, the child her omnipotence, but during development there has to be enough gradually increasing frustration and contact with life's realities so that the adult will have moved on to be able to be loving and creative in her life. Most analysts agree that it is during the second part of a child's second year when a major step is made in transforming primary narcissism into a more adult state. Difficulties or traumas at that time mean that the eventual adult retains narcissism in an unhealthy way (*see* **Fixation**).

Andrea, a 25-year-old who had started medical training, found her course particularly difficult because it required her to work closely and co-operatively with a small group of fellow-students. She rapidly experienced herself as the only 'worthwhile' student in the group, seeing the others as 'frivolous' or 'sex-mad' or 'stupid'. The group refused to collude with Andrea's image of herself and were hostile and condemning of her manner and her lack of interest in their feelings.

At her second assessment her tutor tried to speak to her about these difficulties. Andrea could only return to her basic position of it being everyone else's fault: 'If only the group were better students . . . If only the tutors knew what they were doing . . . If only you [her tutor] could be sensible enough to see what was really happening . . .' When the tutor pointed out that Andrea's work was only of low-to-average standard she became angry with the marking system. Andrea left medical school at the end of her first year and spent 18 months living in a therapeutic community. This intense experience allowed her some insight into the way her belief system and behaviour affected others, and she went on to complete a university course in biology without too much difficulty.

Nigel was an executive for a large computer firm, and at 35 seemed to have everything in life: a good job, nice home, a wife and three children. His wife however felt listless and depressed, especially in his company, and this led to endless arguments. When they came for marital therapy Nigel's high-handed manner immediately annoyed both therapists as he explained to them that he was a professional in an important job while they, the therapists, were mere amateurs who probably did not know very much about marriage. His wife, Suzy, seemed embarrassed by this but commented that it was Nigel's usual style. In the three meetings that followed it became clear that Nigel believed himself to be exceptionally good at and right about everything and viewed any challenge with anger. On the whole Suzy remained quiet, sometimes seeming depressed and withdrawn. Eventually she left him; in the year that followed Nigel lost his job because he had treated his colleagues in the same way as he had treated his wife and the therapists. Finally he came for long-term therapy, his view of self-perfection initially, at least, still undented by his life experience.

Those who remain narcissistic into adulthood demonstrate a remarkable ability to project psychologically all that is bad or unpleasant in themselves onto others. They only recognise badness when they perceive it in others, retaining therefore a perfect sense of themselves. It is both this splitting of the good and bad and this projection that allowed Narcissus to treat those who loved him with contempt and himself with adoration. Narcissism is a defence against ever experiencing envy consciously, since the self is always perceived as more perfect than any other. The experience of envy is thus completely unconscious, but no less destructive. Indeed it may be even more damaging than normal, because the narcissistic individual will deny envy or responsibility for its consequences as well as feeling no need to make amends (*see* **Envy**).

Narcissistic people need to maintain at least an illusion of complete control over their environment as if they were still the omnipotent baby who thinks that the mother is part of him- or herself. In this way narcissistic adults are vulnerable because the reality of life constantly threatens to remind them that they are not the centre of the universe. They have to use considerable denial against that reality in order to maintain their sense of self (*see* **Delusions** and **Denial**). Their greatest fear is of experiencing dependency on anyone, because in order to depend on someone you have to recognise that they have something good to offer which you do not possess. This experience leads to hate and envy and the possibility of betrayal, loss and depression, all of which narcissistic people try to avoid at all costs. Thus they cannot risk relating to anyone closely, and their emotional life is shallow with no truly empathic understanding of the feelings of others. Only those who can be seen as extensions of the self can hold any true worth for such people.

Psychotherapy can help individuals to retrace their developmental footsteps back to the age at which they became 'stuck'. Just allowing an eventual sense of dependency on the therapist, something which fills them with fear and rage initially, may allow narcissists the opportunity for new psychological growth towards an adult form of love of self and others. However this is a painful path which is not open to many and thus, as in the myth, narcissistic people have a tendency to fade in life, their shallowness exposed and their increasing inability to cope with personal realities such as aging and finally death leaving them alone in their world of omnipotent fantasy.

# Need for Punishment
*See* **Punishment**


# Nervous Breakdown
*See* **Emotional Breakdown**


# Neurasthenia

This term was used in the latter half of the 19th century to describe a form of emotional fatigue to which certain personalities appeared to be more susceptible than others. It was said that those of an anxious or obsessional disposition were particularly likely to experience this sense of profound emotional exhaustion. Some famous sufferers took to their beds for years at a time. It may be that this was what we now think of as a post-viral illness.

Personality and constitution do seem to play roles in determining our recovery from both physical and psychological threats and insults to the body. People also vary enormously in how careful and kind they are willing to be to their feelings and physical well-being. Some of these responses are probably learned in childhood but much is probably rooted in our basic characters. (*See also* **Anxiety** and **Obsessive Compulsive Illness**.)


# Neurosis

To be called neurotic carries with it connotations of being silly, attention seeking, and 'not really' unwell. 'I feel neurotic today,' is used in the colloquial sense to mean feeling a bit on edge or stressed. There is also a commonly expressed expectation that those who are 'just' neurotic have only to 'pull themselves together' in order to feel better. This attitude is tantamount to saying to someone with a broken bone, 'Stop moaning about the pain; just think positively!' In psychiatric or psychoanalytic terminology, however, the term neurosis is an important diagnostic category into which all that is not psychotic (psychotic meaning that there are symptoms such as hallucinations, delusions, disorders of thought and a lack of insight into the problem), psychosomatic (emotional distress presented in physical terms) or a perversion (abnormal focus of sexuality) is collected. Thus the neurosis category includes depression, anxiety, panic states, phobias, obsessions, mania, eating disorders, hysterical reactions and a variety of reactive disorders such as post-traumatic stress disorder, compensation and war neurosis. To be neurotic in psychiatric or analytical terminology is to be truly unwell.

Psychiatrists generally think that individuals have a genetic susceptibility for a certain form of neurosis. Like much of what we inherit this genetic susceptibility provides strengths and weaknesses to our character and physique rather than an absolute certainty about which illnesses we will or will not suffer. Our genetic inheritance provides a basic template upon which our lifetime's experience is written.

Some stress factors are so great that it is to be expected that everyone would be affected by them, others so slight that only the most vulnerable to stress or to that particular form of stress will respond with a neurotic illness. Thus there are few reports of personalities which have survived concentration camps undamaged, the level of stress being so high, but lower down the scale, for instance after a large earthquake, a small but significant proportion of the population would be psychologically undamaged. In a war zone the Armed Services expect a rate of approximately 10 per cent of trained men to become neurotically ill, many of whom recover rapidly when removed from immediate danger. Within the range of normal experiences, death of a loved one, divorce and moving house are all high on the list of events likely to cause neurotic illness. Further down the scale, taking out a large mortgage or loan, the birth of a child and a variety of accidents may precipitate distress in some people. For very vulnerable people events which seem small to others, such as a minor disagreement with a friend, will cause enough stress to result in illness.

For each of us, because of previous experience, there are particular 'trigger' stresses which other people would not rate as important. Thus the old woman who did not grieve her husband's death may be especially vulnerable to a grief reaction if her cat dies. Certain times of the year can become 'triggers', as anniversaries of sad events are remembered. This is particularly true for loss events and deaths. Often the most poignant are those anniversaries of miscarriages, abortions or still births when perhaps only the mother is aware of the fact that there is an anniversary to be remembered at all.

Analytical theory looks at the origins of neurosis somewhat differently, believing them based in either sexual frustration or in the psychological conflict between a desired (but forbidden) wish and the defence against its fulfilment. Such theories are based on the notion that our unconscious mind has desires (instincts and drives) which we are taught at an early age to repress and control because they are bad and unacceptable. The internal policeman, the super-ego, controls such feelings and fantasies but can never abolish them. Thus the drive is in perpetual conflict with the prohibition, a state which leaves the individual vulnerable.

In order to develop a super-ego we have to be conditionable in early childhood so that we learn family and social rules in such a way that they become part of us. It may be that the genetic susceptibility makes some individuals more or less sensitive to specific forms of conditioning. The adults in a child's world also provide her with potent models of how to express distress or satisfaction. Illness models are probably just as easy to learn as more healthy models.

A wide range of treatments for neurosis are available and, for the most part, effective, although given the stigma of admitting to these problems, many choose to struggle on alone and unhelped for months or even years. (*See also* **Anxiety, Conflict,**

Depression, Eating Disorders, Grief, Guilt, Hysteria, Idealisation, Mania, Obsessive Compulsive Illness, Panic Attacks, Phobias, and Post-traumatic Stress Disorder.)

# Nightmares
*See* **Dreams**

# Night Terrors
*See* **Insomnia**

# O

## Obsessive Compulsive Illness

The obsessions and rituals of this form of disorder can sometimes be confused with delusions (*see* **Delusions**), so extreme is the patients' need to act out their fears of contagion, dirtyness, lateness or sloppiness. However, unlike those who experience delusions, those exhibiting obsessive compulsive behaviour are able to say that they know that their intrusive thoughts, images and ruminations are 'silly', and to wish that they did not feel compelled to act out on them, often ruining their quality of life in the process.

Obsessive rituals are often incorporated into cleaning programmes or work tasks, because the person fears that without the aid of these rituals he or she will not carry the tasks out properly, and may thus contaminate others.

Usually, early in the illness the person has made attempts to resist the thoughts, knowing them to be a product of 'illness' in his or her own mind rather than some wisdom bestowed from outside, as people normally believe when they are thought-disordered.

The compulsions and their associated ritualised behaviour provide no pleasure for the sufferer. Unlike people who are phobic, whose fears usually centre on a single object or situation, those with obsessional symptoms tend to have more generalised anxiety, and often fear their own rituals more than they fear the dirt, etc. they are trying to rid themselves of.

Often associated with depression, and sometimes with schizophrenia, this disorder tends to follow a chronic course because it is difficult to treat. During a lifetime about 2½ per cent of the population experience these distressing symptoms, with peak 'first episodes' occuring during adolescence and when the patients are in their 20s.

Patients are commonly offered treatment that includes antidepressant or anxiolytic (anti-anxiety) drugs, thought to counteract possible genetic chemical changes in the brain, and also behavioural psychotherapy to work on the learned behaviour involved in the obsessions and rituals. Despite being obviously distressing and damaging to the patients's life, the symptoms seem to be difficult for him or her to relinquish, which would suggest that they confer on the individual some intra-psychic gain. Given the findings of research, which suggest that dynamic psychotherapy does little to change the obsessions, it rarely seems appropriate to offer it to such patients – yet, when working with those who have persuaded me that it is the approach they wish to use, I have been struck by the levels of aggression they can express to family and carers in the form of their symptoms. Equally, among the few I have worked with, there is often a precipitant to the anger they wish to express, albeit disguised and displaced. This anger most usually is about abuse which they have suffered, abuse which they felt powerless to react to when it occurred.

## Oedipus Complex

Had he been around thousands of centuries earlier, Freud would have said that when the Delphic oracle predicted that the baby Oedipus would grow up to murder his father and marry his mother she was merely predicting the great conflict in the lives of all small boys. In the Greek tragedy Oedipus is thrown out of the house at an early age as a result of this prophecy and thus does not recognise his father when he murders him or his mother when he marries her. Hopefully the majority of boys, by staying with both father and mother, have a much better chance of resolving the conflict less dramatically.

As Freud was a man of his times, his explanation of the

conflict experienced by children in their sexual (which he termed *phallic*) stage of development revolves around the male conflict and the male central figure of Oedipus, the little boy, the man-child. Freud says little about Oedipus' mother, Jocasta, although within the story there is some evidence that she does recognise her son at some stage but continues their sexual relationship despite this. By allowing Jocasta silent innocence Freud was reflecting society's image, now as then, of the nurturing good mother, the mother for whom giving birth, (particularly of a son) replaces the experience of loss and inferiority which starts when she discovers that she has no penis. Freud's theory allows for no mention of mothers as sexual beings and most particularly sexual beings towards their sons. This use of the myth has meant that we think of 3- to 5-year-old boys as going through their Oedipus conflict, but, as the analyst and writer Christianne Olivier points out, we never think of women with small sons as going through their Jocasta phase.

Freud did however look upon the Oedipus Complex as having both positive and negative aspects, and the complete form of the complex as being an intricate interweaving of the two. In his theory the positive aspect takes the form of the parent of the opposite sex being loved and the parent of the same sex being the hated rival. The reverse holds true for the negative aspect of the complex, with the parent of the same sex loved while that of the opposite sex is hated. During adolescence the conflict is again aroused and brought to some sort of resolution by the young person choosing (consciously or unconsciously) the object of their passion. Freud talks of the 'primacy of the phallus' in this stage of development, feeling that the boy's personality is organised around his phallic understanding of himself. Thus the importance of the 'how big is my penis as compared to everyone else's?' rivalry so common in boys as they grow.

If boys are to develop to normal manhood, Freud believed that they have to abolish the complex. They do so because their desire for their mother produces in them a fear that father will castrate them as rivals (*see* **Castration Complex**). The centrality of their phallus is by now so great that it apparently becomes reasonable to relinquish the loved mother in order to retain their manhood. Karen Horney suggests that little boys are also unconsciously aware that their infantile penis is too small to satisfy mother and therefore relinquish their hopes of seducing her in order to avoid humiliation. Relinquishing his mother allows the boy to move into a closer identification with his father, which in turn will allow the boy to turn towards sexual relationships with women without fear of castration. Clearly for men who do not resolve the complex and who continue to associate sexual desire with fear of castration women become objects arousing fear as well as excitement. Men are not 'castrated' by women, therefore, but by their inability to resolve satisfactorily the Oedipus Complex.

In Freudian terms normal psychological development in men would seem to suggest that their healthy adult sexuality with women always carries with it a need for identification with the potent father, which we can easily generalise to identification (rather than competition) with all men. Watching adolescent boys swap stories of sexual conquests it is easy to believe that this activity's function is to join them more firmly to the men's group rather than having much to do with relating to women. Freud's theory also leaves men at a phallic-centred stage of development, and many men do have so much anxiety about the phallus that sexual activity becomes a relationship between a man and his penis rather than a man and his partner. Perhaps such limits to development were normal for men of Freud's generation, but they constitute something of a problem for relationships in the 1990s.

Freud did describe an Oedipus Complex of sorts for girls, although he expressed doubts about its validity (*see* **Electra Complex**). He saw this complex as commencing with the little girl's discovery that she lacks a penis, and is therefore already castrated. In her search for a replacement Freud felt that the girl comes to a penis = baby solution. Her flirtation with and love for her father can thus be seen as a desire to have the father's baby rather than to seduce him, and by this solution the daughter is rendered just as asexual as the mother in Freud's treatment of Jocasta.

## Orientation, Difficulties with
*See* **Disorientation**

## Othello Syndrome

Named after the Shakespearean character tricked into believing that his wife Desdemona was unfaithful, this is a form of delusional jealousy (*see* **Jealousy**). No amount of reassurance or proof will dispel the delusion once it is firmly rooted in the person's mind, and his or her behaviour may become erratic and bizarre in the hunt for 'proof' that his or her suspicions are justified.

Such people are often suspicious by nature and may be hypersensitive to any form of criticism, rejection or slight. They tend to be socially isolated, to focus on one central relationship, and to have an inability to understand or believe the views and feelings of others. Freud argued that such people are projecting their own hostility and lack of trustworthiness into important others around them. Certainly these people (usually men) often appear insensitive and arrogant on first acquaintance but are insecure and unhappy inside. Sadly the arrogant external self often leads to people rejecting them, thus confirming their deepest fears about themselves (*see* **Anger**, **Isolation**, and **Oversensitivity**).

Desmond married at the age of 45, having known his fiancée, Marion, for only three weeks. At first Marion welcomed his total dedication, but as the weeks went by his inability to leave her alone even for a moment became apparent and she became restless and desperate to get away for some hours of relief each day. Desmond interpreted this as Marion going to visit a lover, and took to following her and searching her belongings for clues.

This behaviour exasperated Marion further, and she became more secretive about her 'escapes' which in turn fed Desmond's belief that something was going on behind his back. They had many arguments, with Marion protesting her innocence and Desmond attempting to force confessions from her. One night their arguing escalated to the point where Desmond attempted to strangle her.

This syndrome makes people potentially dangerous and likely to act on the basis of their delusional beliefs rather than reality. Most clinicians advise wives of such husbands to leave them, at least during the acute phase of the problem, in order to avoid the possibility of murder or suicide (*see* **Delusions**, **Idealisation**, and **Murder**).

## Overactivity

Many people experience a heightened sense of the need to be active when they are stressed. This is a sensible defence in many cases, as it brings forth the extra energy needed to overcome whatever is stressful. If the stress cannot, at least for the moment, be overcome, then exercise or other outlets for the need for activity reduce the inner stress which can otherwise build up in the face of frustration (*see* **Frustration** and **Stress**).

Amanda, an artist in her late 20s, can only work on new material when her next exhibition is but weeks away. When suitably stressed in this way she has no difficulty working 20 hours a day in order to meet her deadline. This level of activity is very different to her preferred rather sleepy existence which she leads between shows. Many students report similar surges of activity when stressed about forthcoming exams. The activity often extends beyond just studying into all other areas of their lives. I discovered an addiction to housework which I had never felt before, or since, just before my first set of medical exams.

However, like all of our available defence systems, becoming active can go further than is helpful or proportional to the initial stress. After illness some people demonstrate over-enthusiasm about returning to the arduous aspects of their lives, attacking work and play with a rather euphoric approach. This is usually short-lived as their confidence in their health returns. For those who have been given a more long-term prognosis and do not completely return to health however, such as those with multiple sclerosis or diabetes, the euphoria and overactivity can last longer. It is often obvious that this is a defence against the anxiety and depression that they would otherwise experience, and as long as the overactivity is not immediately harmful to their health it remains a workable defence which often allows them to feel better.

When the overactivity occurs in a manic state, the individual usually feels wonderful, both physically and emotionally, and is convinced that his or her hard work is paying great dividends. Occasionally this is true, and some of the most successful people have at least a tendency to be manic. Sadly, and more usually, the overactivity of the manic person merely keeps them going round in circles, often producing work for others who must then clear up the various messes produced (*see* **Mania**).

Charles, a 28-year-old chemistry student, has been working on his Ph.D. for 5 years. During this time he has frequently bombarded the librarian with book lists that are books in themselves, all of which he then claims to have read and understood within days. His tutor often feels exhausted when he tries to help Charles organise his work – Charles' ideas flowing so thick and fast, and Charles being so over-optimistic about their validity, that the tutor feels as if he is attempting to hold back a tidal wave. If by a lucky break Charles can organise one of his great ideas into a workable hypothesis one day he may still get his Ph.D.; it seems more likely, however, that whatever help is offered his overactivity will prove uncontainable, and that it may take recognition of his own failure to finally make Charles realise how distressed he is and how much in need of help.

Some of the addictive drugs, such as amphetamines, have a tendency to make people active. Our thyroid gland, located in the neck, produces a hormone called *thyroxine*, which controls our levels of activity to some extent. Disturbances in the levels of thyroxine can produce dramatic changes in our level of activity. People suffering this brand of overactivity are usually easily distracted, so that they move rapidly from one task to the next, without fulfilling any particular function. Clearly it may be difficult to distinguish this problem from that of a person who is manic or anxious, although in practice those with raised thyroxine levels usually develop additional symptoms such as an inability to tolerate heat and an increased appetite accompanied by weight loss.

## Over-sensitivity

People often accuse others of over-sensitivity. Friends and spouses may make the accusation when someone reacts with anger or sadness to their behaviour. It is far easier to believe that someone is being over-sensitive than that you are being insensitive!

Our understanding of what is over-sensitive stems from what we learn from childhood interpersonal relationships. Different families set different standards of what is or is not sensitive. Thus if the mother of the family is depressed the children may learn that they have to be very sensitive to her feelings. This may lead them to be over-sensitive to the feelings of others throughout life, and rather insensitive to their own. If they have become over-sensitised to their mother's feelings early on in life they will preserve an empathic ability to understand the feelings of others, often to the detriment of their own. We can be so tuned in to others that we cannot hear ourselves, just as extremely loud music can seem to drown out even our own thoughts. If the mother has not been depressed, but instead able to make her own needs understood within the family, the children may grow up with some impression of others' sensitivities without having to ignore their own feelings in the process. In this way family episodes build up our ideas of sensitivity, both our own and that of others.

Notions of sensitivity are not just ideas we absorb, however;

they actually set the tone for the response of our nervous system in future life. If our survival as infants depended on our being ultra-sensitive to our environment, then we will remain highly tuned as adults even if all threat has been removed. Most adults retain some ability to become more sensitive under threat: just as our hearing becomes more acute as we strain to hear again the noise that has frightened us in the night, so too do our emotional sensitivities become heightened when we suspect they are under threat. And just as our skin is more sensitive where it has already been bruised, so our emotions are more sensitive if an event touches a point left 'raw' by our previous experience.

For those who experience a hyper-sensitivity throughout life there is an accompanying sense of fatigue and disinterest. Such people have a greater than average tendency to give up activities, even successful and enjoyable ones, because they tire easily. They tend to end up living alone as the effort required to remain in a relationship is too great for them.

It is sometimes difficult to judge where normal sensitivity ends and over-sensitivity begins, and particularly so in the case of an individual's response to disaster of some kind. On the whole, humans seem to have extraordinary powers of recovery even in the face of great chaos and death, and within a normal grieving process of two or three years' time show a remarkable ability to rebuild even shattered lives (*see* **Grief**).

It would seem as if a number of factors affect our sensitivity to any given event. The size and type of event clearly make a difference. It is often the individual's behaviour, however, which seems most important (*see* **Accident Neurosis**, **Post-traumatic Stress Disorder** and **Trauma**). During the initial grieving process, made up of grief for the self, suddenly experienced as terrifyingly vulnerable, for others, who may have been lost, and for the general sense of security that is shattered by tragedy, there is a generalised over-sensitivity to all other events and traumas. This decreases as time passes, becoming re-activated on anniversaries of the event and whenever reminders of the original trauma occur. Generally, after a period of some three

or four years, the affected person has regained a sense of him-
or herself which may be stronger and more capable than prior
to the disaster. However, for a small minority the incident will
have been like a key turning in the door of their memories,
opening their minds to previous frightening traumas. For such
people the sense of vulnerability remains for longer, and their
over-sensitivity never really lessens.

## Over-valued Ideas

During our childhood we gather together pieces of information
about ourselves, our parents and families, school, friends, and
the world in general, and we weave these bits of information into
some sort of unified whole. This weaving process is made more
complex because the pieces of information often conflict or
contradict one other, and we therefore have to choose (both
consciously and unconsciously) which we adopt as 'fact' and
which we dismiss as 'unlikely' or 'untrue'. As there are very few
absolute truths in life this on-going process operates to build us
a working model, unique for each individual, that allows us
psychological survival in an uncertain and frightening world. As
we grow older events will occur that challenge our model of life,
and we will, to some extent, allow ourselves to be further
moulded by these events. We express this working model to
ourselves in terms of ideas about ourselves, other people, and
events.

Within the model some of the ideas will seem more important
than others, more right, more truthful, more certain and less
questionable. We will have adopted these ideas at times of stress,
trauma or challenge as a way of surviving psychologically, and
any future threat to those ideas resurrects the anxiety we felt at
the time of the original situation. We will therefore defend those
ideas against any change even if we allow ourselves secretly to
doubt them from time to time.

When Graham was 2 years old he had felt abandoned by his
mother, who had to go to hospital for several weeks to have her

second child, Graham's sister Lisa. Graham became an unusually independent child, resenting help when it was offered and ungrateful for anything, whether material or emotional, that was given to him. He strongly resisted all things which he thought of as female, and by the age of 11 had developed a passionate interest in science and maths, and was determination to succeed and never depend on anyone. During adolescence it also became apparent that he was unaware of the feelings of those around him, an aspect of himself which he considered a strength. He came to the attention of a child psychiatrist after he was caught stealing sweets.

During the family session which followed it became obvious that Graham believed that it was all right for him to take anything he wanted as long as he did it in an underhand way. He could not ask for the love he craved as this would mean acknowledging his dependent needs. His ideas on independence, adopted as a defence to anxiety when he was 2, were so over-valued that acknowledging dependence felt like betraying himself. However, having been caught in the act of stealing he had to rethink his ideas and acknowledge some needs more openly. Despite that need to rethink, however, he reappeared for marital therapy 10 years later. His wife's opening words were: 'I feel as if Graham steals love from me in an underhand way and never acknowledges what I give him.' It was clear that he still over-valued his myth of independence.

Other over-valued ideas can stem from commonly acknowledged myth or even old sayings. The notion, for instance, that 'cleanliness is next to godliness' seems to fire many people into over-valuing the goodness of a spotlessly clean home. Many over-valued ideas represent cultural assumptions. In some cultures greed is seen as particularly bad, while in others it is admired. Some cultures think that love and forgiveness are central, while others may find this a daft belief, preferring instead their own notion that avoiding envy is the most important human goal to which we can aspire. These belief systems have a great impact on our developing minds, and often the clashes between cultures are really clashes between each one's over-valued ideas (*see* **Censorship**).

Within psychiatry over-valued ideas fall somewhere between obsessional symptoms – that is, the need to perform actions or thoughts repeatedly even though you know they are stupid, bizarre, or unnecessary (*see* **Compromising** and **Obsessive Compulsive Illness**) – and delusions, where any knowledge or insight into one's thoughts or actions is lost, and the delusions take on an absolute truth for the individual (*see* **Delusions** and **Insight**). For the majority of us our over-valued ideas only become a problem when they are challenged. We can live happily in equilibrium, only occasionally doubting ourselves, until an outer confrontation makes us anxious. The therapist's task is to make the environment and relationship with the patient secure enough to enable questioning of the over-valued ideas without arousing unbearable anxiety, thus allowing new ideas about the self and life to flourish.

Anna was 34 when she started therapy. Her marriage had failed and she was feeling unlovable, a feeling that was familiar to her from an unhappy childhood. Initially she accepted that she was unlovable unquestioningly. She 'knew' she was unlovable and so, presumably, did everyone else. Thus she talked about this basic unlovableness as fact, regrettable but unalterable. This idea about herself, reinforced by her divorce, led her to believe that her life was worthless. During the course of therapy this idea was challenged by the therapist in two ways. First openly, with the therapist asking outright whether there was any evidence of the opposite truth, that people did love Anna? Her life was rich with friends and colleagues who valued her, yet she had not previously noticed their regard. Second, the therapist demonstrated that she herself considered Anna worthwhile, by making sure she always made time for Anna and never missed one of their sessions. Initially it caused Anna some considerable pain and anxiety to question her over-valued idea of her own worthlessness, but gradually she was able to reassess the idea and modify it.

# P

## Paedophilia

Paedophilia is a form of sexual perversion in which an adult finds young children or adolescents sexually exciting.

Children are most likely to be exposed to a paedophile who is already known or related to them, although they are also at risk of an approach by strangers, particularly at times when they are unsupervised. Throughout 1990 there were a spate of reports of bogus social workers attempting to remove children from their homes.

The majority of paedophiles are emotionally under-developed themselves; some are also intellectually impaired. They have difficulty in relating to other adults and often cannot achieve any adult sexual relationships. The vast majority of paedophiles are men, but women do occasionally become involved, often under the influence of a man. Society finds it difficult to believe that women are ever involved in paedophilia because it goes against our images of mothering, and therefore we may be blind to the extent to which women are involved (*see* **Perversion**).

The intensity of interest a paedophile will show can range from looking or touching the child, through to attempted intercourse or rape. Usually the paedophile convinces him- or herself that the child likes the activities, too, and through a combination of bribery and inducing fear can sometimes maintain a relationship of sorts with a child. Some paedophiles have more clearly aggressive and sadistic aims, wanting to torture or kill the child in order to achieve orgasm. Many have been sexually abused themselves as children (*see* **Childhood**

**Sexual Abuse**), and the damage done to their developing psyches by those experiences leaves them unable to understand or appreciate the feelings of others. Abusing children acts as a way of expressing their anger at their own abuse.

An abused child experiences a profound form of helplessness, which may sometimes be combined with sexual arousal in a way that is very confusing for him or her. The paedophile can only feel powerful in relation to children. To have a sexual relationship with another adult would be too much like a repetition of the powerlessness they experienced during their own abuse.

It is difficult to know how common this perversion is, and pressure groups exist that would wish paedophilia to be seen as less perverse and even acceptable. Against this are the feelings of revulsion which most adults express for the notion of children as the 'objects' of choice for sexual arousal. There is, however, a thriving pornographic business based on paedophilia, and regular reports of it not as isolated incidents or within families but also within organised rings of adults.

Paedophilia is against the law and causes great social outrage when discovered. Paedophiles serving prison sentences often have to be protected from fellow prisoners who see them as the lowest of the low. Clearly society should protest on behalf of children too young to protect themselves, but we should not allow ourselves to project too much outrage onto these sick individuals, who have all too often suffered themselves. In a society which is struggling to come to terms with incest and how best to react to abuse within the institution of the family it may be too easy to project into these individuals the sins we should be coping with much nearer home.

## Panic Attacks

A panic attack occurs when anxiety reaches an extreme peak (*see* **Anxiety**). The symptoms include palpitations, tightness in the chest and difficulty breathing, hyperventilation, nausea and a sense of doom associated with a great fear of losing control. It is a physiological as well as psychological event which is usually so frightening that the person will try at all costs to avoid repeating the situation which prompted the attack. Often, however, the sufferers will have no conscious idea of why the attack occurred when it did, and can only associate the immediate environment within which the attack occurred with their sense of panic. Thus, because agoraphobics experience panic when they go out they believe themselves to be frightened of the outside world and confine themselves to their homes, increasingly restricting their lives (*see* **Agoraphobia**). Consciously they can say that they know it does not make sense to be frightened of the outside world, yet their experience of panic starts at the front door. It often comes as a surprise when patients learn in therapy that what originally frightened them was not the outside world but a thought from their inner world which was precipitated by something that happened when they were outdoors.

During a panic attack the heart rate and rate of breathing increase, leaving sufferers in fear of fainting, sometimes in fear that they will have a heart attack and die. One of the reassurances that behavioural therapists often offer patients when encouraging them to face their fears is that no one has ever died of panic. However, in the middle of an attack it feels quite possibly lethal. That fear is underlined by the psychological features of panic, including the sense of imminent doom and the forceful drive to remove oneself from the situation however difficult or dangerous that removal is.

Naomi suffers from claustrophobia and avoids any closed-in spaces. She felt safe enough at her local hairdresser's, however – until she was 'trapped' under a dryer having a perm. As her panic reached its peak Naomi thought nothing of running out of the building with her hair still wrapped in tight perming curls. She said later that she would have gone through any humiliation in order to get away from the terrible choking feeling she was experiencing.

Joanne is frightened of flying, and on one occasion screamed to be allowed off a plane while it was cruising at 30,000 feet. Luckily the flight attendant did not oblige, and Joanne lived to go through a series of graduated steps of familiarisation with planes, airports and flying, which, while still leaving her a slightly reluctant passenger, meant that she can now travel by air when necessary.

The urge to physically remove oneself from the frightening situation is usually great during a panic attack. Presumably, far back in our heritage such determination to escape from fearful things was an advantage to our survival. For those who experience panic attacks, however, this 'flight mechanism' makes them their own worst enemies, as it means that they never stay in the situation causing them to panic long enough for the panic to subside, as it surely will: panic requires energy, and does eventually fade, whatever the stimulus.

We teach children to confront increasingly frightening aspects of life as they grow, and we think they are ready to deal with danger. This is a graduated exposure which leaves them as adults capable of withstanding a fair amount of anxiety without running away from the source. If children are exposed to high-anxiety situations too early their tolerance of anxiety in later life may be decreased.

Pauline was sexually abused by her stepfather for three years, from when she was 6 to 9 years old. As an adult she only half-remembered these episodes, and believed herself to be in some way to blame. When in her early 20s she was on her way home one night when she experienced verbal abuse of the 'Hello darling, what are you doing tonight?' variety from a group of young men standing on the street corner. She was frightened by this incident and increasingly began to stay at home, until 10 years later she considered herself to be agoraphobic; still she felt in some way to blame for the pain her restricted life caused her. It became clear during treatment that the extreme anxiety she experienced during the verbal abuse was closely connected with the unbearably high levels of anxiety she had experienced as a child. She had no way to deal with such anxiety when she was 6, except to tell herself that if she was to blame then at least that meant she must have some sort of control. Thus she dealt with the anxiety she experienced as an adult by restricting her movements and blaming herself for the subsequent isolation: this was the way she stayed 'in control'.

For people like Pauline panic is an alternative to rage and anger in situations where they are too powerless to risk feeling aggressive. Sometimes they remain aware of these emotions crushed in their inner worlds, but often only their unconscious minds remembers their impotent rage, a rage that is projected into the outside world, making it an even more frightening place than their original experience convinced them it was. Sometimes the world is indeed a frightening place, and many women feel panicky travelling home at night alone. Such experiences tend to make them limit their activities rather than question angrily why they should have to live with such fear.

Promotion or the possibility of promotion is often connected with extremely high levels of anxiety, and as these verge on panic so people back away from achieving their full potential, rather than be judged and perhaps rejected or found wanting. Small children are another cause of high levels of anxiety. For two years after my younger son was hurt in a car accident I could not hear squealing brakes without finding my heart in my mouth.

To survive panic we need good relationships which reassure us. Thus self-help groups where people understand one another are often wonderful therapy for those who have experienced panic. Therapists can sometimes become trusted allies as self-confidence is gained through facing up to fear. True bravery is demonstrated by those who, knowing just how fearful it is to be in a panic attack, nevertheless do find the courage to face their fear, be it in their inner or outer worlds.

## Paranoia

When Kraepelin, the father of modern psychiatry, first described paranoia in 1920, it was seen as separate from other mental illnesses, having some symptoms in common with schizophrenia but having a better prognosis with less overall damage to the personality. Today it is regarded increasingly as a symptom of psychotic illness. The word paranoia is Greek for 'beyond reason'.

Paranoid beliefs are those that tell you that you are being persecuted or betrayed in some way, or that you are marked out as an unacceptable human being because of the way you look or the way you smell. Sometimes such beliefs, which are held with delusional conviction, are accompanied by feelings of grandeur, envy, love or hate (*see* **Delusions**, **Envy**, **Grandiose Behaviour**, **Hate**, and **Love**).

Most of us have occasional thoughts that people are 'getting at us'. The joke 'just because I'm paranoid does not mean that they're not really out to get me' reflects this inner element in all our lives. It can be hard to know whether people are persecuting us or merely going about their business in ways that lead us to feel persecuted. For instance a colleague who seems to go out of his way to put you in a bad light with the boss may only be thinking of himself and have no ill-will towards you. On the other hand his motive might be directed towards getting rid of you, as his major competitor. We need to be able to judge situations accurately in order to correctly estimate the degree of persecution levelled against us in any given circumstance (*see* **Persecution Complex**).

Learning to trust others is a fundamental building block in our understanding of interpersonal relationships. That sense of basic trust seems to be established early in life, yet as we grow we also need to learn that not all people are trustworthy, and that everyone may prove untrustworthy in specific situations. These two contradictory pieces of information have to learn to live together in our understanding of the world (*see* **Ambivalence** and **Over-valued Ideas**). Trust however is the more primitive experience, lack of trust a deeply-held component of the deprived person. Once we have established a basic trust we can then learn consciously to 'vet' people at an intellectual level as we grow more knowledgeable about the world's dangers.

Mavis had always been a rather suspicious individual according to her family, someone who had had 'no time' for the neighbours whom she considered 'up to no good'. Even in mid-life she had frequently recommended to her daughters that they should not trust anyone, including banks, with their money. In addition she had always felt herself to be of a higher social class than those around her, and this led to further isolation. When in her 60s she began to have difficulty with her hearing, and at the same time suspected that there was a family campaign against her. She started writing angry letters to all the members of her family, saying that she knew what they were up to and that she was not going to have any of it. She accused various members of her family of a range of offences: Carol, her youngest daughter, was said to be in league with the neighbours, who were tunnelling under the house to get at Mavis' money, while her son, John, was said to be betraying his mother to the Social Services, who would come and kill her for him. Eventually, convinced that she was about to be murdered for her money, Mavis went to the police. Investigation proved that her family were loving and more than a little puzzled.

As babies we use defence mechanisms called splitting and projection in order to protect ourselves from aggressive and sadistic feelings which come both from ourselves and our early experience of the world. We split the good and the bad and we project out of our sense of self into the outside world all that we cannot bear to contain. If we project all our aggressive and sadistic fantasies into the surrounding world, that world becomes a frightening place. In the normal course of development we learn to contain both good and bad feelings, but if there is a lack of a close, trustworthy and containing relationship with a reliable adult figure we do not have that important experience and the world continues to be populated with our own fantasies of persecution and betrayal. It is these fantasies which persecute the individual who is paranoid. As there are always events or persons in the world onto whom it is possible to 'hook' the fantasy, we all retain to some extent the ability to use projection if we feel overloaded with our own aggression. Those with paranoia often choose targets that an outside observer would consider laughable as true persecutors, yet however much reassurance is offered the truly paranoid will continue to believe in their own explanation of things.

Recent research suggests that there is an inherited tendency towards paranoia, one of our genes seeming to have an effect on the development of that part of the brain called the *temporal lobe*. It may be in the temporal lobe that we learn to control our aggressive and sadistic tendencies as children and that this gene inhibits such learning. Childhood experience of paranoid adults also disrupts any hope of learning to trust.

Outside insults to the brain, such as trauma, or prolonged use of drugs or alcohol may also render people more likely to be paranoid. In addition, any restriction on our ability to test reality, such as prolonged social isolation or the personal isolation of the deaf, may also increase the likelihood that we will perceive the world in a paranoid way. (*See also* **Addiction**, **Aggression** and **Isolation**).

## Parasuicide
*See* **Suicide Attempts**

## Parkinson's Disease
*See* **Involuntary Movements**

## Passivity
*See* **Activity and Passivity**

# Penis Envy

Because Freud gave the penis centre-stage in his ideas on the development of male sexuality, he obviously thought that it should be assigned similar importance for women. Thus he assumed that the reason the little girl turns away from mother and towards father (at age 4 to 5) is that she discovers that both she and mother do not have a penis. This leads to a depreciation of mother, who is now seen as significantly lacking, alongside a resentment that mother has failed to give her daughter a penis. The girl turns to father hoping he can rectify matters, and learns that she can only gain a penis through intercourse or, in a modified way, by conceiving father's baby. For Freud little girls equated penis with baby. Many analysts agree with Freud's theory that penis envy remains a corner-stone in women's psychological development, and that even with analysis women cannot hope to completely resolve their feelings about their 'loss'.

Alongside of this central theory run two further threads, namely that the clitoris also has to be relinquished as 'inferior' in favour of only vaginal (that is, passive) orgasm, and that women's sexuality is bound up in procreativity rather than active libidinal enjoyment.

There is undoubtedly some interest in the penis of brothers and other small boys and father too for the average little girl. It is hard to know whether such curiosity is always attended with some envy or whether the child regards her own anatomy as 'lacking' in contrast to the male's. Such emotions must be, in some measure at least, connected to the value placed on maleness and femaleness within the family and the society as a whole. In the loving and equal union of a mother and a father there is presumably a measure of equal sexual and anatomical value to which the growing girl is a witness. If however the father frequently disparages mother, perhaps to the extent of violence and marital rape, then the penis is clearly seen to be more powerful and dominant, and therefore enviable on that basis.

Have men become dominant because they own the penis or

has our image of psychology become penis-centred because men have the power? Do women envy men their power or their penis? Perhaps the ownership of a penis is so central to male psychological development that it is unbelievable for them that it should have little or no meaning for women. In therapy I hear many tales in which women envy men their position within the family they were born into, their education, status and income in adult life and their apparent ability to wield great power with little exercise of responsibility: this is often particularly painful to the women in therapy who seem burdened by heavy responsibilities yet have no power. Occasionally a woman may express distaste or revulsion for the penis, which might, perhaps, be taken as a sign of envy, except that such feelings have usually arisen within the setting of verbal and/or physical abuse during childhood or adulthood rather than as a developmental experience within her psyche.

Women rarely report sexual fantasies involving damaging the penis, whereas both men and women regularly report sexual fantasies about damage to women's breasts and vaginas. This probably reflects the fact that both men and women had their first love/hate relationship with a woman, their mother, whose body conceived, carried, gave birth to and fed them through their dependency with all its concomitant bonding and hostility. Thus it would appear that a woman's body is more heavily invested in sexual imagery for both men and women than is a man's. Karen Horney suggested that the little girl both desires and fears father's penis, knowing that it is too big and may damage her. This fear of the penis, perceived as a weapon of attack rather than an organ of pleasure, certainly survives in the psyche's of many adult women.

Generally women do seem to have lower self-esteem than men in all cultures, and analysts are tempted to see this as a result of unresolved penis envy. It may however be an expression of the fact that mothers experience love towards their sons and daughters differently: from the beginning a daughter may get the message that she is disappointing her mother because she does not have a penis. Such messages would certainly colour the growing daughter's view of male anatomy and its value.

The penis is seen to be an active organ, an organ of penetration and impregnation. The vagina is seen as passively receiving by comparison. This imagery is often extended to cover the whole person rather than just their sexual organ – that is, men are allowed and even expected to be more aggressive, women more accepting and receptive. Women may envy the permission given to men from childhood and throughout adulthood to be more active and aggressive about meeting their own needs, and perhaps this permission is given in the first place simply because the child with the penis is in some way socially over-valued in comparison to the child with the vagina. (*See also* **Activity and Passivity**, **Libido**, and **Womb Envy**.)

# Persecution Complex

During development we perceive important others (mother, father, siblings) and aspects of ourselves (for instance some of our in-turned aggression) as potentially persecutory. These internal and external persecutors cause us great anxiety. As we grow and increase our understanding of relationships and our sense of control over ourselves and our environment this sense of persecution lessens and we are able to get some perspective on the relative dangers around us. Any situation which causes us to regress (that is, which makes us feel psychologically younger) can return us to that earlier developmental position, and we then begin to interpret the signals from others in a paranoid and persecutory way (*see* **Paranoia**). Our own sense of wishing to persecute others may also become stronger in such a situation, although it may be turned inwards because of our fear that others are stronger than ourselves.

Any damage to the brain, such as that caused by degenerating brain diseases (*see* **Dementia**) or chronic alcohol abuse, can make us more persecutory. Fiona, aged 45, had abused alcohol for 25 years before she showed any signs of memory loss. This loss was to her short-term memory more than her memory of distant events, and as a result it became more difficult for her to interpret correctly day-to-day events with her husband and teenage children. She began to express fears about the relationships within the family, saying 'Something terrible is going to happen. I know you all hate each other. One of you will murder us all in our beds.' In her own inner tormented world she also began to have aggressive and murderous thoughts about her family, thinking that they were plotting against her. Of course, because Fiona's behaviour was becoming increasingly strange, her family was indeed talking about her behind her back.

Fiona's sense of persecution became even greater, and eventually she was admitted to hospital, a move which she saw initially as part of the family's plot against her. Sadly Fiona had permanently damaged areas of her brain by her alcohol abuse, but high doses of vitamins made some improvement, and she was able to return home and live more comfortably within her family.

More commonly the sense of persecution that results from alcohol abuse is a temporary phenomenon which abates once the person is sober. The realisation that drinking is causing such problems should stimulate the individual to seek help rapidly to stop the drinking and thus prevent him- or herself from deteriorating to Fiona's sad condition (*see* **Alcoholism**).

As we grow older we often become more suspicious about others, and if this is combined with the beginnings of losing our faculties of memory and reason a sense of persecution can result. Deafness also increases the likelihood of feeling persecuted. It is not unusual for there to be some basis, however vague, for the beginnings of the belief: thus family and neighbours are often targets. An overheard comment or some thoughtless gesture grows in the imagination of an elderly person until it becomes part of the plot against him or her. The caring agencies called in to help in such situations are often viewed in the same persecutory light.

I remember one night being called out to a frail 89-year-old called Lily after neighbours complained that she had been shouting abuse at them for days and had been seen wandering about in the middle of the night with hardly any clothes on. It was a cold, wet night, and the estate on which she lived was dark. I had to park my car some way from her house, and by the time I found her number had begun to feel rather uneasy myself. When I knocked on the door Lily shouted through the letter-box that she was not going to let any 'murdering bastard' into her house. After half an hour of trying to explain who I was and why I was there with Lily still claiming that I was a dangerous lunatic on the loose, I ended up shouting back through the letter-box that I was in considerably more danger of being murdered outside in the dark than she was inside. Clearly she recognised the call from my own sense of persecution enough to trust me, and let me in.

During our emotional development as babies we have angry persecutory ideas towards the 'bad' half of our mothers, the part which is not immediately forthcoming with everything we want and does not always understand what we need. We feel free as infants to hate and imagine attacking this 'bad' mother because we think that she is a separate person from the 'good' mother whom we love and on whom we are dependent. As we begin to realise that there is only one mother, both good and bad, we also begin to see that our fantasies of attack have been towards the mother who is also loved. From this experience we develop a sense of guilt for our actions and also, according to Melanie Klein, a need to make reparation. This important developmental step allows us to begin taking responsibility for our actions within relationships and inspires us with a wish to heal with love that which we may smash with anger (*see* **Aggression**, **Anger**, **Greed**, and **Guilt**).

I have worked with a number of people who experienced persecutory ideas when depressed. Similarly, some of us experience grief in an angry rather than typically sad way, in a form of explosive grief (*see* **Depression** and **Grief**). Often these people cause chaos in their families, and if admitted to hospital on the ward as well. Although desperate to be healed of their pain they are also too angry to allow any caring, and fight off attempts of help, often interpreting the assistance offered as persecution. Whatever is tendered, be it psychotherapy, drugs or ECT, it is seen as an attack rather than a comfort.

Such people hate being at home, yet once admitted to hospital say they wish to be discharged. Everyone is considered to have evil motives behind their offers of help. Thus once home they behave in ways that increase family anxiety enough to necessitate their being readmitted, and so the cycle begins again. Trapped inside a vicious circle of their own making they believe that everyone attacks and hates them. This can become a self-fulfilling prophecy, because such people induce anxiety and distress in those around them, who become increasingly angry in their responses. As recovery begins however it is possible to see the individual growing back to a more reasoned view of the world, and at that stage to develop a sense of guilt for what has been said or done. We need to understand this progress on the part of the patient, through persecution and guilt towards the need to make amends, as a re-growth of his or her original developmental pathway.

## Personality Disorder

May was the only child of rather cold, unattached parents. She came to psychiatric attention after an overdose. Cared for by a variety of nannies because of her mother's post-natal depression (*see* **Post-natal Depression**), she had been remembered as a troubled child. Although apparently successful during adolescence, passing exams and excelling at sport, she had difficulty maintaining friendships because of her tendency to either love or hate people in rapid succession. By her early 20s she was a loner, and experimented with many one-night sexual encounters, drugs and alcohol. She had no friendships or support system and had never stayed in a job longer than a few months. Although clearly desperate for help she expressed resentment at being interviewed by a social worker and psychiatrist on the day after her overdose. She then spent several weeks phoning and visiting the social work office daily, demanding help and saying that she had fallen in love with the male psychiatrist. Eventually she left the area in search of a new job and was not heard from again.

May's experience is typical of someone with borderline personality disorder. This serious disturbance of the personality is characterised by an instability in the way that a person views him- or herself and relates to others. It is a long-standing difficulty that becomes apparent by early adulthood at the latest. Sufferers have unstable moods and often act impulsively in relationships and in their careers, in their eating or drinking and in their spending habits. They may feel empty and/or bored, fear abandonment, will do almost anything to avoid loneliness, and commonly voice suicidal thoughts or even commit suicide. They are prone to extreme outbursts of aggression and violence, followed rapidly by depression or anxiety. They have little permanent sense of who they are (almost like an eternal adolescent trying new personalities to see if one fits) and may make rapid inexplicable changes in their choices of sexual partners or orientation, in their values or beliefs and in their goals (*see* **Aggression, Anxiety, Depression,** and **Mania**).

It is unknown whether people are born likely to develop such a disorder or whether early childhood experiences, within the first two years of life, lead to their alternating black or white image of life. Recent work has suggested that childhood physical and/or sexual abuse may cause disturbances of the personality boundaries, which then makes it impossible for the person to develop emotionally beyond an early stage.

For people with a personality disorder such as this long-term relationships are usually impossible and marriage is rare. Relationships with helping agencies also tend to be fraught with problems, making successful long-term treatment by psychotherapy or drugs difficult.

# Perversion

Perversions are defined as sexual activity and arousal from objects which are not normally considered sexual. Such 'objects' may include animals, clothing, children, or the paraphernalia of sado-masochism (*see* **Paedophilia** and **Sado-Masochism**). Our definition of perversion is blurred, however, and what some people may consider perverse, for example feeling aroused by a 'page-3' girl, would be defined as 'healthy' sexuality by others. Homosexuality used to be considered perverse without argument. It is rare for any homosexual to seek treatment specifically for his or her homosexuality, however, and most would now see their sexual orientation as a genetic endowment or a simple choice with which they are content and proud. Remnants of the idea that homosexuality is perverse are to be found in the general homophobia of society, and many gay men and women say that their sexuality remains a perversion in their own minds, too, causing them much anguish. Identification with other gay people helps to ease such uncertainties.

The most frequent perversion is fetishism. Although it is rarely severe enough to be the cause of treatment, fetishism may become apparent during counselling for other problems. A fetish is an object, usually closely associated with the body, such as leather clothing, or underwear, which a person needs in order to become aroused and achieve orgasm. If a man or woman becomes rigidly attached to a fetish, compulsively demanding its use and unable to achieve satisfaction without it, then it may become a symptom which demands attention.

Freud referred to the fetish as 'a token of triumph over the threat of castration and protection against it', thinking that men who required fetishes for arousal were those who were unduly anxious about their sexuality and feared castration originally in relationship to their mother and father and later in relationships with female partners. Connected to this primitive fear, men also tend to have images of women, and in particular of female genitalia, which are degraded, dirty and mutilated, while also fearing the hidden power of women (*see* **Womb Envy**). Not surprisingly the female partners of such men often feel extremely uncomfortable about their partners' use of fetishes, and yet are also often made to feel that they are 'over-reacting'.

Nicola insisted that her husband Jim seek help when she felt his need for leather clothing when they made love was beyond what she was willing to tolerate. During the initial assessment Jim repeatedly tried to make Nicola seem small-minded and prudish. 'What is wrong with leather underwear?' he asked, attempting to gain the therapist's approval. Nicola felt frustrated that her apparent revulsion could be so easily dismissed by Jim, and the therapist tried to help Jim see how hurt Nicola was. Jim persisted, however, complaining in a 'little-boy' voice that wearing leather was a small thing to ask of a wife and that he could not see why she would want to deny him something that made him happy.

As therapy progressed Jim's narcissistic personality became more obvious (*see* **Narcissism**). Nicola's comment that 'It feels as if you are making love to yourself' prompted an outburst which laid bare Jim's hatred and fear of women. He felt that Nicola should be willing to do anything that gave him sexual pleasure, shouting 'That's what wives are for!' This led the therapist to question Jim about his parents and their marriage. His father worked away from home for much of Jim's first five years, and so his early relationship with his mother had been intense and uninterrupted. Even in adulthood Jim still saw his mother as the powerful force in his life, whom he loved but also hated passionately. Similarly he saw Nicola as unbearably powerful, making him wish to degrade her at every opportunity. It was only by degrading her that he could feel powerful. Nicola confirmed that this was her experience of their relationship, too: 'Jim uses leather clothing to put me down.'

Perversions seem much more common in men and often involve a view of women as both powerful and revolting. However, recent work by Estela Welldon at London's Portman Clinic suggests that women may use their own bodies (or their children's bodies, often seen by women as extensions of their own) to fantasise or act out perversions in a way that is not as obvious as male perversions. Linda, aged 24, asked for help after damaging her nipples during masturbation. She explained that it was only by making her breasts hurt that she could achieve orgasm. She described a relationship with her mother which had regularly involved sleeping in the same bed and mutual masturbation and had continued until she was in her early teens.

Freud felt that small children believed that their mothers had a penis, and that when they discovered that this was not the case either fantasised that the penis was hidden (the concept of concealed power) or that the mother had been mutilated (the concept of women being 'damaged' and 'less than' men). For many men such fantasies lead to a fascination with and fear of women.

Other perversions include transvestism, which is the need to wear clothing of the opposite sex (*see* **Eroticism**), voyeurism, the need to gain arousal by watching others involved in sexual pursuits, and exhibitionism, which is the need to expose the penis (or occasionally the breasts) in public to strangers. There is often an element of sado-masochism in all of these activities, in the desire to shock, hurt or humiliate others while at the same time acting in a way that is likely to humiliate oneself.

## Phobias

Being phobic means being so afraid of something that you feel you have to avoid it whatever the cost to your lifestyle. It may be an intense fear of something which many people would be mildly anxious about, for example snakes, or flying, or it may be a fear of something which others would not find worrying at all, such as the agoraphobic's fear of being away from familiar surroundings (*see* **Agoraphobia** and **Panic Attacks**).

There is usually an initial stressful event which makes the person frightened. The anxiety produced is painful and so the person withdraws from whatever it is that is causing the fear.

This withdrawal makes the sufferer feel comfortable again, and therefore the stressful event is avoided as much as possible. Any exposure to stress makes anxiety levels rise, causing psychic pain sometimes to the point of panic, over-breathing and fainting. Such experiences tend to reinforce the need to avoid the stress in future whatever the cost to the person's freedom or life (*see* **Anxiety** and **Stress**).

Anxiety causes both physical and psychological symptoms which are extremely uncomfortable and frightening in themselves. Thus once we start to be afraid we enter a vicious circle of becoming afraid of the effects of our own anxiety, which then makes us more afraid. Interestingly, the things some of us find frightening other people experience as exciting. The physical responses to anxiety and excitement are similar, and it may be that we learn to 'diagnose' our physical experience in the light of previous experiences. If as children we have been supported during times of potential anxiety so that we have overcome hurdles of various sorts (for example learning to socialise without anxiety or learning to cope with the pressures of being judged and examined by our teachers), our approach to life will be more confident. If, however, we have experienced ourselves as alone, unsupported, unsuccessful, even abandoned during early testing times, then our capacity to cope is limited.

Most children are naturally curious and adventurous. This spirit is curtailed to some extent in all of us – if it were otherwise none of us would survive childhood. However, for many people their spirit is crushed or obliterated by childhood experiences of either great restriction or overwhelming fear. Generally girls are more restricted and less rewarded for their adventurous spirit than boys, and this shows in their adult behaviour and understanding of the world.

Julie was 23 when she first realised that she was terrified of heights. She was on a walking holiday with friends and stopped at a viewpoint on a hillside. Looking out over the valley she suddenly felt cold and clammy. She had palpitations and feared, irrationally, that she might jump over the edge. This experience was painful for her not just because of her symptoms but also because she felt she had made a fool of herself in front of her friends. She avoided going walking after this, avoided contact with this group of friends, and became increasingly withdrawn until her life revolved around work and being alone in her flat. As her flat was on the second floor she became unable to look out of the windows, and even found descending the stairs a nightmare.

During therapy Julie related a childhood of frequent physical abuse from both parents and where she had often felt anxious about what would happen when one or other parent came home. On several occasions she had witnessed her father throwing her brother or mother downstairs, and had had to run and hide thinking he was going to do this to her. It seemed that she had spent much of her childhood in fear and was now repeating that pattern in adulthood.

Many of those who become phobic during their adult lives have experienced some form of verbal, physical or sexual abuse during childhood and have therefore experienced profound feelings of helplessness and humiliation. So terrifying are these experiences that the individual retains a fundamental fear of the world.

In order to quell our natural anxieties we need to have a sense of trust in others and ourselves, and of being in control of our destiny. When events happen that shake these beliefs our fear takes control. We can all be brave when we feel loved and supported, thus for those who are isolated fear can get out of control more quickly. Thus many treatments for phobia involve making a relationship either with a therapist or a group of similar sufferers, in which the individual feels trusting and safe enough to begin to take risks again.

## Post-natal Depression
Twenty-five in 1,000 women who give birth have an episode of serious depressive illness during the first year of their child's life.

A further 400 out of that 1,000 will experience a less severe episode of depression which may linger in a chronic form for years.

The cause of such anguish is due only in part to the woman, the baby, their relationship and their personalities. Most people who deal with these distressed women comment on how normal their personalities are. This reflects the great stress experienced by an adult who is continuously exposed to a new baby with no relief. Fatigue and physical exhaustion coupled with the social isolation and loss of status and income which are often direct results of the baby's birth all take their toll.

Added to this is the fact that our social expectations of mothering are that it is a pleasant, rewarding and fulfilling task, with little mention made of the stressful and wearing side of the job. Thus the realities of life with a new baby can be disconcertingly different to the new mother's fantasies and hopes. Her disillusionment and disappointment lead her to despair.

Because a woman's psychological boundaries are disturbed by pregnancy, labour and the early relationship with her infant she has a great need for security within her other relationships and within the fabric of her home. Thus a poor marital relationship, a husband who is often absent, disinterested with, or worse, envious of the baby, competitive mothers and mothers-in-law, and moving house or building an extension at this vulnerable time will all add to the likelihood of her becoming depressed.

Gloria had a normal pregnancy and had looked forward with excitement to an uncomplicated delivery. Several weeks before she was due, her husband Mark was sent to the Far East on a business trip. Both of them believed he'd be back in time for the birth, but only hours after his plane took off Gloria went into labour. She had to have an emergency Caesarean section because of 'foetal distress', that is, there was a danger that the baby was not getting enough oxygen and had to be delivered very quickly. Gloria lived far away from her parents, and because she and Mark had only recently moved to the area she had no friends nearby. Mark did manage to cut his trip short and fly home, but this still took three days. He arrived to find Gloria apparently coping well despite the fact that baby Amy was in intensive care. He said later that Gloria was renowned in the family for coping with anything and everything. For some weeks all seemed well. Amy improved and went home at 3 weeks old, and physically Gloria healed remarkably rapidly.

When Amy was 10 weeks old Mark began to notice that Gloria was quiet, not eating and often tearful. Initially he put this down to the fact that she was tired; Amy was still not sleeping through the night. Gloria came to therapy when Amy was 4 months old, by which time she had convinced herself she was an unfit mother, that she could never love her baby enough, and that she was the cause of all Amy's crying; that she was, in fact, a 'failed woman'.

In therapy Mark said, with regret, that his initial reaction had been to feel surprised and even annoyed with Gloria. He said that he'd thought 'all women coped with becoming mothers', a theory he based on his own mother's glowing reports of the joys of motherhood. For her part Gloria heard with relief that it was far from unusual for mothers to feel as she was feeling: she was in fact a normal woman who had endured an abnormal and alarming experience totally alone. Given this permission to express herself, Gloria's anger at 'Fate' for the jeopardy of Amy's birth and her feelings of 'abandonment' as she saw it by Mark, 'just when I needed him most,' were allowed to surface. Mark expressed his fears, too, when he recalled being 'trapped' in Bangkok desperately trying to get home and not knowing for several hours whether or not his wife and child had survived. He admitted that he had been less than supportive of Gloria since then because he had been so frightened of the enormity of the responsibility, and at the same time rather envious of baby Amy, who got 'all the attention'.

As Gloria realised that much of her depression was rooted in her feelings of anger and isolation, she also saw that she was not a hopeless mother and could in fact do something about her situation. She joined a group of new mothers, insisted that Mark come home earlier, and allowed Amy to go to a creche twice a week so that she could return to the art classes she had given up when pregnant. When I saw them all about six weeks later Gloria said that she felt much better and Mark said that he was enjoying being more involved in looking after Amy. He had realised that if he gave his daughter some 'quality time' it took some of the stress off Gloria so that she felt more like giving him some attention.

The best protection from experiencing post-natal depression is for mothers to plan realistic programmes for themselves with their babies and get as much supportive, non-critical help as possible. They need to keep their hopes and expectations to realistic levels, remembering that babies do not heal poor relationships, magically make people happy or provide any great fulfilment instantly for the mother. The fulfilment of being a mother is elusive, coming in moments and often gone again before it can be enjoyed for many of the early years of childhood.

Babies are meant to have labile emotions and are born with a fierce will to survive which will pay no heed to the mother's needs. Thus the mother needs to sometimes protect herself. Some mothers do benefit from anti-depressants and/or a course of therapy, but allowing the infant to separate slightly and be looked after by others for periods of each week is often the best and most instant cure for the depression. The whole arena of maternal emotions is explored more fully in my first book, *Motherhood: What It Does To Your Mind*, written under my previous name, Jane Price.

## Post-traumatic Stress Disorder (PTSD)

This complex disorder occurring in normal people after an abnormally stressful event has been apparent in people for as long as history has been recorded. Different generations have had different perceptions of it, however, and different cultures treat it very differently too. In recent years there has been an increase in the professional understanding and help offered to those involved in highly stressful events, but it would be wrong to suggest that this means that we are emotionally weaker than our forefathers were. It has been my experience that even after the most severe stress the British stiff upper lip leads people to believe that they can cope (and make others believe that they can cope) with events which have been emotionally overwhelming for them. Eventually, sometimes months or years later, the results of the stress appear, often complicated by the fact that they have been disguised in the meantime.

It is normal to experience emotional disquiet after a disturbing experience, and particularly after a life-threatening one. For many people this response only lasts for a few weeks, but for those suffering from PTSD the experience continues for longer than a month, sometimes for years. They re-experience the traumatic event in their memories, in their mind's eye and in their nightmares. The emotions connected to the incident come flooding back without warning and they find themselves preoccupied with running through the details again and again, often with crippling guilt about what they did or did not do to save others (*see* **Flashbacks**). Even objects or places only vaguely connected to the original episode can trigger painful memories, and sufferers therefore begin to centre their lives around avoiding such situations. Their emotions often feel flat, and their relatives may think that they are disinterested. It becomes difficult for those affected to 'care' about previously important relationships, and nothing has a sense of permanence or purpose. Alongside their emotional flatness is a form of constant over-arousal which makes for continuous anxiety, difficulty sleeping and concentrating, outbursts of anger or tears, a feeling that they need to be hypervigilant about their own and others' safety and an exaggerated startle response – that is, they jump at every noise.

Work with survivors of tragedies has suggested that some people's brains are so equally divided between thinking and feeling halves that the acute anxiety suffered during a stressful event sets the brain into a kind of overactivity which goes backwards and forwards, first overwhelming their feelings, making them 'numb', and then overwhelming their thinking, making them hyper-aroused. Those of us with a more definitely dominant side to our brains cope either by thinking our way through the weeks after the stress or by feeling all that has been triggered by the experience, but do not suffer both, the painful total, as sufferers of PTSD do.

Analysts have also suggested that however stressful an event it is more symbolic for some of the survivors than others. Even if the stress has continued for some time, most survivors can pinpoint a particular moment which was crucial, the 'key' event, and this is usually an aspect of the situation which has reminded them of earlier painful experiences they went through as children.

Any situation in which we feel helpless and hopeless for ourselves, our loved ones or strangers stirs up powerful anxiety-provoking feelings perhaps not unlike those that the helpless baby experiences. Thus early experiences may to a significant degree dictate our response to later stress (*see* **Anxiety** and **Stress**).

Many people wonder about how they will cope if they are ever exposed to a stressful event such as a national disaster. In reality this is hard to predict, but generally a person's reaction falls into one of three groups: those who become withdrawn and stunned, those who 'collapse' emotionally and look to others for support, and those who become super-practical about rescuing others. The last group have a tendency to break down once the need for immediate action is over. The Armed Services like to believe that their training enables them to take a variety of horrific events in their stride with less than 10 per cent of their number reacting with emotional distress (although even 10 per cent of an Army is a large number of individuals); it seems likely, however, that it is only the external constraints of discipline and morale which safeguard the psyche, and that if and when this is removed, in retirement, for example, the underlying reaction may be unexpectedly unleashed (*see* **Accident Neurosis** and **Adaptive Responses**).

# Pre-Menstrual Syndrome (PMS)

Many women experience sensations of being bloated, clumsy, tired, irritable or aggressive for several days before their period starts. The extent to which this worries them or causes them difficulties varies from woman to woman.

There does seem to be a group of women who suffer because of their hormonal cycles to an extent that incapacitates them or damages their relationships, making normal life impossible for several days, and in extreme cases for a number of weeks, each month. Clearly it is depressing and limiting to be so 'attacked' by your own body on a regular basis. Hormone treatment sometimes controls such symptoms.

There are dangers for women, however, in allowing themselves or others to dismiss their feelings as 'all hormonal'. I have, for example, heard a gynaecologist confidently assert that women cry for the same reasons that they bleed. It is easy to allow our psychological pain, real anger and aggression to be dismissed rather than valued. Whilst it is true that many women report shouting at their families more pre-menstrually than at any other time, it is probably also true that what they are shouting about has some truth in it, and their families should be listening to them, rather than dismissing the anger as 'that time of the month'. Similarly women have been prevented from doing various high prestige jobs, such as flying commercial airlines, on the basis that their hormones make them unpredictable and research has demonstrated that women have more accidents pre-menstrually than at other times. What the research failed to do for many years, however, was compare the extent to which women are accident-prone pre-menstrually and the extent to which men are accident-prone generally. Now we know that men are more accident prone, more clumsy and more aggressive all the time than women are at any time.

There may be emotional advantages to living in a state of emotional flux as hormone levels change. It may, for instance, be the reason why women seem to maintain more emotional flexibility. If viewed positively, hormonal changes certainly allow for a richer and more varied experience of life. Similarly, the time limits imposed by women's biology can be either psychologically stressful or useful and stimulating. Thus it is important to get into perspective the effects of our hormonal changes, and try to see their positive as well as negative aspects. Of course, women who do suffer badly from PMS should seek help, but we should all be alert to the ways in which evidence of hormonal change has been used to control and limit women's behaviour.

## Preoccupation with Death
*See* **Death**

## Psychosomatic Illnesses

It is generally believed that there is an especially close relationship between one's personality and life events on the one hand and the onset or exacerbation of particular illnesses on the other. Theory held that these illnesses included peptic ulceration, asthma, ulcerative colitis, essential hypertension (high blood-pressure) rheumatoid arthritis, thyrotoxicosis and neurodermatitis. Many other physical complaints clearly have an element of psychological precipitation.

It is unknown whether the choice of expressing emotional conflicts via bodily symptoms is inherited or learned. Certainly we are each born with inborn 'bugs' in our physical make-up, which means that there are systems which are for whatever reason more prone to illness under stress. These systems differ both between individuals and between cultures.

We use similar terminology for the body's immune system,

so central to many illness, and psychic function. The notion of defence mechanisms, which cause illness if overactive, for instance, is apparent in both fields; and emotions can play an important part in the body's response to stress. Sean, a 25-year-old lorry driver, had had a peptic ulcer for two years. Medical treatment was excellent at providing short-term relief and cure, but the ulceration reappeared as soon as it was cured. Finally a combination of drugs and psychotherapy allowed the ulcer to stayed healed, but not until much of the aggression which Sean felt to his boss in the here-and-now and his father in the past had been explored and expressed.

This idea of combined physical and psychological treatment may become much more common as our understanding of the complex relationship between mind and body functions increases.

## Punishment

It has long been recognised that some people seem to need their symptoms however painful and disabling, and will hang on to them and put up an enormous resistance to relinquishing them. Freud talked of this 'need for punishment' as part of the death instinct (*see* **Death**), and pointed out that, particularly in the case of obsessional illnesses, a patient can often be seen to be his or her own torturer, performing rituals such as handwashing which cause both mental and physical anguish (*see* **Obsessive Compulsive Illness**).

Within our psychological make-up we have three areas, designated as the id, ego, and super-ego. The id contains the instinctual parts of ourselves as well as early memories and experiences. Much of the energy from the id needs modification in order to be expressed in socially acceptable ways. The ego is the area of rational thought and action, planning and decision-making. It is the part of ourselves which is most easily recognisable both to ourselves and others. The super-ego is the internal policeman, comprised of all the influences – parental, educational, social and religious – which have taught us the rules of how to limit expression of the id (*see* **Unconscious, Conscious and Pre-conscious Minds**).

The power of the super-ego varies according to the experiences of the individual as a young child. Some have excessively strict, moral, conformist super-egos which exert an inflexible strait-jacket on the individual's mind. Such super-egos produce much guilt within an individual, because, being human, he or she can never live up to the unrealistically high standards being internally imposed. This guilt can sometimes be atoned for if the person believes he or she is being sufficiently punished. Painful symptoms can sometimes fulfil the need for punishment that such individuals experience (*see* **Guilt Complex, Insecurity, Over-valued Ideas**, and **Sado-masochism**)

Delia, aged 27, is a portrait painter with considerable talent. She lives in an unhappy relationship with her boyfriend, Alan, who is unemployed, frequently depressed, and demanding of her attention. For several years Delia had been obsessional about the standard of housework she did each day, often rising at 5 a.m. in order to have the house perfect by breakfast time (*see* **Obsessive Compulsive Illness**). As her obsession grew she started buying more and more toxic cleaning fluids in order to achieve the perfection of cleanliness to which she subscribed. She had dreams in which the saying 'cleanliness is next to godliness' played a central part. Eventually, after she developed a severe allergic reaction to an oven cleaning fluid, which had left her hands and forearms raw and bleeding, she sought help.

In therapy it soon became the case that the intensity of Delia's symptoms mirrored the intensity with which the therapist hated the Alan he heard about in her stories. When he suggested that she was angry with Alan, however, Delia expressed outrage with the therapist. It was all her fault she had these stupid symptoms. If they were cured everything would be all right. Gradually however Delia began to see for herself the connection between getting angry, immediately feeling guilty about getting angry, and punishing herself. This translated into a belief that she was a dirty slut who should work harder at keeping a perfectly clean home for Alan. All this happened in an instant, transforming her anger into punishment and thereby granting her a sense of relief from her feelings of guilt.

# R

## Rage

Rage is the sudden and usually brief outpouring of anger, often with an explosive quality. Individuals vary in the amount of rage they experience and/or express. Some of us are much more susceptible than others to 'irritants' such as noise, criticism or frustration. The explosive quality results from the attempt to suppress rising irritation, however brief, followed by a rapid response to a final trigger. Any intoxication, brain damage, disease such as epilepsy, the results (physical and emotional) of old age or the presence of external stress can make us more likely to explode in rage.

Rage is a physiological as well as psychological event, and the heart rate, distribution of blood in the body, and width of the bronchioles in the lungs all alter to prepare the animal to be at its peak for a fight. While the outburst of rage may last just a few seconds these physiological changes take longer to adjust back to normal, and thus leave the individual feeling 'strange' for some time afterwards. During the outburst the person may be unaware of what he or she is doing or saying, at least to the extent of being able to make appropriate judgements about it. This can lead to a sense of despair afterwards if the actions are regretted. Sometimes releasing rage makes an individual feel supremely powerful, and he or she will experience elation in its aftermath.

Rage is a primitive expression of emotion unchecked by the restraints that most of us consider normal. A young baby will express her feelings without thought for the impact this expression has on the people around her. As we grow we learn to moderate this expression so that the feelings of others are taken into consideration along with our own. Many learn this so well that they make other people's feelings more important than their own, and in doing so gradually lose touch with what they feel about anything. Clearly this amount of repression is not healthy for the individual (*see* **Over-sensitivity**, **Repression**, and **Suppressed Feelings**). In order to live comfortably and safely within family and social groups, however, we all have to learn some restraint.

Michael, aged 24, first demonstrated his rage while on his honeymoon. A waiter failed to get an order right and Michael exploded, shouting and breaking some plates and glasses as he overturned the table. His wife, Nicola, put this demonstration down to Michael's extreme tiredness and the champagne they had drunk, thus beginning her pattern of finding excuses for his behaviour. During the first two years of their marriage such explosions were far from unusual, but always directed against younger men who were in a position that made it unlikely that they would fight back.

When Nicola discussed her anxieties about Michael's outbursts with her mother-in-law she was told that he had always had a 'fierce temper' as a child but 'didn't mean any harm.' It therefore came as a painful surprise to Nicola when Michael kicked and punched her when she was pregnant with their first child. He apologised the following day, saying that the 'stress of the pregnancy' was to blame. Nicola, believing by this time that she had little choice, accepted this. It was only in retrospect that she was able to see that her dependency during the pregnancy had placed her in a new light in Michael's eyes. 'I felt that he had started to look down on me, and that after that he could do anything he wanted,' she commented. It was only after two more children and seven years of increasingly regular outbursts of rage levelled at both herself and the children that Nicola finally left. At this point her mother-in-law 'confessed' to Nicola how relieved they had been when Michael left home to marry. She said 'We suddenly realised that we had been

walking around him carefully for years so as not to precipitate
an explosion.' As Nicola had finally recognised, the external
precipitants were only the excuse Michael needed to express his
inner tensions.

We learn control by example from the adults around us when
we are young; thus violent homes tend to rear violent youngsters
who are more likely to explode in rage under provocation than
those reared in a home where outbursts of physical aggression
were not the norm. Within our learning we may become
sophisticated about whom we can or cannot express rage to. The
husband might beat his wife if his tea is not on time and yet
be placatory with male fellow workers. The mother may explode
with her children and yet tolerate all sorts of frustrations from
her husband. In this way it can be seen that the expression of
rage may follow a hierarchical pattern, with the most powerful
expressing their rage freely to everyone and the least powerful –
often the children – having to find ways of containing everyone
else's expressions of rage, at least until they are older.

Because of its explosive nature, rage is sometimes expressed
unexpectedly by previously quiet and restrained individuals,
thus we have the concept of the worm who turns. These people
have often experienced frustration, humiliation and emotional
pain for years, suppressing their feelings and behaving gently
and correctly. They are like walking time-bombs, however, and
when fully 'primed' may explode at a relatively small trigger.

When expressing rage we are all capable of homicide, suicide
and feats of destruction. Because it is a primitive emotion
experienced within our earliest relationships we are most likely
to re-experience it within the context of the family. Often in
crimes of violence the most likely suspects are close family
members. Rage is often expressed in situations where the
individual's need for dependency is thwarted or where
dependency threatens the person too closely. This reflects our
initial rage at our own infantile dependency, a time when we had
to accept the ministering of others to all our needs.

We may yearn once again to return to the blissful state in

which our needs were met, but the reality of dependency is that it is always a far from perfect state. Thus the husband who explodes when his dinner is not on time may have fantasised all day about the perfection of mothering awaiting him in return for his day's hard labours. But he did not receive perfect mothering as a child, and is pained by his dependent needs now, when once again he is faced with imperfection. The wife who colludes with this and attempts to placate as if she was the mother of a troubled youngster instead of the wife of a troublesome adult encourages the fantasies of dependence which are so liable to cause the outbursts of rage.

As adults we cannot repair for each other the lack of parenting we suffered as children. Only by understanding ourselves, acknowledging what we failed to receive, what we feel about being dependent, and that we must take responsibility for that within ourselves, can we hope to produce healing. Thus the myth that 'the love of a good woman' can heal a damaged man is dangerously untrue. Similarly a man cannot heal the childhood damages suffered by a woman. Much rage within adult relationships results from unhealed dependency needs from childhood; we blame our partners for not being able to heal our pain. (*See also* **Addiction**, **Alcoholism**, **Anger**, **Dementia**, **Frustration**, **Irritability**, and **Jealousy**.)

## Rationalisation

Rationalisation is a psychological defence mechanism which we use extensively not only as individuals but also as families and even whole nations. It helps us to 'explain' our emotional experiences in ways that sound plausible and may even be true, at least in part. However, it also allows us to leave a great deal unsaid or unexplained.

Rationalisation is similar to intellectualisation, in which we use our more scientific grasp of life not only to explain but also to distance ourselves from our emotions (*see* **Intellectualisation**). Using rationalisation we may not be so distant from our emotions, acknowledging their existence and even their intensity, but we give them an acceptable but false basis. Even our defences, psychologically, can be rationalised, so that we can keep our instinctual selves well covered. Thus the desire to be dependent may be defended against by the reaction formation of a pseudo-independent personality. In turn Western society's 'cult' of independence may give an external rationale to such a defence.

Given the enormity of the material within our unconscious minds it is impossible for us to be 'in contact' with the roots of our feelings all of the time. By their nature defence mechanisms are unconscious and therefore difficult to understand or appreciate within ourselves (*see* **Defence Mechanisms** and **Unconscious, Conscious and Pre-conscious Minds**). For the most part our feelings would perpetually mystify us unless we could find a 'face-saving' way of explaining them. Thus when we cry at the end of a happy film we do not go to great lengths to justify this rather bizarre reaction; we just say 'I'm crying because I'm so happy.' As a society we accept happiness as a rational explanation for tears without feeling the need to explore their well-spring any further.

Much of every society is ruled by rational explanations of the nature and purpose of life, the roles in life of each individual and the hierarchical structure of the society. Clearly these are man-made constructs, and the fact that they vary between cultures exposes the extent to which they merely seek to explain human emotional experience. It is clear to the objective eye that many of our social institutions – politics, church, scientific ideologies – involve much rationalisation. They allow our instinctual needs and drives to be hidden while at same time allowing them expression.

Political systems allow us to believe we have rational leadership, however blatantly untrue this is. Rationalisation also allows us to believe that our system (our family) is the best and that others are wrong, bad, or dangerous. Clearly it is an advantage for a group of people to feel this about their leadership and structure; it provides the individual or society with security, however illusory this may be in reality. Those within any structure who seek to expose its irrationality are seen as revolutionary. Importantly, both those who turn a (rationally) blind eye to any discrepancies as well as those who wish to expose them are doing so for personal and emotional reasons, although both will believe themselves to be acting on rational political beliefs.

It is difficult to know how truly rational any of us can be, and always much easier to spot the irrationality in another rather than ourselves, not just as individuals but as families, nations, or religions.

## Reality Testing

In order to survive as adults we need to be able to draw a distinction between the reality of our external world of experiences and physical sensation and that of our inner world of memory, instincts, feelings and fantasies. Because of the complexities of the functioning of our inner world this distinction can sometimes become blurred, especially when we are stressed. It then becomes necessary for us to be able to test our external reality.

During our development we have little or no sense of the difference between our inner experiences, such as hunger or satisfaction, and the outer reality of a separate world. What we feel is our reality. This state of affairs changes, however, as we begin to focus our eyes and realise that there are people and things which are non-us, external to ourselves. To some extent we spend the remainder of our lives experimenting to see just how much of an effect we can have on that outside world. One of the most important tasks of early development is the construction of a psychological boundary so that we can distinguish between the 'me' inside and the 'them' and 'it' outside. Without that boundary further development of the 'me' is hampered, and our increasing need to interact with the external world is also frustrated.

Small children frequently have to 'try out' things even when they have been told these are dangerous. Thus they will put their hands on hot objects just seconds after being told not to – they are testing reality. As adults we continue this trial and error approach. It seems that every new generation has to 'try things out', making mistakes and getting hurt before they can believe the experience; simply being told about it by someone else is usually not good enough. As a parent it is often painful watching your children test the reality of the world. The teenager who tells his workaholic father that exams are not important is using himself and his future to test out a part of his father's definition of reality. The adventurer who attempts to climb a mountain or cross a desert 'because it's there' is pushing against the definition of what is realistically possible.

The need to test reality remains with us throughout life. If we perceive a goal in life we may have to reach towards it either physically or metaphorically in order to decide whether our perception of it was accurate: was it externally necessary or was it merely a projection from our inner world of fantasy out into the external world? If we never attempt to reach the goal, however, we may never know how real it was. It is this fine discernment between our dreams and hopes from within and the real limitations, frustrations and dangers of the world outside which is the long-term product of repeated reality testing.

## Regression

During our psychological development we pass through a number of stages that take us from being a totally dependent infant without language to an integrated adult capable of organising ourselves and our lives. As we pass through these stages we do not leave them behind but rather lay them down in layers in our psyches. Therefore, within our adult psyches are all the other stages, laid down, mostly out of sight, but forming the bedrock or foundation of ourselves. Under any form of stress we can regress back to one of these earlier stages of psychological functioning, either in the way we think, feel, or act (*see* **Fixation**).

In many mental illnesses it is clear that the individual is acting and feeling as if he or she were much younger than his or her chronological age. In physical illness, too, most of us experience a kind of regression, a need to retreat back to a time when people looked after us. Nurses have paid attention, in recent years, to how best to prevent patients, particularly if they are in hospital, from regressing too much when they are ill; these nurses feeling that prolonged regression back to helplessness delays the patients' recovery.

Most of us can regress temporarily, knowing all along that life will rapidly require us to 'grow up' again. Some people seem to get 'stuck' at the point they have regressed to: this is called malignant regression.

Julia, aged 25, injured her back in a car accident and had to have bed-rest in hospital for six weeks. During that time her movements were severely restricted and it was impossible for her to feed or clean herself, so nurses were helping her with all the basic requirements of life. This led to a profound regression in Julia's behaviour. She became demanding of her 'favourite' nurses, speaking to them in a baby voice and often saying spiteful things about them behind their backs. When the time came for her to begin exercises that would increase her range of movements and her personal freedom she was resentful of any suggested activity and felt that people were 'getting at' her rather than helping. The more she was encouraged to make progress the more she resisted, saying that she did not feel 'up to it'. The way she said this sounded just as if she were saying, 'But I'm not old enough to do that!' Most people welcome the opportunity to progress from a sick and dependent state to a more healthy and free existence, and so the nurses were quick to recognise that something unusual and unhealthy was happening to Julia.

The nurses were formed into a united group so that Julia could not split them in their determination to help her out of her regression. The doctor then gave her a clear message that they had a graduated programme of exercises and activities over the coming three weeks, and that she was expected to co-operate. Amid much protesting and tears the team stuck to their plan rigorously. Alongside their strict protocol they demonstrated warmth and encouragement with each new achievement. They were model 'good parents', with rules and limitations, warmth and encouragement carefully balanced to push Julia back to adult functioning. A medical team needs to be united and very confident of each other in order to succeed with this sort of programme. Six months after the accident Julia was back at work, living independently. At her follow-up appointment she apologised for her earlier behaviour, saying, 'I don't know what got into me.'

It is sometimes useful to ask yourself, when under pressure, 'Just how old am I today?' The candid answer might be 'I feel just like I'm 5', or, 'About 15'. Knowing from which point you are operating often makes it easier to understand the 'I don't know what got into me' experience. This can be useful when dealing with partners, children and friends, too. If you have some idea of what age they are operating from you can have a hunch about what how best to respond to them. In adolescence, particularly, a person's emotional age can change dramatically from moment to moment, often leaving parents exasperated and bewildered about whether they are dealing with a baby or an adult.

## Repetition Compulsion

The compulsion to repeat past experiences is a powerful internal drive that comes from our unconscious mind. It is this phenomenon that is central to psychotherapeutic and psychoanalytical work, because a patient will attempt to repeat past relationships with his or her therapist. It is always easier to see a pattern being repeated if you are involved with it, and therefore the therapist has the advantage of being involved enough to 'feel' the relationship but also remains uninvolved enough to think about it and reflect on it objectively to the patient. As the pattern of old relationships re-emerges, so the patient can begin to have a conscious understanding of his or her behaviour, which although often repeated has not previously been recognised or understood.

Sylvia was a 33-year-old teacher who had had a series of disastrous relationships with men. During her therapy, with a male therapist to whom I was acting as supervisor, a clear pattern emerged. At first the therapist came to reporting sessions feeling elated: therapy was going extremely well, he said, and he felt that he and Sylvia understood one another perfectly. When we listened together to a tape recording of their session, however, it became clear that they were engaged in mutual admiration rather than therapy, with Sylvia placing her therapist on a high pedestal. The therapist was not inexperienced, but the power of Sylvia's wish to idealise a helping male was so great that he had been swept into her pattern.

The compulsion to repeat is strong, and this is why good therapy requires much regular supervision. When this therapist took a three-week holiday over Christmas the pattern changed abruptly and dramatically. Suddenly he became the betraying, hopeless man, just like all the others who had let Sylvia down. She became hostile to him both openly and in more subtle ways, until he was surprised to find how strongly he disliked her. Some of the men who had previously 'betrayed' Sylvia had during the break-ups been verbally savage with her, a fact difficult to understand when you first met her, but suddenly the therapist could all too easily understand why someone might wish to lash out at her.

Gradually he helped Sylvia see this pattern, something she had repeated at least four times in her adult life and yet had been consciously unaware of. As she grappled with her role in what she had previously seen as external misfortune, the pieces of her personal jigsaw began to fall into place. Her father had been a merchant seaman, absent for much of her childhood, a distant and idealised figure. In therapy she began to remember that whenever he was home however there would be violent rows and she would wish him away again, yet as soon as he was gone she felt a great longing for the ideal dad of her dreams to return. Sylvia had lived on this seesaw for most of her childhood until her father's death when she was 19. Since then she had repeated this pattern of idealisation followed by massive disillusionment and the resulting fury and desire to savage both the man and the relationship.

Sylvia met a new man, Pete, whom she immediately began to idealise. Her therapist reminded her of her pattern and suggested that she try this time to make a more realistic appraisal of Pete. It was a struggle for her to look consciously for his faults as well as his strengths, with her unconscious always attempting to pull her back into the familiar idealisation. With some reminders from her therapist however Sylvia did manage to see that Pete was not perfect, and to accept this without feeling betrayed or disillusioned. When they had their first major argument she was able to be openly angry but did not experience the same need to savage and destroy that she had previously felt. Perhaps this was connected to the fact that much of the anger she felt towards her father had been aired in therapy: the steam had gone out of her feelings in that relationship, taking with it much of the compulsion to repeat it.

Sadly, it is often the traumatic relationships we seek to repeat, as if it is the times we feel hurt, let down or misunderstood that we cannot integrate and accept, needing instead to rework them constantly. Because the compulsion is unconscious the same story tends to get acted out again and again, the conscious mind having no opportunity to get to grips with that part of ourselves and make things different. Within this phenomenon it is possible to make ourselves feel the way we used to feel by placing ourselves in familiar positions or make others suffer what we once suffered. Hence the children who witness violence in their families often go on to either be violent or be the victims of violence themselves.

Many symptoms are compulsive, the inner drive towards fulfilling the compulsion overriding the more healthy part of our psyche which recognises the symptom as 'ridiculous' or 'unnecessary'. Such symptoms occur in many normal people as well as in those suffering a greater psychological disturbance. Some people demonstrate an obsessional personality structure which makes them more likely to revert to compulsive symptoms when they are stressed (*see* **Obsessive Compulsive Illness**).

During our development we all pass through a time when compulsive acts are the norm. Children tend to like repetitive games, feel comfortable watching the same video many times, and have 'magic' rituals that make them feel safer. This may represent a struggle to control a world that without such devices will seem too big or anxiety-provoking. We find traces of this developmental stage in adult superstitions, and organic disease of the brain often makes the patient revert back to compulsive behaviour, clearly as a rather desperate attempt at control. If we are only half-wake or not concentrating we sometimes find that our minds are compulsively repeating something, a quarrel, a problem at work, or the tune of a song. (*See also* **Idealisation** and **Sado-Masochism**.)

## Repression

This is a mental process which allows us to push down into our unconscious minds all the thoughts, memories and fantasies which would be disturbing if they remained in our consciousness.

Laura, aged 32, was convinced that she had cancer, and visited her GP at least once a week with new symptoms that were causing her anxiety. In fact she was a perfectly healthy woman with an apparently happy life style, and her GP was initially puzzled and then increasingly irritated by her pestering. 'Am I missing something?' he wondered, referring her to a psychiatrist specialising in somatisation (a state in which a person calls attention to underlying psychological difficulties by way of physical symptoms) (*see* **Hypochondriasis** and **Psychosomatic Illnesses**).

The therapist suggested to Laura that her situation was rather like a personal detective story: something inside was obviously upsetting her, making her feel ill, and together they had the task of hunting that 'something' out. To begin with Laura continued to talk about her physical symptoms, but as she realised that she was being taken seriously and not 'fobbed off' for being neurotic she also began to speak about her life, her family and her background.

To her surprise she found that counselling sessions were provoking memories of her teenage years; a time which she thought had been reasonably happy yet which she often found herself crying about. It is not uncommon, with memories that have been long repressed, that the emotions connected to them begin to rise into consciousness before the memory itself. This can be a very puzzling experience because, in effect, you are feeling something which is still consciously 'out of sight'. Laura's dreams also seemed to intensify, and she said that she woke up feeling exhausted by her dream activity.

She spoke of her memories emerging 'as if from a thick fog' and accurately said that, 'I must have been frightened by something to hide it away from myself all these years.' What gradually emerged was a horrifying memory of being sexually abused by her grandfather on several occasions when she was 14. She had hidden this from everyone at the time, and then repressed the memory of the experience to hide it from herself. She had been left with a feeling of badness inside of her. 'I felt as if I were rotten,' was how she described it. The death of her grandmother seemed to have provoked the memories enough for that feeling of 'rotten inside' to surface in her mind, although the actual memory of the abuse remained repressed, at least initially. Thus she had translated that sense of rotting into cancer, making the psychological concrete in an attempt to explain to herself why she felt so bad.

The notion of repression, originating with Freud, is the bedrock of understanding that led to psychoanalysis. It is the mental mechanism by which the unconscious mind is kept separate from the conscious (*see* **Unconscious, Conscious, and Pre-conscious Minds**). Our minds are involved continuously in a complicated negotiation about what we will or will not do, think, or remember. Our instincts would take us in one direction, while our socialisation, our desire to be lovable and loved and our need to remain civilised, insists that we curtail instinctual activities to some extent. In order to live in relative mental peace the memories, the fantasies, and thoughts connected to our instincts are all repressed, and thereby we 'translate' them into consciously acceptable forms. Freud talked of the 'return of the repressed' as the time when symptoms herald the fact that repression is no longer working and hidden memories are trying to emerge into our consciousness.

## Resistance

When you feel ill, you seek help with the conscious desire that your illness be treated. Freud noted, however, that when people approached him with psychological problems apparently wanting relief, they were often resistant to the process whereby relief could be obtained.

An example of this may be seen in melancholia, a form of deep depression that seems to afflict women in their 50s who have suffered relationship losses. Any amount of counselling, therapy, drugs or ECT may seem useless. The teams of professionals charged with their care often become despairing themselves, and begin to label such people 'personality disordered' or 'attention seeking' out of their own hopelessness of promoting health. However, with patience, and if such people can be kept safe from their own destructive actions and given 'tender loving care' (a much under-rated but powerful 'medicine'), many eventually recover after several years, apparently spontaneously. No organic illness can be demonstrated in these individuals, rather it seems as if the blanket of depression, often so thick that they quite literally turn their heads to the wall for months, is in some way necessary at the time to help them blot out the even greater pain of real life with all its disappointments and unpredictability (*see* **Grief** and **Melancholia**).

Observations of many patients who appeared to 'need' their symptoms as much as they required being rid of them made Freud formulate the idea that symptoms serve a purpose, and that until this purpose is understood the symptom cannot be relinquished (*see* **Symptoms and Their Meanings**).

Such resistance to treatment and health education is apparent in all forms of medicine. Most of us, as much as we may attempt to avoid illness, also court it with some form of dangerous behaviour, such as drinking, smoking, driving too fast or engaging in dangerous hobbies. Being well means being adult, capable and coping, having to manage, perhaps alone and unsupported. Being ill means being looked after. In simplistic terms, then, it is easy to see why we might resent attempts to cure our symptoms 'too quickly', before we have had enough care and protection from life and feel ready to give them up.

The ego – our conscious, logical mind – presents the symptom first to ourselves and then to others as an indication that something is wrong. However, our ego has also buried whatever is worrying us by means of repression in our unconscious mind. Thus, when attempts are made to understand and treat the symptom the ego is 'on guard', attempting both to maintain this attention and keep the repressed material out of sight by resisting efforts made to liberate it.

The resistance to cure of the presented symptom can be expressed in words or actions. Many people wait months for an out-patient appointment, only to miss it when it eventually arrives. Their feet are acting out their resistance to help even though they want (and need) that help. They are probably also acting out their fury at being kept waiting for extraordinary lengths of time (*see* **Acting Out**). Similarly, patients may be persuasive about wanting psychotherapy yet once this is offered may sit silently in sessions, unable to use the time constructively. Clearly this is puzzling to the patient and potentially infuriating to the helping agencies. One of the benefits of training to be an analyst is that you are yourself analysed; this teaches you how resistant you are, which in turn makes it much easier to be patient and understanding about the resistance of others.

Mary was 32 and had been anorexic for six years. Just prior to starting psychoanalysis she had regained a normal weight. She expressed a commitment to understanding her problems, fearing that her improvement might be only temporary, and therefore arrived for each session full of good intentions about the psychological work she would do. However each session would begin with a recital of why it was impossible to 'get into anything emotional today'. She commented that whereas prior to starting therapy she thought she knew what it was that she wanted to talk about, she had now 'forgotten'. Alongside that she discovered that she could no longer remember years of her childhood. She blamed the therapist for her difficulties and questioned whether she should see someone more experienced.

Several sessions were spent idealising the time when her anorexia had been at its worst. She had been near death, but could now only remember the sense of being cared for in hospital. She compared that with having to live independently, often feeling lonely and unloved. The therapist reflected to her the sense of failure that was so much an aspect of each session, and Mary agreed that failure and fear of failure had been corner-stones in her development. Her father had been a diplomat with obsessionally high standards of dress and appearance. As an adolescent she sensed constantly that her developing femininity was experienced by him as a failure on her part. 'Women are bound to fail,' she said, 'and yet I desperately did not want to fail him.'

The therapist suggested that the anorexia had been a form of ritualised suicide because of Mary's despair about this relationship. During her time in therapy there would be sessions when her relationship with her father could be addressed and then sessions in which Mary 'could not remember' or was 'fed up with talking about it'. Gradually she began to see for herself that some aspects of the anorexia had been enormously satisfying for her, which was what made it so difficult to survive and then beat. During the time of greatest starvation she had felt elation for the amount of self-punishment she could tolerate as retribution for her hatred of her father while at the same time openly punishing him for his lack of acceptance of her by inflicting on him great anxiety for her well-being. Mary talked of her dissatisfaction with every aspect of herself as she gained weight, and how angry she had felt when anyone told her that she was looking better. 'I didn't feel I deserved to be better. It was an agony to give up hating myself and to live with the fact that I hate him, instead.'

As therapy advanced it became clear that she not only hated her father but loved and identified with him as well. She had hoped to be a diplomat too as part of that identification. 'It's strange that I never thought of identifying with my mother,' she commented. There followed a series of memories emerging as though from a distant mist of how unhappy her mother had been, criticised constantly by her father for failing to meet his standards and having to move with him from continent to continent every two or three years. Mary had completely forgotten about her mother's unhappiness, but gradually began to realise that she blamed herself for that, too – another reason she believed herself to be bad. Throughout therapy, at every new step in understanding there would be a period of resistance to movement, new knowledge, new insights. As Mary began to recognise and acknowledge the resistance, so it would crumble to reveal the next piece of the jigsaw.

Freud suggested that five different types of resistance were encountered during psychoanalysis. First, the ego may resist by renewing its original repression of the disturbing memories (forgetting something that was once known); second, the ego may transfer aspects of the self and what worries it onto the therapist (it is the therapist who will fail and not me); third, the ego may also be aware of the gains to be had from remaining ill which act towards maintaining it (symptoms provide intense shorthand to other family members). Fourth, the unconscious for its part desires to repeat early experiences again and again rather than learn about new possibilities (I've failed before so I must fail in therapy); and finally, our super-ego may, from guilt, embrace the symptom as a deserved punishment (I'm bad for hating anyone and so I must hurt myself) (*see* **Guilt, Inferiority Complex**, **Punishment**, and **Sado-masochism**).

## Ruminations

Each of us may ponder over a particular problem or idea from time to time. Something worrying may keep us awake and distract us from everything else. When there are external problems which need to be sorted out this kind of behaviour is helpful to us, focusing our attention until we find a solution. However, for those who have an unusually rigid or obsessional personality this behaviour can dominate their mental lives (*see* **Obsessive Compulsive Illness**). The ruminations may be about irrelevant matters, their thoughts leading them round in circles, yet these ruminations dominate their thoughts to the exclusion of thinking about normal day-to-day activities and issues.

The ruminations may be about disease, and people with such ruminations often have a tendency towards hypochondria. David, aged 35, would spend several hours a day checking his body for signs of illness. He concentrated on breathing and swallowing to such an extent that he inhibited these actions, then, having found himself unable to swallow, would spend time wondering what sort of illness would produce that symptom. Preoccupied with thoughts of death and the possibility of an after-life he would torment himself with questions such as the purpose of life or the reality of death; questions which, despite the hours he devoted to thinking about them, he could not possibly hope to answer. He looked perpetually worn, thin and tense, became unable to work, and destroyed his one close friendship by the extent of his self-preoccupation.

Naomi, aged 42, had been brought up in a strict religious family, for whom cleanliness had been directly associated with godliness. She volunteered that she did not believe in spontaneity, thinking that it allowed the devil into your thoughts. However, much to her shame, she found herself unable to stop thoughts about male genitalia entering her mind. In an attempt to control her ruminations about men and their bodies which took up much of her time she developed counting behaviour, and would count repetitively up to the number 53 many times a day. She was sure that she was suffering from signs of moral decay and would then spend hours in spiritual self-scrutiny, so that she began to lose both her sense of self and of reality.

When ruminations take over in this way people often destroy important aspects of their lives such as their work and relationships. They cannot study effectively and, despite being intellectually bright, often waste that potential. Depression, despair and anxiety frequently overwhelm them as their behaviour makes their lives increasingly stressed and unfulfilling. It is helpful to encourage people who are becoming preoccupied with their ruminations to seek help early, because sadly, by the very nature of the problem, they often become so inward-looking as to be unable to communicate their distress accurately to the outside world, or if they do communicate it they do so by means of endless, apparently trivial visits to their GP with physical ailments, or to their vicar for spiritual answers that cannot be given to their satisfaction. Usually they are referred to psychologists, psychotherapists or psychiatrists some time after the problem started, and by which time much secondary damage has been done to their lives.

Counselling or supportive or educational therapy can be helpful in the early stages, allowing the individuals to explore a variety of areas in their lives and to sort out the real dilemmas from the quite often 'false' difficulties they are persecuting themselves with. Sometimes in-depth analysis will reveal and help to heal basic underlying personality problems which have allowed the problems to arise. Psychologists have a number of thinking exercises that can help the person to control the ruminations by replacing them with other, more healthy thoughts. Such treatment requires a lot of co-operation and commitment from the individual.

Many patients are given mild sedatives or anti-depressants. These are sometimes helpful and can spare the sufferers much psychic pain; however some are addictive psychologically, physically, or both, and therefore need to be taken in restricted amounts for a defined period of time. Some form of counselling may well be needed once the acute pain has past to help the individual back towards a normal and satisfying life.

# S

## Sado-Masochism

Masochism is the experience of pain and/or humiliation which causes arousal, usually sexual arousal, in an individual. Both Freud and Klein connected the childhood experiences of both sadism and masochism with the existence of a death wish or death instinct that is as inherent in human beings, from birth, as is a life wish or life instinct (*see* **Eroticism, Death, Instinct for Survival, Libido,** and **Love**). The anxiety associated with the inner conflict between life and death is lessened by an individual projecting the death wish outwards as aggression or sadism. In order to protect the ones we love from our sadism we may, unconsciously, decide to keep it within us, turned inside as masochism. Freud called this primary masochism. Because this experience happens in connection with our developing abilities to love and be sexual, so our masochism is commonly acted out in sexual and loving relationships. The tendency towards masochism is however always linked with elements of sadism, although the sadism may remain at an unconscious level which is never acknowledged or acted out. Secondary masochism follows a period of time during which the sadism has been turned out onto external objects, people, or animals, and then re-introjected back inside of ourselves as masochism.

It sometimes surprises adults that children can be sadistic, both to each other and to animals and objects – usually things or people who in some way have less power than themselves – and that this is a normal part of development. In families where sadism is openly expressed in contempt or violence this tendency in childhood is greatly exaggerated and the child then develops a distorted sense of how sadism and its consequent masochism are dealt with in normal life.

Freud suggested that one form of masochism was specifically attached to the feminine part of ourselves, a feminine part which can be present in men as well as women. Certainly women seem to report more masochistic tendencies than men, and there are some indications that the stereotypical view of women includes an assumption of suffering, for example in childbirth, which remains painful for many women because our society refuses to turn its high-technology abilities towards rendering it painless, indeed, quite the opposite, high-tech births often being associated with more pain for the mother, for example induced contractions. Men who report sexual fantasies which include the need to be hurt or humiliated tend to be viewed as perverts, while women often report fantasies of enormous masochism (often not acted out) which are regarded as relatively normal. However this view of the normality of feminine masochism has been strongly argued against by many people, such as Paula Caplan, author of *The Myth of Woman's Masochism*, or Jean Baker Miller, author of *Towards a New Psychology of Women*, in which she suggests that the external part of masochism so often connected to a woman's existence is in fact typical of any dominated group and would be seen as clearly amongst young male slaves as amongst middle-aged housewives.

It is certainly true that the expression of sadism requires some form of external power. Without that power the individual, whether child, woman or black person, will resort to an in-turning of his or her own sadism into a form of masochism; if this is extreme enough it may render the individual 'victim-like' to those who retain the external power and express sadism openly.

Masochism is not always directly expressed in a sexual context. Freud described a form of moral masochism in which people seem to experience a need for punishment in order to quell some inner sense of guilt. Such a need can be expressed in many ways within a relationship (*see* **Guilt** and **Punishment**).

Tabatha was a 29-year-old doctor who became depressed as a result of a number of failed relationships. She reported that not only was her love-life disastrous, but that her relationships with colleagues were also tense and unhappy. Within the course of a single interview I found myself infuriated with her, wanting to shout at her or throw her out. I wondered aloud to her how she managed to make people angry with her.

Over a period of time it became clear that Tabatha experienced great guilt about her success in the world. She felt guilty about her great intelligence, which 'made life too easy' for her, about her social position as a doctor which made her feel a fraud, and about the money she earned 'while the rest of the world starved'. One of her ways of coping with this was to make others angry and abusive with her. In this way she gained the punishment she felt she deserved. In all her relationships she adopted such an extreme position of masochism that she managed to extract the sadist out of all but the most saintly around her. She had learned this position as a battered child, and was constantly acting out the cowed infant in the way she attached herself to others. As she began to utilise a small part of her own sadism, she found that others became more pleasant towards her.

It is often suggested that wives who are battered have masochistic personalities and enjoy the cruel treatment they receive. They tend to come from violent families themselves, from which the boys grow into violent men and the girls into abused women. This split suggests that there is a huge social process of expectation as well as individual development at work. It also reflects the great power differential – physical, economic, and social – between men and women. I have never met a woman whom I considered 'addicted' to the beatings she received in the way that masochists are often addicted to their sexual activities. It seems more likely that unrealistic hopes of 'curing' their man by being 'good' wives ('the love of a good woman' myth) is what makes them return many times, alongside the real social and economic disadvantages of leaving.

Regular beatings are rarely associated with arousal for the woman although may well have sexual associations for the man. This reflects the fact that external power gives humans the possibility of expressing sadism. The resultant masochism can be forced onto anyone, masochistic or not by personality, if they have less power. Such a differential is seen in situations of torture and social disintegration on a massive scale as well as within the smaller arena of the family.

There is also some suggestion that women focus any sadism they have onto their children, who have less power than themselves, thus rendering their sadism for the most part invisible to the world and leaving their supposedly masochistic image intact.

## Satisfaction, Experience of
*See* **Experience of Satisfaction**

## Schizophrenia

Just under 1 per cent of the population world-wide suffer from the disorder of their thinking, perception and behaviour known as schizophrenia. Research has suggested that it is a partially inherited illness but that environment both during childhood and adult life is crucial in deciding whether or not the symptoms occur. At least half of the new cases seen have no family history of the disorder, suggesting either a genetic mutation rate or other strong influencing agents in its production. Family dynamics, particularly those which produce misleading or paradoxical messages from adults to children, have been suggested as a psychodynamic cause of the disorder, but family explanations tend to be experienced as apportioning blame by sufferers and their families.

Researchers have demonstrated however that the levels of emotion expressed within a family are associated with the rate of a patient's relapse. Having a schizophrenic relative puts great strain on a family system, and their level of expressed emotion may be a reflection of that strain rather than a pre-existing cause of the illness. Part of the treatment often does, however, need to consist of quiet housing away from relatives. Life events can trigger relapses, suggesting that those vulnerable to schizophrenia have a low tolerance to change.

The pre-schizophrenic personality is said to be introspective, obsessional and emotionally cold. Such people are often rigid in character and go out of their way to avoid stress or change. However, schizophrenia also occurs in people with previously normal personalities.

Research aimed at understanding the biochemistry of the disease has still to come to any provable conclusions. Some believe that normal transmitter substances in the brain may exist in higher quantities in schizophrenics; others feel that the deterioration of personality that is often apparent over time suggests that a slow virus is attacking the brain tissue.

In terms of symptoms, schizophrenia is first and foremost a disorder of thinking, with a characteristic pattern of thought disorder including illogical ideas, thought blocking (where a stream of thought is interrupted), thought insertion or removal (when an outside agency is held responsible for the sudden appearance or disappearance of thoughts), and thought broadcasting (when the sufferer believes that everyone can hear his or her thoughts).

Alongside these problems with thinking, the person may also be deluded – some would say that much of the disordered thought is a result of the patient's desperate attempt to make sense of a delusionally distorted view of the world – and hallucinating (most commonly auditory or visual hallucinations). Emotionally the person will appear incongruous or 'flat' and his or her behaviour may become manneristic, withdrawn and uninterested over a period of months. Work and personal hygiene may be neglected.

The treatment of schizophrenia has improved a little with the onset of the drug chlorpromazine and depot injections to control the more florid and disturbing symptoms. Most specialists would agree, however, that there is still a long way to go before we understand and acceptably treat the problem – an overall approach to both the patient and his life is necessary to achieve and maintain remission.

## Self-Censorship
*See* **Censorship**

## Self-preservation
*See* **Instinct for Survival**

## Senile Dementia
*See* **Dementia**

## Sexual Arousal Disorders

In women the inability to achieve or maintain arousal that used to be termed frigidity is demonstrated by a lack of vaginal lubrication and the subjective experience of lack of pleasure or even disinterest in achieving arousal while at the same time wishing for sexual activity. In men failure to achieve or maintain an erection (previously known as impotence) is the most obvious outward sign of lack of arousal, accompanied by frustration and often a strong sense of humiliation, too.

Sexual activity has become an area of human life which we view as a 'performance' in which we may be judged and found wanting. Many people believe that everyone else is having regular, satisfying sex and therefore judge their own performances or those of their partners critically against what is usually a fantasy of perfectly synchronous orgasms. Because of this, 'performance-quality' sex can provoke anxiety, and anxiety inhibits any possibility of arousal. Having 'failed' once or twice the anxiety becomes worse and the arousal even less likely. Taking away the expectation of intercourse by banning it for days or weeks allows the sexual partners to return to simple pleasuring, much like adolescent exploration, without the anxiety-provoking thought of an eventual performance. This simple measure is frequently sufficient to break the vicious circle.

Education about sexual matters sometimes relieves a sense of guilt or shame that one or both partners may be experiencing. Many women are deeply uncertain and conflicted about whether it is 'good' to be sexy, while many men fear sexual activity much more than they consciously acknowledge to themselves. Early sexual abuse or rape have long-term disastrous consequences for adult enjoyment of sexuality. The presence of a baby or small children in the family is also likely to be an inhibiting factor, and many women feel no need for sexual activity for months or even years after a birth. Depression is also likely to inhibit arousal (*see* **Libido**).

Within a relationship it is possible, perhaps surprisingly, for couples to enjoy sex even if their relationship is not otherwise harmonious. Many couples enjoy sex much more after an argument, for instance. For others, however, one partner's anger towards the other, especially unexpressed resentment, battles about control, dominance and power, or a lack of trust all have negatives effects.

Inhibited orgasms in both men and women are usually connected to strong anti-sex messages from upbringing, fears about homosexuality or social factors such as the fear of unwanted pregnancy. Premature ejaculation is common and relatively easily to treat by means of the 'squeeze' technique taught in psychosexual therapy, in which the penis is squeezed when ejaculation is near to diminish excitement. This is done on a repeated basis helping the man to 'relearn' his sexual response and develop more control. Reports of pain during sexual activity may have physical origins and these certainly need to be considered, however the majority of such complaints are rooted in the lack of or incomplete arousal of one or both partners, usually resulting from ignorance or fear of sexual matters. Occasionally the fear of being hurt is so great that the woman experiences a powerful contraction of her vaginal muscles which prevents penetration. A gentle combination of physical and psychological exploration are frequently helpful in allowing the woman to know and understand her own body before she attempts to share it.

## Sexuality

The sexual instinct, or libido, is an inborn drive with which we are all gifted as well as burdened. In a straightforward understanding, the kind that most religions, cultures and education leans towards, sexuality is the inborn drive of libido used in the service of gaining genital pleasure by the combining of the genitals of two people of opposite sexes (and in some people's understanding this has to lead to conception, or the chance of conception, in order to be 'correctly' gratifying). It takes only the most casual glance at the papers, chat with our friends, the revelations of patients and our knowledge of the wide variety of habits, perversions and pleasures which constitute sexuality for the majority, however, to make us realise that human sexuality is much more complex.

This should not surprise us, given that libido is an inborn instinct, present throughout our many stages of development and therefore affected and influenced by every stage, every experience, in a way that is too powerful for our super-ego to wind up having much control over how we gain sexual pleasure. During his lifetime Freud changed from believing that sexuality only operated along the lines of what he called the 'pleasure principle', by which we use an infantile understanding of sexuality and wish to gain rapid gratification, to thinking that libido was clearly also associated with our life instincts, the drive for both our own lives and for procreation (*see* **Eroticism** and **Libido**). Either way, he felt that we all used much of our energy repressing a variety of sexual thoughts from our conscious minds in order to function in society. His society was, of course, more sexually repressive, but it would be wrong of us to think that we are completely liberated or culturally at ease with sexuality (*see* **Repression**).

Freud talked of 'organ' pleasure, reminding us that the breasts, the mouth and the anus can all be erogenous zones. Humans also have a great ability to fantasise and can gain much pleasure in this way, yet much 'illness' or 'dis-ease' results from peoples' fantasies or partially repressed desires, which they believe to be 'wrong' or unacceptable.

Simon, aged 23, was socially phobic because he thought that others could 'see' that he was homosexual. His desire for men conflicted, in what was for him an unbearably painful way, with his understanding of what he was allowed to feel. Annette, aged 42, was worried by her sado-masochistic fantasies, never acted out, which allowed her to achieve orgasm. Paula, aged 31, felt that she might be promiscuous because she enjoyed sexual activities so much.

Each of these people needed to accept their sexuality for what it was rather than comparing it against an ideal which they considered normal. Simon made contact with a group of homosexual men with whom he experienced feeling normal for the first time since early adolescence. Annette was encouraged to enjoy her fantasies in the understanding that they helped liberate her from a sense of terrible responsibility for sex, which her mother had bestowed upon her. Paula, when confronted with the World Health Organisation definition of promiscuity (three or more sexual partners in a calendar year) laughed and accepted her sexual drive as a positive facet of her relationships. Often we only need permission in order to enjoy our sexual selves.

All these anxieties and many more act to repress our enjoyment of sexuality. Society still actively invades this private aspect of the lives of individuals in order to dictate what is or is not normal. However, within sexual relationships there is often a discrepancy of power between individuals and therefore it is important to assert that 'consenting adults' should always mean 'equal consenting adults' – yet how often do we actually achieve that, even within the confines of the definition of sexuality as socially-monitored heterosexuality. Indeed, for many years marriage has been regarded as the only place for safe and 'proper' sex, even though the structure of marriage was designed to render women unequal. In many ways social repression does as much to turn sexuality into a battlefield as it does to protect us from excesses and perversions which would damage us and society.

## Shame

We experience shame when we break a taboo or moral principle. Unlike guilt, which we experience when we have deliberately done something 'wrong', it is possible to be ashamed unintentionally. Until recently illegitimate children often felt shame without having done anything themselves to deserve it. With guilt we may make atonement, but the pain of shame is not so easily healed. It is possible to feel shame without the cause of that feeling becoming public knowledge. Such a feeling may cause us to want to hide whatever it is that we are ashamed of, and all societies have a need to develop mechanisms by which to distance the object of shame, because psychologically, shame feels contagious. The actions of a few people can shame a nation – for instance the shame we all feel when English football fans behave badly on the Continent.

Of course our experience of shame can vary widely. Some people are very sensitive to any sense of shame, and may even be sub-consciously looking for it all the time; others are more immune, caring less for the belief systems of society or having little sense of principle themselves. Because we tend to hide the things of which we are ashamed we have no way of knowing whether our judgement of how much shame to feel is appropriate or not. Within therapy it is sometimes surprising to the therapist the sorts of things that shame people. Similarly in group therapy, once one member shares something shameful, the group members usually discover that they all have shameful secrets. Such a sense of universality can be curative. Therapy allows people to share experiences which have produced shame in an environment that holds judgement at bay and allows the individual to take a more human, less critical look at their behaviour. In this way many experiences, particularly those of childhood, can be placed in a different perspective and thereby rendered less shameful.

Claire had been anorexic for three years before she joined a weekly out-patient group. She had never spoken about the sexual relationship she had had with her father before she discussed it with the group. When she did choose to share it, the group were initially hushed. 'You must think very badly of me,' Claire said, and immediately the group members said that they were shocked and hurt for Claire, not critical of her. 'You were so little,' remarked Richard, 'how could you possibly know what was right or wrong?' This remark, so obvious in itself, and said with much warmth, had an almost physical effect on Claire, who seemed to straighten and grow in her chair. Over the coming weeks her skin and hair began to glow and she wore more attractive, less concealing clothes. The group regularly reminded her that the source of her shame was illogical, thus immunising her against the terribly destructive effect it had had on her for so long.

The fear of being shamed can limit our growth psychologically and make us restrict ourselves within boundaries that may keep us safe from shame but also inhibit us. There needs to be some healthy balance between growing to fulfil ourselves realistically without breaking the taboos that would most hurt us with shame. Sexual behaviour is often laced with prohibitions that make shame a constant threat. As society changes its code of sexual behaviour people are often left confused about what is or is not shaming. Such ambiguity leads to much distress.

Maria came from Italy to live in England during a training course and became upset and confused by the different sets of cultural rules about sexual relationships here. She complained that she felt 'continually ashamed. I blush all the time' because of the expectations of her English boyfriends. 'What I can get away with here, will cause me great shame at home,' she said. This sort of confusion lays bear just how much our society dictates what is right or wrong for individuals in ways that may well not be very helpful for the individual. The American psychologist Erich Fromm has pointed out that one of the most powerfully limiting aspects to our psychological development is this sense of the imposition placed on us by the time and culture we are born into and from which we have no escape. Indeed, fear of shame is often the policing force of social expectation.

## Sleepwalking
*See* **Insomnia**

## Sorrow
*See* **Grief**

## Stockholm Syndrome
*See* **Identification with Persecutors**

## Stress
We usually experience stress as coming from the outside and bearing down on us, either physically, emotionally or intellectually. Most models of stress, however, emphasise that it can only operate on a limited number of levels. In order to understand it we need to look at the stress level of each situation.

First, we experience a demand: this is the external component of the stress, and is usually easy to identify. It consists of having too much to do in too little time, having to get on with things even if we feel unwell or depressed, having exams, having to face difficult situations at work or troubled relationships. According to 'life events charts' that give a rating to every situation in terms of how stressful the 'average' person might expect to find it, happy events are often just as stressful as unhappy ones: therefore marriage and having a baby, buying a new house (especially one with a big mortgage), getting promoted, and many of the other things which we see as recreation, such as holidays, Christmas, or being with the family, can be stressful.

Second, we recognise the demand: it is sometimes possible to continue in a stressful situation for weeks or even years before acknowledging that it is stressful. We then collapse, either when the stress ends or when someone points out to us just how over-extended we are, which may be the first time we notice it ourselves. Recognising stress is not only a matter of timing but also of how we perceive the stress and our role within it: are we responsible for the stressful event or was it forced on us? Can we do anything about it? Is it helping us towards a wanted goal or pushing us towards an unwanted one? Sometimes we recognise the stress unconsciously, feeling that there is something wrong without being able to put our finger on what it is.

We then respond to the stress in a variety of ways. We may have an internal, physiological response. Exercise can stress our system, in which case our response will be mostly physiological involving our heart rate and breathing. If we become frightened the primary response is also physiological, sometimes to the point of 'freezing' us into a paralysis so that we cannot cope any more.

We may have a psychological response to stress, experiencing anxiety or depression, or making a conscious decision to act either as an individual or with the help of a group, either the family, friends or community. We sometimes think about our reactions to stressful situations: they may be planned responses to the problem or they may be spontaneous.

Finally, in the wake of whatever response we have made we judge whether it was successful. If not, we try to think what else we can do. From these sorts of judgements we learn increasingly what the good and not-so-good ways of handling stress are. At every stage of this process of recognising and managing stress we have feedback systems that monitor the interaction between the stress and ourselves.

Joe, aged 43, worked very hard. He was depressed and drinking too much alcohol when he agreed to join a small psychotherapy group. Although the group did not meet until 8.30 p.m. he was often late, using pressure at work as his excuse. Initially he presented this in such a way that nobody thought to question it, but after a few weeks the group became annoyed with what they saw as a dismissal of themselves, and said 'What is so important at work that it's more important than your health?'; they might have added: 'Or us?'. Joe acknowledged that his wife often said the same, and that she had threatened to leave him if he could not 'sort things out'.

Over the weeks that followed the group continued to challenged Joe's assumption that work came before everything, including himself. He would spend long periods explaining in detail the stresses to which he was subject and how they formed a vicious circle from which he could see no escape. 'Why don't you take a two week break and go away, do something entirely different and then see how it looks?' asked a fellow group member, Anne. 'You don't understand' Joe retorted angrily, 'I've never taken a holiday since starting this job.' Clearly Joe perceived his stress as an inevitable part of his job, while the rest of the world saw that he should take another look at it. It is often true that we become so involved with our own particular stress that we cannot get it into proportion.

Anne then told the group about her experiences of trying to get the family, who had recently all left home, to return for Sunday lunches. She expressed surprise that she did this, as the work involved frequently left her tired and irritable with them when they arrived even though she had looked forward to it all week. 'I feel that I need to be needed,' she said, 'but that need wears me out'.

Joe could identify with this need to be needed. He explained that for years at home he had felt that his wife and the children were a unit that did not appear to need him. 'I used to think I interrupted them whenever I was at home, so I stayed at the office longer and longer. It became a habit which made me very successful: I'm needed at work.' Anne said that she could recognise her own husband in Joe, and wondered whether she had pushed him out of the home. 'I would love to see more of him now,' she commented.

Joe went home that evening and had a long talk with his wife, who said that she did need him. 'Actually,' Joe told the group in amazement the following week, 'she said she had always needed me, even when the children were little, but that she'd thought I was too busy to bother.' Peter, the group leader, pointed out that the group had also felt that Joe was 'too busy to bother' when he had started out by being so late for their sessions.

Joe took a holiday: his work did not collapse. He came back refreshed and found he could do more now that he felt less stressed and also much more supported at home. For Joe the group acted as a feedback loop; he had needed that external reinforcement because he had got used to ignoring his own feedback, which was repeatedly telling him he was tired and stressed. The group's feedback allowed him to modify his perception of his stress, which in turn encouraged him to respond to it in a new, helpful way instead of with his former response of simply trying harder and harder at work.

Our ability to cope with stress varies accordingly with our personalities and what sort of stress it is. Most of us have a range of resources for coping with stress; these include feeling good about ourselves and our intelligence and skills, feeling secure and supported by family and friends, and perceiving ourselves as effective at work, as well as the more material resources such as money, influence and occupation.

We develop particular attitudes towards different sorts of stress depending on whether we see them as unavoidable, desirable, harmful or controllable. If we have had prior experience dealing with a similar stress we will either know that what we did last time worked well or know that we must try something different this time. This may give us more or less strength in facing the stress, depending on how we felt about the previous outcome. In the face of stress we make rapid assessments about the danger that is real or the threat we fear. The amount of danger real or perceived to us and those we love makes an enormous difference to our ability to cope, both in the short term with the immediate stress and in the longer term, with any consequences.

Finally, we have different vulnerabilities to stress. Our inbuilt vulnerability comes from our basic personality and from our early life experiences. To some extent our parents and other important adults will have given us models of coping depending on how they coped. Even those who cope well with the everyday stresses of life can find themselves overwhelmed by a sudden and totally unexpected stress. When this happens it is often hard for them to recover, since the event 'cracks' their vision of themselves as copers, whereas those who constantly view themselves as struggling to cope are less surprised to find themselves overwhelmed and may even welcome the opportunity to give up and allow others to cope for a while. The most difficult stresses to cope with in adult life are those which seem to 'key in' to important and painful events of our childhood, particularly previous deaths or losses. Because the adult event reminds us forcibly of the earlier event, we end up experiencing it as if we were children again, helpless, powerless, uncomprehending. Clearly this adds a new dimension to any stress on the adult (*see* **Anxiety**, **Depression**, **Fixation**, **Flight into Illness**, **Repetition Compulsion**, **Tension**, and **Trauma**).

Thus stress, how we recognise it, respond to it, and judge that response, is a complicated matter: In looking at the effects of stress within yourself each of its elements needs to be evaluated and feedback gained to help you in the coping process.

## Suggestibility

Each of us is, to some extent, suggestible. We believe what someone says to us beyond what may be objective and rational, simply because we invest in the knowledge and ability of that other person. Healers of all sorts have always used this degree of human suggestibility in order to facilitate recovery. When we are ill or in pain we want to believe in the ability of another to make us better, thus we are more suggestible than usual to the healer's influence.

The amount to which we are suggestible varies enormously depending on our personality, past experience, present situation and perception of the honesty and ability of the person making the suggestion. Our suggestibility also varies depending on whether we are familiar with the topic or environment in which the suggestion occurs. An African doctor once told me that each tribe has a special person whose task is to make up unlikely rituals and myths to tell visiting white people about their culture. He convinced me that many famous travellers had been misled by such tales, and to this day I am not sure whether travellers are very suggestible in foreign lands or whether I was very suggestible to this particular doctor, who may have been joking!

There are some illnesses in which one's suggestibility seems to be increased. This often leads to confusion on the part of the doctor trying to diagnose the illness because the person will 'adopt' suggested symptoms as well as experiencing their own initial symptoms. Disseminated sclerosis (also called Multiple Sclerosis or MS) is often associated, particularly in the early days of the illness, with an enhanced suggestibility both in terms of symptoms experienced and recovery. As it is often difficult to diagnose, the sufferer's suggestibility may lead health professionals to think that he or she is being hysterical about the problems, and may lead carers to underestimate both the difficulties and fear he or she is experiencing.

Any illness that affects the structure of the brain may cause an increase in suggestibility; and for heavy drinkers, whose drinking impairs their brains, it may be one of the first signs of long-term damage to their ability to think clearly.

Some of us are by personality extremely suggestible, and this may play an important part in hysterical reactions. An hysterical reaction means we respond to any suggestion made rather than have an accurate perception of what is going on and how it affects us. Even the most resilient of us may prove suggestible when we are in a large group. There was a report of a group of several hundred youngsters who apparently 'collapsed' at a gathering for no obvious reason. It seems as if it took just a few of them to faint in the heat before the group as a whole took up the suggestion, leading to a mass collapse. Certainly most of us are capable of doing things in groups which would normally be out of character, since the group can have more power to suggest than we have individually to resist.

In a now-famous experiment in the USA researchers were able to 'suggest' to their subjects that they should give electric shocks to people (who were in fact actors), even though these people looked to be suffering great pain and even be near death as a result. Less than 5 out of 100 people could resist the suggestion. This is particularly interesting in face of the fact that hypnotists always tell us that they cannot make us do anything by suggestion that we would not normally want to do. Realistically, we all have only limited power with which to resist suggestions from those in authority, whether that authority be perceived or real.

This general suggestibility to those who are powerful in our society should mean that such people are continuously aware of the enormous responsibility this dominance confers on them. Not uncommonly however it leads to them enjoying their power over others and using the potential for suggestion to their own advantage, often disguised as being 'for the good of' others. Within medicine (and education, business, religion, and many other aspects of our society) such suggestibility can be used for good or harm. Perhaps one of the most harmful aspects occurs when the person in power 'suggests' sexual contact with the one who is suggestible to them. Such relationships often end disastrously for the suggestible participant, who will feel used, hurt and angry, but also guilty and shameful. Meanwhile the powerful person from whom the suggestion arose will usually escape any form of judgement on their behaviour and may even feel aggrieved at the outcome of the sexuality, believing (from their own inner suggestion to themselves) that it should have 'cured' or helped the other participant and/or themselves (*see* **Narcissism**).

## Suicide

More than twice as many men kill themselves than do women. They are often older, widowed, lonely or socially isolated people, who may be retired or unemployed. Previous physical and mental ill health are common, and there is a high incidence of associated alcoholism (*see* **Alcoholism**). Almost half of the people who commit suicide have told someone, a relative, friend or doctor, about their low spirits and desire for death within a week or two of the suicide. Although depression is a common precipitant, a concealed hostility towards family or an attempt to act out psychotic hallucinations or delusions may also lead to self-destruction. Assessing the risk and predicting the dangers of suicide is far from easy. Many people will put their affairs in order and give belongings away prior to committing suicide; others will be particularly at risk after distressing news or events.

Suicide is only sought when life appears unendurable and the person believes him- or herself to have exhausted other options or that life no longer has any significance. Almost anyone could come to this point if life was hard enough; the vast majority of us do not, however, because our sense of attachment to others and investment in ourselves carries us through despair. For the lonely, the impulsive and those whose coping mechanisms have ceased to function there is no tether to hold them to humanity.

Commemorations of the deaths of relatives or of significant events are often chosen so as to somehow dignify the suicide with meaning.

Anyone who is felt to be in serious risk of taking his or her own life needs a sustaining relationship to count on, and must be protected from exposure to easy means of death when in the phase of acute despair.

The number of suicides amongst adolescent boys has risen sharply in the last ten years, and mass unemployment has also had an impact on the figures for men. Adolescents are frequently secretive about their feelings and may well conceal the depths of their anguish from family and close friends. Anxieties about sexuality, friendships and exams seem to be common triggers. (*See also* **Suicide Attempts**.)

## Suicide Attempts

Until the 1950s attempted suicides tended to be seen as failed suicides, rather than as a separate experience. Since that time researchers have established that attempted suicides occur among different populations than do suicides. Clearly there is some overlap between the two groups: some people unluckily achieve suicide when they only meant to attempt it; others, whose desire for death is very real, fail to achieve their goal. In an eight-year follow-up of suicide attempters a study in Oxford published in 1988 demonstrated that there was an increased risk of suicide and also of death by other physical illnesses and accidents. Those most at risk of committing suicide after an attempt are men, those people in the older age groups, and those who have either a psychiatric illness (particularly schizophrenia) or a physical illness.

People who attempt suicide are more likely to be responding to a particular distressing incident in their lives – the breakdown of a relationship, failure on an exam, unemployment – and the attempt is often seen as a 'cry for help' when circumstances threaten to overwhelm them. Certainly it was rumoured that there was little attempted suicide during the ambulance drivers' dispute of 1990 – people who might otherwise have wanted to cry for help in this way must have known that their cry might go unheeded, and so were dissuaded from the attempt.

Obviously individuals must feel helpless if they think the only way they can achieve change is by threatening their own lives, and therefore attempted suicide tends to be connected with socio-economic deprivation, and is twice as common in young women as in men. Many external factors can also influence suicidal behaviour. A study done in Ireland suggested that attempted suicide was seasonally related, with the majority of attempts made in the summer months. Self-harm is also often associated with drug or alcohol abuse.

Sharon, aged 19, lives in a fourth-floor council flat with her two young children. She has financial problems, troubles with the neighbours, who complain about the children's noise, and a violent boyfriend. They are a family well known to social services, who were of the opinion that Sharon managed remarkably well in the circumstances. She suffered from an almost continual headache, which meant that she always had stocks of pain-killers at hand. One Friday evening while out drinking with a girlfriend she spotted her boyfriend out with and kissing another woman when he was meant to be home baby-sitting. She described afterwards the sensation of something 'snapping' inside her head. She went home and washed 100 tablets down with a can of beer. She then phoned her friend and told her what she had done.

This is a typical scenario for a suicide attempt. Attempts are therefore associated with acute, intense distress about an aspect of our lives, in situations where we feel unable or inadequate to the task of producing desired change, trapped within a distressing situation, perhaps incapacitated by alcohol or drugs, and without the necessary social support to counteract the despair. It is usually an impulsive rather than well-thought-out event, and one which is aimed at producing enough harm to the self to elicit anxiety and concern on the part of those in our immediate environment. In some families it appears to be almost an accepted method of raising the alarm about situations, and produces the hoped-for result, that is, the individual and his or her distress are finally taken seriously. More often, however, it only infuriates carers because of the worry and upset it causes others. Thus those who attempt suicide tend to receive less than tender loving care from hospitals, doctors and nurses, who often see them as time-wasting and taking up important resources needed for the 'really ill'.

However, to threaten your own life suggests a high degree of despair, and even if that intense hopelessness is short-lived, it is still serious. Thus psychiatric teams usually hope to see all those who attempt suicide admitted to hospital after the attempt. This allows the psychiatric team to sort out the few who are intent on death (and perhaps remain committed to this option) and also to gather appropriate support for those who 'cried for help' because they needed it. For many patients it is the first time someone has taken their feelings seriously; this may be especially true of adolescents, who have often had their feelings dismissed because of their age. Watching adolescent love it is good to remember that Romeo and Juliet were very young – it is all to easy to forget the emotional intensity of youth. Adolescents, it should be remembered, have no adult life to measure up and compare with the feelings they have right now. As we get older we begin to realise that even if today seems black tomorrow may well be better. For those too young, too stuck, too poor, or too trapped to know that, attempted suicide offers some immediate release from the impossible pressures. (*See also* **Suicide**.)

## Suppressed Feelings

There are some feelings which are hard to cope with, either immediately or ever. In order to protect ourselves from being overwhelmed by such feelings we can suppress them into our pre-conscious or unconscious minds, so that they are in storage but out of sight (*see* **Unconscious, Conscious and Pre-conscious Minds**), or we can inhibit feelings to the point of abolishing them, by means of *suppression*.

Suppression differs from repression in that whereas we remain unconscious about what or why we have repressed material, as well as unaware of the material itself, suppression is a more conscious activity, wherein our internal policeman, the super-ego, says 'This won't do,' or, 'I can't cope with this,' and we then decide consciously to put it aside, deal with it another day, turn a blind eye and push it away.

We all have systems of ethics within our super-egos, systems we have been taught from an early age, involving our culture, religion, and 'normal' practice in a variety of situations. Although the core of our super-egos is laid down in early childhood, mostly reflecting parental values, we retain an outer, more flexible super-ego which continues to negotiate with the world, learning new ideas and new values and allowing us to think beyond the narrow confines of our original ideas (*see* **Rationalisation** and **Reality Testing**).

Greta was the 32-year-old daughter of parents who had escaped from what was then East Germany, during the 1960s. Her parents had to struggle with many aspects of Western culture, but out of that struggle arose convictions that seemed to reflect a combination of socialist ideals within a capitalist framework: in this way they combined early values with the ones they had adopted, so that they could continue to function without conflict.

Greta became a doctor, having her training entirely within the NHS. The core values she had received from her parents seemed well-echoed within a system which trained doctors free in the expectation that most of them would, for a few years at least, work extremely long hours without any thought of being paid over-time. In many ways she 'bonded' with the ethos of the NHS, much as if it were a third parent figure. This sense of bonding with an institution, a career, or a firm is not unusual as we take the values of that system into our own understanding of self and the world.

In 1988 Greta became extremely agitated and depressed, and was unable to continue working. It seemed that there were two forces operating within her life that were causing her pain. First, her new husband had suggested she start to work privately to boost their income and help pay their mortgage. Second, she read about planned changes to the NHS and found herself feeling anxious and breathless as she read them. When she first came to be treated she was tearful and distraught, not least because she did not understand what was happening to her.

Throughout her life Greta had been brought up to believe in giving of oneself to the community, on the basis that that behaviour would provide security, respect and self-fulfilment. In order to follow that pathway, however, she had suppressed her feelings of competitiveness and the desire to earn a great deal of money in order to guarantee independence and security. She had always been at least partly conscious of these other feelings – she described them 'like waves that lap on my shores' – but she had pushed them aside time after time because she believed it was right to do so. Now she was faced with a situation where in both her personal life and her work-place she was being told that different values, in fact the values she had suppressed, were the right ones after all. The waves now threatened to overwhelm her as she coped with such a dramatic transition.

Susie Orbach and Luise Eichenbaum have written about the various aspects of personality that women knowingly suppress, particularly in the presence of men, in order to make themselves more 'normal' and acceptable (for instance in their book *Understanding Women*, Penguin, 1985). Such suppression leaves them feeling shifty, manipulative and generally rather bad. And yet if they do not operate such a system of suppression to their sense of competition, fierceness, anger, betrayal, lust and desire for power they will almost certainly be socially outcast in most cultures.

Suppression functions to help us maintain social norms and uphold ethics. However, as with this example, it can be seen that it also presents ethical dilemmas as soon as it is questioned. (*See also* **Conflict** and **Repression**)

## Symptoms and Their Meanings

However much we try to fit symptoms into neat categories for the purposes of diagnosis and treatment, individual presentations tend to dumbfound us with their uniqueness. It seems increasingly likely from genetic and biochemical research that each of us has particular susceptibilities for or resistances to some symptom clusters, but because our emotional make-up is strongly coloured by all our experiences post-conception, that genetic susceptibility will present itself in myriad different ways.

In childhood we are taught by the parental model that some symptoms have more value and are taken more seriously than others. Given that we share genetic make-up with our parents it may well be that the symptoms they demonstrate to us are also the ones we are vulnerable to by inheritance, which will add weight to the possibility that we too will experience such symptoms eventually. However, given the complexity of human response, we may determine that we will never demonstrate the symptoms of our parents. Thus the child of alcoholics may be teetotal, the child of the depressed mother may view depression as a sin to be avoided, and the child of a schizophrenic may regard with horror even the slightest degree of potential madness within him- or herself.

The response of important others to our symptoms continues to influence us throughout life. Thus symptoms have not only primary meaning but rapidly develop secondary meaning based in the response they produce. Freud thought that neuro-psychological symptoms represented the 'return of the repressed'. This means that memories we had put out of sight into our unconscious minds are stirred by something current in our lives and re-emerge in the guise of symptoms (*see*

**Repression**). Sometimes symptoms can be so generalised as to provide a very good disguise for whatever is distressing the individual. Depression, anxiety, phobias and obsessions can all be the hiding place of much more specific worries which the individual remains determined to keep hidden from self or others. Other symptoms are more specific and give direct clues to the underlying distress.

Charles, aged 35, was a vicar who experienced a painful dermatitis on his right hand. This took the form of an ugly red and oozing rash which he found embarrassing and sought to keep hidden. When asked what aspects of his life were most affected he said that he had given up making the sign of the cross as a blessing over each of his congregation during communion because he was so embarrassed about his rash. Longer acquaintance with Charles led to the discovery that he was angry about how his parishioners had treated him, an anger which had stirred up memories of his father's anger whenever Charles did anything wrong as a boy. His father's favourite phrase was 'I'll kill you if I ever catch you doing that again.' In the heat of his argument with the parish council, Charles had found himself thinking about strangling several parishioners as he blessed them. So great was his disgust with himself about this that he 'pushed' the anger down until it reached the end of his right arm and erupted, quite literally, out of his skin.

Thus symptoms can have primary meaning. When we receive care and loving because of illness, the symptoms can come to acquire for us a secondary meaning in terms of gaining and keeping attention. Symptoms can also be effective ways of punishing ourselves or others. Many illnesses have some connection with unexpressed anger, for instance. Usually we are unconscious of the meaning when we experience the symptoms, although it may become apparent in retrospect. Indeed, once the meaning of the symptom becomes clear, the symptom disappears, its function complete. (*See also* **Resistance**.)

# T

## Tension

Most of us have experienced tension at some point in our lives. It produces what most people describe as feelings of being 'strung-up' or 'pulled taut'. It is usually associated with anxiety and/or pressure and in small quantities is even helpful, making us ultra-alert while we deal with a problem. However, long-lasting tension or tension that is so extreme that it distorts or reduces our performance is clearly not helpful (*see* **Overactivity** and **Stress**).

Tension is both a physical and psychological experience. We feel emotionally tense and at the same time our muscles become tense, and often painful. In this way tension produces headaches, stiff necks, backaches and a range of other disorders. All sorts of inner and outer stresses cause tension. A busy, noisy, demanding day can 'wind you up'; a nagging worry can make you feel tense. Unexpected pressure that leaves us feeling unprepared makes us vulnerable to tension. Some women experience more tension pre-menstrually, a tension that is sometimes relieved by 'blowing up' at someone or something.

Clara, aged 34, is a mother of four children, all of whom are under six. She developed chronic backache during her third pregnancy. Her life is devoted to the needs of others and she never has any time designated as 'hers'. She has given up exercise, feeling that she no longer has the time or energy for her dance classes. She has also stopped reading, previously her favourite hobby, and often feels that she is only just keeping a lid on her anger with her children or her husband. The pressures on her seem especially unbearable in the two or three days before her period.

Clara's life is 'winding her up.' Sometimes we set ourselves impossible tasks in life as if we need to challenge our own coping ability. Clara feels perpetually tired, pained and fed up. Her tension is almost tangible. 'It's my tension that's holding me together,' she jokes.

First of all a good friend pointed out to Clara just how much pressure she had placed on herself unnecessarily. That made her question why she would do such an unkind thing to herself. She quickly saw that she was in competition with her mother, who had managed a large family as a farmer's wife without complaint. Clara felt she had to be as good. The friend asked what had happened to Clara's mother, and learned that she had died of breast cancer when Clara was 15. Clara felt that she had to give everything to her family all the time, in case she too died early. She began to see, however, that the amount of tension she was producing was hardly healthy for her or her family.

After some thought about her life style Clara and her friend decided to share child-care more often, giving each other alternate days off during the week. During this time Clara returned to dance classes and again began to enjoy sitting quietly and reading. Her backache disappeared on the day she made the decision to be kinder to herself. After six weeks of her new programme she admitted to feeling occasionally guilty but also much healthier and happier.

## Trauma

Trauma can have a physical cause, such as a head injury, or a psychological one, such as a burglary, or sometimes both, as in a rape. Any of these events triggers psychological excitation, and sometimes this excitation is above and beyond what we can deal with. In such situations we can either feel numb, becoming extremely rational and practical and thus distancing our feelings, or we can be overwhelmed and collapse emotionally.

Whatever the event, the amount of trauma we experience depends on our age, our history, our personality and the amount of support we perceive as immediately available. Thus something which seems horrifically traumatic to one person might be brushed aside as 'nothing much' by another. Sudden death or disaster tend to be traumatic for everyone involved, but even the most dreadful happenings seem to have variable effects on people. Many people prepare themselves in their minds for such disasters by rehearsing 'What if..?' scenarios, although it is usually difficult to predict how anyone will react to a traumatic event. After the event it is not unusual for those involved to feel they have let themselves or others down, to feel guilty that they are safe when others have died or been injured, or to feel angry about the event, asking questions about whose fault it was (*see* **Accident Neurosis** and **Over-sensitivity**).

Colin was 32 and a soldier in Northern Ireland when he witnessed a bomb explosion. Several of his colleagues were killed and a close friend was injured. He felt that the event was his fault, due in some way that he could not explain to his negligence. He felt tearful and physically weak for months afterwards, experienced frightening nightmares, and called off his engagement, saying that he was 'unworthy' of his girlfriend. Increasingly we in the medical professions are beginning to recognise the symptoms of post-traumatic stress disorder, from which Colin was clearly suffering (*see* **Post-traumatic Stress Disorder**).

For some people these feelings last for years. I recently met a man who worked in the police force in Kenya during the up-risings of the 1960s. He still has nightmares and flashbacks of the particularly horrific incidents to which he was a witness. He was helped to some extent by removing the various mementos of Africa that littered his house and which served as constant reminders of the years in which he experienced repeated trauma (*see* **Flashbacks**).

Hungerford is in my catchment area, and even as we approach in 1991 the fourth anniversary of the shootings there, some of those involved remain depressed and frightened about life. They often feel guilty and ashamed of their feelings, thinking that they should be grateful for being alive. They tell themselves, as others tell them too, to 'pull themselves together' and 'get on with life'. They would like to be able to do just that, yet feel that the protective barrier between them and the world was unexpectedly 'torn' by events, so that they feel perpetually unsafe and insecure, wondering what will happen next (*see* **Insecurity**).

Physical trauma also produces strong psychological reactions. This is particularly true of trauma to the head, when the physical and psychological reactions intermingle. People often report feeling as if their personalities have changed for months after they have been concussed, for instance, feeling lethargic and depressed in a way that is 'out of proportion' with the extent of the physical injury.

On the whole we have a cavalier approach to expectations of recovery after a psychological shock. As we mostly over-estimate what we can cope with, we tend to expose ourselves to risks more often than we should, and even though we might be incapable of dealing with the consequences if things do go wrong. As we live in a peaceful country which is rarely subjected to natural disasters we are perhaps more likely to be overwhelmed by catastrophe, if and when it occurs, because it is so unexpected. The acute and chronic shock which results from the unexpected trauma requires recognition, patience and tolerance if it is to be allowed to heal (*see* **Working Through Pain**).

# U

## Unconscious, Conscious and Pre-conscious Minds

In analytical terms the mind is divided into three areas of functioning, based on each area's accessibility to our rational, thinking selves. The conscious mind is that part of our thinking, feeling self which is readily accessible and in use day by day. We are fully aware of the memories, thoughts and feelings in the conscious part of our mind, and are able to compare and contrast facts and feelings, recognise conflicts and come to logical, even scientific decisions. Freud christened this part of our minds the *ego*.

The pre-conscious is the part which is almost accessible to the conscious mind, but because we cannot remember everything all the time acts as an easy reference 'filing cabinet' filled with information waiting to be summoned by our conscious minds. We are all semi-conscious of the fact that we are vetting, shifting, storing, remembering and forgetting things all the time. Emotionally we tend to vet those things which we believe to be wrong or likely to cause us shame or guilt. Our cultural, religious and familial values are probably stored in the pre-conscious area because, for the most part, we do not have to consult them actively to know what we believe to be true or right. In this the pre-conscious functions as a filtering device between full consciousness and the unconscious world, and contains that part of the mind which Freud called the *super-ego*.

The largest area of the mind's function is the unconscious. This contains all our early memories which we were too young to put into words or thoughts and are therefore stored as amorphous emotional memories which we cannot summon up even when we try. Much of our developmental experiences are also stored here. The storage system is also unconscious in that we have mechanisms of repression and suppression, of which we are consciously unaware, to keep hidden those things which have particularly worried us (*see* **Denial**, **Repression**, and **Suppressed Feelings**). Our primitive instincts and drives are buried here, with complex defence systems to keep them in check. Such drives include our instincts for survival, sex and procreation. This area was called the *id* by Freud (*see* **Instinct for Survival**). The super-ego governs what the id can or cannot release into the conscious mind and when it can be released. At times when we are disinhibited, such as when we dream or are tired, angry, or drunk, material can escape more easily from our unconscious world and be expressed consciously. Sometimes we have the experience of being surprised by an idea or feeling which we ourselves have just voiced, because we are hearing our unconscious talk on the subject, maybe for the first time.

Outside events can trigger memories if they are in some way familiar because of past experiences, and can 'stir' the depths of our unconscious, making us uncomfortable and vaguely aware that all is not well. Freud's most famous explanation for psychological distress was that there was conflict between the three areas of functioning. Symptoms, for Freud, were the conscious representation of troubling material from the unconscious and pre-conscious which was trying to be expressed and heard. Psychotherapy and psychoanalysis attempted to make the curtain between these areas more transparent, so that material can be consciously acknowledged rather than buried away (*see* **Conflict** and **Symptoms and Their Meanings**). Because consciousness, unconsciousness and preconsciousness are states of awareness, they can vary, allowing material from one part of the structure of the psyche to move to another. Thus what has been unconscious in the id can become conscious and available for work by the ego.

# W

## Womb Envy

In 1926 the psychologist Karen Horney published a paper entitled 'The Dread of Women'. In it she explored men's ambivalent feelings of yearning for and fear of women, suggesting that this conflict is one of the principle roots of the masculine impulse to creative work (*see* **Ambivalence** and **Conflict**). The vagina and womb are hidden and therefore secretive organs, which contain the great power of life-giving. Horney suggests that little boys know instinctively that their penis is too small to gratify or inseminate mother and thus feel great anxiety connected to a sense of attack on their self-respect. She comments on the possibility that both by loving and glorifying women and by vilifying and disparaging them the object of men's fear and dread is made less anxiety-provoking. By saying that woman is wonderful, beautiful and saintly it is possible to reduce her power, and by disparagement of the sort that makes her vile, inhuman but also weak, a poor thing, the fear is reduced through ridicule.

Within the context of this fear there is also the aggression felt in the relationship with mother when she frustrates the small boy. Such aggression can become sexualised into sadism, with the object of that sadism perhaps being women's genitalia. Within sexual intercourse the man may see himself as penetrating the exciting but frightening inner secrets of women or as being sucked into her as if to his death. This is a reversal of the idea that such acts can lead to conception and therefore life (*see* **Aggression**, **Death**, **Eroticism**, **Greed**, and **Sado-Masochism**). Much envy is also felt towards the mother-figure, who can conceive and grow life and then nurse and comfort that new small being (*see* **Envy**).

Jackie was 23 when she had her first child, a boy called Adrian. Adrian's father, Dick, had been excited about the pregnancy and was present at the birth. In the weeks that followed, however, he felt it was unbearable to be in the same room as Jackie, especially if she was feeding Adrian. He described himself as 'consumed with envy', not for one or the other but for both of them, merged together as he saw them in opposition to himself. He developed a variety of psychosomatic symptoms which meant that he had to stay in bed, requiring nursing from Jackie, who rapidly became exhausted at all the demands being made on her (*see* **Psychosomatic Illnesses**). She was also worried and hurt by the levels of aggression that Dick was expressing.

The experience of Jackie and Dick is not unusual. Many books on baby care tell new mothers 'not to forget the husband, who might be feeling put out' where perhaps they should suggest that new fathers need to explore these feelings as adults rather than have the feelings 'mothered' out of them by already harassed mums.

Much of the social pressure on mothers probably has its roots in the envy of women's ability to be mothers: the message often seems to be 'If you have this amount of power then we will make you suffer for it!' Many women experience obstetric and gynaecological care as an attack on themselves, and this has consequences for their self-esteem as well as their experiences of themselves as sexual beings.

Susan experienced her post-natal examination as an assault. She described the internal examination from a young male doctor as 'a rape. I could feel his fury with me. I could sense how revolted he was by my being female. I felt like a piece of unpleasant meat.' Many feminist therapists have pointed out that the revulsion men experience towards women is a powerful and destructive emotion clearly embedded in their envy of women's procreative powers. The fear of menstrual blood and the sense of taboo applied by many societies, including our own, to menstruation is connected to the fact that it reminds us all of women's power, each month, to give or not to give life. On this basis adverts for tampons were, until recently, banned from TV. Men envy women's power, and women, too are often uncomfortable with it and try to hide it from their menfolk.

Mary underwent three years of investigation and treatment for severe pre-menstrual tension. When I met her it seemed as if her whole life was coloured in an unpleasant and limiting way by her hormones and her body. It transpired that her mother had suffered similarly. Over the course of several months of regular meetings, Mary said that her symptoms were 'a little better'. I commented that she seemed almost ashamed telling me this, and she said that she did experience guilt if she was not 'suffering for being a woman'. She felt uncomfortable demonstrating her abilities in any sphere of her life, but was most uncomfortable with the concept of her feminine power. As Mary improved, her husband, Nick, became depressed. He said that he had always felt inadequate prior to meeting Mary, and that his relationship with her had 'built him up' in his own eyes. Much as if they were on a see-saw, as her inner confidence rose, his appeared to be deflated.

Womb envy should probably stand alongside penis envy in our understanding of relationships between men and women. In early childhood we all harbour the thought of being of both sexes. That hope has to be relinquished as we grow and yet remains entrapped within our envy of the physical attributes and power of the opposite sex (*see* **Penis Envy**).

## Working Through Pain

In psychological terms pain is caused by traumatic events which threaten us and/or cause us loss. Sometimes we push the memories of such traumas, particularly the early traumas of life, deeply into our unconscious mind, where they are stoutly defended by our defence mechanisms (*see* **Defence Mechanisms** and **Unconscious, Conscious and Pre-conscious Minds**).

If we do not 'work' on painful issues, conflicts and events when they occur, they become buried and may later require psychological work to clear up the problems they cause. Psychological work often involves forcing ourselves to focus on things which pain or frighten us until we have found a way of resolving or at least neutralising their effects on us. Such work can take the form of crying at a sad loss, feeling angry at a traumatic event, making amends for something we have done which has worried us, or simply talking over events in a way that allows us to 'let them go' and feel at peace again.

In psychotherapy it becomes clear that people repeat certain patterns of behaviour and relationships again and again if there is unresolved conflict within their make-up. Despite the repetition being destructive to their lives, the defence mechanisms often make it difficult for an individual to understand their own behaviour or stop the repetition (*see* **Repetition Compulsion**). Psychotherapy and psychoanalysis are techniques that allow for resistances and defences to be confronted and interpreted to the patient, in a way and at a time in the process of therapy that grants the individual an emotional understanding of why he or she resists certain options or avoids exploring some areas of his or her experience. This interpretation is rather like the opening up of a wound that will not heal because it is contaminated by a foreign body. Once the wound is opened and the contamination revealed, the work of cleansing can begin and the wound can mend itself. Working through a conflict or memory is the psychological equivalent of cleansing the wound. Once clean it can heal and the individual no longer needs to 'scratch' it psychologically with repetitive behaviour.

Petula, aged 31, found herself ending relationships every spring with monotonous regularity. She felt compelled to act in this way even if she liked the man she was involved with. She explained that she could feel a build-up of tension from the beginning of March and knew that the relationship would soon be over. This often caused her pain and yet the process also left her feeling relieved. As spring approached, her male therapist interpreted her need to leave therapy as a need to get away from him before he abandoned her. He also drew her attention to how her pattern was repeating itself even within therapy. She thus made a conscious decision to stay, although she felt increasingly anxious and unhappy. During this time she was conscious of a sensation that 'something' was happening inside of herself that was causing psychological pain. When asked what it felt like she said 'grieving'. She had no memory of the date of her father's death as she had only been three years old at the time, but when she checked with her mother she learnt that it had been during April. The following spring she was able to maintain a relationship and understood why she felt slightly uneasy during April (*see* **Idealisation**).

## PART 2

# WHY DOES IT HAPPEN?

# INTRODUCTION

The search to give meaning to and find explanations for our emotional and mental experiences is an important quest for most people. Understanding our reactions often makes them more bearable; thus to be depressed for an obvious, external reason, for instance a loss, is although painful more easily tolerated than to be depressed without evident cause. We are all unique in our reactions and yet, despite that, there is much common ground which allows us to theorise about the causes of emotional and mental anguish. In this section we are going to explore some of those theories.

Those who work in the field of mental health are often split as a result of investing all their belief in one or other of these theories as the sole cause for mental illness. This investment then leads on logically to theories about how such illness should be treated. The brain is however an extraordinarily complicated organ and its functions and malfunctions so diverse that our understanding can only be partial. Thus explanations for our emotions and mental experiences will only ever answer part of the question 'Why has this happened to me, and why now?'

For some people it is easier to believe in a basic biological explanation, as it is often felt that this removes the responsibility and stigma from the sufferer. If a problem is caused by our genes or our biochemistry then it is not our fault. As there is still considerable stigma attached to being mentally ill this is an important consideration. Individuals who might otherwise be judged as morally weak, or parents who might be blamed for their children's problems, find great relief in being told that they are dealing with an illness with a biochemical basis. Other people find the concept of a physical illness in their mind frightening and would rather see their problems as being related to or caused by external factors such as life events, over which they can exercise some control.

During the course of a lifetime we all experience some emotional anguish. Clearly some people experience a great deal more than do others, and some of us are more resilient than others. It is a lucky person who has never felt depressed or anxious – or is it? These are profoundly human experiences and, although painful, often prompt us to a deeper understanding of ourselves and greater compassion for others. Thus are the concepts of mental illness or health somewhat different to those in other fields of medicine. It would be unthinkable to say that a small dose of appendicitis was good for you! It is however true that people often grow to greater maturity through a phase of depression, and rather than have 'illness' diagnosed need support and love from others to help them through the phase towards a positive outcome.

Life causes distress, it turns our feelings upside-down with monotonous regularity. There is much to be gained from surviving and learning from these emotional upheavals rather than seeing them as 'illnesses' which need rapid relief. It is pointless, however, to suffer mental pain or be frightened by mental experiences if for any reason that suffering is out of proportion with normal expectations. It is at that point, as our mental health slides towards dis-ease, that we need help. A central part of that professional help is the ability to offer an explanation of why we are experiencing more-than-to-be-expected mental pain at this point in our lives.

# GENETIC AND BIOCHEMICAL EXPLANATIONS

Genetic material, inherited from both mother and father, holds a key role in every cell in our body. The pattern of genes in paired chromosomes laid down as sperm meets egg is repeated exactly in each cell, and forms our basic template as unique individuals who bear some likeness, both physical and psychological, to relatives from both sides of the family. We inherit both strengths and weaknesses in this way. Genes can have modifying effects on each other, either enhancing or decreasing the potential of individual genes. The fact that they are paired, one from the mother and one from the father, within each cell, means that the degree of modification that they exert over each other is considerable, but there are genes which are dominant, that is, their effect is powerful enough to overcome modification. In terms of susceptibility to illness there are some dominant genes, and if you inherit such a gene then you will develop the illness associated with it. Other genes merely render a person more likely than most to develop a specific illness under stress.

Twins provide us with a golden opportunity to study the importance of genetic influence in the production of illness. There are two forms of twins, one monozygotic – where two individuals result from a splitting of one fertilised egg and who are therefore genetically identical – and the second dizygotic – the result of two fertilised eggs implanting in the uterus at the same time. These twins are no more or less genetically similar than normal brothers and sisters would be. When rates of mental illness are compared in these groups it becomes evident that there is some genetic influence in the production of certain illnesses but it is not absolute.

Studies have demonstrated that it is probably a gene that sits on part of a sex chromosome that renders a person more likely to have a mental illness than a member of the general population. The fact that it is on a sex chromosome may explain why different illnesses have different rates in men and women. In the past it was hoped that a specific gene would be found for each specific illness. However, in diagnosis, it is obvious that despite attempts to describe these specific disease entities there is much overlap between different illnesses. This clinical finding seems to have been underlined by the discovery that there is probably one gene that renders a person more vulnerable overall to a number of related mental and emotional conditions, from schizophrenia through manic depression to psychotic depression and other non-reactive depressions. While the person is more likely to develop the illness demonstrated by other family members if they become ill, the same gene also renders him or her more likely to develop the other illnesses on this spectrum too.

It is thought that this gene affects the development of the temporal lobe of the brain, although it is, as yet, unclear why this should then make people more vulnerable to severe mental illness. Even in the presence of the gene mental illness is not a certainty, and many people with the gene will never show signs of illness even under stress. Therefore it is clear that the gene is only part of the causation of illness, and other factors have to be found to explain why it has important effects for some people and not others.

This uncertainty makes it difficult to counsel people with schizophrenia and related illnesses in their family, who wish to have children but are unhappy at the thought of reproducing that illness in their children. Many of the larger psychiatric facilities now have a counselling programme, however, which can give them up-to-date information about the risks that they may be taking. Often this can be reassuring, for instance, if your mother has had a diagnosed schizophrenic illness the chance of one of your children also developing it is only 3 per cent (as against 1 per cent for the general population). This would be considered a low-risk genetic factor. Even if other close family members were also affected the risk would not necessarily rise beyond 10 per cent. If, however, both parents were diagnosed as schizophrenic then it is thought that the risk to a child might be as high as 50 per cent. For such families the risk of passing on a gene which renders the children more susceptible to illness is only one of a number of considerations. The effect of pregnancy and parenthood on the parents' mental health and the effect on the foetus in utero of various drugs may be at least as significant factors as the genetic ones.

There seems to be clear evidence that manic-depression (also known as bipolar illness, or illness that has both manic and depressive swings) clusters in families, with relatives facing a 20 per cent chance of developing a similar illness as compared to the 1-2 per cent risk present for the general population. If one monozygotic twin develops the illness the second has a 65 per cent risk of becoming ill, while dizygotic twins face only a 15 per cent risk. Although this demonstrates an important genetic element to the illness, it also shows that the genetic risk is only one factor, and that others must also make a powerful contribution, for 35 per cent of monozygotic twins do not experience the same illness as their twin despite the fact that their genetic make-up is identical.

Much research attention has also been paid to the biochemistry of the brain. Nerve cells are connected by synapses, which are gaps through which the electrical message crosses as a chemical transmitter (the *neurotransmitter*), which then provokes a new electrical message in the neurone on the other side. These neurotransmitters are released from the pre-synaptic neurone (the nerve cell before the synapse) and attach themselves to receptor sites on the post-synaptic neurone (the nerve cell on the other side of the gap). Some nerve cells function with more than one kind of neurotransmitter; others release neurohormones, which circulate throughout the body and have a more general effect than that of the neurotransmitters.

In understanding these chemicals, research has concentrated on their initial production and storage in the pre-synaptic neurone, their mechanism of release, how they bind to the receptor site and how they then produce their actions. Many drugs used in the treatment of mental illness act to change one or more of these steps in the neurotransmitters' life. The important transmitters discovered so far include *dopamine*, *adrenaline* and *noradrenaline*, *serotonin*, *acetylcholine* and *histamine*.

Raised levels of dopamine have been implicated in theories of the causes of schizophrenia and mania, while lowered levels are thought to be found in depressed people whose movements are slowed down by their depression. Much of the evidence for such theories comes from the effects of drugs used to control or cure these illnesses. Noradrenaline and serotonin underactivity has also been suggested as a cause for depression.

There are also three groups of opiods (that is, naturally occurring opiate derivatives) – the encephalins, the endorphins and the dynorphins – that take part in an electro-biochemical inhibition/excitation feedback loop in the brain, which seems to regulate a person's amount of emotional sensitivity (including perceptions of pain) as against his or her degree of mental/intellectual alertness. These pathways may be important in our understanding of the power of thought and emotions in causing physical illness, as well as our appreciation of pain and its relief, for instance by acupuncture.

The study of developmental psychobiology suggests that environmental circumstances, particularly at critical times of development, may have subtle but permanent effects on the regulation of the functions of these transmitters.

Clearly the phenomena we associate as arising in our minds must be related to the electrical and biochemical function of our brains. In the past the distinct representations of on the one hand brain function as pure anatomy and physiology, and on the other the emotional experience and behaviour of the mind, have obscured the fact that a successful model of how we function mentally needs to incorporate both these aspects.

Recent models have suggested that we need to look carefully at the relationship between different regions of the brain and the processes by which that relationship is formed, rather than attempt a simple 'map' of different parts of the brain, each having different functions. This model suggests not only that illness would result from multiple changes in the physiological or biochemical working of the brain, because of the close interaction between the different regions, but that these changes might be precipitated and repeatedly transformed by inter-personal relationships and social processes. Thus vulnerability to mental illness might be a generalised vulnerability to internal biochemical change from external stressors, to which other people, lacking this in-built vulnerability, either react less or have the biological ability to react more to balance the brain regions involved.

Even in the type of illness that is clearly related to external stimuli, such as post-traumatic stress disorder, the response might be viewed as an imbalance between left and right sides of the brain, the left struggling to moderate the overexcitement caused by intense fear while the right reacts emotionally, perhaps overwhelming the left side. This inner battle for control between the two sides of the brain may explain the phenomena often reported by those with this disorder, that is, the experience of swinging from emotional numbness to overwhelming fear and back again. There has been a suggestion that those individuals with less 'lateralised' brain function, the ambidextrous for instance, may be significantly more at risk of developing this disorder than those with one side of the brain clearly dominant.

# PSYCHODYNAMIC AND PSYCHOLOGICAL EXPLANATIONS

The structure of the mind as described in psychodynamic explanations of dis-ease is not an anatomical or chemical structure but rather a functional and developmental one. The mind is divided into regions which have different functions and abilities and which relate to each other in ways that reflect the developmental experience of the person. Such a model states that conflict between these different regions is inevitable as part of the human condition, and that it is the person's capacity for dealing with that conflict as well as the nature and intensity of the conflict that makes him or her susceptible or resilient to a variety of emotional or mental disturbances.

The unconscious region holds our instincts, early memories and much that has been actively repressed (that is pushed 'out of sight') by our conscious minds. Sigmund Freud talked of *psychic determinism*, by which he meant that emotional and mental events always have explanations and never arise by chance, even though many of those explanations are buried in our unconscious mind and therefore difficult to get at and consciously understand. Such material is much like the evidence of previous civilisations, which lies buried under thousands of years of history and can only be uncovered and understood by archaeologists. There can be no doubt that previous civilisations have all had an impact on our present-day life, and each of us can learn about today by studying history, yet as we go about our day-to-day lives we are probably unaware of what it is that influences us from this cultural past. Similarly we may be totally unaware of what is influencing us from our personal past: indeed, as it is often the traumatic that is repressed we may be blind and forgetful to the very aspects of our past which could if revealed throw light on our present difficulties.

The pre-conscious mind holds material that can be made conscious if we make an effort, those thoughts and memories that are only out of sight because our conscious mind cannot be expected to contain all our memories all the time. The conscious mind is the rational, thinking and remembering part of ourselves, with which we are most familiar. In personality terms it is the tip of the iceberg, perched on top of the pre-conscious and unconscious, and greatly influenced by them.

During development a child has much to learn about the emotional nature of life as well as struggling to master both physical control of his body and the necessary intellectual skills. The difficult balance between the pleasure principle of meeting needs and the reality principle of life as a frustrating and containing place must be achieved. Social rules of behaviour need to be acquired early so that the child can begin to meet with and enjoy the company of others. The placing of boundaries on the child's behaviour causes frustration and anger. The small baby experiences this as murderous rage and survives such powerful emotions by believing that he hates the bad parent and loves the good one, as if mother or father were split into two. Mending that split, realising that the people we love and depend on are good and bad, and cause us to feel both love and hate, is the first great emotional step in development.

During infancy we each have to build up an image of ourselves and others as we separate from our parents and begin to see ourselves as unique, distinct people. We do this in part by taking in images of ourselves as reflected in the feelings of others and their treatment of us. Thus if our mother and father radiate love and concern towards us we feel loved and worthy of concern: this view of ourselves is taken in so that we have introjected their love of us and made it into our own positive self-esteem. We take in much of the parental emotions and behaviour, including an understanding of how they cope with our demands. From their coping behaviour we come to some understanding of how much we can demand from life, how much attention we are worth. Much of this development is centred around feeding, which involves both sucking and biting, and it is thought of as the *oral* (or oral-sadistic) stage, which takes up the first year of life.

Next, from the ages of 1 to 4 years, the child has to master her body in order to move with co-ordination and be able to control her sphincters; thus this is called the *anal* phase. These developmental steps then allow for the child's greater personal freedom and increasing sense of mastery over the environment as well as over herself. Interference in this development will hinder that growing sense of being powerful and in control. Children who are not allowed to achieve this sense of control for themselves may always have trouble mastering problems or exercising personal boundaries, always feeling an underlying disquiet that someone else is imposing boundaries upon them. Freud believed that people became obsessional if something went wrong in this stage of development and that the child became over-controlled and overanxious about control.

Freud concentrated on the sexual development of young children (having thought that the energy for both oral and anal stages of development was libidinal) in the *phallic* phase (ages 4 to 6 years), when they compete with the parent of the same sex for the attentions of the parent of the opposite sex. The importance of this phase lies in the fact that the child is fantasising about sexual activity and needs to be free to have fantasies without any fear that these fantasies will be acted out. Increasingly we are coming to know (much as Freud discovered and then, too shocked, ignored) that a percentage of adults, often the parents or guardians of the child, break the boundaries between fantasy and reality and have sexual activity with the child while he or she is still very young. 'Soul murder' is the term used by many of the survivors of abuse and by those who work with them in an attempt to describe the enormity of the damage done to a child's developing psyche by this betrayal of trust. Destroying the boundaries between fantasy and reality robs children of further childhood sexual innocence, and means that they grow into a precocious adult sexual interest which negatively influences their future relationships. The burden of secrecy that both abuser and society still place on the victim/survivor of abuse often compounds this damage with a sense of shame, guilt and blame, which the children carry with them, as a central part of their understanding of themselves, into adulthood.

Psychoanalysis explains psychosis as a 'rupture' of the conscious mind through which elements of the unconscious are exposed, without defence. Many of the symptoms experienced are seen as the conscious mind's desperate attempt to make sense of this uncontrollable projection of the unconscious mind. Thus, if a person's own persecutory thoughts are exposed without defence, they might be projected out so that that person believes the world to be a persecutory place. In order to make sense of that vision of the world the person must then alter his or her understanding and perception of the environment so that it is in line with his or her unconscious mind rather than external reality.

Neurosis is seen as a conflict between a wish, desire or need on the one hand and a defence against that wish on the other. The desire to seek sexual fulfilment, for instance, can be surrounded by great anxiety because of restrictive social norms. Many people are defended against their need for satisfying sexuality, but if then placed in a situation where that need is aroused, may experience symptoms of mental distress as their defensive resistance is threatened.

Throughout our lives there are developmental steps we need to conquer and external traumas which have to be dealt with. In early childhood we are especially vulnerable to the blocking of these hurdles, and the insults of early childhood, be they failed emotional development and/or external trauma, render us susceptible to further, adult insults. A large part of the three vital stages of development occurs before we can actively remember, and therefore our experiences of that development are stored in our unconscious mind. Thus much which worried or traumatised us, or which was repressed as we conformed with social and family expectations for our behaviour, has been pushed out of sight of our conscious minds before we can have any memory of it. Experiences of adult life may re-activate such early memories and leave us struggling between a need to remember and make sense of our feelings and a continuing necessity to repress past material. Symptoms of mental distress can be the external sign of such a conflict.

The psychological or behaviorist explanation of our conduct and emotions suggests that personality is an acquired pattern which each of us learns during childhood and which is constantly modified by our environment. This approach emphasises the fact that our behaviour can be conditioned into patterns by our interaction with a rewarding or punishing environment. Rewards or reinforcing factors can be either primary – those which satisfy our innate needs – such as food or sex, or secondary, such as money or the approval of important others. If the environment withdraws the reward our conditioned behaviour will lessen and then cease: this is described as extinction of that behaviour. The predictability with which the reward is presented influences how strong the conditioning for a form of behaviour will be. If we are always rewarded for being thoughtful towards others by being accepted socially, for instance, we will tend to retain thoughtful behaviour. If we suddenly find ourselves in a situation where we receive no positive feedback our social behaviour would be modified.

Interestingly, intermittent feedback appears to produce stronger conditioning than does continual feedback. Parents need to bear this in mind if they are attempting to modify their children's behaviour: family rules that are applied intermittently will be reinforced very strongly. However, intermittent feedback can also strongly reinforce unwanted behaviour in amongst the desired behaviour. Punishment for unwanted behaviour may not produce the desired results either, as the child may perceive spanking and shouting as positive –

the attention she was seeking. Often 'time out', such as five minutes alone in her room, has a much more powerful effect in extinguishing anti-social behaviour, although this then needs to be combined with a reinforcer for appropriate behaviour immediately afterwards.

Sibling rivalry often causes parents anxieties, especially if one child is larger and more physically aggressive than his brothers and sisters. The aggressive behaviour can be modified by sending the child up to his room immediately, then after a few minutes bringing him back and demonstrating that he is loved and needed within the family by showing that playing with the brother or sister with whom he was just fighting is still possible. The alternatives of either ignoring the behaviour or angry shouting and smacking will reinforce the unwanted behaviour, the first by failing to draw clear boundaries and the second by confirming to the child that he is naughty and less loved than the sibling, the underlying fear which aroused his aggression in the first place.

We also modify our behaviour by observing the behaviour of those around us and by becoming influenced by social expectations and values. Much culturally-related behaviour is absorbed in this way so that we are continuously influenced by it and yet relatively unaware of it until presented by the close proximity of different cultural values and behaviour. In order to model ourselves on others we have to be able to identify with them to some extent. Our behaviour is also influenced by the degree to which we feel we have control over ourselves and our environment. Our behaviour under stress or during illness will reflect much of what we have learned behaviorally as well as in response to the expectations of others.

Recent work has concentrated on the psychological attributes that people need in order to stay emotionally healthy. Work by Abraham Maslow in the 1960s suggested that we have a hierarchy of needs, from the basic physiological needs of food and sex, through needs for physical safety and 'belonging' to a group or a society, up to the need for self-esteem and, eventually, the time when other needs are met to achieve self-actualisation. Much of what we know or theorise about emotional development and its pitfalls comes from the study of distressed or ill people. Maslow attempted to correct this imbalance by also studying those he believed to be not only mentally healthy but also fulfilled. He discovered that such people manage to maintain certain child-like attributes such as spontaneity and the ability to relish peak emotional experiences, which makes them creative and humorous, while at the same time encompassing the more adult understanding of reality, self-sufficiency and democracy. Fulfilment in adult life seems closely linked to the ability to be both intimate with others and yet also need and cope with privacy. Events that hinder development block our path to such 'all-rounded emotional adulthood'. Certainly the adults who can reach such heights of maturity are probably psychologically protected from most emotional distress, although even they, if stressed enough by events, are not completely protected.

# LIFE EVENT
# EXPLANATIONS

We are all aware of the fact that the events that occur in our lives change the way we feel about ourselves and others. Sad events most commonly make us sad, and happy ones, happy. Some of us are probably more sensitive than others to this impact of the outside world on our inner world of feelings: women, for instance, are thought to be generally more sensitive than men to the effect of both positive situations such as having supportive personal relationships and negative ones such as the loss of an important relationship. This difference may be because women invest more heavily in relationships than do men, or because they have less in their lives outside of relationships to distract and/or fulfil them. Research during the early 1980s in Camberwell in London demonstrated that negative or threatening life events had a precipitating role in depressive illness. Those who were diagnosed as depressed had had significantly more life events in the proceeding month than had other, non-depressed people, and the volume of life events was unusual for them, so that it was clear that people were not precipitating life events because they were becoming depressed, but rather becoming depressed because of an unusually high rate of life events.

Life events can be divided into those representing chronic adversity on the one hand, for example bad housing, low income, and ill health, and on the other more immediate events, of both a positive or negative appearance, which threaten the stability and normality of a person's immediate environment. Thus immediate life events can have as big an effect as can chronic ones if, for example, they take the form promotion or unemployment, a new baby or an abortion, a family loss or a desired move, marriage or divorce. Tables have been constructed so that each life event can be rated as to how disturbing it would usually be to a person. Losses by death or divorce, or gains by marriage or birth always rate highly, but moving, changing jobs, and taking out large loans also rate high up on the stress-factor chart.

As well as precipitating illness, life events can help or hinder recovery. 'Neutralising' events which give the person time and space to adapt may be more helpful than positive or negative ones. Social support, for instance, may be more curative than an intense new interpersonal relationship. For those with psychotic illnesses, particularly schizophrenia, the degree of expressed emotion within the family or living environment in response to any event may decide whether that event produces a detrimental effect or not. Advice is offered to families about how to deal calmly with events so that the vulnerable member with an illness will not be disturbed. Ill members cause life events (for example, hospital admissions) to a family, the members of which may then respond with outbursts of anxiety, distress or anger. These emotional outbursts, although very understandable in the circumstances, can be detrimental to the ill family member and therefore to the family as a whole.

Marriage and parenthood are the two most common stress events for young adults, who are often unprepared for the fact that such apparently happy events can have such disastrous consequences for their mental well-being. There is clear evidence that having three or more children who are under 14 years of age is a powerfully depressing factor for many women, particularly those without female social support and those who have lost their own mothers, through death or parents' divorce, before they were themselves 14 years old. As the rate of multiple births rises in line with the success of infertility treatments, mothers report that it is emotionally impossible to care for the needs of three or more infants without a great emotional toll being taken on the parents, most commonly the mother, for at least the first four or five years of the children's lives.

The research into the effects of life events is only ever as good as the design of the life events charts. Thus early in this research events such as miscarriage and abortion, sexual abuse or rape did not feature, although most women would say, if asked, that all of these are highly-charged and significant emotional events. More recent research evidence has suggested that life events have less effect on the elderly, but this seems more likely to reflect a bias in the design of the research towards 'young' life events: the elderly often have to cope with the multiple losses of friends and family and also of parts of the self, such as the loss of employment, physical freedoms, and a steady, good income.

Major life events such as bereavement and abuse during childhood probably render the people involved more vulnerable to future events than they would have been constitutionally. Increasing evidence from the USA suggests that multiple personalities, for instance, are only seen in people who have suffered physical and sexual abuse associated with much fear and humiliation. Such life events might mean that the person has to produce a 'protected' part of themselves which is quite separate to the 'victim' part from an early age, so that these splits become built into his or her personality structure.

Life events which have particular significance to us in the light of previous experience probably have a greater impact on our psychological well-being than events without that special significance. Events that render us powerless or helpless often evoke painful memories of past events when, as children, we were also powerless to protect or help ourselves.

Once a depressive illness has been precipitated by life events it is possible that people begin to construe all future life events with a more negative, depressive view. This shift in their perception of life may account for the fact that many depressed people seem to cling tenaciously to their depression. Perhaps, after feeling betrayed by life, it feels safer to look on the black side of things.

# FAMILY AND CULTURAL EXPLANATIONS

Every family functions slightly differently, with different rules, myths and roles for each member. The unique nature of our family of origin is imprinted on our personalities and our understanding of all future relationships. However, within a single culture there are generally accepted family rules and roles. Our descriptions of healthy or unhealthy families all originate from studies of Western families, thus concepts such as clear boundaries between family members and the goal of self-differentiation for each family member are seen as vital for family health. Such concepts would have less value for a culture where an extended family network was the norm, in which case loyalty to family and remaining interdependence into adulthood would be seen as healthy goals. Families are mini-cultures, and they prepare us for the culture in which we are expected to live. It is extremely difficult for an adult to adapt psychologically to a culture that is different from the one for which their family of origin prepared them.

The psychiatrist Murray Bowen worked with the families of schizophrenics in the 1960s, and was the first to suggest that emotional problems which remain unresolved in one generation are passed down to the next. For him the health of the family was reflected in the degree of emotional independence of each of the family members. Families with schizophrenic children were said to have poorly developed boundaries between family members and impervious boundaries between the family and the rest of the world. In order to achieve this state of affairs the family members developed ways of communicating which produced the characteristic thought disorders of schizophrenia.

More recent work has suggested that it is unlikely that family boundary disturbance would be enough, in itself, to produce schizophrenia in a family member, although repeated exposure to what the psychologist Gregory Bateson described as the 'double-bind' experience certainly produces disturbed communications within the whole family. Double-bind messages are those which demand some response yet to which the respondent cannot give a sensible response, thus they place a family member in a no-win situation as regards another family member. Paul and his father, Victor, provided an example of this, when Victor suggested to Paul that it was time he got a job, but went on within a sentence or two to explain why Paul was not bright enough to get a job and that anyway his mother needed him at home. Paul struggled to explain to the interviewer why he was unemployed; Victor took up the position opposing whichever side of the discussion Paul represented.

Families have also been studied as biological 'systems' based on the work of Ludwig von Bertalanffy. His work emphasised the importance of feedback systems in human communications; families with disturbed family members often perpetuate faulty systems through inadequate or misleading feedback. A system needs to be able to interact with its surrounding environment and yet also keep its integrity. Thus the family needs to maintain an adequate communication with the society in which it exists, and at the same time uphold the boundary that differentiates it from other members of that society. Systems also need ways of reaching decisions and pursuing goals. For instance, parents need to have a way of communicating supportively between themselves and expressing clear messages about a joint parental policy to their children. As children often attempt to pursue a policy of divide and conquer with their parents it is particularly important for family stability that the parents can achieve some form of solidarity, and yet for the parents' individual stability they may also need to disagree. Families must continually resolve such conflicts between individual and group needs.

Families often have elaborate systems of myths about

themselves and the world. Individual family members have to incorporate these myths in order to 'belong'. Some of the myths may be about health and illness. The Spicer family presented their 15-year-old daughter Amanda as 'the problem', but in their first interview reported that 'women in this family have always been neurotic'. It was clear that Amanda believed that the way to become an accepted woman in the family was to have symptoms of emotional distress, and that if she were to grow into healthy adulthood this would separate her from her female relatives.

As we grow up we are increasingly exposed to the larger 'family' of our culture, first through school and friends and then through work, relationships and the need to form our own, new families. Almost inevitably there will be some conflicts or inconsistencies between what we learned about the rules and roles at home and those we find operating out in the world. The disturbances of adolescents may be related to the need to work our way through some of those conflicts, and both individuals and families need to have a degree of flexibility in their understanding of the self and others if healthy adjustments are to be made.

In cultures which are in the process of social change that flexibility needs to be maintained if we are to feel we 'belong' both to our family and our culture. Different or conflicting models of normality tax our sense of belonging and can leave us feeling alienated. Many women of the 1990s live totally different lives and have different expectations of themselves and others than did their mothers or grandmothers. This can lead to inter-generational stress with an accompanying decrease in the amount of support and understanding one generation can offer to another. Such social separation can be emotionally uncomfortable to the individuals concerned. A possible explanation for the high rate of marital stress in the Western world today may be that women's expectations and values have changed more rapidly than men's have over the last two or three decades, causing social isolation between men and women.

For those who emigrate to a different culture the stress caused by their sense of alienation can be enormous and long-lasting. On the whole individuals naturally tend to group themselves with people who share their basic values, traditions and rules because it is less psychologically stressful. The need to belong is a fundamental human requirement, and our emotional well-being is directly related to the balance we achieve between belonging (and the compromises necessary in order to belong) and achieving psychological separation from those with whom we belong.

# PHYSIOLOGICAL
# EXPLANATIONS

Our brains are totally dependent on the systems of the body, both to provide them with nutrition and oxygen and to remove the waste products of their metabolism. Thus our life style and its effect on our physical well-being has in turn a pronounced effect on our feelings and mental experiences. A healthy diet, adequate rest from stress and gentle exercise will produce a greater sense of psychological well-being than will more self-persecutory life styles. If we are kind to ourselves we feel better about ourselves, and if we feel good about ourselves we are more likely to be kind to our bodies. Thus there is a circle of care and concern for self and feeling happy about the self, which can operate in a positive or negative direction. This circle can be influenced by both emotional and physical illness. Depressed people often feel that they cannot be bothered to take care of themselves physically, people with flu often feel depressed too. Sometimes we need others to intervene and care for our physical or emotional well-being in order to restore the circle to a healthy, positive direction.

Almost any form of ill health can produce emotional consequences, either directly because of its effects on our brain's functioning or indirectly because of our feelings about the limitations it will place or consequences it will have on us. Many physical illnesses also seem to have psychological elements, which can precipitate the illness and affect its course and outcome. This interaction is complex, and often even the person suffering cannot say how much of his or her suffering is emotional and how much physical. Both components are just as real, however: to say something has a psychological element is no more of a dismissal than saying an illness has a physical basis, although people sometimes do feel outraged at the suggestion that there is an emotional basis to physical complaints.

The post-viral illness commonly called ME (myalgic encephalitis) illustrates the complexity of this physiological/psychological interaction. The first stage of ME involves infection by a virus which circulates via the bloodstream and causes ill health in a variety of organs, including the brain. Some would theorise that we are more likely to be susceptible to both the original infection and being physically overwhelmed by it if we have been feeling either physically or emotionally run down before being exposed to the virus. During the acute stage of the infection the sense of illness includes feeling depressed, both directly because of the affect of the virus on the brain, and indirectly because the rest of the body feels unwell. The immediate infection is then defeated by the body's defence mechanisms, but its effects on the systems of the body do not seem to heal, and the sense of illness both physical and emotional persists, sometimes for months or even years. This leads the person to alter his or her life style to accommodate for the fatigue, lethargy and overwhelming sense of being unwell, but that alteration may then, secondarily, add to the symptoms rather than help in the healing process.

There is, for instance, much controversy about the amount of exercise that people should attempt when still feeling lethargic and when even minimal physical effort seems to make them feel worse rather than better. Clinically, muscles which are not exercised rapidly lose strength, thus prolonged bed rest would make even minimal exercise a painful prospect. Physical lethargy and depression have a close relationship. For those who find themselves in this negative spiral of physiological and psychological interaction a combined programme aimed at tackling both aspects often proves more powerfully restorative. Thus therapy and/or anti-depressants to combat the psychological effects provides the support necessary for the body to begin a climb back to physical health. Without that support the body may feel unable to contemplate the gradual resumption of normal life.

Any trauma or illness that directly affects the brain will have at least as powerful an affect on the emotions and mental experiences as it has on other brain functions. Concussion, for instance, after a blow to the head which produces unconsciousness, may not leave residual damage to the physical functions of the brain but often leaves the person feeling 'unreal' and depressed for several weeks. Some people have reported personality changes which last for months after relatively minor head trauma.

The organs concerned with purifying the blood of toxins and waste products of metabolism – the kidneys, liver and lungs – are all extremely important for normal brain functioning, and any disease that affects their ability to function will also compromise brain function. Similarly, those organs that take in nutrition and oxygen – the digestive tract and lungs, and the heart, which enables the blood to distribute these nutrients – are also important for brain function.

Common abuses to the body, such as smoking and alcohol, have direct effects on our emotional well-being and also have longer-term indirect consequences because of the damage they do to other organs. Freud postulated that we all have a death instinct as well as a life instinct, and this may explain why we do not all choose healthy life styles to keep our bodies and brains functioning as well as possible, but rather choose regularly to insult and challenge ourselves.

# PART 3

# WHAT IS IT CALLED?

# INTRODUCTION:
# DIAGNOSING DISTRESS

In order to produce a structure for the way in which we think about psychological problems, a series of diagnoses have been developed both in the UK and abroad over the last century. A diagnosis is usually based on a set of symptoms which commonly occur together, and by making a diagnosis it is possible to decide which group of treatments are necessary and what the likely outcome will be. This is a medical model of the way human beings work, adopted by psychiatrists from their earlier training in general medicine. It sees the individual as a separate entity, with symptoms directly relating to the function of organs within the body. For the more simple branches of medicine dealing with much less complex organs than the brain this straightforward approach to illness has allowed many breakthroughs in treating and understanding illness.

This approach has many critics, however, who say that it is over-simplified, a reductionist view of human beings. Many other professionals, for example psychologists, nurses, social workers and occupational therapists, also treat psychological problems, and have different methods for categorising people. Certainly, within an individual each organ affects the others, and this is most true of the brain, which oversees the remainder of the body. It is therefore probably a medical mistake to ignore the role of the emotional in both illness and recovery. Research still in progress in Birmingham in 1991, for instance, has demonstrated that the manner in which a surgeon speaks to patients being investigated for breast cancer on the night before they are operated on may influence the physical and emotional consequences of their treatment. The patients who do best seem to be those who are allowed an opportunity to discuss their emotional responses with the surgeon. Other research has suggested that patients who either 'take on' their illnesses in an aggressive way, determined to beat it, and even those who ignore and deny their illness, have better recovery and survival rates than those who feel immediately despondent and beaten by their disease.

In order to make diagnosis a more sophisticated skill, increasingly a multi-directional (multi-axial) approach is being adopted. This approach allows for many aspects of the patients' lives to be taken into account. Thus their physical and emotional health would be only two of the many issues investigated. Other stress factors, such as poverty, poor housing, difficult relationships, tension in the family background, and employment difficulties, clearly have an impact on people's emotional and physical health. At the same time the personalities of the individual and close family members make a difference to how he or she interacts with other problems.

Within psychiatry there is an on-going conversation between those who adopt an organic approach to problems, believing that diagnosis and physical treatments such as drugs and ECT are the positive solution to people's distress, and those who feel that more often than not the distress is a symptom of a disorder in the patient's life experience, past, present, or both, and that whatever you do physically to 'cure' the distress it will return again and again unless the underlying problems are discovered and rectified.

The first approach suggests that there is a fault of some sort within the tissue or transmitters in the brain. It is often believed that this fault is inherited, and needs to be chemically rebalanced. The second approach sees the individual as part of a family and social system which has an on-going effect on the health of that individual from conception. The sorts of diagnosis made vary between these approaches as they view people in different ways. An organic psychiatrist may diagnose depression in one case while a marriage guidance counsellor might see marital troubles and their consequences. The reality is that both diagnoses may be accurate and useful, and that the person concerned might be helped by either approach, or by a combined approach. Too often different approaches to diagnosis are seen as embattled one against the other, with practitioners on both sides feeling that they have the only answer. In this section we will look at the diagnoses most commonly made in British psychiatry and psychotherapy today.

It is useful to think of making a diagnosis on a number of different levels. *Symptom diagnosis* is a descriptive entity, reflecting the patient's verbalised complaints. *Structural diagnosis* allows us to describe the way in which the individual's personality is structured, so gaining added colour about the way that individual will react both to the symptoms and the treatment. A *psychodynamic diagnosis* allows us to describe the underlying conflicts of the individual, which adds a further depth to our understanding of the problems and difficulties that may be encountered in treatment. There may also be good reason to look at a *family diagnosis* – it is not unusual for the wrong member of the family to turn up for treatment – or even a *social diagnosis*, as for instance it has been my experience with post-natal depression that the best treatment is for the mother to go back to work, with adequate provision made for child care.

It is fundamentally important to listen to the patients' vocabulary, which discloses what they think about their symptoms. It may be that they are only willing to consider diagnosis and help at one or two of these levels, and will be resistant to any other explanation for their distress. Attempting to explain symptoms at a level in which the patient cannot believe them does no good. Thus the depressed housewife will probably feel rejected and ignored when the GP tells her it is her neurotransmitters that are at fault and gives her anti-depressants, while the schizophrenic may suffer endless distress without medication, whatever the accuracy of the diagnosis of family dynamics. It is important that all clinicians remember that it is not their pride in being right about a diagnosis at any level which makes them therapeutic, but rather their ability to aim the diagnosis at the correct level to be helpful to the patient.

Patients can also help carers to help them more effectively if they have ideas about the origins of their problems and what they are willing to suffer in order to put things right. It is not helpful to be over-compliant, accepting on the surface what is diagnosed or suggested as treatment while challenging or ignoring it underneath. Many accept prescriptions, for instance, and yet feel angry that this is what they have been offered. Others will enter therapy, but as a 'hidden agenda' will have already decided that it is useless for them. Expectation of accurate diagnosis and cure and a belief in the carer all have a positive effect on the outcome, and it is therefore important that each person feels that he or she has been listened to correctly, at the right level of functioning for self and family. This can be more easily achieved if the patient has already reflected on his or her experiences and has some prior knowledge of what he or she wants from the professionals.

# PSYCHIATRIC DIAGNOSIS

The World Health Organisation (WHO) produces an International Classification of Diseases (ICD), Chapter V of which has always been for psychiatric diseases. It takes years of communication and discussion between psychiatrists of many nations to produce a chapter with international acceptability, as well as a chapter which fits in with the basic format and goals of the ICD as a whole. The tenth edition of the ICD is due to come into practice during the early 1990s.

Another system of classification, named DSM-III-R, is widely used in the USA. Comparisons between the two systems show that there are differences of opinion as to the way in which to group, label and describe symptom complexes as illnesses. These differences show that we have conceptual problems with drawing boundaries around groups of illnesses and with knowing what to include within any one category and what to exclude. Such problems are particularly taxing within psychiatry because there are many 'grey' areas between groups of symptoms. For instance, it is not unusual to find that a person who is depressed also experiences anxiety, or that a person who is unduly anxious is also often depressed. These illnesses form two overlapping groups descriptively, so that while the extreme forms of depression or anxiety are easy to separate, in many cases there is considerable overlap. This is reflected by the use of a third descriptive category within the classifications, namely 'mixed depressive/anxiety disorder', which is useful when it comes to international communication about research, statistics about the rates of illnesses in various countries, and the multi-national education of psychiatrists.

Similarly there is on-going discussion about the relationship between anxiety and obsessional disorders. Some believe them to be related to anxiety in much the same way as depression is, others believe them to be separate. Thus in ICD-10 they will be classified separately while in DSM-III-R obsessional disorder is regarded as a type of anxiety disorder. The benefits of such systems of diagnosis, even when they disagree, are clear to the clinician. They allow for the structuring of our understanding in ways that mean we can communicate to one another about the sorts of distress we are seeing, which leads on to being able to research illness and its treatment. DSM-III-R is often thought of as the best research tool because it contains precise descriptions in all categories. Clinicians say that such precision is only achieved by arbitrary inclusion and exclusion criteria within categories, and that the more flexible approach of ICD-10 is better for clinical practice.

Clearly, however, much is lost in reducing a group of complaints into a single 'disorder'. When a strictly medical diagnosis is made it usually tells the clinician about the cause, treatment and likely outcome of the illness. This is not true in psychiatry, when for the most part the diagnosis is simply descriptive. It is only in those illnesses where we know that there is structural damage to the brain, for instance the dementias, that the diagnosis also tells us about the cause and effect of the symptoms as well as describing those symptoms.

In the second half of the twentieth century there has been a resurgence of interest in attempting to make diagnoses in psychiatry, spurred on by the advent of drugs with powerful effects on mental experiences and emotions. As all drugs need to be tested in trials which can be repeated with similar patients, a way to group patients meaningfully was needed. Psychiatry has become increasingly medicalised, and so doctors have used their understanding of diagnosis in other organs of the body and imposed this on the structural understanding of our mental and emotional experiences. In its desire to compare and contrast psychiatric illness in many countries the WHO also stimulated interest in finding a common way of recognising which illness we are talking about. Even within a country, doctors have to communicate with other agencies such as the courts or Social Services, and diagnosis undoubtedly makes that communication easier, although also potentially less accurate for the individual concerned.

Many criticise the practice of making a diagnosis at all, in psychiatry, saying that it always has an aspect of negative labelling for patients which stigmatises them in the eyes of their family, friends, employers and society. Psychoanalysis and psychology tend to view individuals within the context of their development, learning, and life experiences, and sociologists point to the illness in society, to which much individual distress is directly related. Thus all these professionals would see diagnosis as unacceptably reductionist and unlikely to benefit the individual who is experiencing the distress.

However, against these arguments many 'biological' psychiatrists would argue that psychiatry is an accepted branch of medicine generally, and that it therefore merits research into the biochemical and biological aspects of illness. They believe that eventually, after enough research, we will be able to diagnose specific entities of illness and have precise knowledge of the cause of the illness as well as specific treatment to cure it. For this group, probably the most influential in both Europe and the USA at present, psychoanalysis and psychology merely provide explanations in terms of the meaning of symptoms without naming a cause or a specific treatment. Furthermore, they hold that the explanations offered by psychoanalysis and psychology are only theories, as yet unproven. Perhaps sadly, and despite extensive research, it is no easier, indeed apparently almost impossible, for these psychiatrists to demonstrate biological cause and effect, although they have achieved success in predicting the outcome of treatment and in identifying genes which appear to 'mark' inherited tendencies towards groups of mental illnesses.

Nevertheless, psychiatric diagnosis influences the practice of all those who attempt to deal with mental health issues. For some it is the guiding light, and the attempt to make the correct diagnosis through the use of interview and examination is seen as the central clinical skill; others may use diagnosis in a more peripheral way, preferring models that help them understand individuals rather than illnesses.

## Making a Psychiatric Diagnosis

Recognising psychiatric illness requires that a system for examining aspects of a person's behaviour, mood, perception, thoughts, and cognition (that is, intelligence, memory, orientation in time and space and concentration) by question-and-answer method is taught, and that we have some way of deciding between normality and abnormality in these areas. Such a system is made up of taking a personal history and examining the patient's mental state in the here-and-now of the assessment interview. The history will include the reason for referral to a psychiatrist, either in the patient's own words, or if this is not possible, then by description from a relative or other involved person. A family history places the person within the context of the family of origin (whether mum and dad are still alive, how many brothers and sisters, etc.) and also explores whether there is any history of previous psychiatric problems within the family. A personal history records the development of the individual, noting any problems from birth onwards. School and work history are included. Usually the menstrual and psychosexual history is also questioned, including note of fantasies or abnormal practices. Relationships, marriage and parenthood are next explored. The history of past illnesses, both physical and psychiatric, may give clues to the present problem, and an attempt is made to gain an image of the person's personality before he or she became ill – these are areas which when illuminated help to put the individual and the present problem into context. The history then turns to the present problem.

During this interview the clinician will have been looking for clues to the present behaviour of the individual. From these clues he or she will deduce how aware of the surroundings, how co-operative, how active, or how agitated the person being interviewed is. Any mannerisms or gestures will be noted, and the level of relationship which the patient finds possible to establish with the interviewer will also be commented on. By both description and observation the interviewer will come to conclusions about the mood and stability of mood which the person is presenting, and also record observations about his or her form (how fast, slow, fluent or interrupted) and content (principle preoccupations) of speech.

The content of the person's expressed thoughts is examined, with particular reference to hypochondriacal ideas about their health which may or may not be based in actual bodily symptoms, obsessive compulsive ideas about their habits of cleanliness or of rituals, and delusional ideas. Perceptual disturbances, most notably visual or auditory hallucinations but also those affecting the senses of smell, taste or touch are also questioned. The cognitive testing often takes the shape of 'games' of memory and concentration, asking the person about orientation in terms of which day of which month of which year it is, and attempting through general information to get a (rough) guide to his or her level of intelligence. At the end of all this the clinician makes an observation on the level of insight the individual seems to have into his or her illness.

There follows a physical examination, sometimes backed up with laboratory tests of the blood, or X-rays, and further psychological testing.

A diagnosis will be made on the basis of this kind of interview. Jonathan, aged 42, complained of extreme fatigue. On examination he was found to be a quiet man who had difficulty finding the energy to express his thoughts. He moved very little throughout the interview, seeming tired. He said that he had felt depressed for four weeks for no apparent reason, that he had suddenly lost his appetite, had difficulty sleeping and felt no interest in life. His outlook on life was pessimistic, quite at odds with his wife's description of his normal out-going personality. He was not deluded, however, and was fully aware of the fact that he was ill and that his pessimism was an aspect of that illness. Jonathan was diagnosed as having a straightforward depression which would statistically have a good chance (probably on the order of two out of every three patients with a similar complaint) of responding well to anti-depressants.

Each diagnosis has a list of features, some or all of which need to be present in order to make the diagnosis. Thus in order to diagnose schizophrenia the clinician would be looking for signs of schizophrenic thought disorder, with its accompanying indications of difficulty in thinking, thought blocking (when one topic is suddenly dropped and another, unassociated topic begun), and the patient's subjective experience that thoughts are being inserted into or withdrawn from his or her head. The clinician will also take note of any signs of hallucinations (most commonly the patient hears voices talking about him or her) and of delusions, sometimes including thoughts that the TV is talking to or about him or her, or 'passivity feelings', that is, the patient feels that his or her body and mind are being controlled by others. Emotional and behavioural disturbances would also be noted.

The term 'differential diagnosis' refers to the skill of deciding from the symptoms and signs discovered on examination what exact illness this person suffers from. When presented with someone who may be schizophrenic, the clinician will be running through a list of possible other diagnoses as he or she makes the final decision. Other diagnoses might include a drug-induced psychosis – because the symptoms of schizophrenia are mimicked in people who take amphetamines or LSD – an organic psychosis produced by a physical illness, a personality disorder, hysteria, a depressive illness, or a paranoid state. As each would require different treatment a correct diagnosis helps the clinician to help the patient. In fact there is still considerable disagreement about the basis for diagnosing schizophrenia, although most British psychiatrists would agree that signs of thought disorder, hallucinations, delusions, emotional blunting, a marked deterioration in the person's everyday functioning, an onset of the illness before the age of 40 and a duration of at least weeks or months rather than hours or days are necessary prior to this diagnosis being made.

# PSYCHODYNAMIC DIAGNOSIS

This is a system of diagnosis based on the concepts of analysis from Freud onwards. It is theoretical in the sense that it is scientifically unproven and unprovable; it attempts to look at the totality of an individual's internal world and how that relates to the external world. Most analysts work by making diagnoses at various levels of functioning (symptom diagnosis, structural diagnosis, etc.): thus they might note a symptom diagnosis based on the major complaints of the person, for example depression. They would then make a structural diagnosis of the predominant mode of functioning of the personality, followed by a psychodynamic diagnosis which would describe the individual's major conflicts and the role played by his or her psychological defences. Many would say that there are two fundamental forms of conflict: either pre-Oedipal – the struggle within individuals with a part of themselves which they experience with a life-or-death intensity, or Oedipal – the conflict between three aspects of the self, often represented by others in their lives, a conflict in which one of the three aspects is excluded. Conflicts of either type make it difficult for individuals to sustain relationships or communicate with others because they function by means of self-concealment and self-isolation, either hiding aspects of themselves from their conscious minds or by isolating various aspects of their inner worlds from each other so that their personality is not in any sense integrated.

This system of diagnosis depends on an understanding of the structure of the mind that is not based in either biology or biochemistry but rather focuses on how the mind functions. It requires that there is a large unconscious area of the mind, from which we are protected by our defence mechanisms. Within the unconscious all early memories and experiences are stored, including our primary instincts of survival, life, procreation, death, and sexuality. As we grow so we quickly learn that many aspects of that inner experience are unacceptable to our families and society at large. We store the knowledge of what is unacceptable within our super-ego, which acts as an internal policeman over our expression of feelings and our behaviour. The super-ego has a solid nucleus of ideas and values which we internalise at an early age, learned from our parents, and which is relatively impervious to change in later life, whatever our subsequent experiences. Around that core is a much more flexible area of the super-ego which continues to interact with the external world throughout our lives, meaning that we can take on new values and question old ones. Our conscious mind is the tip of the iceberg of the remainder, showing a little of what we remember, what we have experienced, and allowing us rational control over some aspects of our lives. However much we struggle to be scientific and rational, the unconscious still holds enormous power over our thoughts and feelings: how we express those to ourselves and others depends on the relationship between unconscious (the id), super-ego, and conscious mind (the ego).

The model suggests that conflicts arise between these areas of the mind which cause the individual psychic pain, which is either directly experienced as a psychological symptom or acted out against the self or others as a form of behaviour. The distinction between neurotic symptoms and personality disorders is often seen in terms of the type of defence and the type of ego reaction to stress. Individuals with personality disorders are often said to have *alloplastic* defences, meaning that they react to stress by attempting to change external factors. If a relationship looks likely to disillusion them, for instance, thereby representing a threat to their psychological well-being, they may threaten retaliation or in some way manipulate the other person into meeting their wishes, thereby avoiding the disillusionment. People with neurotic disorders have *autoplastic* defences which react to stress by attempts to change their internal world. Thus if they are in a disillusioning relationship they may deny the disillusionment or take the blame for it themselves. Similarly, those with personality disorders view their personality defects as *ego-syntonic*, that is, they find themselves acceptable and unobjectionable in any situation; while those with neurotic disorders view their shortcomings as *ego-dystonic*, that is, unacceptable and alien to the self.

## Making a Psychodynamic Diagnosis

Within the various models of psychoanalysis and psychotherapy the diagnosis may be made primarily in the first few sessions, although it will almost certainly be modified by further experience within therapy. Such a diagnosis rests on an interflow of communication between patient and therapist. The therapist will want, initially, to collect a historical overview of the patient's life in a way that allows him or her to draw meaning from the developmental experiences of the individual. Thus, *what* happened is less important than the *feelings* connected to any particular happening.

In order to make connections between past and present experience a detailed history of the person's past needs to be acquired. Alongside the concrete details of dates and order of events, the therapist will be trying to extract some ideas about repeating patterns in the person's life, either in the way the person views him- or herself or how he or she relates to others.

Judith aged 32, wanted psychotherapy in order to help her make sense of two failed marriages. She felt that she was to blame for the fact that both of these relationships proved unworkable, and wished to change aspects of herself which she perceived as 'ugly'. Judith was the second of three children born within four years to a mother who was described as being post-natally depressed until her youngest child was 5 and Judith 6½.

Judith could vaguely remember her mother lying on the sofa, apparently asleep, for many hours each day, and spoke of starting school at 4 as 'a relief'. She had no memories of her father at all until she was 10, at which point he seemed to appear suddenly in their lives and 'take over'. In fact he had had a job which took him away for weeks at a time, and, finding the atmosphere at home intolerable, had therefore capitalised on the amount he could avoid it. Talking to Judith about these early experiences the therapist felt rather lost and directionless. Judith would talk brightly about the way the three children 'got on with everything' as if they were castaways on a desert island, enjoying themselves with the game of survival but lacking clear long-term goals. He told Judith that he experienced her description of childhood as 'without direction' and she instantly agreed, taking his comment as a positive one, that there had been few boundaries or rules to restrict them.

This ability to see positive benefit to herself in every situation, however outwardly terrible, was reflected in her view of both of her divorces. She saw the battles for money and custody as 'making me grow up', rather than feeling embittered or outraged about her experiences, although her therapist often experienced just these feelings 'for her'. Within four sessions the therapist was able to say to Judith that he thought that early on in life she had learned to be grateful for very little, because that was all that was available. Her basic personality had allowed her to take some good out of relationships, even fundamentally unsatisfactory ones, but she had forced herself to become blind to many disappointments when her needs were not met. She tended to idealise anything that was offered and deny that there were outstanding needs still unmet. She also lacked a sense of inner direction. In order to acquire this we need to have consistency, both in the care we are offered and in our perception of the world, when we are young. For Judith the world was unpredictable and uncontrollable, and simply had to be 'coped with'.

It was clear to the therapist that both of these factors,

originating in her early life, had taken their toll within Judith's marriages and made the events leading to her divorces much more comprehensible. It was also clear that within the predictable boundaries of therapy Judith would benefit and grow in ways that would allow her to identify her needs more accurately and develop a realistic expectation that those needs could sometimes be met. In order to do this Judith would have to 'grieve' for the parenting she had not received and express some of the anger and resentment which she had hidden within her psyche so carefully that even she could not see it any more.

Furthermore, the long absence of her father during her early years had created an idealisation of men in Judith's psyche, without any ideas or expectations of how to relate to them 'in person'. Because of this she had no way of gauging whether the demands of either of her husbands had been reasonable, and little expectation that she could demand anything of them. This uncertainty had been reflected in her sexual experiences, in which she had been unsatisfied and even humiliated without being able to name or emotionally respond to these events. The male therapist quickly recognised that Judith would be likely to be an 'over-grateful' patient, and would need to assert herself against him one day and survive the experience if she was to grow in her relationships to men.

In talking to distressed people it is sometimes useful to ask yourself 'How old, emotionally, does this person sound now?', because when stressed we slide back to developmental stages of our earlier life, stages which we have in some way failed to complete. Every age of life requires that we jump certain psychological hurdles. This need for growth and enrichment goes on until late in life, but during infancy the developmental stages are clustered together in the first few years. As we grow through adulthood we get more time to explore and resolve each stage. Freud talked of oral, anal and sexual stages of development, all occurring before we are 5 or 6 years old. Melanie Klein believed that from day one we are thrown into the frenzy of our inner world. How we complete these complex stages depends on our innate personality, the inherited part of ourselves, and our external experience of the world around us, especially our experience, in those early years, of our parents.

Erik Erikson (an analyst who trained with Anna Freud) worked in the USA from the early 1930s and developed a scheme of eight stages through which he felt we grew psychologically until we died. In his scheme each individual must accomplish major 'tasks' before he or she can move competently on to the next stage.

Stage I, which occurs in the first year of life, he called *Trust versus Mistrust*. If the infant receives 'good enough' parenting in which the parents respond to her individual needs empathically, then by the time she is a year old she will have developed a basic sense of trust in herself and the world. If, however, the infant's needs have not been met, or have been met in a chaotic way in no sense related to her demonstration of need, then the one-year-old will have a sense of loneliness and unpredictability, and may wish to withdraw into herself and away from the un-loving world. Attachments to other human beings will never come easily to such people.

Stage II, which occurs between the ages of 1 and 3, is called *Autonomy versus Shame and Doubt*. This is the age of discovery. Based on the previous foundation of trust in a loving environment the infant sets out to use his newly acquired co-ordination and muscular skills to interact with the world, returning regularly to check that a dependable figure is there for comfort when needed. Gradually his circle of discovery widens. Alongside this, the infant is struggling for control, both over his own body as he gains sphincter control and becomes clean and dry, and over his environment, seeing just what he can 'get away with'. By the age of three the infant should have a sense of mastery over himself and a sense of security in his environment which is not entirely dependent on his parents. Over-stressed bodily control may have led the infant to experience shame and a desire to conceal aspects of himself from others. Failure to explore safely may lead to a need for 'sameness', and the inability to relate to others, acquired (or inherited) in the first year will now become more obvious.

Stage III, occurring between 3 and 6 years, is called *Initiative versus Guilt*. The child is now ready to discover what kind of person she is, and does this by identifying with either mummy or daddy, both of whom are seen as simultaneously beautiful and dangerous. The fantasy of replacing the parent of the same sex and satisfying the parent of the opposite sex causes rivalry as well as anxiety. The child is faced with the fact that she is still much smaller, weaker and sexually unproductive, and therefore falls back on an identification with the parent of the same sex. This leads to the 'grown-up life' of facing the world of school and new activities with enjoyment of competition, a desire to pursue goals, and increasing pleasure in attaining external goals. Failure to resolve this stage means that the child remains timid, frightened of the challenges of the world and potentially guilty because she remembers the yearnings of early, precocious sexuality.

Stage IV occurs between the ages of 6 and 12 and is called *Industry versus Inferiority*. During this time the child is still young, small and can easily be made to feel inferior to the many challenges that are waiting. What is needed are goals that allow enough challenge to stretch the individual but which are also within the resources of a child of that age. With this form of teaching the child's intellectual world begins to expand, and gradually thinking can move from the entirely concrete (question and answer) to more creative lateral thinking. Parents and their opinions become less important as society begins to have an impact on the developing child. By 12 a child needs to have established a sense of his own skills and abilities which is acceptable, lovable and realistic: gaining this attitude is fundamentally important in later finding the right niche in the working world. Early failures can cause the individual to underachieve in a way that is bound to be unsatisfying to the adult. Childhood ends and the tasks of adulthood now emerge.

Stage V, occurring between 12 and 20 years, is called *Identity versus Role Confusion*. Erikson coined the term 'identity crisis' to describe the normal disruptive process of adolescence, as the individual begins to match his or her inner experience with outside adult expectations. There are also many physical changes as the person's body prepares for the onset of adult sexuality. Best friends become important, and fashions are essential, in order to feel a sense of belonging to the group. There is a need to experiment with roles, within the relatively safe structure of support from home. 'Falling in love' is often the grand finale to this stage because it feels like a validation of the chosen identity. Confrontation with parents is also a common reaction. The adolescent needs to react against as well as towards conformity, and parents need to help both in freeing the youngster to move away while at the same time upholding adult boundaries and a sense of security. The very quiet adolescent may not necessarily be weathering this phase better than the highly disruptive one. By the late teens, a sense of the consolidation of the self will enable the fully developed adolescent to emerge into adult life, making choices that are realistic and yet also hopeful. For those who fail to emerge, adult life with all its varied experiences cannot psychologically begin.

Stage VI, occurring between 20 and 30 years of age, is called *Intimacy versus Isolation*. Once a sense of self has been established it becomes possible to have a relationship based on mature interdependence and intimacy with another. At the same time the individual is making decisions about his or her needs: the biological (should I have children?), the social (which group do I mix best with?), and the professional and economic (what do I want to gain for what I do?). These decisions often come down to a basic conflict between wanting to settle down and wishing to move on. Freud, when asked what a normal adult should be able to do, said 'to love and to work'. This is the phase when the individual discovers whether he or she is capable of meeting such simple and yet such high ideals.

Stage VII occurs between the ages of 30 and 65 and is called *Generativity versus Self-Absorption and Stagnation*. The tasks for this phase are to achieve external, productive creations, either in terms of children, of projects, or both. Jung talked about the need not to expect to resolve or solve everything but instead to be engaged in working at ourselves incessantly. Mid-life is a time for taking stock and allowing previously unexpressed parts of the self some space. The individuals who retreat from these challenges, usually because of having failed to resolve earlier hurdles, become absorbed in themselves and stagnate into rigid and generally rather unsatisfied adulthood.

Stage VIII usually occurs from age 65 until death and is called *Ego Integrity versus Despair.* During the aging process a person has to cope with many blows to his or her ego. The body may fail and friends will die. Work no longer provides external structure to life and a new, inner reason for living and enjoying life has to be found. Clearly, in many ways this is the most difficult stage of all, and yet for those who have worked through the previous hurdles of living, it can also be the most peaceful and pleasurable, a time for looking back at life with satisfaction and not too many regrets.

With such a range of developmental tasks throughout life, it is clear to any therapist that whatever the age of the person seeking help, some psychological work is always ready to be done.

# PERSONALITY DIAGNOSIS

Given the unique nature of each of us it is hard to produce a way of defining personality which allows us to make comparisons and judge what is normal. We can either measure personality on a number of parameters and then define normality as a statistical entity from which a small proportion of the population deviate, or we can describe personality and use the more subjective but potentially more useful definition offered by the American psychiatrist Kirt Schneider, as 'abnormal personalities who suffer from their abnormalities or cause others to suffer'.

DSM-III defines personality traits as 'enduring patterns of perceiving, relating to and thinking about the environment and oneself . . . exhibited in a wide range of important social and personal contexts.' When such patterns become rigid and fixed and cause impairment in the functioning or relationships of individuals they are seen as personality disorders.

Such traits or disorders have usually been apparent from the early years of an individual's life, indeed many of the behaviours demonstrated by an adult that would be considered unusual or abnormal are normal parts of childhood experience which the individual has failed to grow through and leave behind. Obsessional personalities, for instance, often use ritual and repetition to keep their anxieties within bearable limits. Many childhood games are based on ritual and repetition for the same purpose.

# Making a Diagnosis of Personality Traits and Disorders

Such a diagnosis is made on the basis of the individual's behaviour, either observed or described, alongside his or her explanations for such behaviour.

Mary is 24, and arrives to her psychiatric out-patient appointment wearing a see-through blouse, to which she brings the psychiatrist's attention, asking for compliments about how hard she has tried to look nice for him. She cannot see anything inappropriate in this behaviour, but instead presses for reassurances about her physical attractiveness to him. When describing a minor problem with her neighbour which has been the apparent precipitant to her wish for the appointment she sobs uncontrollably for a few minutes and then suddenly becomes cheerful again. Her argument with the neighbour appears to be centred in Mary's desire to know what is going on next door and to be in some way involved. When the neighbour objected Mary felt rejected to the extent of threatening to take an overdose.

Mary has a long history of desperately seeking attention, particularly sexual attention, yet being unable to sustain emotional contacts with people for more than a few weeks. Her descriptions of others are often superficial, demonstrating the degree to which her primary interest is self-centred and based in her great need for the immediate gratification of her wishes. Any obstruction to her wishes provokes extreme outbursts. She has been diagnosed as having a histrionic personality disorder.

Josephine, aged 42, also puts on impressive displays of emotion, but does this within her job as an actress. Although she too has difficulty sustaining relationships, she is more willing to accept some responsibility for their breaking up than Mary is. She is aware of other people as separate individuals whose primary responsibility is not to her, and demonstrates an ability to delay gratification. While Josephine probably has histrionic traits in her personality, she had put these to good use, of benefit to herself and others, rather than being overwhelmed by them as Mary is.

Charles, aged 43, has always been suspicious of the motives of others, and expects to be betrayed or hurt by everyone eventually. He is constantly on guard against any threat of humiliation and will take offence quickly. Any sense of slight or injustice provokes intense rage; he never forgets or forgives. His interpersonal relationships are severely limited by these problems, and he has been diagnosed as having a paranoid personality disorder.

Nigel is 54 and has always lived alone. He has no desire to be a part of a family and says he does not need friends. All his hobbies are solitary and he maintains a constant mood of neutrality, claiming never to have experienced anger or joy. He is happy with his chosen life style and does not hurt others, whom he keeps at a distance: thus although demonstrating a schizoid trait he would not be diagnosed as having a schizoid personality disorder.

Peter, on the other hand, who is also 54 and who demonstrated similar traits in younger life, wanted to try marriage and parenthood. Sadly for all concerned, his personality was too rigid to be able to blossom; he became unable to stand the interpersonal demands and eventually withdrew. His indifference to his wife's praise or criticism and his cool and distant behaviour with his children caused much anguish.

From these examples it becomes obvious that a person who is aware of his or her limitations and fits life to suit them can live with extreme traits of personality without necessarily looking disordered, whereas those who are blind to themselves often attempt to make themselves and their lives into situations which stress them, making their limitations more apparent and more disruptive.

Those with personality disorders are often difficult to live with and may well come to diagnostic attention because their spouses are exhausted from trying to cope with them. An example of this was Pauline, who arrived complaining of post-natal depression. Within the first hour of the interview a picture of her husband as a supremely narcissistic person began to emerge, raising the suspicions of the psychiatrist that the wrong member of the family was asking for a diagnosis. When Jeremy was asked to accompany his wife to her next appointment, his demanding nature became obvious at reception where he explained that he was an important person who should not be kept waiting and deserved some special attention from the doctor immediately. Once with the doctor he attempted to make a 'special' relationship, talking about 'men like us', and regaling the doctor with stories of his success and his sense of puzzlement at Pauline's sadness when he had made such a wonderful life for them. The extent of his envy of the baby became apparent when he talked about her as 'a demanding and unreasonable creature' to whom Pauline was 'over-attached'. The baby was 3 weeks old. Jeremy lacked any insight into the feelings of either Pauline or the baby, and when confronted, gently, by the doctor about his demands on Pauline at a difficult time, exploded in rage and told the doctor that he had 'every right to make demands on her'.

Society also 'diagnoses' some personality disorders because of the probability that they will someday lead to the law being broken. Lily had been cruel to animals since early childhood, then 'graduated' on to truanting and eventually setting light to her classroom. When she had had three convictions before the age of 25 there was general agreement to a diagnosis of an anti-social personality disorder. Ted was convicted of GBH (Grievous Bodily Harm) when he was 30. He felt no remorse for his victim, a widower of 80 whom he had blinded, and detailed an adult life in which he had travelled without a fixed home and had had many short-term relationships. He said with pride that he thought he might have fathered 'hundreds of bastards' and 'never had to take care of any of them'. His anti-social personality was also noted.

At another end of the personality spectrum are those who avoid relationships because of fear of themselves or others. Sally, aged 31, is too easily hurt by minimal criticism to risk a relationship and will avoid social occasions, if possible. When forced at work to socialise she becomes tongue-tied, and fears that she will blush and make a fool of herself. Whenever any exciting new opportunity is offered, she decides that the risks, which she exaggerates, are too great.

Catherine, – aged 34, cannot make everyday decisions, allowing others to do this for her, even if she knows that they are wrong. She goes to great lengths to make people like her and fears being left alone and abandoned. The threat of a relationship ending is devastating to her, and she is willing to continue to demean herself so long as the relationship continues. This dependent trait in her personality is causing her increasing distress because of the violent nature of her relationship, and if she cannot find the flexibility and strength to make the decision to leave and face her fears, this trait will soon grow into being a dependent personality disorder.

Some of the most difficult people to live with are those with compulsive personality disorders who are constantly preoccupied with details and desire perfection in all things. For such people work is like a religion, and they will insist that others do things just the way they themselves would do them. Such people often have difficulty making decisions because they are so determined to get exactly the right answer and cannot bear to compromise. They will be inflexible about their chosen religion or values, regardless of the feelings of others. Mean with affection and material goods, they are often great hoarders of useless things.

From these descriptions it can be seen that many of those whose traits of personality become disorders can make exceptionally annoying friends, spouses or patients. However, most of us have annoying traits which we demonstrate in certain situations and which we counterbalance with our personality assets. In assessing personality it is important to look to the positive strengths of the individual as well as those negative aspects, particularly because when someone is distressed he or she tends to forget that each personality is made up of strengths and assets as well as weaknesses. Many people will forget that they are funny and loving when they become depressed, or capable and constructive when they are anxious. They need to be reminded of their 'other side' if we want to help them examine the less enhancing aspects of their personality.

# FAMILY DIAGNOSIS

The family is the most usual 'home-base' from which we function, both as children and adults. It is not, however, a concrete entity, like a building, but rather a flexible and forever moving system constructed between people and held together by bonds of blood or affection. Within the family there are many types of relationships, requiring different and changing roles to be adopted by the members; also, not all the members will like, respect and love each other – the fact that we do not choose our relatives is an old truism. Thus the base upon which we depend as a retreat from the threatening world, a place to be ourselves, a place to find and give love and nurturing, is also the place of heated argument, conflicting loyalties and needs, envy, abuse and hatred. Many more murders are committed within families than between strangers. Today there are many different family patterns, and little research to tell us which, if any, work best.

The true role of the family can be seen as having evolved from tribe and extended family, which were themselves attempts to keep as many members of the unit as safe and secure as possible. However, geographical mobility and very different working and socialising patterns have led to families becoming increasingly 'nuclear': cut off from all but immediate relatives. Many people yearn for a more extended family now and feel lonely within the small group that a nuclear family can provide. Many members of the minority ethnic groups in the UK still preserve a more extended family network, to the clear benefit of some members, although perhaps to the limitation of others. The flip side of the loneliness one can feel within a nuclear family is the great freedom it affords you to become an individual and seek your own destiny.

Family groupings may be reconstituted because of divorce or death, and women raising children alone is more common and accepted than in the past. Statistics suggest that only 11 per cent of households are nuclear families in the traditional sense. New family structures have benefits and difficulties much as older patterns of the extended or nuclear family had. Therapy is aimed at diagnosing the particular problem for that grouping of people, whatever their chosen pattern of family structure.

What makes a family structure sick? This question raises another: namely, what role do we now expect families to play in our lives? It has been the generally accepted view that family structures were for the benefit of children, and also women while they were having and bringing those children up. Thus most referrals to family therapists occur because a child or adolescent has problems or symptoms which seem related to the dynamics of the entire family. Many therapists would now question the understanding that families do function for the benefit of children. Multi-national surveys, like the one that Professor Anthony Clare conducted for television on the nature of marriage, seem to suggest that the system exists primarily to provide a stable, well-tended male work force, and only secondarily for the good of women and children, via the income thus generated. This would perhaps explain why so many fathers fail to attend family therapy appointments, being 'too busy at work'.

Families, like individuals, acquire a certain level of maturity which usually reflects the maturity of one or both of the adults involved. It is difficult for adults to help their children to surmount developmental tasks which they themselves have still to face. Such limitations within a family may go unnoticed for years before the stress that will specifically attack their weakness arises. Family limitations are handed down for generations . . . if the sin of the father is indeed visited on the son, it is the sin of not resolving his own problems and developing fully as an adult but instead having some hopes that his children will do this work for him.

A study conducted in the USA, called the Timberland Study, described the repeating patterns that were demonstrated in healthy, mid-range, or severely disturbed families. The healthy family showed a clear demarcation between the parents and children in terms of roles and decision-making authority, although most decisions were reached through a process of negotiation between the equally empowered parental coalition and the children. High levels of individual responsibility were the norm for such families, and each family member seemed able to uphold a firm identity while at the same time intimacy between family members was maintained. Because the 'basics' of relationships were thus secured, these families could communicate directly and spontaneously, and were open to new ideas and challenges. In these families the ambivalence of powerful emotions was openly accepted, but each individual could reasonably expect a positive, warm response to a positive approach. The adults engaged in a warm and sexually satisfying relationship.

The mid-range families were those which showed 'breakdown' when stressed, usually with one family member presenting the distress for everyone else. Such families were led by a rigid parent who was either engaged in a battle for dominance over the other parent or who had a partner who had already submitted to his or her dominance. There is much role-stereotyping within these families, with little spontaneity, and the sense of any personal identity is only maintained by keeping each other emotionally distant. Communication may be clear but is rigid and unable to change when stressed; it also has the quality of monologue, with one family member voicing his or her say in the presence of the others, rather than being a true dialogue. Such families tend to believe in the basic 'evil' of mankind, which thus requires much repression in each member: this tends to mean an unhappy and unfulfilling parental relationship.

Severely dysfunctional families have at least one very sick member, but often the whole family is showing signs of the disorder in the system. In such families one parent (most commonly the mother) enters into powerful coalitions with one or all of the children. There is little sense of responsibility within the family, and roles and boundaries are blurred, and each member's experience of 'self' is tinged with a sense of being invaded by the others. Communication is complex and confused, depending on rather magical and mysterious explanations which are often contradictory or evasive. The ambivalence in feelings remains completely split and there are therefore sudden and extreme swings of mood, often with no obvious provocation and later denied. The parental relationship is negative or non-existent.

Experiences of separation, loss and death tend to throw families back to a basic mode of functioning, and it is, therefore, at these moments that the fundamental health or illness of the family system becomes apparent. Healthy families have a clear perception of reality, even under extreme stress.

Stephen, aged 11, started to play truant from school. His mother Judy, 34, was frequently in tears to the teacher as she related her inability to get him 'to behave'. Stephen's sister Claire, aged 9, had nightmares which woke the house and still regularly wet the bed for no apparent physical reason. Judy was desperate for help but seemed unable to get the whole family, including her 36-year-old husband, Ben, to the meetings. She clearly felt responsible for the behaviour of all the family members. As an attempt to overcome that basic assumption, the therapy team sent individual invitations to all four family members for the next appointment, reminding them that it was, for each of them, a personal responsibility to get there on time. Rather surprisingly this ploy worked and all four did turn up, although both Stephen and his father were sulky and initially uncooperative.

It seemed that both the truanting and the nightmares had started soon after the death of Judy's mother six months previously. In eliciting this information, the structure of the family and the way in which it functioned as a team became apparent. Judy took responsibility for all the explaining, bringing Claire in as prime reinforcer of the story. Ben was, for the most part, quiet, but when he did intervene it was to tell Judy and Claire that they had 'got it wrong again', but offering no clarification. When pushed for further explanations he answered 'They always get it wrong!' Stephen looked distressed but was unforthcoming, often glancing at his father as if in hopes that he could pair up with him in the way that Mum and Claire were so clearly a team. Ben was plainly a 'loner', however, who seemed impervious to his son's glances.

At the first meeting the therapy team spelled out what they had observed so far in the way that the family functioned, attempting as much as possible to put each member's behaviour into a positive light. It was suggested to Ben that his wife needed his support in order to keep the children 'steady', and that maybe he did not understand or appreciate how important he was in the family. The team also suggested that Judy should attempt to talk to Ben rather than Claire about the problems with Stephen, if Ben was willing to listen. The team told Claire that they thought she had done a very good job supporting her mother through a difficult time, when grandmother died, but that now was the right time to allow Mum and Dad more space to talk to each, so that she could relinquish some of the adult responsibility that she had taken upon herself. Last, but not least, one team member went and put an arm around Stephen's shoulders and said that he knew that Stephen was upset and just did not know what was the acceptable way of expressing grief in the family, when everyone else was so strong in the face of loss. 'Sometimes' the team member went on, apparently to Stephen, but also to the remainder of the family, 'the strongest thing is being able to express the grief which everyone rightly feels when someone important dies.'

The family returned for three further sessions over the next four months. Judy and Ben had tried to talk to each other and take a more equal and shared parental role with Stephen. Ben had become responsible for getting Stephen up and dropping him off at school, and this attention seemed to have worked magic over the truanting. Stephen looked a happier child. Claire also looked more like a child and less like 'mother's little helper', a transition which seemed to have been helped by Judy's having taken a part-time job. This seemed to have reduced the tension under which Claire laboured in her attempts to support her mother, and not surprisingly the bedwetting and nightmares had also ceased. The team warmly congratulated all the family members on their positive attempts to put things right, and reminded them that they needed to give time and attention to the way the family functioned in the future.

The major threats to family security occur when a family member either arrives or leaves, for whatever reason. Most families are in states of transition for much of the time because of the development of the children and their different needs. Such changes do not happen on a continuous spectrum of activity but rather in a stop/start fashion. It is at the times of crisis and threat that symptoms, psychological or physical, will occur in one or all members of an unhealthy family. Healthy families will have their own coping strategies, and for them the stress becomes a challenge to make changes and move on to the next stage.

# PSYCHOSOCIAL DIAGNOSIS

The demographic distribution of some forms of mental illness varies from one part of a community to another and from one culture to another; social psychiatrists wish to find explanations for these differences.

Generally speaking, the highest rates of schizophrenia and personality disorders are found in the lowest social class, while the neuroses (depression, anxiety, obsessional illness, phobias, eating disorders, etc.) and bipolar (manic and depressive) illnesses are found more commonly in the upper or upper-middle classes.

There has been much argument over these figures as attempts are made to find an explanation which is upheld by research findings. Some researchers have felt that having a mental illness would lead to the individual's occupying a position in a lower social class (because the illness led to the fragmenting of his or her working and social life, and to feelings of low self-esteem); others have felt that the experiences and stresses of being in a lower social class were, in themselves, enough to create or induce mental illness (because it has been demonstrated that more damaging life events occur, and that individuals have less control over them, in the lower social classes). There have been theories of social drift, in which ill people move down through society as a result of their illness, and of social segregation, in which those members of the lowest social class who are ill or handicapped will be the ones least likely to escape the confines of their class.

Not all of the movement between or restriction within social class will be directly due to illness. Some of it will be related to the adequacy and availability of help, particularly in countries where mental health units require insurance certificates or payment, and some of it will be related to the stigma experienced by those diagnosed with a mental illness. There is an on-going discussion within psychiatry about on the one hand how a rapid diagnosis of serious disorders leads to help and support and perhaps prevents some of the long-term and irreversible damage to the personality which can occur, versus a more cautious diagnosis so as to avoid the problems of stigmatisation as much as possible, as well as not encouraging the individual to adopt a sick and dependent role, as for example a patient with chronic schizophrenia might do.

There is much evidence to suggest the life events are connected with the onset of both physical and mental illness. In a study in London, G.W. Brown and T. Harris demonstrated that the loss of a relationship, status or love was directly connected with women becoming depressed. Moreover, they demonstrated that those women who were most at risk had had earlier life events which left them vulnerable to loss, and had present-day stresses that limited their coping capacity. The factors which rendered these women most at risk included having no intimate, confiding relationship, having three or more young children at home, not having an outside job, and having lost their own mothers before the age of 14.

The relationship between life events and illness is probably not as direct as originally thought but involves both a previous vulnerability for a specific or more generalised event and a lack of care or tremendous present-day demands on the individual which together further deplete his or her ability to cope.

Despite the stigma of mental illness it is surprisingly common in all cultures. Epidemiologists have studied both the prevalence (the number of existing cases at a point in time or within a period of time) and the incidence (the number of new cases within a period of time), and have usually demonstrated that within any one period of time between 18 and 22 per cent of the population are experiencing symptoms of mental illness of some sort. Many of these people will not come to the attention of professional help, but it is this high prevalence which makes most of us sensitive to the presence of such illness and fearful for our own sanity. Unlike many physical illnesses where we can be sympathetic with the sufferer reasonably safe in the knowledge that we will not get the same illness, we all have the uncomfortable feeling in the presence of mental illness that 'There but for fortune . . .', and hence have in the past believed madness to be contagious and in need of 'putting away'.

In a study conducted in 1980 by the Mental Health Unit in the USA, epidemiologists discovered that 18.7 per cent of the population has a diagnosable psychiatric illness within any six-month period. Such figures would be in agreement with (and are even slightly lower than) figures from a Manchester survey taken over a similar period. This 18.7 per cent is mostly divided between cases involving substance (drug and alcohol) abuse: 6.4 per cent and anxiety and depression: 9.8 per cent, with only 1.0 per cent having schizophrenia.

Despite these figures, psychiatric services have had to maintain a balance between cure, care and control, and containment. Thus these services are often geared to the minority who cause the greatest alarm to others and are more at risk themselves, but who are often resistant to cure and most in need of care and control. This has been at the expense of the majority who may be in as great distress but do less to alarm themselves and others, and who may be easily curable but cannot find the help that they need.

Psychiatry has always been the Cinderella service within the NHS, with successive governments preferring to put money into high-tech medicine and surgery, presumably reflecting the feelings of the general population. With the changes enacted in 1990/91 much of the responsibility for caring as opposed to curing passed (along with the finances) to Social Services. Sadly, this means that there is a large group of depressed and anxious people who do not seek help, and who may not find appropriate help even if they do seek it.

Social control has always been an aspect of psychiatry which warrants mention and examination. For instance, in the Soviet Union psychiatry was clearly used as a part of state control (disagreement with the State was defined as schizophrenia, for example); this greatly angered the international psychiatric bodies, to the extent that they expelled the Soviet Union as a member and have still to allow her full membership, and will do so only when it is clear that the situation has been greatly improved. Accusations have been made that psychiatry is similarly used in the Western world. It is certainly an area in which we need to take the greatest care to make sure that it is the patient's interests which are to the fore, as far as the caring services are concerned, leaving the police and court system to protect society when it sees fit. However, because of the Mental Health Act, which authorises compulsory admission and treatment, and because psychiatrists are asked to make 'expert' statements about the dangerousness of individuals, there is an overlap between the rights of the patient and the demands of society which the profession has to carefully monitor at all times.

Determining dangerousness is one of the most difficult aspects of assessment, often falling back on the common-sense position of 'If the person has done something dangerous previously then he or she is more likely to do it again.' Some mental illnesses make individuals less controlled or less aware of what they are doing, and until these illnesses are cured or under control these individuals remain dangerous. However, the decision often falls to the 'intuition' and experience of the assessment team. Luckily this seems adequate in the great majority of cases, and although we hear in the media of the rare occasions where re-offending occurs, it is also true that Broadmoor discharges a large proportion of its population every year, as cured, who never cause trouble again. It may be that such assessment, while mostly fair to the community, is unfair to the many individuals who would be capable of good citizenship if released.

There are many forms of social control, and it may be that

we should be more anxious about those which are covert and apparently sought by the patient rather than fought against. An example of this may be the widespread use of the minor tranquillisers that took place for over 20 years, prescribed mostly to housewives experiencing stress, distress or depression, until in the 1980s their use was questioned. Even now these prescriptions take up a vast section of the pharmacological budget, and many women are still struggling to relinquish their 'mother's little helpers'. What might have happened to society if all these women had been forced to voice their discontent rather than having it tranquillised?

Jayne, aged 43, had been on Valium for 14 years, having first been prescribed it when her children were little and causing her distress. She reported many years during which she would wait until 2.30 p.m. and then wash down some Valium with a small sherry in order to fortify her against the children's return from school. She had four children and they did seem to make enormous demands on her which she was unable to limit or control. Of course, the effects of the Valium and sherry made her less rather than more able to limit and contain their demands, although they did transform her into this ethereal being who could float over her family apparently being all-good and providing, never losing her temper and never making demands herself. When she felt needy she took an extra tablet. She explained, with some pride, that she felt that the tablets had helped her live up to the image of motherhood which she felt society expected of her.

Her husband Brian, aged 49, had been aware of the medication for many years, but had never questioned its use. He was often absent on business, and seemed to feel that if the Valium helped her cope then it was fine. 'She has been a perfect wife and mother,' he said at the one meeting he could attend. When I suggested that the pursuit of social perfection had greatly impoverished his wife's emotional world he seemed bemused. 'We are her world,' he contended, 'and she is happy with that.' I persisted: 'If she is happy why is she taking tablets?'

Again he seemed momentarily puzzled, and then said 'But I think a lot of women do, don't they? It seems socially normal to me.' Sadly, in terms of statistics this scenario was surprisingly normal for a whole generation of women, thanks to a society which wanted perfect mothers and wives far more than it wanted happy, fulfilled women!

There are many situations within psychiatry and psychotherapy where the practitioner is faced by a person in great distress and with a choice of whether to give him or her something that will immediately relieve that distress, an option which allows both patient and carer rapid gratification but often does little to address the underlying problems, or to take the approach that distress is a human phenomena which provides us with clues about what we should be addressing in our lives. It may be our right to pursue happiness as according to the American Constitution, but we all know that happiness is not a regular or predictable experience, nor one we can capture for ever. Unhappiness often does teach us things, so long as we can feel supported while we bear it. In my experience, male practitioners when faced with distressed female patients have an almost overwhelming need to make them better as quickly as possible, and thus will go to great therapeutic lengths rather than stay with the pain and attempt to help her learn from the ordeal. Although apparently kind in the first instant, this does nothing to cure the underlying problems. Thus the choice of whether to diagnose the individual or the social mode of his or her life may be crucial to the long-term good of both the patient and the health of the community.

# PHYSICAL
# DIAGNOSIS

The body and mind are closely linked and can exert considerable influence over one another. Thus illness in the body can cause mental illness and illnesses of the mind can cause physical disease.

Clearly physical illnesses of the brain are most likely to affect the emotions, but disease in other systems of the body will also have a major impact on the mind. The brain depends on the body to perform successfully, for example to supply oxygen and nutrients and to eliminate waste products. Any failure in the body's systems will mean that the brain will function less effectively and eventually cease to function at all. Similarly, the body's systems receive a nerve supply from the brain and so stress, unhappiness and illness within the brain will affect this innervation. Each of us probably has specific vulnerabilities to both mental and physical illness, and therefore these stresses, operating as they do in both directions, will leave us open to experiencing specific forms of either physical or mental illness, or both.

It was thought during the 1950s that there were seven 'classical' psychosomatic illnesses, which the emotions played a major role in producing and strengthening. These illnesses were peptic ulcers, bronchial asthma, rheumatoid arthritis, ulcerative colitis, essential hypertension, thyrotoxicosis and neurodermatitis. More recent research has demonstrated the complexity of the relationship between many more physical illnesses and the emotions. The example of peptic ulcer demonstrates this complexity. Evidence at first suggested that peptic ulcers occurred especially within a group of people who required love and nurturing from others but who felt guilty and ashamed when they experienced these needs because it was equally important to them to appear as capable adults. The conflict between a desire for dependence and a need to be independent was expressed by these people by increased (acid) gastric secretions in their stomachs which eventually led to ulceration. It was suggested that in order to produce a disease the individual needed a particular set of psychological conflicts, a life event which reactivated these conflicts, and a biological vulnerability to the conflicts being expressed via gastric secretions. Further research suggested that if these individuals reacted to stress with increased gastric secretions, as infants they may have been touchy and difficult to feed, and may have often felt that their needs were not being adequately met, however much their mother tried. Thus their biological vulnerability might have been instrumental in producing the underlying conflict as well as in communicating it.

The political theorist Friedrich Engels, who himself suffered a heart attack on the last day of the period of mourning (as observed by the Jewish religion) for the death of his twin brother, noted that both sudden and fatal illnesses were often connected with life events which involved the loss of a loved one. He believed that such physical illnesses were the sign that the individual had 'given-up' on self and on life. Certainly when I was practising general medicine and surgery it was my experience that a patient's will to live (or die) made a substantial difference to his or her recovery or decline. We have all read in fiction of people dying of a broken heart, but in reality this seems close to the truth, with the death rate among newly-bereaved spouses several times higher than that of non-bereaved people of a similar age. There is also increasing evidence that the emotions play a part in regulating the body's immune system, which in turn protects us from both infection and cancer. Personality also affects physical health. The type A personality, who works over-hard and is pushy, and driven to achieve, has a greatly increased chance of a heart attack than the remainder of the population.

Physical illness can also accompany mental illness problems. As previously stated, infections of or tumours in the brain and epilepsy can all produce a wide range of mental illness symptoms. Other illnesses, such as Parkinson's Disease and MS, as well as trauma to the brain, can also produce many symptoms. Problems in the hormone (endocrine) systems are also likely to produce psychological as well as physical symptoms. The thyroid (a gland in the neck producing thyroxine, which maintains the body's metabolic rate) can either over- or under-function. Either of these possibilities causes a change in the person's psychological functioning as well as in their physical well-being, mimicking a depression if under-active and mania if over-active.

The pituitary gland (situated on the underside of the middle of the brain and producing a number of stimulating hormones which modify the function of other glands in the body) can exert its influence over the production of blood cortisol, which is necessary for much of the smooth functioning of the body's regulation of the electrolyte inner world, as well as giving us diurnal rhythm. Whether the pituitary instructs an over-production of cortisol (Cushing's Disease) or an under-production (Addison's Disease), the patient may present an anxiety-coloured depression or appear retarded, although occasionally in Cushing's Disease the person is apparently elated. Diabetes (lack of insulin to control blood-sugar levels) can also produce dramatic personality changes if badly controlled.

Many women experience psychological symptoms at specific times in their menstrual cycle, depending on the peaks of the level of sex hormones secretion. For some this is so severe as to be incapacitating, and treatment with hormones seems advantageous. For the majority a planned programme of sensible eating and exercise can be helpful, plus a sensitivity to their needs for greater rest at some phases of their cycle.

Ruth is a 28-year-old mother of two who finds herself restless, aggressive and clumsy for several days prior to her period. She finds herself unable to be understanding with the children and also shouts at her husband, who is generally sympathetic to the problem. When first seen, Ruth made no allowances for herself during these difficult days despite acknowledging the problem. Looking at her life it was possible to see that she could organise herself and the family so that she could rest more and feel less stressed during that time. She also reorganised her eating so that she was taking more fruit and vegetables and less starch, salt, and fat for that week. She allowed her craving for chocolate a freer rein, however, having saved calories on the other changes. These simple changes made a considerable difference to how she felt, and she experienced herself as 'back in control'. She also suggested to the family that some of the things she shouted about for those three days were really things she had a right to shout about every day, and that they should take more notice and be less dismissive. Taking responsibility for both her body and her feelings gave Ruth a sense of empowerment and renewed self-esteem.

The interface between the psychological and physical can never be ignored. A person is an entity, and just as our feelings are reflected in our bodies, so too are our bodies powerful in determining how we feel.

---

## PART 4

---

# WHAT CAN BE DONE?

# INTRODUCTION

Methods of treating mental illness can take several forms: *psychological* treatments include behaviour therapy and cognitive therapy; *psychotherapeutic* treatments include supportive, educational and exploratory therapy. *Counselling* represents the 'common sense' part of the psychotherapeutic spectrum, in that counsellors befriend in a way that encourages the recipient to discuss his or her difficulties and share problems. *Marital and family therapy* and *group therapy or analysis* are other possible treatments; *psychoanalysis* includes long-, medium- or short-term dynamic therapy, individually or in groups, with a particular 'flavour' depending on which school the analyst trained with. All these treatments have been demonstrated to be equally successful, both with each other and with other forms of treatment (for example drug treatment of depression). Thus the form of therapy is a personal choice, depending as much on availability as specific treatment for specific problems. Much of the research into the effectiveness of therapy suggests that a good patient/therapist match in terms of personality is more important to the outcome than is the form of therapy. Certainly therapy is unlikely to be helpful if the patient does not like or respect the therapist. The experience of the therapist only seems to make an impact on the outcome of therapy with people with personality disorders, with trainee therapists under supervision often achieving good results.

*Self-help groups* offer the comfort of being with people who can relate to our problems and experiences and who can provide a supportive and accepting environment. *Drug treatment* offered within the context of psychiatry has achieved many positive results when used either in the short or long term; and the *physical treatments* of ECT (Electro-convulsive Therapy) and psychosurgery can seem to work magic on patients who have long been suffering with the darkness of depression.

In this section we will explore all of these treatments; each has its positive and negative aspects, and each has been of help and benefit to a variety of patients.

# THERAPIES

## Psychological Treatments

The underlying assumption of this form of therapy is that the client has disorders of behaviour which demonstrate themselves as symptoms, and that the client and therapist then negotiate together to agree on target problems and explore what seems to make those problems better or worse. This is a *behavioural* analysis of the symptoms and is undertaken in great detail because the client may be initially unaware of what is precipitating or potentiating his or her problem behaviour. Treatment involves asking the client to change aspects of behaviour so as to produce a modification of the problems, by decreasing the patterns which make the symptoms worse and increasing 'healthy' behaviour. In both behavioural and *cognitive* therapy the therapist is actively involved in directing and advising the patient, who has to do 'homework' that includes taking action as well as thinking, feeling and understanding. Unlike other forms of therapy, here patients are seen as capable of changing their behaviour without necessarily having to change their personality or their understanding of past events in their lives.

There are a number of techniques used to help clients mould their behaviour. First we are all more likely to continue to do things which are rewarded and to cease activities which are either ignored or punished. This approach is therefore used in many treatment packages to encourage normal behaviour, for instance in treating anorexia – not eating is seen as the target problem behaviour, the patient is rewarded for eating and putting on weight while privileges are withdrawn when weight is lost. Of course the patient has to be motivated to co-operate if these factors are to have an impact on his or her behaviour, and staff and patient need to feel they are working together to achieve a mutually agreed goal rather than it being a question of staff enforcing a cure on the patient.

Secondly, if we learn to associate something unpleasant with a previously pleasing but unhealthy activity, such as drinking too much, then we eventually associate the activity with a sense of displeasure which makes us less likely to continue it. Thus if an alcoholic takes medication which makes him or her sick every time he or she has a drink, then alcohol is perceived as not as agreeable as it once was. Furthermore the alcoholic learns that avoiding alcohol makes him or her feel well. Punishment also extinguishes unwanted behaviour, and small electric shocks have been used to discourage behaviours ranging from drug abuse to sexual perversion. Again, the patient's co-operation is of course essential.

Relaxation is often used to help patients gain a state of mind which is incompatible with any anxiety or fear they might feel when they are confronted (little by little) with whatever they have been afraid of. While in a state of relaxation they either use their imagination to place themselves in the worrying situation, for example a shopping centre for an agoraphobic, or they are actually exposed in the company of their therapist to the frightening stimulus, which may be anything from a spider to flying. Most therapists believe that prolonged exposure to the frightening stimulus is more effective than brief exposure, which may act to reinforce the fear rather than extinguish it.

In cognitive therapy thoughts and actions are combined to alter behaviour. The therapist teaches the client to use visual imagery to stop the sequence of thoughts which lead to unwanted behaviour and to replace it with a positive series of thoughts which will lead to healthy behaviour. The underlying assumption is that people's emotional experience of life is largely determined by how they think about it. Therefore people become depressed because they are selectively taking the unhappy aspects of their life and magnifying them while ignoring or undermining the happy experiences. They may also be setting themselves false goals, believing that they are unhappy because they cannot be famous, for instance, even when famous people are clearly seen to be unhappy sometimes; or perhaps they are worrying themselves with false dilemmas which allow them to ignore real choices and options in their lives. Therapy seeks to question their black interpretations of life and help them to focus on the positive.

## Psychotherapeutic Treatments and Counselling

The underlying assumption of all psychotherapeutic treatments is that people need to talk about what worries them with a neutral but concerned person who listens actively and makes comments designed to help them understand their problems. Supportive psychotherapy offers clients a chance to talk about their problems in a friendly atmosphere in which they will not be criticised or attacked. The therapist can take a neutral stance because he or she is not involved in the way that relatives or friends might be. Being outside the problem he or she can help the client see it from a number of new perspectives, and can also help to place the problem within the on-going context of the client's life and relationships. The therapist will probably not offer advice or directives, or have an opinion about what the client should do, but rather will construct a sense of acceptance within the sessions so that the client can freely explore options without undue influence from the therapist.

Counselling takes place within a similarly friendly, non-critical atmosphere, but counsellors are trained to give advice and make suggestions alongside of providing the psychological relief the client gains from unburdening him- or herself of problems by discussing them.

Educational psychotherapy builds on the basic supportive therapy as the therapist attempts to teach the client about his or her feelings. Simply helping a client to understand that what happens in life affects the emotions is often eye-opening: I have often said to people that if I was living the life they were trying to cope with I would be depressed, too. Many people believe that they have to accept what is handed to them without questioning it or making any attempts to change it, be it in terms of their working life, home or relationships, and no matter how unhappy they become as a consequence. The educative process may be a process of learning how to question that assumption. Some people do not realise that what occurred to them as children has any effect on how they feel as adults. They may even feel guilty about 'blaming' parents who did their best. Therapy is not about blame, however, but about understanding and acceptance. In order to reach that position the past often has to be explored with new eyes in order to learn from it in a way that helps the present.

Exploratory psychotherapy often uses techniques which are drawn from the psychoanalytical understanding of the structure of the mind and of the way people repeat their relationship problems through a phenomenon known as transference. We all transfer the feelings we have about important people in our lives onto others, and can sometimes even make those others behave as if they were just like the people we remember.

Joseph asked me why he had the misfortune to have the worst therapist in Britain. I suggested that it might be connected to the fact that he also believed himself to have had the worst mother in the world. Although he replied that yes, he did seem to get all the bad luck, the comment sank in and a few weeks later he said that maybe he viewed all his relationships rather negatively. The therapist can use his or her knowledge of the fact that what transpires in therapy is a repeat of earlier, intense relationships, feeding this knowledge back to the patient in a non-hostile way which the client can understand and 'swallow'; in this way it is possible for people to experience a shift in the way they view themselves and others.

Most psychotherapy is conducted in weekly sessions of

between 30 minutes and an hour, 50 minutes being the 'magic' time of much therapy. It is available on the NHS in most districts, although waiting lists are often long. The therapist will contract with the client when and where they will meet, how often and for how long. These are important parameters to set clearly from the start as they provide structural boundaries within which the client can feel more secure. Within the NHS clients are usually allocated to therapists, many of whom will be in training under supervision. Although lacking experience such therapists often provide good help, partly because they are at the beginning of their careers and anxious to do their best and partly because what they hear from the client is all new. Older therapists suffer from having heard it before, although they benefit from increasing experience too. Some attempt is usually made to 'match' therapist and client, within the limits of who is available, because research suggests that a therapist's own experience of life needs to have some similarities with the client's for optimum progress to be made. However, I have not infrequently supervised young male trainee psychiatrists from Nigeria and Uganda who were working with middle-aged housewives from Berkshire, and been amazed at the universality of all of our experiences, whatever our origins, sex or age.

Psychotherapy of all sorts is also available privately. In 1992 those advertising themselves as psychotherapists will have to have undergone some form of specialised training, but for the time being anyone can call themselves a psychotherapist. The important things for a client to know are which training, if any, the therapist they consult has had, how long and intensive was that training (did it, for example, require the therapist to have personal therapy?) and has he or she achieved some form of qualification. Personal recommendation is often a good guide to the therapist's ability; the client also needs to question whether he or she can intuitively trust the therapist.

Some forms of therapy require action as well as words. The world of *gestalt* therapy uses the body, movement and action techniques to help stimulate the exploration of the client's inner world. The basic statement used is 'Don't just tell me – show me' and, of course, in telling and showing others we sometimes learn ourselves. Psychodrama is a specialised technique in which the client or protagonist is asked to recreate in drama an experience from his or her life, using others in the group to people the drama. The client is then asked to replay the experience in the way he or she would have liked it to be. Jacob Moreno, who invented this technique, said that Freud analysed people's dreams, whereas he allowed people to live their dreams. Drama therapy uses a range of exercises to help the client work through particular issues or experiences. For example, a story might be related by the group leader, who then asks the group to replay it with each member selecting a role. At the end discussion might concentrate on why each person chose a particular role and what it felt like for him or her. All of these techniques include active, non-critical feedback from other members of the group.

Others forms of therapy use art, music, singing, writing and play in order to help people express things which cannot easily be expressed in words. Many of the most creative therapists use humour, not as a defence against pain, but as an enabling tool we can use to express the things which worry or hurt us most.

## Marital and Family Therapy

The basic assumption of these therapies is that dis-ease may lie within the structure of a relationship or relationships rather than within an individual. The therapist's main task is to retain neutrality in a situation where blame or illness is often focused on one member of the marriage or family, and to attempt to understand the dynamics of the system and then explain them to the participants.

## Group Therapy or Analysis

Group therapy is conducted by as wide a range of therapists as is found in individual therapy, and therefore the spectrum of goals ranging from support through learning and on to inner exploration is similar. Here, however, a group of clients or patients is like a 'mini-society' and can therefore offer a context in which people can learn about their relationships in a wider and more comprehensive way than is ever possible in individual, marital or family work. One of the myths of therapy is that only the therapist, whom the client believes to have life 'worked out', can help him or her sort out any problems. Patients have asked what possible help someone with as many problems as they have can offer. The answer is that sometimes the person who seems to have more problems may well understand the patient even more than the therapist can, and that because of this level of sensitivity will be of great help. The role of the therapist varies according to the style of the group, but many are more active and involved with the group than they might be in other therapies. The main task of the leader is to help the group reflect on itself as a group as well as individuals, because this helps each member understand his or her position in the 'whole', which often reflects his or her position in many other aspects of life.

Some groups will be formed with people who share a problem. These groups tend to be supportive and educational. In analytical groups the leader will attempt to have a 'mix' of people, as this stimulates more exploration and allows for a wide range of possible interrelationships within the group. Most groups function with rules. These may be basic rules about time, place, punctuality and confidentiality, or they may be more explicit, such as a ban on relationships forming outside of the group. Every group is different, and whatever the orientation of the leader, the group members produce a unique group culture. This culture is called the group matrix, a criss-crossing of the strands of relationship, understanding and experience to which each member contributes and which forms the basis for reflection and understanding.

# Psychoanalysis

The important technique in psychoanalysis, originally described by Sigmund Freud, is *free association*. The patient is encouraged to allow thoughts, feelings, dreams and memories to come into consciousness and to communicate them directly to the analyst without vetting them, however illogical and bizarre they may seem. The analyst then uses the structure of his or her particular school of analysis to make this flow comprehensible and useful to the patient. The patient lies on a couch and the analyst sits behind him or her so that there is nothing to distract the patient's flow. Such therapy is open-ended in its duration, the contract between patient and analyst being 'as long as it takes to get a reasonable result or to explore all the areas that need exploration'. It is usually conducted in daily sessions of 50 minutes, although some analysts have modified that intensive regime to three or four times weekly.

Psychoanalysis is based on a structural understanding of the mind in which the id (unconscious) contains material which has been actively repressed (buried) because of its worrying nature, and to which the patient is resistant to regaining access. Despite this the material continues to cause conflict in the patient's inner world, always threatening to appear in the ego (consciousness) against the instruction of the super-ego, which polices our inner lives. This conflict causes psychic pain and symptoms of distress. Free association is the technique which encourages the material to come into the open in the safety of a therapeutic relationship in which it can be contained and understood. The analyst interprets the meaning of the material to the patient (*analysand*), and during the course of therapy the same issue will appear on a number of occasions, each time slightly changed by its previous exploration so that the conflict is gradually worked through.

Such analysis aims to produce long-lasting changes to the personality, and in this most intense form is suitable for those with severe personality difficulties. It also provides a 'window' onto the inner workings of all of our minds and is therefore a useful research tool whose results influence the practices of the other, less intense or long-term therapies.

Many of the famous analysts have added their own flavour to the practice of analysis. Freud, father of them all, described the structure of the mind, developed free association, indicated the importance of dreams as 'the golden road to the unconscious', and described a number of developmental stages – oral, anal and genital – through which we all pass on the way to maturity. He is probably best known for the concept of the Oedipus Complex, that is, the son's competition with father for the love of mother, which raises the son's anxieties that father will castrate him, and so eventually the son relinquishes mother and instead identifies with father.

Melanie Klein worked with children in analysis and described earlier developmental steps in the baby and infant, including a paranoid position in the young baby, who splits good and bad and loves and hates with great energy these split-off bits of her mother. As the depressive position is then worked through, the baby puts the good and bad together, realises that she has hated and (in fantasy) attacked part of the good and loved mother, and wishes to make amends. The baby has to relinquish the hope of an ideal in order to perceive and cope with reality. These theories formed the starting point for the object-relations school of analysis, whose theory is that we construct our egos from parts of others and parts of our relationships with others which we take into ourselves (introjecting). Material within us which is unacceptable or incompatible may be pushed out onto others (projecting) and often once we have projected it onto others we hate them for it, in reality hating our own, projected weaknesses.

Carl Gustav Jung was a spiritual man, interested in the collective unconscious, that is, an unconscious we all share in terms of myths, fairy stories and culture, and its effect on individuals. Mid life and its accompanying psychological changes, with their impact on the second half of life, fascinated him.

Psychoanalytic psychotherapy uses much of the theory and

practice of psychoanalysis but does not base itself on free association and is often time-limited. Within the NHS it is this form of analysis which is most frequently practised. This less intense form of analysis is suitable treatment for many emotional problems. The therapist attempts to help the patient form a positive and dependent relationship which allows expression of needs and wishes and a re-enactment of earlier relationships which can then be analysed. Modern schools of analysis include the existentialists, who are particularly interested in the universal concerns such as death, loneliness, freedom, responsibility, and meaninglessness in life, and the ways in which each of us chooses to defend against or deal with such concerns, and feminist analysts, who have described new understandings of female psychology, including the fundamental importance of the mother/daughter relationship, women's need for other women, and the impact of social position on psychological development.

There follows a list of training centres and associations. By contacting them it is possible to get details of the sort of therapy they offer, the training provided, and a list of trained graduates who live in your area.

## Behavioural Therapies

These are often available from NHS practitioners and specialist nurses and psychologists.

*The Academic Dept of Psychiatry* at the Middlesex Hospital Medical School, London W1P 8AA; tel. 071 636 8333 (ext. 7370) runs treatment and training leading to a diploma in behavioural psychotherapy.

*The Maudsley Hospital*, Denmark Hill, London SE5; tel. 071 703 6333 has an in-patient and out-patient treatment facility run on behavioural lines.

Privately, you can contact the *British Association of Behavioural Psychotherapy*, c/o Dr Taylor, Psychology Department, Dykebar Hospital, Grahamston Road, Paisley, Renfrewshire, Scotland PA2 1DE; tel. 041 884 5122 (ext. 213).

## Cognitive Therapies

*The Centre for Personal Construct Psychology*, 132 Warwick Way, London SW1V 4JD; tel. 071 834 8875.

*Rational Emotive Therapy*, 14 Winchester Avenue, London NW6; tel. 071 624 0732.

Focus is on one's individual belief system about oneself and one's life, and encouragement given to take responsibility for one's own life.

*Transactional Analysis*. There are three centres within London, at:

The International Transactional Analysis Association, 13 North Common Road, London W5; tel. 071 579 2505;

South London Transactional Analysis Centre (SOLTAC), 122 Charlton Lane, London SE7 8AB; tel. 081 853 3643; or via Lilly Stuart at the South London Psychotherapy Training Centre, 106 Heathwood Gardens, London SE7 8ER, tel. 081 854 3606.

## Psychotherapy

*The Adlerian Society of Great Britain*, 11 Osbourne House, 414, Wimbledon Park Road, London SW19; tel. 081 789 8086.

*Antioch University*, Regent's College, Regent's Park, London NW1; tel. 071 487 7552, offers existential therapy on a one-to-one basis.

*The British Association of Psychotherapists*, 121 Hendon Lane, London, N3 3PR; tel. 071 346 1747. Practises psychoanalytical psychotherapy.

*The Lincoln Centre and Institute for Psychotherapy*, The Lincoln Tower, 77 Westminster Bridge Road, London SE1 7HS; tel. 071 928 7211.

*The London Centre for Psychotherapy*, 19 Fitzjohn's Avenue, Swiss Cottage, London NW3 5JY, tel. 071 435 0873.

Many health care workers train within the NHS to high standards of psychotherapeutic practice, and it is worth finding out about psychotherapy provision in your area. A number of universities offer diplomas or MSCs in psychotherapy, which usually involve more theoretical work than supervised practice, although admission to such courses often depends on the therapists already having a wide practical experience. Aberdeen, London, Oxford, Leeds, Liverpool, Sheffield and Warwick Universities presently offer such courses.

## Counselling

There are many courses, both theory-based, offered at universities such as Reading, and practical, offered around the country. Both produce well-trained counsellors each year. The best way of judging the quality of training is to ask how many patients the counsellor saw while he or she was being supervised.

*Westminster Pastoral Foundation*, 23, Kensington Square, London W8 5HN; tel. 071 937 6956.

## Humanistic Therapies

*The Centre for Biosynthesis*, BCM, Chesil, London WC1.

*Centre for Transpersonal Psychology*, 7 Pembridge Place, London W2 4XB.

*The Facilitator Development Institute*, The Norwich Centre, 7 Earlham Road, Norwich NR2 3RA; tel. 0603 617709.

*The Gestalt Centre* 64 Warwick Road, St Albans, Herts; tel. 0727 64806.

*Institute of Psychosynthesis*, 310 Finchley Road, London NW3; tel. 071 486 2588.

*Metanoia Humanistic Psychotherapy Training Centre*, 11 Tring Avenue, London W5 3QA; tel. 071 992 3035.

*Minster Centre*, 57 Minster Road, London NW2 3SH; tel. 071 435 9200.

*Psychosynthesis and Education Trust* 50 Guildford Road, London SW8 2BU; tel. 081 720 7800.

All these therapies require action as well as reflection. There are also courses throughout the country in art and drama therapy. The centre for psychodrama in the UK is run by Marcia Karp and Ken Sprague at the *Holwell Centre for Psychodrama and Sociodrama*, East Down, Barnstaple, Devon; tel. 0271 82597

# Family and Marital Therapies

*Hampstead Child Therapy Course and Clinic*, 21 Maresfield Gardens, London NW3 5SH; tel. 071 794 2313.

*Institute of Family Therapy*, 43 New Cavendish Street, London W1; tel. 071 935 1651.

*Institute of Marital Studies*, Tavistock Centre, Belsize Lane, London NW3 5BA; tel. 071 435 7111.

*Relate* (formerly known as Marriage Guidance). Local branches can be found in your local telephone directory.

*Scottish Institute of Human Relationships*, 56 Albany Street, Edinburgh EH1 3QU; tel. 031 556 6454.

# Psychoanalysis

*British Psychoanalytical Society*, 63 New Cavendish Street, London W1; tel. 071 580 4952. They can put you in contact with a wide range of Freudian and Kleinian analysts working throughout the country.

*The Group Analytic Practice*, 88 Montague Mansions, London W1H 1LF; tel. 071 935 3103/3085 and *The Institute of Group Analysis*, 1 Daleham Gardens, London NW3. For group analysis.

*Society of Analytical Psychology*, 1 Daleham Gardens, London NW3; tel. 071 435 7696. For Jungian analysts.

*Tavistock Clinic*, 120 Belsize Lane, London NW3; tel. 071 435 7111. This is an NHS national centre for many forms of analysis and family therapy.

*The Women's Therapy Centre*, 6 Manor Gardens, London N7; tel. 071 263 6200. Practise a mainly psychoanalytical approach with feminist psychoanalytical theory as their basis.

# SELF-HELP GROUPS

Group therapy and group analysis have always recognised the patients', clients' and fellow-sufferers' potential for helping one another. Indeed in most groups, if all is going well, the therapist or analyst can sit back and watch in admiration as the group works with and helps itself. However there are still issues of authority, imposed theory and practice and the (often wrong) notion that the therapist is completely 'together' and therefore cannot understand the patient, which makes a leader counter-productive to group work. In some situations it is difficult for the therapist to understand the feelings that someone experiences, and a fellow sufferer, particularly someone who has already begun to journey along the road to recovery, can seem more helpful.

Self-help groups of all sorts have been running for more than 20 years, with increasing variety and levels of experience. There is considerable benefit to be derived from simply being with people who are like ourselves and can relate to our own experience of life. Life often feels alien to people with problems, as if they are outcasts, and meeting with others who are struggling with similar difficulties gives them a warm feeling of belonging and being supported which often forms a healthy bedrock on which to lay the foundations for a full recovery. Some people take the initiative and form self-help groups to discuss specific issues that relate to their own experiences. MIND (the National Association for Mental Health) 22, Harley Street, London W1N 2ED have published a book entitled *Finding Our Own Solutions* which details many of the self-help groups currently running (see Appendix C).

Sheila Ernst produced a book called *In Our Own Hands* (see Appendix C) describing the process of setting up such groups. Often the group starts with one or two enthusiastic people realising that they have a need to talk to like-minded people; they then advertise for others to join them. The group will need to set its own boundaries such as time and place, frequency, and trust between members sharing information, and also decide on goals. Many of the groups have social as well as therapeutic aspects – for some the social activities are in themselves therapeutic.

Women have been particularly active in starting self-help groups, because they often feel that the services they are offered either through the NHS or privately are not 'woman-friendly' and wish to produce a better and more caring atmosphere for themselves. Rape crisis lines and child abuse lines have become a source of help to which many carers refer women after sexual abuse in preference to the regular services. Women's centres all over the country have spent time and effort training members to facilitate groups and counsel, always with the underlying concept of women learning to help themselves and one another.

Listed below are a number of the self-help agencies active in the UK. Most have local branches whose address and telephone number can be found in your local directory or by asking at your GP's surgery or the Citizen's Advice Bureau. This list is not all-inclusive and there may be other groups available near you. Many Health Districts have conducted a 'Good Practices in Mental Health' audit of both NHS and Social Service and self-help groups for particular areas on behalf of the International Hospital Federation, copies of which should be available at the Community Health Council, from District Health Authorities or from your local Psychiatric Out-patient Department.

*Age Concern:* This is a national organisation with over 1,000 branches which receives both voluntary and national funding. Each branch will differ slightly in its history and the services it can provide, but most will attempt to provide sitting services for the elderly infirm, including transport, lunch clubs, drop-in centres, advice, information and a wide range of practical supportive services. The aims of Age Concern are to support the elderly person who is in need as well as his or her carers, as an addition to and not a substitute for NHS and Social Service provision.

*Alcohol Services:* Most Health Districts provide NHS alcohol out-patient services and some provide in-patient 'drying-out' facilities too. In addition *Alcoholics Anonymous* has a long established reputation for the support of those wishing to give up alcohol: its famous advice is 'take it one day at a time'. Most work occurs in groups, and there are often telephone support numbers within the groups to help the individual overcome the loneliness and despair which often accompany the early days of withdrawal. AA continues to offer support over many years to the rehabilitated alcoholic. *AlAnon* presents help to families of alcoholics and *Alteen* makes special provision for the adolescent children of alcoholics.

*Alzheimer's Disease Society* is a national organisation founded in 1979. It is an informal self-help group which distributes information and offers support for the carers of those with dementia.

*Cruse* has a national network which provides voluntary counselling for the bereaved. Each counsellor undergoes an intensive training programme before beginning work.

*Home Start* aims to help improve the home environment for the under-fives and their parents by offering friendly support and advice for families experiencing difficulties. Volunteers are usually parents themselves who have been trained to help new parents under stress.

*MIND* is an active campaigning group which aims to support the rights of all those with any form of mental illness or distress. As well as funding research and establishing its own hostels for the mentally ill, MIND plays an important political role is revising laws and policy effecting patients and their relatives.

*National Childbirth Trust (NCT)* is a large national organisation which aims to help mothers prepare for childbirth and parenthood. Its volunteer workers are mothers who have trained to teach and counsel others.

*National Association for the Welfare of Children in Hospital (NAWCH)* gives support and is willing to take up any complaints on behalf of parents. Members also sit on Health Care Planning Teams to influence hospital policy.

*National Council for Carers and their Elderly Dependants* acts as a pressure group and support group for the carers of elderly relatives.

*National Stepfamily Association* offers support, advice and information and publishes a quarterly newsletter for stepfamilies.

*National Schizophrenia Fellowship (NSF)* has 150 local branches run by sufferers of schizophrenia, their families and carers, and has an active role in campaigning for the rights of sufferers and providing support for the patient and family.

*Parents Anonymous* offers a telephone support system for distressed parents.

*Richmond Fellowship* is a national organisation which finances the setting up and running of 'halfway' houses for those who are attempting to live in the community after a time in hospital. As well as accommodation these houses offer friendship, group activities and staff guidance to their residents.

*Samaritans* offer a nation-wide 24-hour telephone counselling and support service to those contemplating suicide, feeling distressed, despairing, alone or abandoned.

*Tranx* offer a mail service to those wishing to give up tranquillisers: send s.a.e. to 2, St John's Road, Harrow, Middlesex.

In most communities there are now well-established *Women's Centres*, which may include *Well-Women Clinics*, run by volunteer staff to provide health advice and counselling for women in distress. *Women's Refuges* are also available for women who have suffered from violence in the home, and although the telephone numbers and addresses of these often remain (quite rightly) a well-kept secret in the community, a Women's Centre will be able to make contact. *Rape and Child Abuse* helplines are also available locally, in addition to the well-known national *ChildLine* founded by Esther Rantzen.

*Asian, Indian and Caribbean Community groups* are also founded locally, providing a wide range of supportive networks and advice centres.

*Gay and Lesbian helpline and self-help groups* operate in many districts, providing information, support, advice, friendship, activities and group work.

# Drug
# Treatment

The drugs used in psychiatry fall within one of three groups: *sedatives* (hypnotics and anxiolytics) prescribed to treat anxiety and/or insomnia, *anti-psychotic* or *anti-manic* drugs used as major tranquillisers in serious psychiatric illnesses, and *anti-depressants*. Drugs are known by their generic (chemical) names and by the names which drug companies ascribe to them. Changes made in 1987 to NHS practice mean that many of the brand-name medications are no longer prescribed under the NHS; drugs are instead prescribed by their generic names only. This simplifies prescribing and usually means for the patient a cheaper form of the same drug than that produced under a brand name. Throughout this text I have used the generic names but have placed brand names in brackets where appropriate to help in the recognition of medication.

## Sedatives

Sleeping tablets (hypnotics) should be used for short-term insomnia (sleeping difficulties), usually for no longer than three weeks, and it is recommended that even within that time it is beneficial to go several nights without taking them. Long-term insomnia is rarely helped by medication, indeed it is sometimes caused by a mild dependence on the very tablets meant to have cured it. Occasional doses of hypnotics are used to help those with transient insomnia from jet lag or shift work. In general short-acting drugs are better than those with a prolonged action, which have a tendency to produce morning 'hangovers' and to accumulate in the body, making the person increasingly dozy during the day.

Drugs used as sleeping tablets include the benzodiazepines: *nitrazepam* (Mogadon), *flunitrazepam* and *flurazepam* (Dalmane), which have prolonged action, and *loprazolam*, *lormetazepam*, *temazepam* and *triazolam* (Halcion), which are shorter-acting, *choral hydrate* (Welldorm), *chlormethiazole* (Heminevrin) and *zopiclone*.

Sedatives used to treat anxiety should also be prescribed and used cautiously, and only to treat serious anxiety which is significantly affecting the quality of a person's life and even then, usually, as a short-term measure. It is possible to become both physically and emotionally dependent on medication, which then exposes the person to withdrawal symptoms of insomnia and anxiety if the withdrawal is gradual and convulsions and severe confusion if it is abrupt. Some sedatives produce the paradoxical effect of making the person more anxious, excited or aggressive than he or she was in the first place.

Drugs used as anxiolytics include *diazepam* (Valium), *alprazolam*, *bromazepam*, *chlordiazepoxide* (Librium), *clobazam*, *lorazepam* (Ativan) and *oxazepam*. These were once called 'minor' tranquillisers, but that term has fallen into disrepute with our increased understanding of the potency of their effects. All should be used in the lowest doses possible and for the shortest periods of time. Many people are faced with the daunting task of coming off long-term use of these drugs; current advice is that first the person should be transferred to diazepam in a dosage equivalent to that of his or her usual medication; then the dosage should be reduced gradually, in fortnightly steps of 2 to 2.5 mg (it is better to reduce too slowly than too quickly). Diazepam is used for withdrawal because it is metabolised more slowly by the body; therefore levels of the tranquilliser in the bloodstream change gradually, where sudden shifts might have caused anxiety or panic. Complete withdrawal can take from 4 weeks to several months and takes courage and support. After years of medication with tranquillisers life can seem a frightening place, and self-help groups, therapy groups and individual therapy can all help people make this step towards independence.

*Buspirone* is also used as an anxiolytic; it takes two weeks to be effective against anxiety and is presently thought not to produce withdrawal symptoms, however it is a relatively new product. *Propranolol*, a beta-blocker, is sometimes used in small doses to control anxiety's physical symptoms, such as sweating and palpitations.

## Anti-psychotic Drugs

Anti-psychotic drugs act both as tranquillisers to quiet disturbed patients and also specifically to relieve symptoms such as hallucinations, delusions and thought disorder, which may have caused their disturbance initially. These drugs can produce positive relief from psychotic symptoms and allow a person to return to feeling and behaving normally. However, long-term medication is often necessary, administered either by mouth or injection. They produce their effects by interfering with chemical transmission in the brain; this means that they also produce marked side-effects for some people, most importantly tremor, abnormal facial and body movements, restlessness, and tardive dyskinesia, a longer-term disruption of muscle movements in the mouth, lips, face and body. All except tardive dyskinesia will improve if the drug is withdrawn or if treatment is combined with *procyclidine hydrochloride* or *benzhexol hydrochloride*. Patients taking *chlorpromazine* need to protect their skin from bright sunlight, as the drug makes the skin very sensitive to ultraviolet light.

Anti-psychotic drugs vary in their sedative power: of the phenothiazines, *chlorpromazine*, *methotimeprazine* and *promazine* can have strong sedative actions; *pericyazine*, *pipothiazine* and *thioridazine* have moderate sedative action; and *fluphenazine*, *perphenazine* and *prochlorperazine* have little sedative action. Those with moderate sedative potency also tend to produce fewer side-effects. Other anti-psychotic drugs have less sedative action and include the butyrophenones: *benperidol, droperidol* and *haloperidol*, the diphenylbutylpiperidines: *fluspirilene* and *pimozide*, and the thioxanthenes: *flupenthixol* and *zuclopenthixol*. Some, for example chlorpromazine, thioridazine and flupenthixol, can sometimes have an anti-depressant action, while others can exacerbate depression, for example, fluphenazine and pimozide. All of these drugs require careful supervision and a degree of trial and error to find which is the right drug and the right dose for each person, individually. Withdrawal needs to be monitored carefully, as there is a risk of relapse which may only manifest itself several weeks after treatment has stopped.

As long-term maintenance is sometimes required, anti-psychotic drugs are also produced in depot injection form lasting for between one and four weeks. A small test dose is given initially in case the drug produces side-effects which would then be as long lasting as the drug. It is a serious decision of both doctor and patient to start any therapy which is going to be long term and has the possibility of unwanted side-effects, however many patients report that the positive contribution that these drugs make to their lives outweighs any of the disadvantages. The relationship between doctor (and often community nurse) and patient is of even greater importance than usual in this situation. Depot injections include *flupenthixol decanoate, fluphenazine decanoate, fluspirilene* and *haloperidol decanoate*.

Anti-psychotic drugs are also used in the treatment of mania, particularly in its acute phase. Longer-term treatment to prevent further episodes of mania can be achieved with *lithium* (Camcolit, Priadel) or *carbamazepine*. Lithium takes several days to produce its mood-stabilising effects and is therefore used, after discussion with the patient, to prevent further episodes of mania, manic depression or recurrent depression. It is crucial to be able to monitor the blood levels of lithium so that it is high enough to have a maximal effect on maintaining mood stability but not so high that it goes into the toxic range, where it can cause convulsions, damage to the kidneys, and even death. Even in therapeutic doses there is concern on the part of some professionals that it may damage the kidneys if its use is prolonged. Thus most patients would need to re-discuss and reconsider long-term medication every two or three years. Many do feel that it is worth taking the risk of side-effects because of the benefits that regular, well-monitored use of lithium can produce for them.

## Anti-depressants

*Amitriptyline* (Lentizol, Tryptizol) is probably the most commonly prescribed anti-depressant, and it produces relief for as many as 75 per cent of those whose depressive symptoms include biological features such as changes in their sleeping and eating patterns. The anti-depressant effect takes two weeks to achieve, although amitriptyline is also a sedative and if taken at night can restore normal sleeping rapidly. *Imipramine* (Tofranil) is less sedative in its action and therefore of more use to people who feel emotionally flat and apathetic.

Both of these drugs have been widely used and have good safety records, but also have dangerous side-effects for those with any heart problems or if taken in overdose. Clearly, as depressed people are at risk from taking overdoses of their tablets, such risks are especially important to consider in the case of anti-depressants, which leads doctors to prescribe them in small numbers, at least until some of the benefits of the treatment can be felt by the patient. *Lofepramine* is also a tri-cyclic anti-depressant of the same chemical 'family' as amitriptyline and imipramine, but less sedative and not as dangerous in overdosage. *Dothiepin* (Prothiaden) is sedative but also probably safer than amitriptyline in overdose (individual response is very variable). *Mianserin* is also sedative but has been found to produce disorders of the red and white blood cells, especially in the elderly, which means that monthly blood checks are recommended for patients who take this drug.

*Amoxapine* is thought to act more quickly than the average two weeks between the commencement of treatment and an improvement in depressed mood being achieved, although this claim is not always substantiated in clinical practice, and the drug is known to produce side-effects in women patients such as menstrual irregularities and swollen breasts. *Trazodone* seems to produce fewer side-effects and may be particularly useful in older patients, who are more sensitive to drug actions.

All of these drugs tend to cause dry mouth, drowsiness, blurred vision, constipation and sweating, particularly in the first few weeks of treatment. These side-effects do improve sometimes once the patient's body develops some tolerance to the drugs. Effects on the functioning of the heart have been known to cause changes in the rhythm of the heart beat and may cause sudden death by heart attack. Changes in the functioning of both liver and blood cells have also been reported. Although few in number, these serious side-effects mean that treatment with such an anti-depressant needs to be considered only in the face of moderate to severe depression with clear biological symptoms, and not as a panacea to the pain of ordinary life. It is important for each patient to have an opportunity to choose a treatment in the full knowledge of possible side-effects, although when seriously depressed it is often hard for people to muster any enthusiasm to listening to or deciding on what is best for them.

*Monoamine-oxidase inhibitors* (MAOIs) are used more rarely to treat depression, often after other treatments have failed. *Phenelzine* (Nardil) is the most commonly prescribed, and patients with phobic or hypochondriacal symptoms associated with their depression are said to respond best. Treatment cards detailing dietary restrictions are essential for all patients who are on these drugs, and the range of food which produces dangerous effects when combined with MAOIs is extensive, including cheese, pickled fish, broad beans, any meat or yeast extract, and alcohol. Dangerous interactions cause a serious rise in blood-pressure, producing a throbbing headache as an early warning sign. It is generally considered dangerous to combine these drugs with other anti-depressants, although occasionally this approach is used in a person whose depression has proved resistant to everything else. Because of the risk of suicide (and sometimes the accompanying murder of close family members), depression has to be viewed as a potentially dangerous illness; this sometimes justifies using drugs singularly or in combination which are known to have serious side-effects.

Other anti-depressant drugs include a relatively new group of *5-hydroxytryptamine re-uptake inhibitors*. *Fluvoxamine* seemed to produce many gastric side-effects such as nausea and vomiting and has not proved very popular. *Fluoxetine*, however, seems more promising especially as it does not produce the cardiac side-effects of the tri-cyclics. People with obsessive symptoms as well as depression seem to gain some benefit from these drugs, although their use in cases of moderate-to-severe depression is less tested.

Peoples' response to these drugs is individual, and treatment does not always produce a cure. For some it is a matter of finding the right medication for them, for others the depression is a symptom of problems with life rather than an illness, and thus not curable by drug treatment. Depression is a painful experience, and for many these drugs, used accurately, within a short time span, and adapted to their particular needs, can save them from much distress.

# PHYSICAL
# TREATMENTS

## Electro-convulsive Therapy (ECT)

This treatment is conducted while the patient is under a general anaesthetic, with accompanying muscle relaxants and a mask to administer oxygen while he or she is unconscious. Electrodes are applied to the top of the patient's head, usually on both sides (bilaterally), and an electric current, which is closely monitored to be of the right size and wave form, is passed between the electrodes, causing the patient to have a fit much like an epileptic fit but under controlled conditions.

This treatment is usually used in the treatment of depression that is resistant to other forms of help. A course of ECT may include between six and twelve separate treatments administered over two or three weeks, and as recovery from the anaesthetic is rapid, it can be conducted on an out-patient basis as well as for those in hospital.

It is an intrusive and, to some, unaesthetic treatment which has been banned in some of the states of the USA. For those who respond well however it can seem to work magic, particularly if they have been suffering for weeks or even months under the cloud of depression. The Royal College of Psychiatrists in the UK have laid down strict guidelines about the use of ECT. It can only be given with the patient's consent, except in exceptional circumstances, such as where there is the risk of suicide in a patient mute with depression and therefore unable to give consent.

How ECT works is still unclear. It was first used after doctors noted that epileptics often felt high in spirits immediately after a fit. Some patients see it as punishment, others welcome it with relief, some say that there are no side-effects, others experience memory problems for days, weeks or even months after the treatments. Patients need to be able to explore alternatives and to understand the treatment fully before considering giving their consent.

## Psychosurgery

It has become rare for a psychiatrist to consider any form of psychosurgery, and this is reflected in the fact that few units now exist that specialise in it. However there is a unit at Guy's Hospital in London that will offer assessment and, if recommended, treatment to the few for whom no other therapy offers relief of their symptoms. Modern neurosurgical techniques mean that pathways between brain centres can be accurately located and cut. Clearly once cut it is not possible to reverse the process, and because of this it has become a treatment of last resort.

# APPENDIX A: THE PROFESSIONALS INVOLVED IN A MENTAL HEALTH CARE TEAM

Psychiatry has attempted to evolve a multi-disciplinary form of offering service under the NHS. Each professional brings a different perspective to a person's problems and, by working together, we also influence one another's concepts of illness and treatment.

## Psychiatrists

Psychiatrists initially train as doctors, and then specialise in psychiatry. Their specialist training involves a minimum of three years as a Senior House Officer and Registrar, working in a variety of subspecialities within psychiatry so that they gain an overall knowledge of the subject. Alongside the practical training of working with patients and other staff under the supervision of a Consultant, they also learn the theory behind the practice, and have to pass a two-part examination before proceeding to the next part of their training. The examination known as *Membership* allows them to become Members of the Royal College of Psychiatrists. They then spend between three and five years as Senior Registrars, during which time they may specialise in a particular area of psychiatry. They learn to take responsibility for the supervision of others and become increasingly more autonomous and less in need of supervision in their day-to-day work. Eventually they become Consultants responsible for a particular area of service and the training of others.

Although all psychiatrists are meant to be exposed to supervised practice in the psychological (talking) therapies during their training, their educational basis in medicine often means that they take a primarily organic or biological view of mental illness, taking personal, psychological and social elements into account secondarily. They are qualified to diagnose, treat patients with drugs, and prescribe physical methods of treatment; they also have access to other forms of help such as specialised psychological treatments, to which they can refer patients. They have access to hospital beds and are in overall responsibility for the care of in-patients. They can also visit patients at home (domiciliary visits), for which they are paid extra. Doctors also operate on-call rotas, meaning that there is a duty psychiatrist available in all areas at all times.

Within psychiatry there are a number of subspecialities:

- General psychiatry deals with the adult population as a 'front-line' resource, offering a quick response in emergencies and referring patients on to subspecialities where that is appropriate. The service usually consists of in-patient, out-patient and day-patient elements, depending on the level of patient need. The general psychiatric team will be able to offer a wide range of services and treatments.
- Child and adolescent psychiatry deals with those under 18 years of age. It tends to concentrate on dealing with the family as an entity rather more than general psychiatry does.
- Psychiatry of the elderly (psychogeriatrics) deals with those over 65 or 70 years of age. The interaction between physical and emotional illness is particularly relevant with people in this age group.
- Psychotherapy specialises in the treatment of problems by psychological means rather than physical treatments.
- Forensic psychiatry deals with those patients who have committed offences while ill.
- Liaison psychiatry helps patients who have mixed physical and emotional problems.
- Rehabilitation psychiatry specialises in helping those who have had serious mental illness resume their lives as normally as possible, which usually involves a combination of physical and psychological treatments.
- Community psychiatry offers help on an out-patient basis. It is often located within a general practice, and attempts to treat people early in their difficulties so that the problems do not become serious enough to justify admission to hospital.
- Day-hospital psychiatry offers group and individual programmes on a sessional or daily basis, often providing a stepping stone between hospital and normal life.
- Therapeutic community psychiatry offers either residential or out-patient intensive therapy within a large group of patients, and is combined with activities of normal life, for example eating and cooking together.
- Alcohol and addiction psychiatry offers specialist help to those attempting to give up their addictions.

# Psychologists

Psychologists working in clinical practice in the NHS have a dual training, initially theory-based, gaining a degree in Psychology, and then more practically orientated, training in clinical psychology over a period of three years. Each District in the NHS has a team of psychologists who can accept direct referrals or act as a part of a team. They are trained to diagnose and treat a range of emotional and behavioural problems and to conduct complicated tests of people's emotional or intellectual functioning. With training they will be able to treat patients by means of psychological cures, often with a behaviouristic or cognitive theoretical base. There are also educational psychologists who have special training in assessing the needs of children.

## Psychotherapists

Psychotherapists often have one of the trainings described above and belong to a professional group before undertaking a psychotherapy or psychoanalytic training. Until 1992 almost anyone can call themselves a therapist whatever their background or training. After 1992 European law will enable us to limit this title to those with training. The trainings vary because there are many styles of therapy, and the length and intensity of training tends to reflect the style of therapy which is taught. Generally all trainings consist of three elements, however: the theoretical, the supervised practice with patients, and the personal therapy of the psychotherapist. Whatever their background, people describing themselves as psychotherapists or analysts will specialise in one of a variety of 'talking' cures, and even if they are also doctors will almost certainly not make physical diagnoses nor prescribe drugs for their clients.

## Nurses

Nurses who work within mental health may be trained by a scheme operated by the Royal College of Mental Nurses (RMNs), for which a three year practical and theoretical course with assessments and exams is necessary, or may have a general nurse training and then later specialise in mental nursing. During their training they learn to function in all the many aspects of psychiatric care – the wards, the clinics, the day hospitals and the community – with a wide range of patients in terms of their ages and illnesses. Many go on to further training by specialising in a particular area of psychiatry. A team of nurses always has a clear hierarchical structure for supervision and management, leading up to a single nurse who is in overall charge of a hospital or mental health unit. Many nurses have training in the psychological treatments and are capable of diagnosing and treating people in the community (CPNs – Community Psychiatric Nurses), either at the patient's home or at GP surgeries.

## Social Workers

Social workers have to complete a specialised training in psychiatry in order to fulfil their obligations under the Mental Health Act. They also offer a wide range of psychological, family and practical support services to patients and their relatives.

# Occupational Therapists (OTs)

OTs complete a three-year general training before specialising in psychiatry. They are trained to assess peoples' capacities and limitations over a wide range of activities, and to offer help in improving these if possible. They work both within the hospital and the community.

# APPENDIX B:
# THE MENTAL
# HEALTH ACT

The Lunacy Acts of the 1890s underlined the pessimism felt about treating the mentally ill, providing as they did for custodial care and not even allowing for the possibility of voluntary admission for care. The Mental Treatment Act of 1930 made it possible for people to be admitted to a mental institution on request and then, as treatments became more successful, a further act (The Mental Health Act of 1959) took the regulation of admissions and detention out of legal hands and gave it over to the medical arena. Most psychiatrists felt that this system worked well, but increasing pressures from patients and relatives, complaining in particular that the Act gave doctors a 'paternal' role in the patient's treatment, meant that a further Mental Health Act was passed in 1983. This Act installed the Mental Health Act Commission as overseers, made second opinions necessary for any forced detention of patients, and generally weighed the law towards patient liberties. This Act is still in the process of refinement in its operation, most particularly in terms of considering the restrictions necessary to enable some patients to be treated safely within the community.

The 1983 Mental Health Act is divided into ten parts, which define the terms used and then deal with a variety of settings in which patients come to the attention of or are treated by psychiatrists. The important definitions are:

*Mental disorder*: mental illness, arrested or incomplete development of mind, psychopathic disorder, or any other disability or disorder of the mind.

*Severe mental impairment*: a state of arrested or incomplete development of mind which includes severe impairment of intelligence and social functioning and is associated with abnormally aggressive or seriously irresponsible conduct. (Mental impairment is similarly defined but adds the condition 'not amounting to severe mental impairment'.)

*Psychopathic disorder*: a persistent disorder or disability of mind (with or without mental impairment) which results in abnormally aggressive or seriously irresponsible conduct.

*Mental illness*: the Act leaves this undefined, and operational definition is left to clinical judgement.

*Medical treatment*: this includes nursing care, rehabilitation and care under medical supervision.

The law is divided into numbered 'Sections', that is, the orders which have to be completed and signed as the 'paperwork' for the Act, and each of which is applicable in different situations. Part 2 of the Act consists of Sections 2 to 34, which deal with compulsory admission to hospital and guardianship.

Section 2 allows for compulsory admission to hospital for 28 days if the patient is mentally ill 'of a nature or degree which warrants detention' for assessment alone and/or assessment followed by treatment, or if the patient is considered to be a risk to him- or herself or to others. Sections require an application (usually from a relative or an approved social worker) and then, as in Section 2, the medical recommendations of two doctors, usually the patient's GP and a psychiatrist who is approved as having specialised knowledge of mental illness. Discharge can occur only one of the following stipulations are met:

a) 28 days have elapsed since the patient was admitted;
b) the RMO (Responsible Medical Officer, usually the Consultant Psychiatrist) discharges the patient considering that he or she no longer needs detention;
c) 3 members of the hospital management (District Health Authority) discharge the Section;
d) the nearest relatives (after 72 hours notice) discharge the patient – the RMO can however block this with a barring certificate);
e) the Mental Health Tribunal hear an appeal and discharge the Section; or
f) the patient goes absent without leave and remains absent up to the expiry point fixed by the Section.

Most Sections operate in a similar form but, as with Section 3, allow for different periods of time or treatment settings. Section 3 allows for 6 months' detention, which can be extended first by a further 6 months and then annually, while Section 4 allows for 72 hours admission for assessment, and then only in an emergency. Section 5 allows for detention of patients already in a mental health unit.

For many who are not directly concerned with treating mental illness the operation of the law to detain people for health care often seems incomprehensible and even morally wrong. Within psychiatric and social work practice there is a continuing debate as to how much the Mental Health Act should be used, and it would be untrue to say that there is easy consensus on the subject. Each year, however, the well-informed and monitored use of the Mental Health Act undoubtedly saves many lives and improves the eventual quality of many others. It might be seen as a form of 'seat belt act', which takes from us certain liberties – like a seat belt, however, it undoubtedly saves many of us from death or injury every year.

The Mental Health Act Commission has not only improved the policing of the Act but also means that its operation is regularly questioned and policies updated, always seeking to combine effective containment of behaviour that is dangerous to the self and others and realistic treatment of disturbing illness with ensuring civil liberties as much as possible. Many patients, when well, will thank staff for restraining them from suicidal or dangerous actions when ill, and say that if they are ever in the same state again they would wish the staff to repeat their methods.

# APPENDIX C: REFERENCES AND USEFUL READING

The lists of references given here represent only the tip of the iceberg. Much is published each year which offers new ideas and opinions; our thoughts on mental health and illness never stand still. I think it is possible to gain as great an understanding of human nature from fiction as from the more factual accounts, and would recommend the reader search in both areas of writing for whatever it is he or she is seeking.

## General Reading

Abraham, K., *Dreams and Myths: A Study in Race Psychology*, Karnac, 1971 (reprint of 1913 edition).

Freud, Sigmund, *The Complete Works*, Hogarth Press, 1951.

Hendrick, C. (ed), *Close Relationships*, Sage, 1989.

Hojat, Mohammadreza (ed), *Loneliness*, Sage, 1989.

D. Klein, D. and Aldous, J., *Social Stress and Family Development*, Guildford Press, 1988.

Mash, E. and Terdal, L., *Behavioural Assessment of Childhood Disorders*, Guildford Press, 1988.

Meth, R.L., *Men in Therapy: The Challenge of Change*, Guildford Press, 1990.

Sandler, J. (ed), *Dimensions of Psychoanalysis*, Karnac, 1990.

Spacapan, Shirley, *The Social Psychology of Aging*, Sage, 1989.

Suttie, Ian, *The Origins of Love and Hate*, Free Association Press, 1988.

## Aggression

De Bono, E., *Conflicts: A Better Way to Resolve Them*, Pelican, 1986.

Eichenbaum, Luise and Orbach, Susie, *Bittersweet: Facing Up to Feelings of Love, Envy, and Competition in Women's Friendships*, Century, 1987.

Formaini, Heather, *Men: The Darker Continent*, Heinemann, 1990.

Lewis, H., *Psychic War in Men and Women*, New York, NYU Press, 1976.

Schoenewolf, *Sexual Animosity Between Men and Women*, Jason Aronson, 1989.

Storr, A., *Human Aggression*, New York, Bantam Books, 1970.

## Anxiety

Barlow, D.H. and Cerny, Jerome, *Psychological Treatment of Panic*, Guildford Press, 1988.

Bowlby, *Attachment and Loss*, vol 2, 'Separation: Anxiety and Anger', Hogarth, 1962.

Bretton, Sue, *Don't Panic: A Guide to Overcoming Panic Attacks*, London, McDonald and Co.

Freud, Sigmund, *The Problem of Anxiety*, New York, Norton, 1936.

Greist, Jefferson, and Marks, *Anxiety and Its Treatment: Help is Available*, New York, Warner.

Harvey, *If I'm so Successful, Why do I Feel Like a Fake? The Impostor Phenomenon*, New York, Bantam Books.

Kelly, *Anxiety and Emotions*, Thomas.

Marks, Isaac, *Living with Fear*, New York, McGraw-Hill,1978.

Menzies Lyth, Isabel, *Containing Anxiety in Institutions*, Free Association Books.

Priest, Robert, *Anxiety and Depression*, McDonald and Co, 1988.

Weekes, Claire, *Peace from Nervous Suffering*, Angus and Robertson, 1972.

——, *Self-Help for Your Nerves*, Angus and Robertson, 1962.

# Depression

Alloy, L.B. (ed), *Cognitive Processes in Depression*, Guildford Press, 1988.

Berne, E., *Games People Play*, Penguin, 1970.

Friedman, R. and Katz, M. (eds), *The Psychology of Depression, Contemporary Theory and Research*, Washington, D.C., Winston and Sons, 1974.

Gomberg, E., and Franks, D. (eds), *Gender and Psychopathology. Sex Differences in Disordered Behaviour*, Brunner/Mazel, 1979.

Gove, W.R. and Geerken, M., 'The Effect of Children and Employment on the Mental Health of Married Men and Women', *Social Forces*, 5, pp. 66- – 75, 1977.

Gove, W.R. and Tudor, J., 'Adult Sex Roles and Mental Illness', *American Journal of Sociology* 77, pp. 812 – 2D35, 1973.

Pearlin, L., 'Sex Roles and Depression', in Datan, N. and Ginsberg, L.H. (eds), *Life Span Developmental Psychology. Normative Life Crisis*, New York, Academic Press, 1975.

Rowe, Dorothy, *Depression. The Way Out of Your Prison*, Routledge, 1989.

Sargant, W., *Battle for the Mind*, Heinemann, 1957.

Weissman, M. M. and Klerman, G. L.,'Sex Differences and the Epidemiology of Depression', *Archives of General Psychiatry*, 34, pp. 98 – 111, 1977.

# Eating Disorders

Bovey, Shelley, *Being Fat is Not a Sin*, Pandora, 1988.

Orbach, Susie, *Fat is a Feminist Issue*, Arrow, 1984.

# Manic Depression

*Understanding Manic Depression*, MIND Publications, 1987.

## Schizophrenia

*Understanding Schizophrenia*, MIND Publications, 1987.

Arieti, S., *Interpretation of Schizophrenia*, New York, Basic Books, 2nd edition.

Atkinson, Jacqueline, *Schizophrenia: A Guide for Sufferers and Their Families*, Turnstone Press Ltd, 1985.

Kay, S.R., Opler, L.A., and Fiszbein, A., 'Significance of Positive and Negative Syndromes in Chronic Schizophrenia', *British Journal of Psychiatry*, 149, p. 439, 1986.

Laing, R.D., *The Divided Self*, Pelican, 1965.

Strauss, J.S., *The Psychotherapy of Schizophrenia*, Plenum Press, 1980.

## Women's Issues

Blum, H. (ed), *Female Psychology. Contemporary Psychoanalytic Views*, Madison, CT, International Universities Press, 1977.

Caplan, Paula, *The Myth of Women's Masochism*, Methuen, 1986.

Chesler, Phyllis, *Women and Madness*, Allen Lane, 1972.

de Beauvoir, Simone, *The Second Sex*, Penguin, 1972.

Diner, H., *Mothers and Amazons*, New York, Anchor Press, 1973.

Dinneage, Rosemary, *One to One*, London, Viking.

Eichenbaum, Luise and Orbach, Susie, *Understanding Women*, Penguin, 1985.

——, *What Do Women Want?*, Fontana, 1984.

Ernst, Sheila, *In Our Own Hands*, Women's Press, 1981.

*Finding Our Own Solutions*, MIND Publications.

Greer, Germaine, *The Female Eunuch*, McGibbon & Kee, 1970.

Hancock, Emily, *The Girl Within*, Pandora, 1990.

Horney, K., *Feminine Psychology*, New York, Norton, 1967.

Howell, E. and Bayes, M. (eds), *Women and Mental Health*, Basic Books, 1981.

Kaplan, Louise J., *Female Perversions*, Pandora, 1991.

Knight, Lindsey, *Talking to a Stranger*, Fontana, 1986.

Miller, Jean Baker, *Toward a New Psychology of Women*, Penguin, 1978.

Millet, K., *Sexual Politics*, New York, Doubleday, 1970.

Mitchell, J., *Psychoanalysis and Women*, Vintage, 1974.

Norwood, R., *Women Who Love Too Much*, J.P. Tarcher, 1985.

Price, Jane, *Motherhood: What It Does to Your Mind*, Pandora, 1988 (reprinted 1990).

Rich, Adrienne, *Of Woman Born: Motherhood as Experience and Institution*, New York, Norton, 1977.

Rosaldo, M. and Lamphere, L. (eds), *Women, Culture and Society*, Palo Alto, CA, Stanford University Press, 1974.

Rowbotham, S., *Women: Resistance and Revolution*, New York, Random House, 1974.

Scaffer, R., 'Problems in Freud's Psychology of Women', *Journal of the American Psychiatric Association*, 22, 3, pp. 459 – 2D485, 1974.

Scarf, J., *Unfinished Business*, New York, Doubleday, 1980.

Strouse, J. (ed), *Women and Analysis*, New York, Dell, 1974.

Walsh, Mary R. (ed), *The Psychology of Women. On-going Debates*, New Haven, CT, Yale University Press, 1987.

# INDEX

lithium, 454
liver, 46, 102, 163, 384
Liverpool University, 444
lofepramine, 455
London Centre for Psychotherapy, 443
London University, 444
loneliness, 52, 53, 199, 239, 247, 286, 442; *see also* isolation
loprazolam, 452
lorazepam, 30, 452
lormetazepam, 452
love, 51, 103, 156, 164, 227, 236–41, 277, 316, 322, 369, 420, 441; and envy, 116; food as substitute for, 103
love and hate, link between, 41–2, 89, 112, 117, 164, 167, 284–5
low blood sugar, 102
LSD, 30, 396
'ludes' (methaqualone), 30
Lunacy Acts, 465
lungs, 384

Madonna and Child image, 181
magic mushroom (psilocin), 30
malingering, 45
Manchester, 15
mania, 33, 35, 94, 106, 201, 242–5, 257, 270, 286, 427
manic-depressive psychosis, 47, 94–5, 106, 126, 127–8, 174, 244, 245–6; class basis of, 419; genetic basis of, 364–5; and grandiose behaviour, 146; inhibition in, 187; insomnia in, 200–1; intelligence and, 215; irritability and, 222
marital rape, 280
marital therapy, 34, 270, 438, 445
marriage, 111, 376, 394; helplessness connected with, 171; and loss of libido, 236; love and, 240–1; power in, 123, 149, 172; two-culture, 65; women's responsibility for success of, 160
Marriage Guidance, 445
masculinity, and instinct for mastery, 204
Maslow, Abraham, 373–4
masochism, 235, 322, 324, 325; *see also* sado-masochism
mastery, instinct for *see* instinct for mastery
masturbation, 50, 108, 289
Maudsley Hospital, 442
ME (myalgic encephalitis), 383
measles, 220
medical treatment, 466
melancholy, 246–7, 315, 316; *see also* grief
memories, 313, 314
memory problems, 36, 63, 80, 89, 282–3, 318; resulting from ECT, 459; *see also* amnesia
menstrual problems, 427; *see also* pre-menstrual syndrome
menstruation taboos, 356

Mental Health Act, 196–7, 421, 422, 463–4, 465–7
Mental Health Act Commission, 465
Mental Health Unit, 421
mental illness, 467
Mental Treatment Act, 465
metabolic disorders, 214
metabolic rate, 427
*Metamorphosis* (Ovid), 252
Metanoia Humanistic Psychotherapy Training Centre, 444
methadone, 30
methaqualone ('ludes'), 30
methotimeprazine, 453
mianserin, 455
Middlesex Hospital Medical School, 442
mid-life changes, 75, 142, 406, 441
Miller, Jean Baker, 323
MIND (National Association for Mental Health), 446, 448
Minster Centre, 444
miscarriage, 258
Mogadon, 453
monoamine-oxidase inhibitors (MAOIs), 456
mood swings, 86, 92, 106
Moreno, Jacob, 438
morphine, 30
mother/daughter relationship, 109, 111–12, 148; *see also* Electra complex; Oedipus complex
mother/son relationship, 62, 125, 354–5; *see also* Oedipus complex
motherhood, 93–4, 116–17, 119, 158, 179–80, 206, 375–6; envy of, 354–6; idealisation of, 110, 160, 181, 305
*Motherhood: What It Does To Your Mind* (Price), 294
'mothering', need for, 77, 147, 305
mourning, 149, 151, 155, 426; *see also* grief
moving house, 257
MS *see* multiple sclerosis
multiple personality, 377
multiple sclerosis (MS), 266, 338, 427
mumps, 220
Munchausen's syndrome, 248
murder, 32, 83, 248–50, 265, 304, 413; desire to, 33, 34, 69, 227, 283
music therapy, 438
mutism, 250–1, 265
myalgic encephalitis (ME), 383
myth, and collective unconscious, 441
*Myth of Woman's Masochism, The* (Caplan), 323

narcissism, 252–5, 288
Nardil, 456
National Association for the Welfare of Children in Hospital (NAWCH), 449
National Childbirth Trust (NCT), 448–9
National Commission on Marijuana and Drug Abuse, 30